JERRY B. JENKINS
CHRISTIAN
WRITERS
GUI

D0822631

THE CHRISTIAN WRITER'S
MARKET GUIDE
2013

YOUR COMPREHENSIVE RESOURCE FOR GETTING PUBLISHED

JERRY B. JENKINS

TYNDALE HOUSE PUBLISHERS, INC.
CAROL STREAM, ILLINOIS

Visit Tyndale online at www.tyndale.com.

Visit Jerry B. Jenkins Christian Writers Guild at www.christianwritersguild.com.

E-mail: marketguide@christianwritersguild.com

The 2013 Christian Writer's Market Guide: Your Comprehensive Resource for Getting Published

Designed by Beth Sparkman

Edited by Susan Taylor and Erin Gwynne

ISSN 1080-3955

ISBN 978-1-4143-7640-0

Printed in the United States of America

18 17 16 15 14 13 12
7   6   5   4   3   2   1

CONTENTS

PART 2: PERIODICAL PUBLISHERS

INTRODUCTION

Hardly any industry has ever changed as much in so short a time as publishing has in the last few years. Traditional methods of seeing your writing get to the printed page have broadened so dramatically that many veterans hardly recognize the publishing landscape anymore. Besides royalty-paying book publishers and fee-paying periodical markets, opportunities abound for anyone who wants to be published electronically, on demand, in blogs, or through self-, vanity- or subsidy-publishing means.

Regardless, good writing rises like cream and must be crafted, edited, proofread, honed, and polished.

Some publishers say writers who submit to them don't read their guidelines first—some even drop their listings from this guide for that reason. Most publishers carry their guidelines on their websites, so most of our listings include the addresses to find those. Carefully read the guidelines before submitting—a critical step if you want to sell in today's tighter market.

More and more publishers are dropping their fax numbers or even their addresses and depend almost entirely on e-mail or website contacts.

A number of periodical publishers are accepting assignments only, so it is important that you establish a reputation in your areas of interest and expertise. Once you have acquired credits in a given field, write to some of those assignment-only editors, asking for an assignment.

Carefully check out agents before signing with them. See the introduction to the agent section for tips on that. Because agents have become more important in a writer's quest for publication, we list which conferences have agents in attendance.

Attending conferences is one of the best ways to contact agents as well as publishers.

If you are new to this Guide or only want to find specific markets for your work, check out the supplementary lists throughout the book. Read through the glossary and learn terms.

Also be sure to study the "How to Use This Book" section. It will save you time, and it's full of helpful hints.

One of the most common complaints from publishers is that the material they receive is not appropriate for their needs. Editors tell me they are looking for writers who understand their periodical or publishing house and its unique approach to the marketplace. With a little time and effort, you can meet an editor's expectations, distinguish yourself as a professional, and sell what you write.

Godspeed to you as you travel the exciting road to publication. You have been given a mission for which you might often feel inadequate. Just remember that the writing assignments God has given you could not be written the same by anyone else.

Finally, special thanks to my executive assistant Debbie Kaupp for developing and overseeing the database we use to produce the guide. Through her efforts the listings are as up to date as they can be, and the guide has been streamlined to be easier to use than ever. Thanks also to Kerma Murray, Janice Mitchell, Julie Adams, and Tanya Shtatman for their help with the guide.

Jerry B. Jenkins

P.O. Box 88288, Black Forest, CO 80908
719.495.5835
Fax: 719.494.1299
Christian Writers Guild: 719.495.5177 or 866.495.5177
E-mail: marketguide@jerryjenkins.com
Website: www.christianwritersguild.com
Blog: www.jerry-jenkins.com
Facebook: facebook.com/jerry.b.jenkins
Twitter: twitter.com/JerryBJenkins

For additional books or pamphlets to help with your writing needs, visit the bookstore on our website, www.christianwritersguild.com.

HOW TO USE THIS BOOK

The Christian Writer's Market Guide is designed to make it easier for you to sell your writing. It will serve you well if you use it as a springboard for becoming thoroughly familiar with those markets best suited to your style and areas of interest and expertise.

Start by getting acquainted with the setup of the guide. The table of contents carries comprehensive listings of periodical and book topics. Cross-referencing may be helpful. For example, if you have a novel that deals with doctor-assisted suicide, you might look at the list for adult fiction and the list for controversial issues and look for publishers on both lists.

Read listings carefully to see whether your target market pays, requires an agent, etc. Each book publisher listing carries the following information (as available):

- Name of publisher
- Address, phone and fax numbers, e-mail address, website
- Denomination or affiliation
- Name of editor—This may include the main editor, followed by another editor to whom submissions should be sent. In some cases, several editors are listed with the types of books each is responsible for. (It's always best to submit to a specific person, never just "Sir" or "Madam" or "To Whom It May Concern.")
- Statement of purpose
- List of imprint names
- Number of inspirational/religious titles published per year, followed by formats of books published (hardcover, trade paperbacks, mass-market paperbacks, coffee-table books). Note that coffee-table books are also represented in the topical listings.
- Number of submissions received annually
- Percentage of books published from first-time authors
- (Usually) whether the publisher accepts, prefers, requires, or doesn't accept manuscripts through agents
- Percentage of books from freelance authors they subsidy publish (if any). This does not refer to percentage paid by author. If percentage of subsidy is over 50 percent, the publisher will be listed in a separate section under "Subsidy Publishers."
- Whether they reprint out-of-print books from other publishers
- Preferred manuscript length in words or pages; "pages" refers to double-spaced manuscript pages.
- Average amount of royalty, if provided, and whether it is based on the retail (cover price) of the book or on the net receipts (wholesale price to bookstores or distributors)
- Average amount paid for advances and whether the publisher pays an advance against royalties. Not all publishers answer this, so if nothing is mentioned, that doesn't necessarily mean none is offered.
- Whether they pay flat fees rather than royalties
- Average number of copies in first printing
- Average length of time between acceptance of a manuscript and publication
- Whether they consider simultaneous submissions. This means you can send a query or proposal or even a complete manuscript simultaneously, as long as you indicate to each that you are doing so.
- Length of time it should take them to respond to a query/proposal or to a complete manuscript (when two lengths of time are given, the first refers to a query and the latter to a complete manuscript). Give them a one-month grace period beyond that, and then send a polite follow-up letter.

- Whether a publisher "accepts," "prefers," or "requires" manuscripts sent electronically. (Sending hard copies is almost unheard of now.)
- Which Bible version the publisher prefers
- Whether they do print-on-demand publishing
- Availability and cost of writer's guidelines and book catalogs. Most of these will be available online or via e-mail, but if the publisher offers hard copies, ask directly whether there's a charge, postage costs, etc.
- Nonfiction and Fiction sections indicate preference for query letter, book proposal, or complete manuscript, and whether they accept phone, fax, or e-queries. (Most do not.) If they want a query letter, send a letter describing your project. If they want a query letter/ proposal, add a chapter-by-chapter synopsis and 2-3 sample chapters.
- Special Needs
- Ethnic Books—Specifies which groups they target
- Also Does—Indicates which publishers also publish booklets, pamphlets, tracts, or e-books
- Photos/Artwork—Indicates whether they accept freelance photos for book covers.
- Tips

At the end of some listings you will find an indication that the publisher receives book proposals from ChristianManuscriptSubmissions.com (see website or index).

In each periodical listing you will find the following information (as available) in this format:

- Name of periodical
- Address, phone and fax numbers, e-mail address, website
- Denomination or affiliation
- Name of editor to submit to
- Theme of publication
- Format, frequency of publication, number of pages, and circulation size
- Subscription rate for a one-year subscription. (You might want to subscribe to at least one of your primary markets every year to become acquainted with its focus.)
- Date established, if 2007 or later
- Openness to freelance submissions; percentage of unsolicited freelance submissions accepted versus assigned articles
- Preference for query or complete manuscript also tells whether they want a cover letter with complete manuscripts and whether they accept phone or e-mail queries. If there is no mention of cover letters or phone or e-mail queries, assume they do not accept them.
- Payment schedule, payment on acceptance or publication, and rights purchased. (See glossary for definitions.)
- If a publication does not pay or pays in copies or subscription, that is indicated in bold capital letters.
- If a publication is not copyrighted, you should ask that your copyright notice appear with your published piece so your rights will be protected.
- Preferred word lengths and average number of manuscripts purchased per year (in parentheses)
- Response time—The time they usually take to respond to your query or manuscript submission
- Seasonal and holiday material—should reach them by at least the specified length of time in advance.
- Acceptance of simultaneous submissions and reprints—whether they accept submissions sent simultaneously to several publishers. It's best to send to non-overlapping markets (such

as denominational), and be sure to indicate that it is a simultaneous submission. Reprints are pieces you have sold previously but to which you hold the rights (which means you sold only first or one-time rights to the original publisher and the rights reverted to you).

- Whether they accept, prefer, or require submissions electronically. Most prefer them now. Some indicate whether they want submissions as attached files or copied into the message.
- Average kill-fee amount (see glossary)
- Whether they use sidebars (see glossary)
- Their preferred Bible version, if any. See glossary for "Bible Versions."
- Whether they accept submissions from children or teens. "Young-Writer Markets" are also found in the topical listings.
- Availability and cost for writer's guidelines, theme lists, and sample copies—most now have guidelines available by e-mail or website.
- Poetry—Name of poetry editor. Average number of poems bought each year. Types of poetry. Number of lines. Payment rate. Maximum number of poems you may submit at one time.
- Fillers—Name of fillers editor. Types of fillers accepted; word length. Payment rate.
- Columns/Departments—Name of column editor. Names of columns in the periodical (information in parentheses gives focus of column); word-length requirements. Payment rate. Be sure to see sample before sending ms or query. Most columns require a query letter first.
- Special Issues or Needs
- Ethnic
- Contest Information. See "Contests" chapter for full list of contests.
- Tips
- Some listings also include Evangelical Press Association winners, annual awards from the trade organization for Christian periodicals.

Adhering closely to the guidelines set out in these listings will mark you as a professional.

If your manuscript is completed, be sure the slant fits the publisher you have in mind.

If you have an idea for an article, short story, or book but you have not written it yet, the topical listing will help you decide on a possible slant or approach. If your idea is for an article, do not overlook writing on the same topic for different periodicals listed under that topic. For example, you could write on money management for a general adult magazine, a teen magazine, a women's publication, or a magazine for pastors. Each would require a different slant, but you would get a lot more mileage from that idea.

If you run into words you're not familiar with, check the glossary at the back of the book.

If you need someone to evaluate your material or to give it a thorough editing, look up "Editorial Services." That often will make the difference between success or failure in publishing.

If you are a published author, you may be interested in finding an agent. Some agents consider unpublished authors (their listing will indicate that), but even they require you to have a completed manuscript before being considered (see agent list). The list also includes secular agents who handle religious/inspirational material.

Check the "Clubs/Groups" list to find a chapter to join in your area.

Go to the "Conferences" list to find one you might attend this year. Attending a conference every year or two is almost essential to your success.

Do not rely solely on the information provided in this guide. Use it to familiarize yourself with target markets, but then interact personally with an editor to be sure you're providing what they want. It is important to your success that you learn to use writer's guidelines and study book catalogs or sample copies before submitting to any publisher.

PART 1

Book Publishers

1

Topical Listings of Book Publishers

One of the most difficult aspects of marketing yourself is determining which publishers might be interested in your book. This list will help you do just that.

If you don't find your topic of interest, check the table of contents and look for related topics. Next, secure writer's guidelines and book catalogs from those publishers. Just because a particular publisher is listed under your topic, don't assume it would automatically be interested in your book. You must determine whether your approach will fit within the scope of that publisher's catalog. It is also helpful to visit a Christian bookstore to actually see some of the books produced by each publisher you are interested in pursuing.

(a) before a listing indicates the publisher accepts submissions only through agents.

AFRICAN AMERICAN MARKETS
(a) Abingdon Press
(a) Doubleday Relig.

American Binding
Booklocker.com
Bridge Logos
CLC Publications
Franciscan Media
InterVarsity Press
Judson Press
Lift Every Voice
Moody Publishers
New Hope
Praeger Publishers
Tate Publishing
Whitaker House

APOLOGETICS
(a) Bethany House
(a) FaithWords
(a) Kregel
(a) Nelson, Thomas

Aaron Book
Abingdon Press
ACW Press
Ambassador Intl.
American Binding
AMG Publishers

Blue Dolphin
BMH Books
Booklocker.com
Bridge Logos
Brown Books
Canticle Books
Charisma House
Christian Heritage
Creation House
Crossway
CSS Publishing
Discovery House
Earthen Vessel
Eerdmans Pub., Wm. B.
Essence
Fairway Press
Faith Books & More
Grace Acres Press
Guardian Angel
Hensley Publishing
Howard Books
InterVarsity Press
Lighthouse Publishing
Lutheran Univ. Press
Magnus Press
NavPress
New Leaf
Our Sunday Visitor
Parson Place
Randall House

Salt Works
Tate Publishing
VBC Publishing
Whitaker House
WinePress
Word Alive
Zoë Life Publishing

ARCHAEOLOGY
(a) Baker Academic
(a) Baker Books
(a) Doubleday Relig.
(a) HarperOne
(a) Kregel

Aaron Book
Abingdon Press
ACW Press
American Binding
Blue Dolphin
BMH Books
Booklocker.com
Brown Books
Christian Writer's Ebook
Comfort Publishing
Conciliar Press
Eerdmans Pub., Wm. B.
Essence
Fairway Press
Faith Books & More

Lighthouse Publishing
NavPress
New Leaf
Pacific Press
Tate Publishing
VBC Publishing
White Fire Publishing
WinePress
Word Alive
Yale Univ. Press

ART, FREELANCE

Aaron Book
Abingdon Press
Ambassador Books
Ambassador Intl.
AMG Publishers
Blue Dolphin
Booklocker.com
CrossLink Publishing
Dawn Publications
Dove Inspirational
Earthen Vessel
Eerdmans/Yg Readers
Essence
Faith Books & More
Focus on the Family
Grace Acres Press
Group Publishing
Guardian Angel
Halo Publishing Intl.
JourneyForth/BJU
Judson Press
Legacy Press
Lighthouse Publishing
Marcher Lord Press
New Leaf
Parson Place
Parsons Publishing
Pauline Kids
Pelican Publishing
Rainbow Publishers
Randall House
Ravenhawk Books
Salt Works
Sunpenny Publishing
VBC Publishing
Warner Press
WinePress

AUTOBIOGRAPHY

(a) Baker Books
(a) Doubleday Relig.
(a) FaithWords
(a) HarperOne
(a) Nelson, Thomas
(a) WaterBrook Press

Aaron Book
ACW Press
Ambassador Intl.
American Binding
Blue Dolphin
Bondfire Books
Booklocker.com
Bridge Logos
Brown Books
Charisma House
Christian Heritage
Christian Writer's Ebook
CLC Publications
Comfort Publishing
Creation House
CrossLink Publishing
Deep River Books
Earthen Vessel
Essence
Fairway Press
Faith Books & More
Grace Acres Press
INO Publishing
Kirk House
Lighthouse Publishing
Pacific Press
Parson Place
Parsons Publishing
Tate Publishing
White Fire Publishing
WinePress
Word Alive
Zoë Life Publishing

BIBLE/BIBLICAL STUDIES

(a) Baker Academic
(a) Baker Books
(a) Bethany House
(a) Cook, David C.
(a) Doubleday Relig.
(a) Kregel
(a) WaterBrook Press

Aaron Book
Abingdon Press
ACW Press
Ambassador Books
Ambassador Intl.
American Binding
AMG Publishers
Blue Dolphin
BMH Books
Bondfire Books
Booklocker.com
Bridge Logos
Brown Books
Canticle Books
Christian Writer's Ebook
Conciliar Press
Contemporary Drama
CrossLink Publishing
CSS Publishing
DCTS Publishers
Deep River Books
Discovery House
Earthen Vessel
Eerdmans Pub., Wm. B.
Essence
Fairway Press
Faith Books & More
Gospel Publishing
Group Publishing
Hannibal Books
Harrison House
Hensley Publishing
Inkling Books
INO Publishing
InterVarsity Press
JourneyForth/BJU
Lift Every Voice
Lighthouse Publishing
Lutheran Univ. Press
Magnus Press
NavPress
New Hope
On My Own Now
Our Sunday Visitor
Pacific Press
Parson Place
Parsons Publishing
Pauline Kids
Randall House Digital
Salt Works

Tate Publishing
VBC Publishing
Wesleyan Publishing
Whitaker House
WinePress
Word Alive
Yale Univ. Press
Zoë Life Publishing
Zondervan

BIBLE COMMENTARY

(a) Baker Books
(a) B&H Publishing
(a) Cook, David C.
(a) Doubleday Relig.
(a) Kregel
(a) Tyndale House

Aaron Book
Abingdon Press
ACW Press
Ambassador Books
Ambassador Intl.
American Binding
AMG Publishers
Blue Dolphin
BMH Books
Bondfire Books
Booklocker.com
Bridge Logos
Brown Books
Christian Writer's Ebook
Conciliar Press
CrossLink Publishing
CSS Publishing
Discovery House
Eerdmans Pub., Wm. B.
Essence
Fairway Press
Faith Books & More
Harrison House
Inkling Books
INO Publishing
InterVarsity Press
Lighthouse Publishing
Lutheran Univ. Press
NavPress
Our Sunday Visitor
Tate Publishing
VBC Publishing
WinePress

Word Alive
Yale Univ. Press
Zoë Life Publishing
Zondervan

BIOGRAPHY

(a) Baker Books
(a) Ballantine
(a) Doubleday Relig.
(a) HarperOne
(a) Nelson, Thomas
(a) WaterBrook Press

Aaron Book
ACW Press
Ambassador Intl.
American Binding
Blue Dolphin
Bondfire Books
Booklocker.com
Bridge Logos
Brown Books
Charisma House
Christian Heritage
Christian Writer's Ebook
CLC Publications
Comfort Publishing
Conciliar Press
Creation House
CrossLink Publishing
Deep River Books
Discovery House
Eerdmans Pub., Wm. B.
Essence
Fairway Press
Faith Books & More
Franciscan Media
Grace Acres Press
Guideposts Books
Hannibal Books
Inkling Books
INO Publishing
Kirk House
Lighthouse Publishing
New Leaf
On My Own Now
Pacific Press
Parson Place
Parsons Publishing
Pauline Books
Pauline Kids

Ravenhawk Books
Tate Publishing
Whitaker House
White Fire Publishing
WinePress
Word Alive
Yale Univ. Press
Zoë Life Publishing

BOOKLETS

Aaron Book
American Binding
Bondfire Books
Charisma House
Christian Writer's Ebook
Creation House
Essence
Fruitbearer Pub.
InterVarsity Press
Life Cycle Books
Our Sunday Visitor
Pacific Press
Randall House
Salt Works
Tate Publishing
Trinity Foundation
WinePress
Word Alive

CANADIAN/FOREIGN

Essence
Sunpenny Publishing
Word Alive

CELEBRITY PROFILES

(a) Baker Books
(a) FaithWords
(a) Hay House
(a) Nelson, Thomas

Aaron Book
ACW Press
American Binding
Blue Dolphin
Bondfire Books
Booklocker.com
Brown Books
Charisma House
Christian Writer's Ebook
Comfort Publishing
Deep River Books

Essence
Fairway Press
Faith Books & More
Grace Acres Press
Howard Books
Lighthouse Publishing
On My Own Now
Ravenhawk Books
Tate Publishing
Whitaker House
WinePress
Word Alive

CHARISMATIC
(a) Nelson, Thomas

Aaron Book
ACW Press
American Binding
Blue Dolphin
Booklocker.com
Bridge Logos
Canticle Books
Charisma House
Chosen Books
Comfort Publishing
Creation House
CSS Publishing
Destiny Image (books)
Eerdmans Pub., Wm. B.
Essence
Fairway Press
Faith Books & More
Fruitbearer Pub.
Gospel Publishing
Harrison House
Lighthouse Publishing
Lutheran Univ. Press
Magnus Press
Parsons Publishing
Salvation Publisher
Tate Publishing
Whitaker House
WinePress
Word Alive
Zoë Life Publishing

CHILDREN'S BOARD BOOKS
Ambassador Books
Eerdmans/Yg Readers

Faith Books & More
Halo Publishing Intl.
Pauline Kids
Tate Publishing
WinePress
Word Alive

CHILDREN'S DEVOTIONALS
Bondfire Books
Essence
INO Publishing
New Leaf
Pauline Books
Warner Press
Zoë Life Publishing

CHILDREN'S EASY READERS
(a) Baker Books
(a) Cook, David C.
(a) Tyndale House

Aaron Book
Ambassador Books
Booklocker.com
Brown Books
Charisma House
Conciliar Press
Creation House
Dawn Publications
Deep River Books
Essence
Fairway Press
Faith Books & More
Guardian Angel
Inkling Books
INO Publishing
JourneyForth/BJU
Legacy Press Lift
   Every Voice
Lighthouse Publishing
Our Sunday Visitor
Pacific Press
Pauline Books
Pauline Kids
Pelican Publishing
Standard Publishing
Tate Publishing
VBC Publishing
Warner Press

Word Alive
Zoë Life Publishing

CHILDREN'S PICTURE BOOKS (NONFICTION)
(a) Baker Books
(a) Bethany House
(a) Cook, David C.
(a) Tyndale House
(a) WaterBrook Press

Aaron Book
Abingdon Press
Ambassador Books
Bridge Logos
Brown Books
Conciliar Press
Creation House
Dove Inspirational
Eerdmans Pub., Wm. B.
Eerdmans/Yg Readers
Essence
Faith Books & More
Fruitbearer Pub.
Guardian Angel
Halo Publishing Intl.
INO Publishing
Lighthouse Publishing
New Leaf
Pauline Books
Pauline Kids
Pelican Publishing
Standard Publishing
Tate Publishing
Warner Press
WinePress
Zoë Life Publishing

CHRIST
(a) Bethany House
(a) Cook, David C.
(a) Doubleday Relig.
(a) Nelson, Thomas

Aaron Book
ACW Press
Ambassador Intl.
American Binding
Barbour
Blue Dolphin
BMH Books

Bondfire Books
Booklocker.com
Brown Books
Canticle Books
Charisma House
Christian Heritage
Christian Writer's Ebook
CLC Publications
Creation House
CrossLink Publishing
CSS Publishing
Deep River Books
Discovery House
Earthen Vessel
Eerdmans Pub., Wm. B.
Essence
Fairway Press
Faith Books & More
Grace Acres Press
Guardian Angel
Guideposts Books
INO Publishing
JourneyForth/BJU
Lift Every Voice
Lighthouse Publishing
Lutheran Univ. Press
Magnus Press
NavPress
New Leaf
Our Sunday Visitor
Parson Place
Pauline Kids
Salt Works
Tate Publishing
VBC Publishing
WinePress
Word Alive
Yale Univ. Press
Zoë Life Publishing

CHRISTIAN BUSINESS
(a) Cook, David C.
(a) Doubleday Relig.
(a) Nelson, Thomas
(a) WaterBrook Press

Aaron Book
ACW Press
Ambassador Intl.
American Binding

Blue Dolphin
BMH Books
Bondfire Books
Booklocker.com
Brown Books
Charisma House
Christian Writer's Ebook
Comfort Publishing
Creation House
CSS Publishing
Cupola Press
Deep River Books
Eerdmans Pub., Wm. B.
Essence
Fairway Press
Faith Books & More
Grace Acres Press
Hannibal Books
Howard Books
InterVarsity Press
JourneyForth/BJU
Kirk House
Lift Every Voice
Lighthouse Publishing
Lutheran Univ. Press
NavPress
New Leaf
Ravenhawk Books
Salvation Publisher
Tate Publishing
Trinity Foundation
VBC Publishing
Whitaker House
White Fire Publishing
WinePress
Word Alive
Zoë Life Publishing

CHRISTIAN EDUCATION
(a) Baker Academic
(a) Baker Books
(a) Cook, David C.
(a) Doubleday Relig.
(a) Kregel

Aaron Book
ACW Press
Ambassador Intl.
American Binding
Blue Dolphin

Bondfire Books
Booklocker.com
Brown Books
Christian Heritage
Christian Writer's Ebook
Church Growth Inst.
Contemporary Drama
CSS Publishing
DCTS Publishers
Eerdmans Pub., Wm. B.
Essence
Fairway Press
Faith Books & More
Gospel Publishing
Grace Acres Press
Group Publishing
Halo Publishing Intl.
Hensley Publishing
InterVarsity Press
Judson Press
Kirk House
Lift Every Voice
Lighthouse Publishing
Lutheran Univ. Press
Meriwether
New Leaf
Our Sunday Visitor
Pacific Press
Rainbow Publishers
Reference Service
Salvation Publisher
Standard Publishing
Tate Publishing
Trinity Foundation
VBC Publishing
White Fire Publishing
WinePress
Word Alive
Zoë Life Publishing

CHRISTIAN HOMESCHOOLING
(a) Baker Books

Aaron Book
ACW Press
American Binding
Blue Dolphin
BMH Books
Bondfire Books

Booklocker.com
Brown Books
Christian Writer's Ebook
CrossHouse
CSS Publishing
Eerdmans Pub., Wm. B.
Essence
Fairway Press
Faith Books & More
Fruitbearer Pub.
Grace Acres Press
Hannibal Books
Inkling Books
Lift Every Voice
Lighthouse Publishing
New Leaf
Pacific Press
Parsons Publishing
Standard Publishing
Tate Publishing
White Fire Publishing
WinePress
Word Alive
Zoë Life Publishing

CHRISTIAN LIVING
(a) Baker Books
(a) B&H Publishing
(a) Bethany House
(a) Cook, David C.
(a) Doubleday Relig.
(a) FaithWords
(a) HarperOne
(a) Multnomah
(a) Nelson, Thomas
(a) Revell
(a) Tyndale House
(a) WaterBrook Press

Aaron Book
Abingdon Press
ACW Press
Ambassador Books
Ambassador Intl.
American Binding
Barbour
Blue Dolphin
Bondfire Books
Booklocker.com
Brown Books

Canticle Books
Charisma House
Christian Writer's Ebook
CLC Publications
Comfort Publishing
Creation House
CrossLink Publishing
Crossway
CSS Publishing
Cupola Press
DCTS Publishers
Deep River Books
Destiny Image (books)
Discovery House
Eerdmans Pub., Wm. B.
Essence
Fairway Press
Franciscan Media
Faith Books & More
Grace Acres Press
Guideposts Books
Howard Books
Inheritance Press
INO Publishing
InterVarsity Press
JourneyForth/BJU
Judson Press
Life Cycle Books
Lift Every Voice
Lighthouse Publishing
Lutheran Univ. Press
Magnus Press
Moody Publishers
NavPress
New Hope
New Leaf
On My Own Now
Our Sunday Visitor
Parsons Publishing
Pauline Kids
Port Hole Public.
Randall House
Salvation Publisher
Standard Publishing
Sunpenny Publishing
Tate Publishing
VBC Publishing
Wesleyan Publishing
White Fire Publishing
WinePress

Word Alive
Zoë Life Publishing

CHRISTIAN SCHOOL BOOKS
(a) Baker Books

Aaron Book
ACW Press
American Binding
Blue Dolphin
Bondfire Books
Booklocker.com
Christian Writer's Ebook
CrossLink Publishing
CSS Publishing
Eerdmans Pub., Wm. B.
Essence
Fairway Press
Faith Books & More
Grace Acres Press
Inkling Books
JourneyForth/BJU
Lighthouse Publishing
Our Sunday Visitor
Pacific Press
Pauline Kids
Tate Publishing
Trinity Foundation
White Fire Publishing
WinePress
Word Alive
Zoë Life Publishing

CHRISTMAS BOOKS
Bondfire Books
Cupola Press
Essence
Warner Press
White Fire Publishing
Zoë Life Publishing

CHURCH GROWTH
(a) Kregel

Aaron Book
Ambassador Intl.
Booklocker.com
Brown Books
CrossHouse
Dove Inspirational

Eerdmans/Yg Readers
Essence
Faith Books & More
Grace Acres Press
Guardian Angel
INO Publishing
Legacy Press
NavPress
New Leaf
Pauline Kids
Pelican Publishing
Randall House
Salt Works
White Fire Publishing
WinePress
Zoë Life Publishing

CHURCH HISTORY
(a) Baker Books
(a) B&H Publishing
(a) Doubleday Relig.
(a) HarperOne
(a) Kregel

Aaron Book
Abingdon Press
ACW Press
Ambassador Intl.
American Binding
Blue Dolphin
Bondfire Books
Booklocker.com
Christian Heritage
Christian Writer's Ebook
Creation House
CrossHouse
CrossLink Publishing
Crossway
CSS Publishing
Earthen Vessel
Eerdmans Pub., Wm. B.
Essence
Fairway Press
Faith Books & More
Franciscan Media
Hannibal Books
INO Publishing
InterVarsity Press
Kirk House
Lighthouse Publishing

Loyola Press
Lutheran Univ. Press
NavPress
Our Sunday Visitor
Pacific Press
Pauline Books
Randall House
Tate Publishing
Trinity Foundation
White Fire Publishing
WinePress
Word Alive
Yale Univ. Press
Zoë Life Publishing
Zondervan

CHURCH LIFE
(a) Baker Books
(a) Bethany House
(a) Doubleday Relig.
(a) HarperOne
(a) Kregel
(a) Nelson, Thomas

Aaron Book
Abingdon Press
ACW Press
Ambassador Intl.
American Binding
Blue Dolphin
Bondfire Books
Booklocker.com
Charisma House
Christian Writer's Ebook
CLC Publications
Creation House
Crossway
CSS Publishing
DCTS Publishers
Deep River Books
Destiny Image (gifts)
Discovery House
Earthen Vessel
Eerdmans Pub., Wm. B.
Essence
Fairway Press
Faith Books & More
Grace Acres Press
Hannibal Books
Harrison House

Howard Books
INO Publishing
InterVarsity Press
Judson Press
Kirk House
Lift Every Voice
Lighthouse Publishing
Lutheran Univ. Press
NavPress
New Hope
Pacific Press
Pauline Kids
Randall House
Tate Publishing
Wesleyan Publishing
White Fire Publishing
WinePress
Word Alive
Zoë Life Publishing

CHURCH MANAGEMENT
(a) B&H Publishing
(a) Doubleday Relig.
(a) Kregel

Aaron Book
Abingdon Press
ACW Press
Ambassador Intl.
American Binding
Blue Dolphin
BMH Books
Booklocker.com
Charisma House
Christian Heritage
CLC Publications
Creation House
CSS Publishing
Eerdmans Pub., Wm. B.
Essence
Fairway Press
Faith Books & More
Grace Acres Press
Group Publishing
Hannibal Books
Harrison House
JourneyForth/BJU
Judson Press
Kirk House
Lighthouse Publishing

Lutheran Univ. Press
Our Sunday Visitor
Randall House
Tate Publishing
Wesleyan Publishing
White Fire Publishing
WinePress
Word Alive
Zoë Life Publishing

CHURCH RENEWAL
(a) Baker Books
(a) Doubleday Relig.
(a) HarperOne
(a) Kregel

Aaron Book
Abingdon Press
ACW Press
Ambassador Intl.
American Binding
Blue Dolphin
BMH Books
Bondfire Books
Booklocker.com
Bridge Logos
Canticle Books
Christian Writer's Ebook
Church Growth Inst.
CLC Publications
Creation House
CSS Publishing
Deep River Books
Destiny Image (books)
Destiny Image (gifts)
Earthen Vessel
Eerdmans Pub., Wm. B.
Essence
Fairway Press
Faith Books & More
Grace Acres Press
Hannibal Books
Howard Books
INO Publishing
InterVarsity Press
Judson Press
Lighthouse Publishing
Lutheran Univ. Press
Magnus Press
NavPress
Pacific Press

Parson Place
Randall House
Salvation Publisher
Tate Publishing
Wesleyan Publishing
White Fire Publishing
WinePress
Word Alive
Zoë Life Publishing

CHURCH TRADITIONS
(a) Baker Books
(a) Doubleday Relig.
(a) Kregel
(a) Nelson, Thomas

Aaron Book
Abingdon Press
ACW Press
Ambassador Intl.
American Binding
Blue Dolphin
Booklocker.com
Christian Heritage
Christian Writer's
    Ebook
Conciliar Press
Creation House
CSS Publishing
Deep River Books
Earthen Vessel
Eerdmans Pub., Wm. B.
Essence
Fairway Press
Faith Books & More
Franciscan Media
Howard Books
Inkling Books
InterVarsity Press
Lighthouse Publishing
Lutheran Univ. Press
NavPress
Our Sunday Visitor
Pacific Press
Pauline Kids
Praeger Publishers
Tate Publishing
White Fire Publishing
WinePress
Word Alive
Zoë Life Publishing

COFFEE-TABLE BOOKS
Aaron Book
ACW Press
Ambassador Intl.
Brown Books
Creation House
Deep River Books
Essence
Halo Publishing Intl.
Kirk House
Lutheran Univ. Press
Salt Works
WinePress
Zoë Life Publishing

COMPILATIONS
(a) Doubleday Relig.
(a) WaterBrook Press

Aaron Book
ACW Press
Ambassador Intl.
American Binding
Barbour
Bondfire Books
Booklocker.com
Charisma House
Christian Heritage
Christian Writer's Ebook
CLC Publications
Creation House
Cupola Press
Deep River Books
Earthen Vessel
Eerdmans Pub., Wm. B.
Essence
Fairway Press
Faith Books & More
Group Publishing
InterVarsity Press
Lighthouse Publishing
NavPress
Salt Works
Tate Publishing
White Fire Publishing
WinePress
Word Alive
Zoë Life Publishing

CONTROVERSIAL ISSUES
(a) Baker Books
(a) Doubleday Relig.

(a) FaithWords
(a) HarperOne
(a) Hay House
(a) Kregel

Aaron Book
ACW Press
American Binding
AMG Publishers
Blue Dolphin
Bondfire Books
Booklocker.com
Bridge Logos
Canticle Books
Charisma House
Christian Writer's Ebook
Comfort Publishing
Conciliar Press
Creation House
Deep River Books
Destiny Image (books)
Destiny Image (gifts)
Earthen Vessel
Eerdmans Pub., Wm. B.
Essence
Fairway Press
Faith Books & More
Hannibal Books
Howard Books
Inkling Books
InterVarsity Press
Judson Press
Life Cycle Books
Lighthouse Publishing
Magnus Press
MountainView
NavPress
Ravenhawk Books
Salt Works
Tate Publishing
White Fire Publishing
WinePress
Word Alive
Zoë Life Publishing

COOKBOOKS
(a) Ballantine
(a) Nelson, Thomas

Aaron Book
Adams Media

American Binding
Barbour
Booklocker.com
Bridge Logos
Brown Books
Charisma House
Christian Writer's Ebook
CrossHouse
Dove Inspirational
Essence
Fairway Press
Faith Books & More
Guardian Angel
Halo Publishing Intl.
Hannibal Books
Pacific Press
Pelican Publishing
Sunpenny Publishing
Tate Publishing
WinePress
Word Alive
Zoë Life Publishing

COUNSELING AIDS
(a) Baker Books
(a) Kregel
(a) Nelson, Thomas

Aaron Book
ACW Press
Ambassador Intl.
American Binding
Blue Dolphin
Bondfire Books
Booklocker.com
Bridge Logos
Brown Books
Charisma House
Christian Writer's Ebook
CSS Publishing
Deep River Books
Eerdmans Pub., Wm. B.
Essence
Fairway Press
Faith Books & More
InterVarsity Press
JourneyForth/BJU
Langmarc
Life Cycle Books
Lighthouse Publishing
On My Own Now

Randall House
Reference Service
Tate Publishing
WinePress
Word Alive
Zoë Life Publishing

CREATION SCIENCE
Aaron Book
ACW Press
Ambassador Intl.
American Binding
Blue Dolphin
BMH Books
Bondfire Books
Booklocker.com
Bridge Logos
Charisma House
Christian Writer's Ebook
Eerdmans Pub., Wm. B.
Essence
Fairway Press
Faith Books & More
Inkling Books
INO Publishing
Lighthouse Publishing
New Leaf
Pacific Press
Parson Place
Salt Works
Tate Publishing
Whitaker House
WinePress
Word Alive
Zoë Life Publishing

CULTS/OCCULT
(a) Baker Books
(a) HarperOne
(a) Kregel

Aaron Book
ACW Press
American Binding
Booklocker.com
Christian Writer's Ebook
CLC Publications
Comfort Publishing
Conciliar Press
Eerdmans Pub., Wm. B.
Essence

Fairway Press
Faith Books & More
Lighthouse Publishing
Ravenhawk Books
Tate Publishing
Whitaker House
WinePress
Word Alive

CURRENT/SOCIAL ISSUES
(a) Baker Academic
(a) Baker Books
(a) B&H Publishing
(a) Bethany House
(a) Doubleday Relig.
(a) FaithWords
(a) HarperOne
(a) Kregel
(a) Nelson, Thomas
(a) Tyndale House

Aaron Book
ACW Press
American Binding
AMG Publishers
Ampelos Press
Blue Dolphin
Bondfire Books
Booklocker.com
Bridge Logos
Brown Books
Charisma House
Christian Writer's Ebook
Comfort Publishing
Conari Press
Creation House
CrossLink Publishing
DCTS Publishers
Deep River Books
Destiny Image (gifts)
Eerdmans Pub., Wm. B.
Essence
Fairway Press
Faith Books & More
Hannibal Books
Howard Books
Inkling Books
InterVarsity Press
JourneyForth/BJU
Judson Press
Life Cycle Books

Lighthouse Publishing
Loyola Press
Lutheran Univ. Press
NavPress
New Hope
New Leaf
On My Own Now
Ravenhawk Books
Salt Works
Tate Publishing
VBC Publishing
Whitaker House
White Fire Publishing
WinePress
Word Alive
Yale Univ. Press
Zoë Life Publishing

CURRICULUM
(a) Cook, David C.

Aaron Book
Bondfire Books
CrossLink Publishing
Eerdmans Pub., Wm. B.
Fairway Press
Gospel Light
Gospel Publishing
Grace Acres Press
Group Publishing
Hannibal Books
Inheritance Press
Lighthouse Publishing
New Leaf
Randall House Digital
Standard Publishing
Tate Publishing
WinePress
Word Alive
Zoë Life Publishing

DATING/SEX
(a) Ballantine
(a) Bethany House
(a) Cook, David C.
(a) Doubleday Relig.
(a) FaithWords
(a) HarperOne
(a) Kregel
(a) Nelson, Thomas
(a) WaterBrook Press

Aaron Book
ACW Press
American Binding
Barbour
Blue Dolphin
Bondfire Books
Booklocker.com
Bridge Logos
Charisma House
Christian Writer's Ebook
Comfort Publishing
Deep River Books
Destiny Image (books)
Eerdmans Pub., Wm. B.
Essence
Fairway Press
Faith Books & More
Lift Every Voice
Lighthouse Publishing
NavPress
On My Own Now
Pauline Books
Tate Publishing
Whitaker House
White Fire Publishing
WinePress
Word Alive
Zoë Life Publishing

DEATH/DYING
(a) Baker Books
(a) Cook, David C.
(a) Doubleday Relig.
(a) HarperOne
(a) Kregel
(a) Nelson, Thomas
(a) WaterBrook Press

Aaron Book
Abingdon Press
ACW Press
American Binding
Blue Dolphin
Bondfire Books
Booklocker.com
Bridge Logos
Brown Books
Charisma House
Christian Writer's Ebook
Comfort Publishing
Creation House

CSS Publishing
Cupola Press
Deep River Books
Discovery House
Eerdmans Pub., Wm. B.
Essence
Fairway Press
Faith Books & More
Guardian Angel
Halo Publishing Intl.
Life Cycle Books
Lift Every Voice
Lighthouse Publishing
Loyola Press
Lutheran Univ. Press
NavPress
Pacific Press
Pauline Books
Tate Publishing
Whitaker House
White Fire Publishing
WinePress
Word Alive
Zoë Life Publishing

DEVOTIONAL BOOKS
(a) Baker Books
(a) Bethany House
(a) Cook, David C.
(a) Doubleday Relig.
(a) FaithWords
(a) HarperOne
(a) Kregel
(a) Nelson, Thomas
(a) Tyndale House
(a) WaterBrook Press

Aaron Book
Abingdon Press
ACW Press
Ambassador Books
Ambassador Intl.
American Binding
Ampelos Press
Barbour
Blue Dolphin
Bondfire Books
Booklocker.com
Brown Books
Charisma House
Christian Heritage

Christian Writer's Ebook
CLC Publications
Contemporary Drama
Creation House
CrossLink Publishing
CSS Publishing
Cupola Press
Deep River Books
Discovery House
Eerdmans Pub., Wm. B.
Essence
Fairway Press
Faith Books & More
Franciscan Media
Fruitbearer Pub.
Group Publishing
Guideposts Books
Hannibal Books
Harrison House
Howard Books
Inheritance Press
Inkling Books
INO Publishing
Judson Press
Legacy Press
Lift Every Voice
Lighthouse Publishing
MOPS Intl.
NavPress
New Hope
New Leaf
On My Own Now
Parson Place
Parsons Publishing
Pauline Books
Salt Works
Salvation Publisher
Standard Publishing
Tate Publishing
VBC Publishing
Warner Press
Wesleyan Publishing
White Fire Publishing
WinePress
Word Alive
Zoë Life Publishing

DISCIPLESHIP
(a) Baker Books
(a) B&H Publishing

(a) Bethany House
(a) Cook, David C.
(a) Doubleday Relig.
(a) HarperOne
(a) Kregel
(a) Nelson, Thomas
(a) WaterBrook Press

Aaron Book
Abingdon Press
ACW Press
Ambassador Intl.
American Binding
Barbour
Blue Dolphin
BMH Books
Bondfire Books
Booklocker.com
Bridge Logos
Brown Books
Charisma House
Christian Heritage
Christian Writer's Ebook
CLC Publications
Comfort Publishing
Creation House
Crossway
CSS Publishing
Cupola Press
DCTS Publishers
Deep River Books
Destiny Image (books)
Discovery House
Eerdmans Pub., Wm. B.
Essence
Fairway Press
Faith Books & More
Gospel Publishing
Grace Acres Press
Group Publishing
Harrison House
Hensley Publishing
Howard Books
Inheritance Press
Inkling Books
INO Publishing
InterVarsity Press
JourneyForth/BJU
Judson Press
Lift Every Voice
Lighthouse Publishing

Lutheran Univ. Press
Moody Publishers
NavPress
New Hope
New Leaf
On My Own Now
Pacific Press
Parson Place
Pauline Books
Randall House
Salt Works
Salvation Publisher
Standard Publishing
Tate Publishing
Whitaker House
White Fire Publishing
WinePress
Word Alive
Zoë Life Publishing

DIVORCE
(a) Baker Books
(a) Bethany House
(a) Cook, David C.
(a) Kregel
(a) Nelson, Thomas
(a) WaterBrook Press

Aaron Book
ACW Press
Ambassador Books
Ambassador Intl.
American Binding
Blue Dolphin
Bondfire Books
Booklocker.com
Bridge Logos
Brown Books
Charisma House
Christian Writer's Ebook
Comfort Publishing
Creation House
CSS Publishing
Deep River Books
Earthen Vessel
Eerdmans Pub., Wm. B.
Essence
Fairway Press
Faith Books & More
Guideposts Books

Halo Publishing Intl.
INO Publishing
InterVarsity Press
Lighthouse Publishing
Pacific Press
Pauline Books
Tate Publishing
WinePress
Word Alive
Zoë Life Publishing

DOCTRINAL
(a) Baker Books
(a) Bethany House
(a) Doubleday Relig.
(a) Kregel
(a) Tyndale House

Aaron Book
ACW Press
Ambassador Intl.
American Binding
Blue Dolphin
Booklocker.com
Brown Books
Canticle Books
Christian Heritage
Christian Writer's
    Ebook
CLC Publications
Creation House
Crossway
DCTS Publishers
Earthen Vessel
Eerdmans Pub., Wm. B.
Essence
Fairway Press
Faith Books & More
InterVarsity Press
Lighthouse Publishing
Lutheran Univ. Press
Pacific Press
Randall House
Tate Publishing
Trinity Foundation
VBC Publishing
White Fire Publishing
WinePress
Word Alive
Zoë Life Publishing

DRAMA
(a) Kregel

Aaron Book
American Binding
Contemporary Drama
Fairway Press
Faith Books & More
Guardian Angel
Halo Publishing Intl.
Lighthouse Publishing
Meriwether
Ravenhawk Books
Salt Works
Tate Publishing
WinePress
Word Alive

E-BOOKS
(a) Tyndale House

Ambassador Intl.
Blue Dolphin
Bondfire Books
Booklocker.com
Christian Writer's Ebook
Comfort Publishing
CSS Publishing
Cupola Press
Faith Books & More
Grace Acres Press
Guardian Angel
InterVarsity Press
Lighthouse Publishing
NavPress
New Leaf
Randall House Digital
Salt Works
Sunpenny Publishing
Westbow Press
White Fire Publishing
White Rose
Word Alive
Zoë Life Publishing

ECONOMICS
(a) Baker Books

Aaron Book
ACW Press
American Binding

Blue Dolphin
Booklocker.com
Brown Books
Christian Writer's Ebook
Creation House
Deep River Books
Eerdmans Pub., Wm. B.
Essence
Fairway Press
Faith Books & More
Lighthouse Publishing
New Hope
New Leaf
Praeger Publishers
Salvation Publisher
Tate Publishing
Trinity Foundation
WinePress
Word Alive
Zoë Life Publishing

ENCOURAGEMENT
(a) Doubleday Relig.
(a) WaterBrook Press

Aaron Book
ACW Press
American Binding
Barbour
Blue Dolphin
Bondfire Books
Booklocker.com
Brown Books
Charisma House
CLC Publications
Comfort Publishing
Creation House
CSS Publishing
Cupola Press
Discovery House
Earthen Vessel
Eerdmans Pub., Wm. B.
Essence
Fairway Press
Faith Books & More
Grace Acres Press
Guardian Angel
Howard Books
INO Publishing
JourneyForth/BJU

Lift Every Voice
Lighthouse Publishing
NavPress
New Hope
On My Own Now
Parson Place
Port Hole Public.
Randall House
Salvation Publisher
Tate Publishing
VBC Publishing
White Fire Publishing
WinePress
Word Alive
Zoë Life Publishing

ENVIRONMENTAL ISSUES
(a) Baker Books
(a) Doubleday Relig.

Aaron Book
ACW Press
American Binding
Blue Dolphin
Booklocker.com
Christian Writer's Ebook
Cladach Publishing
Dawn Publications
Deep River Books
Eerdmans Pub., Wm. B.
Essence
Fairway Press
Faith Books & More
InterVarsity Press
Judson Press
Lighthouse Publishing
New Leaf
Praeger Publishers
Ravenhawk Books
Sunpenny Publishing
Tate Publishing
WinePress
Word Alive

ESCHATOLOGY
(a) Baker Books
(a) Kregel
(a) Nelson, Thomas

Aaron Book
ACW Press

American Binding
Blue Dolphin
BMH Books
Booklocker.com
Bridge Logos
Charisma House
Christian Heritage
Christian Writer's Ebook
Creation House
CSS Publishing
DCTS Publishers
Eerdmans Pub., Wm. B.
Essence
Fairway Press
Faith Books & More
Grace Acres Press
Kirk House
Lighthouse Publishing
Lutheran Univ. Press
Nelson, Thomas
Pacific Press
Parson Place
Strong Tower
Tate Publishing
VBC Publishing
WinePress
Word Alive
Zoë Life Publishing

ETHICS
(a) Baker Books
(a) Kregel

Aaron Book
ACW Press
American Binding
Blue Dolphin
Bondfire Books
Booklocker.com
Christian Heritage
Christian Writer's Ebook
CLC Publications
Conciliar Press
Creation House
Crossway
Deep River Books
Earthen Vessel
Eerdmans Pub., Wm. B.
Essence
Fairway Press

Faith Books & More
Franciscan Media
Grace Acres Press
Guardian Angel
Hannibal Books
Howard Books
Inkling Books
InterVarsity Press
Kirk House
Life Cycle Books
Lift Every Voice
Lighthouse Publishing
Lutheran Univ. Press
Our Sunday Visitor
Pacific Press
Paragon House
Randall House
Ravenhawk Books
Salt Works
Tate Publishing
Trinity Foundation
Whitaker House
White Fire Publishing
WinePress
Word Alive
Yale Univ. Press
Zoë Life Publishing

ETHNIC/CULTURAL

(a) Baker Books
(a) Doubleday Relig.
(a) HarperOne
(a) Kregel

Aaron Book
ACW Press
American Binding
Blue Dolphin
Booklocker.com
Bridge Logos
Christian Writer's Ebook
CLC Publications
Creation House
Deep River Books
Eerdmans Pub., Wm. B.
Essence
Fairway Press
Faith Books & More
Franciscan Media
Guardian Angel

Howard Books
InterVarsity Press
Judson Press
Kirk House
Lift Every Voice
Lighthouse Publishing
Lutheran Univ. Press
Moody Publishers
NavPress
New Hope
Pacific Press
Praeger Publishers
Standard Publishing
Sunpenny Publishing
Tate Publishing
Whitaker House
WinePress
Word Alive
Yale Univ. Press
Zoë Life Publishing
Zondervan

EVANGELISM/ WITNESSING

(a) Baker Books
(a) Cook, David C.
(a) Kregel
(a) Nelson, Thomas
(a) Tyndale House

Aaron Book
ACW Press
Ambassador Intl.
American Binding
Blue Dolphin
BMH Books
Bondfire Books
Booklocker.com
Bridge Logos
Charisma House
Christian Heritage
Christian Writer's Ebook
Church Growth Inst.
CLC Publications
Creation House
CrossHouse
CrossLink Publishing
CSS Publishing
DCTS Publishers
Deep River Books

Discovery House
Earthen Vessel
Eerdmans Pub., Wm. B.
Essence
Fairway Press
Faith Books & More
Gospel Publishing
Grace Acres Press
Group Publishing
InterVarsity Press
Judson Press
Lift Every Voice
Lighthouse Publishing
Lutheran Univ. Press
Moody Publishers
NavPress
New Hope
Pacific Press
Parson Place
Randall House
Salt Works
Tate Publishing
VBC Publishing
Wesleyan Publishing
White Fire Publishing
WinePress
Word Alive
Yale Univ. Press
Zoë Life Publishing

EXEGESIS

(a) Baker Books
(a) Doubleday Relig.
(a) Kregel

Aaron Book
Abingdon Press
ACW Press
American Binding
Blue Dolphin
BMH Books
Bondfire Books
Booklocker.com
Canticle Books
Christian Writer's Ebook
CLC Publications
CSS Publishing
Deep River Books
Earthen Vessel
Eerdmans Pub., Wm. B.

Essence
Fairway Press
Faith Books & More
Grace Acres Press
INO Publishing
InterVarsity Press
Lighthouse Publishing
Lutheran Univ. Press
Salt Works
Tate Publishing
VBC Publishing
WinePress
Word Alive
Yale Univ. Press
Zoë Life Publishing

EXPOSÉS

(a) Baker Books

Aaron Book
ACW Press
American Binding
Blue Dolphin
Booklocker.com
Christian Writer's Ebook
Eerdmans Pub., Wm. B.
Fairway Press
Faith Books & More
Lighthouse Publishing
Ravenhawk Books
Salt Works
WinePress
Word Alive
Zoë Life Publishing

FAITH

(a) Baker Books
(a) B&H Publishing
(a) Bethany House
(a) Doubleday Relig.
(a) FaithWords
(a) HarperOne
(a) Kregel
(a) Nelson, Thomas
(a) Tyndale House
(a) WaterBrook Press

Aaron Book
Abingdon Press
ACW Press
Ambassador Books

Ambassador Intl.
American Binding
Barbour
Blue Dolphin
Bondfire Books
Booklocker.com
Bridge Logos
Brown Books
Charisma House
Christian Heritage
Christian Writer's Ebook
CLC Publications
Comfort Publishing
Creation House
CrossLink Publishing
Cupola Press
DCTS Publishers
Deep River Books
Destiny Image (books)
Destiny Image (gifts)
Discovery House
Earthen Vessel
Eerdmans Pub., Wm. B.
Essence
Fairway Press
Faith Books & More
Fruitbearer Pub.
Grace Acres Press
Group Publishing
Guardian Angel
Guideposts Books
Halo Publishing Intl.
Harrison House
Hensley Publishing
Howard Books
Inheritance Press
InterVarsity Press
JourneyForth/BJU
Judson Press
Lift Every Voice
Lighthouse Publishing
Loyola Press
Lutheran Univ. Press
Magnus Press
NavPress
New Hope
On My Own Now
Pacific Press
Parson Place
Parsons Publishing

Pauline Books
Randall House
Salt Works
Salvation Publisher
Tate Publishing
VBC Publishing
Wesleyan Publishing
Whitaker House
White Fire Publishing
WinePress
Word Alive
Zoë Life Publishing

FAMILY LIFE

(a) Baker Books
(a) B&H Publishing
(a) Bethany House
(a) Cook, David C.
(a) FaithWords
(a) HarperOne
(a) Kregel
(a) Nelson, Thomas
(a) Tyndale House
(a) WaterBrook Press

Aaron Book
Abingdon Press
ACW Press
Ambassador Books
Ambassador Intl.
American Binding
Barbour
Blue Dolphin
Bondfire Books
Booklocker.com
Bridge Logos
Brown Books
Charisma House
Christian Writer's Ebook
Cladach Publishing
Comfort Publishing
Conari Press
Creation House
CrossLink Publishing
Crossway
Cupola Press
DCTS Publishers
Deep River Books
Destiny Image (books)
Destiny Image (gifts)

Discovery House
Dove Inspirational
Eerdmans Pub., Wm. B.
Essence
Fairway Press
Faith Books & More
Focus on the Family
Franciscan Media
Grace Acres Press
Guardian Angel
Guideposts Books
Halo Publishing Intl.
Hannibal Books
Hensley Publishing
Howard Books
INO Publishing
InterVarsity Press
JourneyForth/BJU
Judson Press
Langmarc
Legacy Press
Life Cycle Books
Lift Every Voice
Lighthouse Publishing
Loyola Press
MOPS Intl.
MountainView
NavPress
New Hope
New Leaf
Our Sunday Visitor
Pacific Press
Pauline Books
Pelican Publishing
Port Hole Public.
Randall House
Salvation Publisher
Tate Publishing
VBC Publishing
Vision Forum
Whitaker House
White Fire Publishing
WinePress
Word Alive
Zoë Life Publishing

FICTION: ADULT/ GENERAL

(a) Ballantine
(a) FaithWords
(a) HarperOne
(a) Kregel
(a) Multnomah
(a) Nelson, Fiction, Thomas

Aaron Book
Ambassador Intl.
American Binding
Blue Dolphin
Bondfire Books
Brown Books
BRP Publishing
Charisma House
Cladach Publishing
Comfort Publishing
Creation House
Essence
Halo Publishing Intl.
Howard Books
INO Publishing
Lighthouse Publishing
Love Inspired
MountainView
New Leaf
Parson Place
Ravenhawk Books
Whitaker House
White Fire Publishing

FICTION: ADULT/ RELIGIOUS

(a) Baker Books
(a) Ballantine
(a) B&H Publishing
(a) Bethany House
(a) Doubleday Relig.
(a) FaithWords
(a) HarperOne
(a) Kregel
(a) Multnomah
(a) Nelson, Fiction, Thomas
(a) Revell
(a) WaterBrook Press

Aaron Book
ACW Press
Adams Media
Ambassador Books
Ambassador Intl.
American Binding

Barbour
Bondfire Books
Booklocker.com
Bridge Logos
Brown Books
BRP Publishing
Charisma House
Christian Writer's
    Ebook
Cladach Publishing
Comfort Publishing
Creation House
CrossHouse
Deep River Books
Destiny Image (books)
Destiny Image (gifts)
Earthen Vessel
Eerdmans Pub., Wm. B.
Essence
Fairway Press
Faith Books & More
Focus on the Family
Fruitbearer Pub.
Guideposts Books
Halo Publishing Intl.
Hannibal Books
Howard Books
INO Publishing
Lift Every Voice
Lighthouse Publishing
Love Inspired
Moody Publishers
MountainView
NavPress
New Leaf
OakTara
Pacific Press
Parson Place
Parsons Publishing
Port Hole Public.
Salt Works
Sunpenny Publishing
Tate Publishing
Vision Forum
Whitaker House
White Fire Publishing
White Rose
WinePress
Word Alive
Zoë Life Publishing

FICTION: ADVENTURE

(a) Baker Books
(a) Multnomah
(a) WaterBrook Press

Aaron Book
ACW Press
Ambassador Books
Ambassador Intl.
American Binding
Barbour
Bondfire Books
Booklocker.com
Bridge Logos
Brown Books
BRP Publishing
Charisma House
Christian Writer's Ebook
Comfort Publishing
Creation House
Deep River Books
Eerdmans/Yg Readers
Essence
Fairway Press
Faith Books & More
Halo Publishing Intl.
Howard Books
INO Publishing
JourneyForth/BJU
Lift Every Voice
Lighthouse Publishing
MountainView
New Leaf
Parson Place
Parsons Publishing
Pauline Kids
Port Hole Public.
Ravenhawk Books
Salt Works
Sunpenny Publishing
Tate Publishing
White Fire Publishing
WinePress
Zoë Life Publishing

FICTION: ALLEGORY

(a) Baker Books
(a) Multnomah

Aaron Book
ACW Press

American Binding
Barbour
Bondfire Books
Booklocker.com
Bridge Logos
Brown Books
Charisma House
Christian Writer's Ebook
Creation House
Deep River Books
Destiny Image (books)
Essence
Fairway Press
Faith Books & More
Howard Books
Lighthouse Publishing
OakTara
Port Hole Public.
Salt Works
Tate Publishing
WinePress
Zoë Life Publishing

FICTION: BIBLICAL

(a) Baker Books
(a) Multnomah
(a) Nelson, Fiction,Thomas
(a) WaterBrook Press

Aaron Book
Abingdon Press
ACW Press
Ambassador Intl.
American Binding
Bondfire Books
Booklocker.com
Bridge Logos
Brown Books
BRP Publishing
Charisma House
Christian Writer's Ebook
Cladach Publishing
Creation House
Deep River Books
Destiny Image (books)
Destiny Image (gifts)
Earthen Vessel
Eerdmans Pub.,Wm. B.
Eerdmans/Yg Readers
Essence

Fairway Press
Faith Books & More
Guideposts Books
Hannibal Books
Howard Books
Lift Every Voice
Lighthouse Publishing
Moody Publishers
NavPress
OakTara
Pacific Press
Parsons Publishing
Port Hole Public.
Salt Works
Tate Publishing
WinePress
Zoë Life Publishing

FICTION: CHICK LIT

(a) Multnomah
(a) Nelson, Fiction, Thomas
(a) WaterBrook Press

Aaron Book
ACW Press
Ambassador Books
Ambassador Intl.
American Binding
Bondfire Books
Booklocker.com
Brown Books
BRP Publishing
Charisma House
Christian Writer's Ebook
Creation House
Deep River Books
Essence
Faith Books & More
INO Publishing
Lighthouse Publishing
Love Inspired Suspense
Port Hole Public.
Ravenhawk Books
Whitaker House
WinePress
Zoë Life Publishing

FICTION: CONTEMPORARY

(a) Avon Inspire
(a) Baker Books

(a) Ballantine
(a) B&H Publishing
(a) Bethany House
(a) FaithWords
(a) Kregel
(a) Multnomah
(a) Nelson, Fiction, Thomas
(a) Revell
(a) Tyndale House
(a) WaterBrook Press

Aaron Book
ACW Press
Ambassador Books
American Binding
AMG Publishers
Barbour
Bondfire Books
Booklocker.com
Brown Books
BRP Publishing
Charisma House
Christian Writer's Ebook
Creation House
Deep River Books
Desert Breeze Pub.
Destiny Image (books)
Destiny Image (gifts)
Eerdmans/Yg Readers
Essence
Fairway Press
Faith Books & More
Focus on the Family
Howard Books
INO Publishing
JourneyForth/BJU
Lift Every Voice
Lighthouse Publishing
Love Inspired
Moody Publishers
MountainView
NavPress
New Leaf
OakTara
Parson Place
Pauline Books
Pauline Kids
Port Hole Public.
Ravenhawk Books
Salt Works
Sunpenny Publishing

Tate Publishing
Whitaker House
White Fire Publishing
WinePress
Zoë Life Publishing

FICTION: COZY MYSTERIES

Ambassador Intl.
Bondfire Books
BRP Publishing
Comfort Publishing
Essence
INO Publishing
Zoë Life Publishing

FICTION: ETHNIC

(a) Baker Books
(a) Ballantine
(a) Multnomah

Aaron Book
ACW Press
American Binding
Booklocker.com
Charisma House
Christian Writer's Ebook
Deep River Books
Destiny Image (gifts)
Essence
Fairway Press
Faith Books & More
Focus on the Family
Lift Every Voice
Lighthouse Publishing
Sunpenny Publishing
Tate Publishing
White Fire Publishing
WinePress
Zoë Life Publishing

FICTION: FABLES/ PARABLES

(a) HarperOne

Aaron Book
ACW Press
American Binding
Blue Dolphin
Booklocker.com
Brown Books

BRP Publishing
Deep River Books
Essence
Faith Books & More
Lighthouse Publishing
Parson Place
Pauline Books
Salt Works
Tate Publishing
White Fire Publishing
WinePress
Zoë Life Publishing

FICTION: FANTASY

(a) Ballantine
(a) Multnomah
(a) WaterBrook Press

Aaron Book
ACW Press
American Binding
AMG Publishers
Barbour
Bondfire Books
Booklocker.com
BRP Publishing
Charisma House
Christian Writer's
    Ebook
Comfort Publishing
Creation House
Deep River Books
Desert Breeze Pub.
Destiny Image (books)
Destiny Image (gifts)
Eerdmans Pub., Wm. B.
Essence
Fairway Press
Faith Books & More
INO Publishing
Lighthouse Publishing
Marcher Lord Press
MountainView
OakTara
Parsons Publishing
Port Hole Public.
Ravenhawk Books
Tate Publishing
Whitaker House
WinePress
Zoë Life Publishing

FICTION: FRONTIER

(a) Baker Books
(a) Bethany House
(a) Multnomah
(a) Nelson, Fiction, Thomas

Aaron Book
ACW Press
Ambassador Intl.
American Binding
AMG Publishers
Booklocker.com
Brown Books
BRP Publishing
Charisma House
Christian Writer's Ebook
Cladach Publishing
Deep River Books
Essence
Fairway Press
Faith Books & More
Guardian Angel
JourneyForth/BJU
Lighthouse Publishing
MountainView
Parson Place
Port Hole Public.
Ravenhawk Books
Tate Publishing
Whitaker House
WinePress
Zoë Life Publishing

FICTION: FRONTIER/ ROMANCE

(a) Baker Books
(a) Bethany House
(a) Multnomah
(a) Nelson, Fiction,
    Thomas

Aaron Book
ACW Press
Ambassador Intl.
American Binding
AMG Publishers
Barbour
Bondfire Books
Booklocker.com
Brown Books
BRP Publishing

Charisma House
Christian Writer's Ebook
Deep River Books
Desert Breeze Pub.
Essence
Fairway Press
Faith Books & More
Lighthouse Publishing
MountainView
Parson Place
Port Hole Public.
Ravenhawk Books
Tate Publishing
Whitaker House
White Fire Publishing
White Rose
WinePress
Zoë Life Publishing

FICTION: HISTORICAL

(a) Avon Inspire
(a) Baker Books
(a) Ballantine
(a) B&H Publishing
(a) Bethany House
(a) FaithWords
(a) Kregel
(a) Multnomah
(a) Nelson, Fiction, Thomas
(a) Revell
(a) WaterBrook Press

Aaron Book
Abingdon Press
ACW Press
Ambassador Books
Ambassador Intl.
American Binding
AMG Publishers
Blue Dolphin
Bondfire Books
Booklocker.com
Bridge Logos
Brown Books
BRP Publishing
Charisma House
Christian Writer's Ebook
Cladach Publishing
Comfort Publishing
Deep River Books
Earthen Vessel

Eerdmans Pub., Wm. B.
Eerdmans/Yg Readers
Essence
Fairway Press
Faith Books & More
Focus on the Family
Hannibal Books
Howard Books
INO Publishing
JourneyForth/BJU
Lift Every Voice
Lighthouse Publishing
Moody Publishers
MountainView
NavPress
OakTara
Parson Place
Parsons Publishing
Pauline Books
Pauline Kids
Port Hole Public.
Ravenhawk Books
Salt Works
Sunpenny Publishing
Tate Publishing
Vision Forum
Whitaker House
White Fire Publishing
WinePress
Zoë Life Publishing

FICTION: HISTORICAL/ ROMANCE

(a) Baker Books
(a) B&H Publishing
(a) Bethany House
(a) Multnomah
(a) Nelson, Fiction, Thomas
(a) Tyndale House
(a) WaterBrook Press

Aaron Book
Abingdon Press
ACW Press
Ambassador Intl.
American Binding
AMG Publishers
Barbour
Bondfire Books
Booklocker.com
Brown Books

BRP Publishing
Charisma House
Christian Writer's Ebook
Comfort Publishing
Deep River Books
Desert Breeze Pub.
Essence
Fairway Press
Faith Books & More
Hannibal Books
INO Publishing
Lift Every Voice
Lighthouse Publishing
MountainView
Parson Place
Port Hole Public.
Ravenhawk Books
Tate Publishing
Whitaker House
White Fire Publishing
White Rose
WinePress
Zoë Life Publishing

FICTION: HUMOR
(a) Baker Books
(a) Ballantine
(a) FaithWords
(a) Multnomah

Aaron Book
ACW Press
Ambassador Books
American Binding
Bondfire Books
Booklocker.com
BRP Publishing
Charisma House
Christian Writer's Ebook
Creation House
Deep River Books
Eerdmans/Yg Readers
Essence
Fairway Press
Faith Books & More
Halo Publishing Intl.
JourneyForth/BJU
Lighthouse Publishing
MountainView
Parson Place

Parsons Publishing
Port Hole Public.
Ravenhawk Books
Salt Works
Sunpenny Publishing
Tate Publishing
White Fire Publishing
WinePress
Zoë Life Publishing

FICTION: JUVENILE (AGES 8-12)
(a) Baker Books
(a) Kregel
(a) Tyndale House

Aaron Book
ACW Press
Ambassador Books
American Binding
AMG Publishers
Barbour
Blue Dolphin
Booklocker.com
Brown Books
Charisma House
Comfort Publishing
Creation House
CrossHouse
Deep River Books
Eerdmans Pub., Wm. B.
Eerdmans/Yg Readers
Essence
Fairway Press
Faith Books & More
Fruitbearer Pub.
Guardian Angel
Halo Publishing Intl.
INO Publishing
JourneyForth/BJU
Lift Every Voice
Lighthouse Publishing
Moody Publishers
Pacific Press
Parson Place
Pauline Books
Pauline Kids
Port Hole Public.
Salt Works
Standard Publishing

Tate Publishing
Warner Press
WinePress
Word Alive
Zoë Life Publishing

FICTION: LITERARY
(a) Baker Books
(a) Ballantine
(a) Bethany House
(a) FaithWords
(a) HarperOne
(a) Multnomah
(a) Nelson, Fiction, Thomas
(a) WaterBrook Press

Aaron Book
ACW Press
Ambassador Books
American Binding
Bondfire Books
Booklocker.com
Brown Books
BRP Publishing
Charisma House
Christian Writer's Ebook
Deep River Books
Eerdmans Pub., Wm. B.
Eerdmans/Yg Readers
Essence
Fairway Press
Faith Books & More
Focus on the Family
JourneyForth/BJU
Lighthouse Publishing
Moody Publishers
NavPress
Port Hole Public.
Ravenhawk Books
Salt Works
Sunpenny Publishing
Tate Publishing
WinePress
Zoë Life Publishing

FICTION: MYSTERY/ ROMANCE
(a) Baker Books
(a) Ballantine
(a) B&H Publishing

(a) Bethany House
(a) Kregel
(a) Multnomah
(a) Nelson, Fiction, Thomas
(a) Summerside Press

Aaron Book
ACW Press
American Binding
Barbour
Bondfire Books
Booklocker.com
Brown Books
BRP Publishing
Charisma House
Christian Writer's Ebook
Comfort Publishing
Deep River Books
Desert Breeze Pub.
Destiny Image (gifts)
Essence
Fairway Press
Faith Books & More
Guideposts Books
Howard Books
INO Publishing
Lift Every Voice
Lighthouse Publishing
Love Inspired Suspense
MountainView
Parson Place
Port Hole Public.
Tate Publishing
White Fire Publishing
White Rose
WinePress
Zoë Life Publishing

FICTION: MYSTERY/ SUSPENSE
(a) Baker Books
(a) Ballantine
(a) B&H Publishing
(a) Bethany House
(a) Kregel
(a) Multnomah
(a) Revell
(a) Tyndale House

Aaron Book
ACW Press

Ambassador Books
American Binding
Blue Dolphin
Booklocker.com
Brown Books
BRP Publishing
Charisma House
Christian Writer's Ebook
Comfort Publishing
Creation House
Deep River Books
Desert Breeze Pub.
Eerdmans/Yg Readers
Essence
Fairway Press
Faith Books & More
Focus on the Family
Guideposts Books
Howard Books
INO Publishing
JourneyForth/BJU
Lift Every Voice
Lighthouse Publishing
Love Inspired Suspense
Moody Publishers
MountainView
New Leaf
OakTara
Parson Place
Parsons Publishing
Pauline Books
Pauline Kids
Port Hole Public.
Ravenhawk Books
Salt Works
Sunpenny Publishing
Tate Publishing
White Fire Publishing
WinePress
Zoë Life Publishing

FICTION: NOVELLAS
(a) Baker Books

Aaron Book
ACW Press
American Binding
Barbour
Bondfire Books
Booklocker.com

BRP Publishing
Christian Writer's Ebook
Essence
Fairway Press
Faith Books & More
Halo Publishing Intl.
Lighthouse Publishing
MountainView
Salt Works
WinePress
Zoë Life Publishing

FICTION: PLAYS
American Binding
CSS Publishing
Essence
Fairway Press
Guardian Angel
Meriwether
Salt Works

FICTION: ROMANCE
(a) Baker Books
(a) Ballantine
(a) Bethany House
(a) Multnomah
(a) Nelson, Fiction, Thomas
(a) Summerside Press
(a) Tyndale House
(a) WaterBrook Press

Aaron Book
ACW Press
American Binding
Barbour
Bondfire Books
Booklocker.com
Brown Books
BRP Publishing
Charisma House
Christian Writer's Ebook
Comfort Publishing
Creation House
Deep River Books
Essence
Fairway Press
Faith Books & More
Hannibal Books
INO Publishing
Lift Every Voice

Lighthouse Publishing
Love Inspired
Love Inspired Suspense
MountainView
OakTara
Parson Place
Port Hole Public.
Sunpenny Publishing
Tate Publishing
Whitaker House
White Fire Publishing
White Rose
WinePress
Zoë Life Publishing

FICTION: SCIENCE FICTION

(a) WaterBrook Press

Aaron Book
ACW Press
American Binding
Bondfire Books
Booklocker.com
BRP Publishing
Charisma House
Christian Writer's Ebook
Comfort Publishing
Creation House
Deep River Books
Desert Breeze Pub.
Destiny Image (gifts)
Essence
Fairway Press
Faith Books & More
INO Publishing
Lighthouse Publishing
Marcher Lord Press
MountainView
OakTara
Port Hole Public.
Sunpenny Publishing
Tate Publishing
White Fire Publishing
WinePress
Zoë Life Publishing

FICTION: SHORT STORY COLLECTIONS

(a) Baker Books
(a) Ballantine

Aaron Book
ACW Press
American Binding
Bondfire Books
Booklocker.com
BRP Publishing
Christian Writer's Ebook
Comfort Publishing
Deep River Books
Earthen Vessel
Eerdmans Pub., Wm. B.
Essence
Fairway Press
Faith Books & More
MountainView
Parson Place
Pauline Books
Pauline Kids
Port Hole Public.
Salt Works
Tate Publishing
White Fire Publishing
White Rose
WinePress
Zoë Life Publishing

FICTION: SPECULATIVE

(a) Baker Books
(a) Multnomah

Aaron Book
ACW Press
American Binding
Booklocker.com
Charisma House
Christian Writer's Ebook
Deep River Books
Essence
Faith Books & More
INO Publishing
Lighthouse Publishing
Marcher Lord Press
MountainView
OakTara
Port Hole Public.
Salt Works
Tate Publishing
White Fire Publishing
WinePress
Zoë Life Publishing

FICTION: TEEN/YOUNG ADULT

(a) Baker Books
(a) FaithWords
(a) Kregel
(a) Multnomah
(a) Nelson, Fiction, Thomas
(a) WaterBrook Press

Aaron Book
ACW Press
Ambassador Books
American Binding
AMG Publishers
Barbour
Blue Dolphin
Bondfire Books
Booklocker.com
BRP Publishing
Charisma House
Christian Writer's Ebook
Comfort Publishing
Creation House
Deep River Books
Eerdmans Pub., Wm. B.
Eerdmans/Yg Readers
Essence
Fairway Press
Faith Books & More
Fruitbearer Pub.
INO Publishing
JourneyForth/BJU
Kirk House
Legacy Press
Lift Every Voice
Lighthouse Publishing
Moody Publishers
MountainView
NavPress
Parson Place
Parsons Publishing
Ravenhawk Books
Tate Publishing
Warner Press
Watershed Books
White Fire Publishing
WinePress
Word Alive
Zoë Life Publishing

FICTION: WESTERNS

(a) Baker Books
(a) Multnomah

Aaron Book
ACW Press
American Binding
Booklocker.com
Brown Books
BRP Publishing
Charisma House
Christian Writer's Ebook
Deep River Books
Desert Breeze Pub.
Essence
Fairway Press
Faith Books & More
JourneyForth/BJU
Lighthouse Publishing
MountainView
Parson Place
Ravenhawk Books
Salt Works
Tate Publishing
Whitaker House
WinePress
Zoë Life Publishing

FORGIVENESS

(a) B&H Publishing
(a) Doubleday Relig.
(a) FaithWords
(a) HarperOne
(a) Kregel
(a) Nelson, Thomas

Aaron Book
Abingdon Press
ACW Press
Ambassador Intl.
American Binding
Barbour
Blue Dolphin
Bondfire Books
Booklocker.com
Bridge Logos
Brown Books
Charisma House
Christian Writer's Ebook
CLC Publications
Comfort Publishing

Creation House
CrossLink Publishing
CSS Publishing
Cupola Press
DCTS Publishers
Deep River Books
Destiny Image (books)
Discovery House
Eerdmans Pub., Wm. B.
Essence
Fairway Press
Faith Books & More
Grace Acres Press
Guardian Angel
Halo Publishing Intl.
Hensley Publishing
Howard Books
InterVarsity Press
JourneyForth/BJU
Judson Press
Lift Every Voice
Lighthouse Publishing
Lutheran Univ. Press
NavPress
New Hope
On My Own Now
Pacific Press
Parson Place
Parsons Publishing
Pauline Books
Salt Works
Salvation Publisher
Tate Publishing
VBC Publishing
White Fire Publishing
WinePress
Word Alive
Zoë Life Publishing

GAMES/CRAFTS

(a) Baker Books

Booklocker.com
Contemporary Drama
Essence
Fairway Press
Faith Books & More
Group Publishing
Guardian Angel
Legacy Press
Lighthouse Publishing

Rainbow Publishers
Standard Publishing
Tate Publishing
Warner Press
Zoë Life Publishing

GIFT BOOKS

Aaron Book
Blue Dolphin
Bridge Logos
Brown Books
Charisma House
Creation House
Cupola Press
Eerdmans Pub., Wm. B.
Essence
Faith Books & More
Fruitbearer Pub.
Howard Books
Lighthouse Publishing
Ravenhawk Books
Salt Works
WinePress
Zoë Life Publishing

GRANDPARENTING

(a) Bethany House
(a) Nelson, Thomas

Aaron Book
Abingdon Press
ACW Press
American Binding
Blue Dolphin
Bondfire Books
Booklocker.com
Bridge Logos
Brown Books
CLC Publications
Comfort Publishing
Creation House
CrossLink Publishing
Cupola Press
Discovery House
Eerdmans Pub.,
     Wm. B.
Essence
Faith Books & More
Howard Books
Lighthouse Publishing
New Hope

Parson Place
Salvation Publisher
VBC Publishing
Whitaker House
White Fire Publishing
WinePress
Zoë Life Publishing

GRIEF
(a) Bethany House

Aaron Book
ACW Press
American Binding
Blue Dolphin
BMH Books
Bondfire Books
Booklocker.com
Charisma House
Comfort Publishing
Creation House
CrossLink Publishing
Cupola Press
Discovery House
Eerdmans Pub., Wm. B.
Essence
Faith Books & More
Franciscan Media
Howard Books
INO Publishing
Lift Every Voice
Lighthouse Publishing
NavPress
Pauline Books
Port Hole Public.
Ravenhawk Books
Salvation Publisher
White Fire Publishing
WinePress
Zoë Life Publishing

GROUP STUDY BOOKS
(a) Baker Books

Aaron Book
Abingdon Press
ACW Press
American Binding
AMG Publishers
BMH Books
Bondfire Books
Booklocker.com

Bridge Logos
Christian Writer's Ebook
CrossHouse
CrossLink Publishing
CSS Publishing
Deep River Books
Eerdmans Pub., Wm. B.
Essence
Fairway Press
Gospel Publishing
Grace Acres Press
Group Publishing
Hannibal Books
Hensley Publishing
InterVarsity Press
Judson Press
Lighthouse Publishing
New Hope
Pacific Press
Parson Place
Randall House
Salt Works
Tate Publishing
White Fire Publishing
WinePress
Word Alive
Zoë Life Publishing

HEALING
(a) Baker Books
(a) Cook, David C.
(a) FaithWords
(a) Hay House
(a) Nelson, Thomas

Aaron Book
ACW Press
American Binding
Blue Dolphin
Booklocker.com
Bridge Logos
Brown Books
Canticle Books
Charisma House
Christian Heritage
Christian Writer's Ebook
CLC Publications
Comfort Publishing
Creation House
CSS Publishing
Cupola Press

Deep River Books
Destiny Image (books)
Destiny Image (gifts)
Eerdmans Pub., Wm. B.
Essence
Fairway Press
Faith Books & More
Harrison House
Lighthouse Publishing
Loyola Press
Lutheran Univ. Press
Magnus Press
NavPress
Pacific Press
Parson Place
Parsons Publishing
Pauline Books
Salvation Publisher
Tate Publishing
Whitaker House
White Fire Publishing
WinePress
Word Alive
Zoë Life Publishing

HEALTH
(a) Baker Books
(a) Ballantine
(a) FaithWords
(a) Hay House
(a) Nelson, Thomas

Aaron Book
ACW Press
Ambassador Books
American Binding
Blue Dolphin
Booklocker.com
Brown Books
Canticle Books
Charisma House
Christian Writer's Ebook
Cladach Publishing
Comfort Publishing
Creation House
Deep River Books
Destiny Image (books)
Eerdmans Pub.,Wm. B.
Essence
Fairway Press
Faith Books & More

Franciscan Media
Guardian Angel
Langmarc
Life Cycle Books
Lighthouse Publishing
Loyola Press
Magnus Press
MountainView
New Hope
Pacific Press
Parsons Publishing
Salvation Publisher
Sunpenny Publishing
Tate Publishing
VBC Publishing
WinePress
Word Alive
Zoë Life Publishing

HISPANIC MARKETS
(a) Doubleday Relig.

Abingdon Press
American Binding
B&H Publishing
Booklocker.com
Bridge Logos
Charisma House
InterVarsity Press
Judson Press
Pacific Press
Parsons Publishing
Praeger Publishers
Tate Publishing
Tyndale Español
Whitaker House

HISTORICAL
(a) Baker Academic
(a) Baker Books
(a) Doubleday Relig.
(a) HarperOne
(a) Kregel
(a) Nelson, Thomas

Aaron Book
ACW Press
Ambassador Books
American Binding
AMG Publishers
Blue Dolphin
Booklocker.com

Bridge Logos
Brown Books
Christian Heritage
Christian Writer's Ebook
Comfort Publishing
Conciliar Press
Creation House
CrossLink Publishing
Earthen Vessel
Eerdmans Pub., Wm. B.
Essence
Fairway Press
Faith Books & More
Inkling Books
InterVarsity Press
Kirk House
Lift Every Voice
Lighthouse Publishing
Loyola Press
Lutheran Univ. Press
Salt Works
Sunpenny Publishing
Tate Publishing
Trinity Foundation
Vision Forum
WinePress
Word Alive
Yale Univ. Press
Zoë Life Publishing

HOLIDAY/SEASONAL
(a) Cook, David C.
(a) FaithWords
(a) HarperOne

Aaron Book
Abingdon Press
ACW Press
Ambassador Books
American Binding
Barbour
Blue Dolphin
Bondfire Books
Booklocker.com
Charisma House
Christian Writer's Ebook
CSS Publishing
Deep River Books
Discovery House
Essence
Fairway Press

Faith Books & More
Guardian Angel
Guideposts Books
Howard Books
Judson Press
Lighthouse Publishing
Meriwether
New Hope
Pauline Books
Ravenhawk Books
Salt Works
Standard Publishing
Tate Publishing
Warner Press
WinePress
Word Alive

HOLINESS
(a) Bethany House

Aaron Book
ACW Press
Ambassador Intl.
American Binding
Blue Dolphin
Bondfire Books
Booklocker.com
Bridge Logos
Brown Books
Charisma House
Christian Heritage
CLC Publications
Creation House
Eerdmans Pub.,
    Wm. B.
Essence
Faith Books & More
Grace Acres Press
Howard Books
InterVarsity Press
Lighthouse Publishing
NavPress
Parson Place
Parsons Publishing
Pauline Books
Salt Works
Salvation Publisher
Tate Publishing
Wesleyan Publishing
White Fire Publishing
WinePress

HOLY SPIRIT
(a) Kregel
(a) Nelson, Thomas

Aaron Book
ACW Press
American Binding
Blue Dolphin
Bondfire Books
Booklocker.com
Bridge Logos
Canticle Books
Charisma House
Christian Heritage
Christian Writer's Ebook
CLC Publications
Comfort Publishing
Creation House
CSS Publishing
Deep River Books
Destiny Image (books)
Destiny Image (gifts)
Eerdmans Pub., Wm. B.
Essence
Fairway Press
Faith Books & More
Gospel Publishing
Harrison House
InterVarsity Press
Lift Every Voice
Lighthouse Publishing
Lutheran Univ. Press
Magnus Press
NavPress
Pacific Press
Parson Place
Parsons Publishing
Salvation Publisher
Tate Publishing
VBC Publishing
Whitaker House
White Fire Publishing
WinePress
Word Alive
Zoë Life Publishing

HOMESCHOOLING RESOURCES
(a) Baker Books

Aaron Book
ACW Press

American Binding
Bondfire Books
Booklocker.com
Christian Writer's Ebook
CrossHouse
CrossLink Publishing
Eerdmans Pub., Wm. B.
Essence
Fairway Press
Faith Books & More
Grace Acres Press
Guardian Angel
Hannibal Books
JourneyForth/BJU
Lighthouse Publishing
New Leaf
Salt Works
Tate Publishing
WinePress
Word Alive
Zoë Life Publishing

HOMILETICS
(a) Baker Books
(a) Kregel

Aaron Book
Abingdon Press
ACW Press
American Binding
Bondfire Books
Booklocker.com
Christian Writer's Ebook
CSS Publishing
DCTS Publishers
Deep River Books
Earthen Vessel
Eerdmans Pub., Wm. B.
Essence
Fairway Press
Faith Books & More
Judson Press
Lighthouse Publishing
Lutheran Univ. Press
NavPress
Salt Works
Tate Publishing
VBC Publishing
WinePress
Word Alive
Zoë Life Publishing

HOW-TO
(a) Baker Books
(a) Ballantine
(a) Nelson, Thomas
(a) Revell

Aaron Book
ACW Press
Adams Media
American Binding
Blue Dolphin
Bondfire Books
Booklocker.com
Bridge Logos
Christian Writer's Ebook
Church Growth Inst.
Deep River Books
Destiny Image (gifts)
Essence
Fairway Press
Faith Books & More
Gospel Light
Guardian Angel
Halo Publishing Intl.
Howard Books
Inkling Books
Kirk House
Lighthouse Publishing
Meriwether
MountainView
Our Sunday Visitor
Pacific Press
Parson Place
Salt Works
Salvation Publisher
Standard Publishing
Tate Publishing
VBC Publishing
WinePress
Word Alive
Zoë Life Publishing

HUMOR
(a) Baker Books
(a) Ballantine
(a) Cook, David C.
(a) FaithWords
(a) Nelson, Thomas

Aaron Book
ACW Press

Ambassador Books
American Binding
Barbour
Blue Dolphin
Bondfire Books
Booklocker.com
Bridge Logos
Christian Writer's Ebook
Comfort Publishing
Creation House
Cupola Press
Deep River Books
Essence
Fairway Press
Faith Books & More
Guideposts Books
Kirk House
Lighthouse Publishing
Loyola Press
Meriwether
MOPS Intl.
NavPress
On My Own Now
Pacific Press
Parson Place
Salt Works
Salvation Publisher
Tate Publishing
White Fire Publishing
WinePress
Word Alive
Zoë Life Publishing

INSPIRATIONAL
(a) Baker Books
(a) Bethany House
(a) Doubleday Relig.
(a) FaithWords
(a) Hay House
(a) Nelson, Thomas
(a) Tyndale House
(a) WaterBrook Press

Aaron Book
Abingdon Press
ACW Press
Adams Media
Ambassador Books
American Binding
Barbour
Blue Dolphin

Bondfire Books
Booklocker.com
Bridge Logos
Brown Books
Canticle Books
Charisma House
Christian Writer's Ebook
CLC Publications
Comfort Publishing
Creation House
CrossHouse
CrossLink Publishing
CSS Publishing
Cupola Press
DCTS Publishers
Deep River Books
Destiny Image (books)
Destiny Image (gifts)
Discovery House
Dove Inspirational
Earthen Vessel
Essence
Fairway Press
Faith Books & More
Franciscan Media
Fruitbearer Pub.
Guardian Angel
Harrison House
Howard Books
INO Publishing
JourneyForth/BJU
Judson Press
Kirk House
Langmarc
Lighthouse Publishing
Loyola Press
Lutheran Univ. Press
Magnus Press
MountainView
NavPress
New Leaf
On My Own Now
Pacific Press
Parson Place
Parsons Publishing
Pauline Books
Pelican Publishing
Port Hole Public.
Ravenhawk Books
Salt Works

Salvation Publisher
Sunpenny Publishing
Tate Publishing
VBC Publishing
Wesleyan Publishing
Whitaker House
White Fire Publishing
WinePress
Word Alive
Zoë Life Publishing

LAY COUNSELING
Bondfire Books
Randall House
Zoë Life Publishing

LEADERSHIP
(a) Baker Books
(a) B&H Publishing
(a) Bethany House
(a) Cook, David C.
(a) Kregel
(a) Nelson, Thomas
(a) WaterBrook Press

Aaron Book
Abingdon Press
ACW Press
Ambassador Intl.
American Binding
Blue Dolphin
BMH Books
Bondfire Books
Booklocker.com
Bridge Logos
Charisma House
Christian Writer's Ebook
Church Growth Inst.
CLC Publications
Creation House
CrossLink Publishing
Crossway
CSS Publishing
DCTS Publishers
Deep River Books
Destiny Image (gifts)
Eerdmans Pub., Wm. B.
Essence
Fairway Press
Faith Books & More
Gospel Publishing

Grace Acres Press
Group Publishing
Guardian Angel
Harrison House
InterVarsity Press
Judson Press
Kirk House
Lift Every Voice
Lighthouse Publishing
Lutheran Univ. Press
NavPress
New Hope
New Leaf
Parson Place
Parsons Publishing
Randall House
Ravenhawk Books
Salt Works
Salvation Publisher
Standard Publishing
Tate Publishing
VBC Publishing
Wesleyan Publishing
Whitaker House
White Fire Publishing
WinePress
Word Alive
Zoë Life Publishing

LIFESTYLE
Bondfire Books
Cladach Publishing
Comfort Publishing
Halo Publishing Intl.
NavPress
New Leaf
Zoë Life Publishing

LITURGICAL STUDIES
(a) Baker Books
(a) Doubleday Relig.

Aaron Book
ACW Press
American Binding
American Cath. Press
Bondfire Books
Booklocker.com
Christian Heritage
Christian Writer's Ebook
Conciliar Press

CSS Publishing
Eerdmans Pub., Wm. B.
Fairway Press
Faith Books & More
Group Publishing
InterVarsity Press
Lighthouse Publishing
Lutheran Univ. Press
Parson Place
Ravenhawk Books
Salt Works
Tate Publishing
White Fire Publishing
WinePress
Word Alive
Zoë Life Publishing

MARRIAGE
(a) Baker Books
(a) B&H Publishing
(a) Bethany House
(a) Cook, David C.
(a) Doubleday Relig.
(a) FaithWords
(a) HarperOne
(a) Kregel
(a) Nelson, Thomas
(a) Revell
(a) Tyndale House
(a) WaterBrook Press

Aaron Book
ACW Press
Ambassador Books
Ambassador Intl.
American Binding
Barbour
Blue Dolphin
Bondfire Books
Booklocker.com
Brown Books
Charisma House
Christian Writer's Ebook
Comfort Publishing
Creation House
CrossHouse
CrossLink Publishing
Crossway
CSS Publishing
Cupola Press
Deep River Books

Destiny Image (books)
Destiny Image (gifts)
Discovery House
Earthen Vessel
Eerdmans Pub., Wm. B.
Essence
Fairway Press
Faith Books & More
Focus on the Family
Franciscan Media
Grace Acres Press
Guideposts Books
Halo Publishing Intl.
Hannibal Books
Hensley Publishing
Howard Books
InterVarsity Press
JourneyForth/BJU
Judson Press
Lift Every Voice
Lighthouse Publishing
Loyola Press
MOPS Intl.
NavPress
New Hope
New Leaf
Pacific Press
Parson Place
Parsons Publishing
Randall House
Standard Publishing
Tate Publishing
VBC Publishing
Whitaker House
White Fire Publishing
WinePress
Word Alive
Zoë Life Publishing

MEMOIRS
(a) Baker Books
(a) Ballantine
(a) Doubleday Relig.
(a) FaithWords
(a) HarperOne
(a) Nelson, Thomas

Aaron Book
ACW Press
Ambassador Intl.
American Binding

Bondfire Books
Booklocker.com
Brown Books
Christian Heritage
Christian Writer's Ebook
Cladach Publishing
Creation House
Deep River Books
Essence
Fairway Press
Faith Books & More
Franciscan Media
Fruitbearer Pub.
Grace Acres Press
Guideposts Books
Halo Publishing Intl.
Inheritance Press
INO Publishing
Lighthouse Publishing
On My Own Now
Pacific Press
Salvation Publisher
Sunpenny Publishing
Tate Publishing
White Fire Publishing
WinePress
Word Alive
Zoë Life Publishing

MEN'S BOOKS
(a) Baker Books
(a) B&H Publishing
(a) Bethany House
(a) Doubleday Relig.
(a) Kregel
(a) Nelson, Thomas
(a) WaterBrook Press

Aaron Book
ACW Press
Ambassador Books
American Binding
AMG Publishers
Barbour
Blue Dolphin
BMH Books Bondfire Books
Booklocker.com
Bridge Logos
Charisma House
Christian Writer's Ebook
Comfort Publishing

Creation House
CrossLink Publishing
Crossway
Deep River Books
Eerdmans Pub., Wm. B.
Essence
Fairway Press
Faith Books & More
Franciscan Media
Halo Publishing Intl.
Hensley Publishing
Howard Books
Inkling Books
InterVarsity Press
Lift Every Voice
Lighthouse Publishing
Loyola Press
NavPress
New Leaf
Pacific Press
Parson Place
Randall House
Ravenhawk Books
Tate Publishing
VBC Publishing
Whitaker House
White Fire Publishing
WinePress
Word Alive
Zoë Life Publishing

MINIBOOKS
American Binding
Charisma House
Harrison House
Legacy Press
Lighthouse Publishing
Salt Works
Tate Publishing

MIRACLES
(a) Baker Books
(a) HarperOne

Aaron Book
ACW Press
American Binding
Blue Dolphin
Bondfire Books
Booklocker.com
Charisma House

Christian Heritage
Christian Writer's Ebook
Comfort Publishing
Creation House
CrossLink Publishing
CSS Publishing
Deep River Books
Destiny Image (books)
Essence
Fairway Press
Faith Books & More
Guideposts Books
Harrison House
Lighthouse Publishing
Loyola Press
On My Own Now
Pacific Press
Parson Place
Parsons Publishing
Salvation Publisher
Tate Publishing
Whitaker House
White Fire Publishing
WinePress
Word Alive
Zoë Life Publishing

MISSIONS/MISSIONARY
(a) Baker Books

Aaron Book
ACW Press
Ambassador Intl.
American Binding
Ampelos Press
Bondfire Books
Booklocker.com
Brown Books
Charisma House
Christian Heritage
Christian Writer's Ebook
CLC Publications
Comfort Publishing
Creation House
CrossHouse
CSS Publishing
Deep River Books
Discovery House
Earthen Vessel
Eerdmans Pub., Wm. B.
Essence

Fairway Press
Faith Books & More
Grace Acres Press
Hannibal Books
InterVarsity Press
Lift Every Voice
Lighthouse Publishing
Lutheran Univ. Press
NavPress
Pacific Press
Parson Place
Parsons Publishing
Randall House
Salt Works
Tate Publishing
VBC Publishing
White Fire Publishing
WinePress
Word Alive
Yale Univ. Press
Zoë Life Publishing

MONEY MANAGEMENT
(a) Baker Books
(a) Cook, David C.
(a) FaithWords
(a) Nelson, Thomas
(a) WaterBrook Press

Aaron Book
ACW Press
Ambassador Intl.
American Binding
Barbour
Blue Dolphin
BMH Books
Bondfire Books
Booklocker.com
Charisma House
Christian Writer's Ebook
Creation House
Deep River Books
Eerdmans Pub., Wm. B.
Essence
Fairway Press
Faith Books & More
Hannibal Books
Hensley Publishing
JourneyForth/BJU
Judson Press

Lift Every Voice
Lighthouse Publishing
Moody Publishers
MountainView
NavPress
New Hope
New Leaf
Pacific Press
Parson Place
Ravenhawk Books
Reference Service
Salvation Publisher
Tate Publishing
VBC Publishing
WinePress
Word Alive
Zoë Life Publishing

MUSIC-RELATED BOOKS
(a) Baker Books

Aaron Book
American Cath. Press
Blue Dolphin
BMH Books
Booklocker.com
Christian Writer's Ebook
Contemporary Drama
Deep River Books
Destiny Image (books)
Eerdmans Pub., Wm. B.
Essence
Fairway Press
Faith Books & More
Guardian Angel
Lighthouse Publishing
Lutheran Univ. Press
Standard Publishing
Tate Publishing
WinePress
Word Alive
Zoë Life Publishing

NOVELTY BOOKS
FOR KIDS
(a) Baker Books

Brown Books
Fairway Press
Guardian Angel
Legacy Press

Lift Every Voice
Salt Works
Standard Publishing
Tate Publishing
Word Alive
Zoë Life Publishing

PAMPHLETS
Christian Writer's Ebook
Essence
Fruitbearer Pub.
Lift Every Voice
Our Sunday Visitor
Salt Works
Trinity Foundation

PARENTING
(a) Baker Books
(a) Ballantine
(a) B&H Publishing
(a) Bethany House
(a) Cook, David C.
(a) FaithWords
(a) Kregel
(a) Nelson, Thomas
(a) Revell
(a) Tyndale House
(a) WaterBrook Press

Aaron Book
ACW Press
Adams Media
Ambassador Books
Ambassador Intl.
American Binding
AMG Publishers
Barbour
Blue Dolphin
Bondfire Books
Booklocker.com
Brown Books
Christian Writer's Ebook
Comfort Publishing
Conari Press
Conciliar Press
Creation House
CrossLink Publishing
Cupola Press
Deep River Books
Destiny Image (books)

Discovery House
Eerdmans Pub., Wm. B.
Essence
Fairway Press
Faith Books & More
Focus on the Family
Franciscan Media
Grace Acres Press
Halo Publishing Intl.
Harrison House
Hensley Publishing
Howard Books
INO Publishing
InterVarsity Press
JourneyForth/BJU
Langmarc
Lift Every Voice
Lighthouse Publishing
MOPS Intl.
NavPress
New Hope
New Leaf
Our Sunday Visitor
Pacific Press
Parsons Publishing
Pauline Books
Port Hole Public.
Randall House
Salt Works
Standard Publishing
Sunpenny Publishing
Tate Publishing
VBC Publishing
Whitaker House
White Fire Publishing
WinePress
Word Alive
Zoë Life Publishing

PASTORS' HELPS
(a) Baker Academic
(a) Baker Books
(a) B&H Publishing
(a) Kregel

Aaron Book
ACW Press
Ambassador Intl.
American Binding
Blue Dolphin

Booklocker.com
Bridge Logos
Christian Writer's Ebook
Church Growth Inst.
Creation House
CrossLink Publishing
CSS Publishing
DCTS Publishers
Deep River Books
Earthen Vessel
Eerdmans Pub., Wm.
Essence
Fairway Press
Faith Books & More
Gospel Publishing
Group Publishing
Lighthouse Publishing
Lutheran Univ. Press
NavPress
Randall House
Standard Publishing
Tate Publishing
VBC Publishing
Wesleyan Publishing
White Fire Publishing
WinePress
Word Alive
Zoë Life Publishing
Zondervan

PERSONAL EXPERIENCE
(a) Baker Books
(a) HarperOne
(a) Kregel
(a) Nelson, Thomas

Aaron Book
ACW Press
Ambassador Intl.
American Binding
Ampelos Press
Blue Dolphin
Bondfire Books
Booklocker.com
Bridge Logos
Canticle Books
Charisma House
Christian Writer's Ebook
Comfort Publishing
Creation House

CrossLink Publishing
Cupola Press
DCTS Publishers
Deep River Books
Destiny Image (gifts)
Essence
Fairway Press
Faith Books & More
Fruitbearer Pub.
Guideposts Books
Halo Publishing Intl.
Hannibal Books
INO Publishing
Lighthouse Publishing
On My Own Now
Pacific Press
Ravenhawk Books
Salvation Publisher
Tate Publishing
White Fire Publishing
WinePress
Word Alive

PERSONAL GROWTH
(a) Baker Books
(a) B&H Publishing
(a) Bethany House
(a) FaithWords
(a) HarperOne
(a) Hay House
(a) Kregel
(a) Nelson, Thomas
(a) Tyndale House
(a) WaterBrook Press

Aaron Book
ACW Press
Ambassador Books
Ambassador Intl.
American Binding
AMG Publishers
Barbour
Blue Dolphin
BMH Books
Bondfire Books
Booklocker.com
Bridge Logos
Canticle Books
Charisma House
Christian Writer's Ebook

CLC Publications
Comfort Publishing
Conari Press
Creation House
CrossLink Publishing
Cupola Press
DCTS Publishers
Deep River Books
Destiny Image (books)
Destiny Image (gifts)
Discovery House
Essence
Fairway Press
Faith Books & More
Franciscan Media
Guideposts Books
Halo Publishing Intl.
Hannibal Books
Hensley Publishing
Howard Books
INO Publishing
InterVarsity Press
JourneyForth/BJU
Lift Every Voice
Lighthouse Publishing
NavPress
New Hope
On My Own Now
Pacific Press
Parson Place
Parsons Publishing
Pauline Books
Ravenhawk Books
Tate Publishing
White Fire Publishing
WinePress
Word Alive

PERSONAL RENEWAL
(a) Baker Books
(a) HarperOne
(a) Kregel
(a) Tyndale House

Aaron Book
ACW Press
American Binding
Barbour
Blue Dolphin
BMH Books

Bondfire Books
Booklocker.com
Bridge Logos
Canticle Books
Charisma House
Christian Writer's Ebook
Cladach Publishing
CLC Publications
Comfort Publishing
Conari Press
Creation House
DCTS Publishers
Deep River Books
Destiny Image (books)
Destiny Image (gifts)
Essence
Fairway Press
Faith Books & More
Halo Publishing Intl.
Hannibal Books
Hensley Publishing
Howard Books
INO Publishing
Kirk House
Lift Every Voice
Lighthouse Publishing
NavPress
New Hope
On My Own Now
Pacific Press
Ravenhawk Books
Tate Publishing
White Fire Publishing
WinePress
Word Alive
Zoë Life Publishing

PHILOSOPHY
(a) Baker Books
(a) Doubleday Relig.
(a) HarperOne
(a) Kregel

Aaron Book
ACW Press
American Binding
Blue Dolphin
Bondfire Books
Booklocker.com
Christian Writer's Ebook

Creation House
Deep River Books
Eerdmans Pub., Wm. B.
Essence
Fairway Press
Faith Books & More
Inkling Books
InterVarsity Press
Lighthouse Publishing
Lutheran Univ. Press
Paragon House
Port Hole Public.
Salt Works
Tate Publishing
Trinity Foundation
White Fire Publishing
WinePress
Word Alive
Zoë Life Publishing

**PHOTOGRAPHS
(FOR COVERS)**
Abingdon Press
Ambassador Books
Ambassador Intl.
American Binding
Blue Dolphin
Booklocker.com
Bridge Logos
Charisma House
Church Growth Inst.
Comfort Publishing
Conciliar Press
Creation House
CrossHouse
CrossLink Publishing
Earthen Vessel
Essence
Faith Books & More
Fruitbearer Pub.
Guardian Angel
Lift Every Voice
Lighthouse Publishing
Lutheran Univ. Press
Marcher Lord Press
MountainView
New Hope
Our Sunday Visitor
Parson Place
Pauline Kids

Ravenhawk Books
Sunpenny Publishing
Tate Publishing
Trinity Foundation
WinePress
Zoë Life Publishing

POETRY
Aaron Book
ACW Press
American Binding
Blue Dolphin
Bondfire Books
Booklocker.com
Christian Writer's Ebook
Creation House
Earthen Vessel
Eerdmans Pub., Wm. B.
Essence
Fairway Press
Faith Books & More
Halo Publishing Intl.
Lighthouse Publishing
Port Hole Public.
Tate Publishing
WinePress
Word Alive
Zoë Life Publishing

POLITICS
(a) Baker Books
(a) Doubleday Relig.
(a) HarperOne
(a) Nelson, Thomas

Aaron Book
ACW Press
American Binding
AMG Publishers
Blue Dolphin
Bondfire Books
Booklocker.com
Christian Writer's Ebook
Creation House
Deep River Books
Eerdmans Pub., Wm. B.
Essence
Fairway Press
Faith Books & More
Howard Books

Inkling Books
Lighthouse Publishing
Praeger Publishers
Ravenhawk Books
Salt Works
Tate Publishing
Trinity Foundation
White Fire Publishing
WinePress
Word Alive
Yale Univ. Press
Zoë Life Publishing

POPULAR CULTURE
Bondfire Books
Comfort Publishing
Essence
Pauline Books
White Fire Publishing
Zoë Life Publishing

POSTMODERNISM
Essence
White Fire Publishing
Zoë Life Publishing

PRAYER
(a) Baker Books
(a) Bethany House
(a) Cook, David C.
(a) Doubleday Relig.
(a) FaithWords
(a) HarperOne
(a) Kregel
(a) Nelson, Thomas
(a) Tyndale House
(a) WaterBrook Press

Aaron Book
Abingdon Press
ACW Press
Ambassador Books
Ambassador Intl.
American Binding
Ampelos Press
Barbour
Blue Dolphin
BMH Books
Bondfire Books
Booklocker.com

Bridge Logos
Charisma House
Christian Heritage
Christian Writer's Ebook
CLC Publications
Creation House
CrossHouse
CrossLink Publishing
CSS Publishing
Cupola Press
DCTS Publishers
Deep River Books
Destiny Image (books)
Destiny Image (gifts)
Discovery House
Earthen Vessel
Eerdmans Pub., Wm. B.
Essence
Fairway Press
Faith Books & More
Franciscan Media
Fruitbearer Pub.
Gospel Publishing
Guideposts Books
Halo Publishing Intl.
Harrison House
Hensley Publishing
Howard Books
INO Publishing
InterVarsity Press
JourneyForth/BJU
Legacy Press
Lift Every Voice
Lighthouse Publishing
Loyola Press
Lutheran Univ. Press
Moody Publishers
NavPress
On My Own Now
Our Sunday Visitor
Pacific Press
Pauline Books
Pauline Kids
Port Hole Public.
Salvation Publisher
Standard Publishing
Tate Publishing
VBC Publishing
Wesleyan Publishing
Whitaker House

White Fire Publishing
WinePress
Word Alive
Zoë Life Publishing

PRINT-ON-DEMAND
Aaron Book
ACW Press
American Binding
Blue Dolphin
Booklocker.com
Bridge Logos
Christian Writer's Ebook
CrossLink Publishing
CSS Publishing
Faith Books & More
Hannibal Books
Inkling Books
Lighthouse Publishing
OakTara
Randall House Digital
Ravenhawk Books
Salvation Publisher
Strong Tower
VBC Publishing
Word Alive

PROPHECY
(a) Baker Books
(a) Kregel

Aaron Book
ACW Press
American Binding
Blue Dolphin
BMH Books
Bondfire Books
Booklocker.com
Bridge Logos
Charisma House
Christian Writer's Ebook
Comfort Publishing
Creation House
CSS Publishing
Deep River Books
Destiny Image (books)
Eerdmans Pub., Wm. B.
Essence
Fairway Press
Faith Books & More

Harrison House
Lighthouse Publishing
Lutheran Univ. Press
Pacific Press
Parson Place
Parsons Publishing
Ravenhawk Books
Salvation Publisher
Tate Publishing
White Fire Publishing
WinePress
Word Alive
Zoë Life Publishing

PSYCHOLOGY
(a) Baker Academic
(a) Kregel
(a) Tyndale House

Aaron Book
ACW Press
Adams Media
American Binding
Blue Dolphin
Bondfire Books
Booklocker.com
Christian Writer's Ebook
Comfort Publishing
Creation House
Deep River Books
Eerdmans Pub., Wm. B.
Essence
Fairway Press
Faith Books & More
InterVarsity Press
Lighthouse Publishing
MountainView
On My Own Now
Paragon House
Tate Publishing
White Fire Publishing
WinePress
Word Alive
Zoë Life Publishing

RACISM
(a) Baker Books

Aaron Book
ACW Press
American Binding

Blue Dolphin
Booklocker.com
Charisma House
Christian Writer's Ebook
DCTS Publishers
Deep River Books
Destiny Image (gifts)
Eerdmans Pub., Wm. B.
Essence
Fairway Press
Faith Books & More
Howard Books
InterVarsity Press
Judson Press
Kirk House
Lift Every Voice
Lighthouse Publishing
New Hope
Salt Works
Tate Publishing
White Fire Publishing
WinePress
Word Alive
Zoë Life Publishing

RECOVERY
(a) Baker Books
(a) HarperOne
(a) Tyndale House
(a) WaterBrook Press

Aaron Book
ACW Press
Ambassador Books
American Binding
Blue Dolphin
Bondfire Books
Booklocker.com
Brown Books
Charisma House
Christian Writer's Ebook
Comfort Publishing
Creation House
CSS Publishing
Deep River Books
Earthen Vessel
Eerdmans Pub., Wm. B.
Essence
Fairway Press
Faith Books & More

Halo Publishing Intl.
Hannibal Books
Howard Books
Langmarc
Lighthouse Publishing
NavPress
Parsons Publishing
Pauline Books
Randall House
Tate Publishing
VBC Publishing
WinePress
Word Alive
Zoë Life Publishing

REFERENCE

(a) Baker Academic
(a) Baker Books
(a) Bethany House
(a) Cook, David C.
(a) Doubleday Relig.
(a) HarperOne
(a) Kregel
(a) Tyndale House

Aaron Book
Abingdon Press
ACW Press
Ambassador Intl.
American Binding
AMG Publishers
Barbour
BMH Books
Bondfire Books
Booklocker.com
Bridge Logos
Christian Heritage
Christian Writer's Ebook
Creation House
CrossLink Publishing
Eerdmans Pub., Wm. B.
Essence
Fairway Press
Faith Books & More
Guardian Angel
InterVarsity Press
Life Cycle Books
Lighthouse Publishing
Our Sunday Visitor
Paragon House

Reference Service
Tate Publishing
VBC Publishing
White Fire Publishing
WinePress
Word Alive
Zoë Life Publishing
Zondervan

RELATIONSHIPS

(a) Bethany House
(a) FaithWords
(a) Kregel
(a) Nelson, Thomas

Aaron Book
ACW Press
Adams Media
Ambassador Books
Ambassador Intl.
American Binding
Barbour
Blue Dolphin
Bondfire Books
Booklocker.com
Bridge Logos
Brown Books
Charisma House
Church Growth Inst.
Cladach Publishing
CLC Publications
Comfort Publishing
Creation House
CrossHouse
CrossLink Publishing
Cupola Press
Discovery House
Eerdmans Pub., Wm. B.
Essence
Faith Books & More
Halo Publishing Intl.
Hannibal Books
Hensley Publishing
Howard Books
INO Publishing
InterVarsity Press
Judson Press
Lift Every Voice
Lighthouse Publishing
MOPS Intl.

NavPress
New Hope
New Leaf
On My Own Now
Pauline Books
Port Hole Public.
Randall House
Ravenhawk Books
Salt Works
Tate Publishing
Whitaker House
White Fire Publishing
WinePress
Zoë Life Publishing

RELIGION

(a) Baker Academic
(a) Baker Books
(a) Ballantine
(a) B&H Publishing
(a) Doubleday Relig.
(a) FaithWords
(a) HarperOne
(a) Nelson, Thomas
(a) Revell
(a) Tyndale House
(a) WaterBrook Press

Aaron Book
Abingdon Press
ACW Press
Ambassador Books
Ambassador Intl.
American Binding
American Cath. Press
Blue Dolphin
Bondfire Books
Booklocker.com
Brown Books
Charisma House
Christian Heritage
Christian Writer's Ebook
Church Growth Inst.
CLC Publications
Comfort Publishing
Creation House
CrossLink Publishing
CSS Publishing
Deep River Books
Eerdmans Pub., Wm. B.

Essence
Fairway Press
Faith Books & More
Grace Acres Press
Halo Publishing Intl.
Harrison House
InterVarsity Press
Kirk House
Life Cycle Books
Lighthouse Publishing
Loyola Press
Lutheran Univ. Press
NavPress
New Leaf
Our Sunday Visitor
Pacific Press
Parsons Publishing
Pauline Books
Praeger Publishers
Salt Works
Tate Publishing
Trinity Foundation
Whitaker House
White Fire Publishing
WinePress
Word Alive
Yale Univ. Press
Zoë Life Publishing

RELIGIOUS TOLERANCE
(a) Baker Books
(a) FaithWords

Aaron Book
ACW Press
American Binding
Blue Dolphin
Bondfire Books
Booklocker.com
Charisma House
Christian Writer's Ebook
Creation House
Deep River Books
Eerdmans Pub., Wm. B.
Essence
Fairway Press
Faith Books & More
Howard Books
Judson Press
Lighthouse Publishing
On My Own Now

Paragon House
Tate Publishing
White Fire Publishing
WinePress
Word Alive
Yale Univ. Press
Zoë Life Publishing

RETIREMENT
(a) Baker Books

Aaron Book
ACW Press
American Binding
Blue Dolphin
Bondfire Books
Booklocker.com
Charisma House
Christian Writer's Ebook
Cladach Publishing
Cupola Press
Eerdmans Pub., Wm. B.
Essence
Fairway Press
Faith Books & More
Kirk House
Lighthouse Publishing
Tate Publishing
WinePress
Word Alive
Zoë Life Publishing

SCHOLARLY
(a) Baker Academic
(a) Baker Books
(a) Cook, David C.
(a) Doubleday Relig.
(a) Kregel

Aaron Book
Abingdon Press
ACW Press
American Binding
Blue Dolphin
Bondfire Books
Booklocker.com
Christian Heritage
Christian Writer's Ebook
Deep River Books
Eerdmans Pub., Wm. B.
Essence
Fairway Press

Faith Books & More
Grace Acres Press
Guardian Angel
Inkling Books
InterVarsity Press
Life Cycle Books
Lighthouse Publishing
Lutheran Univ. Press
Paragon House
Tate Publishing
Trinity Foundation
VBC Publishing
White Fire Publishing
WinePress
Word Alive
Yale Univ. Press
Zoë Life Publishing
Zondervan

SCIENCE
(a) Baker Books
(a) Doubleday Relig.

Aaron Book
ACW Press
American Binding
Blue Dolphin
Booklocker.com
Christian Writer's Ebook
Eerdmans Pub., Wm. B.
Essence
Fairway Press
Faith Books & More
Guardian Angel
Inkling Books
InterVarsity Press
Lighthouse Publishing
New Leaf
Parsons Publishing
Salt Works
Tate Publishing
Trinity Foundation
WinePress
Word Alive
Zoë Life Publishing

SELF-HELP
(a) Baker Books
(a) Ballantine
(a) HarperOne
(a) Hay House

(a) Nelson, Thomas
(a) Revell
(a) Tyndale House
(a) WaterBrook Press

Aaron Book
ACW Press
Adams Media
Ambassador Books
American Binding
Blue Dolphin
Bondfire Books
Booklocker.com
Bridge Logos
Brown Books
Charisma House
Christian Writer's Ebook
CLC Publications
Comfort Publishing
Creation House
CrossLink Publishing
Cupola Press
DCTS Publishers
Deep River Books
Destiny Image (gifts)
Essence
Fairway Press
Faith Books & More
Franciscan Media
Guideposts Books
Halo Publishing Intl.
Howard Books
Langmarc
Lighthouse Publishing
MountainView
On My Own Now
Salvation Publisher
Tate Publishing
VBC Publishing
WinePress
Word Alive
Zoë Life Publishing

SENIOR ADULT CONCERNS
(a) Baker Books
(a) Cook, David C.

Aaron Book
ACW Press
American Binding

Blue Dolphin
Bondfire Books
Booklocker.com
Charisma House
Christian Writer's
   Ebook
Cupola Press
Deep River Books
Discovery House
Eerdmans Pub., Wm. B.
Essence
Fairway Press
Faith Books & More
Focus on the Family
Langmarc
Lighthouse Publishing
New Hope
Tate Publishing
WinePress
Word Alive
Zoë Life Publishing

SERMONS
(a) Baker Books
(a) Kregel

Aaron Book
Abingdon Press
ACW Press
American Binding
Bondfire Books
Booklocker.com
Christian Writer's Ebook
Church Growth Inst.
CrossLink Publishing
CSS Publishing
DCTS Publishers
Deep River Books
Earthen Vessel
Eerdmans Pub., Wm. B.
Essence
Fairway Press
Faith Books & More
Group Publishing
Judson Press
Lighthouse Publishing
MountainView
NavPress
Pacific Press
Salt Works
Salvation Publisher

Tate Publishing
WinePress
Word Alive
Zoë Life Publishing

SINGLES' ISSUES
(a) Baker Books
(a) Bethany House
(a) Cook, David C.
(a) FaithWords
(a) Kregel

Aaron Book
ACW Press
Ambassador Books
American Binding
Barbour
Blue Dolphin
Bondfire Books
Booklocker.com
Charisma House
Christian Writer's
   Ebook
Creation House
Deep River Books
Destiny Image (gifts)
Eerdmans Pub., Wm. B.
Essence
Fairway Press
Faith Books & More
Fruitbearer Pub.
Hensley Publishing
INO Publishing
InterVarsity Press
Judson Press
Lift Every Voice
Lighthouse Publishing
NavPress
New Hope
On My Own Now
Pacific Press
Parsons Publishing
Pauline Books
Salt Works
Tate Publishing
VBC Publishing
Whitaker House
White Fire Publishing
WinePress
Word Alive
Zoë Life Publishing

SMALL-GROUP RESOURCES
Bondfire Books
Essence
Franciscan Media
Grace Acres Press
INO Publishing
NavPress
Randall House
Zoë Life Publishing

SOCIAL JUSTICE ISSUES
(a) Baker Books
(a) FaithWords
(a) HarperOne
(a) Nelson, Thomas

Aaron Book
ACW Press
American Binding
Ampelos Press
Blue Dolphin
Bondfire Books
Booklocker.com
Charisma House
Christian Writer's Ebook
Comfort Publishing
DCTS Publishers
Deep River Books
Destiny Image (books)
Destiny Image (gifts)
Eerdmans Pub., Wm. B.
Essence
Fairway Press
Faith Books & More
Howard Books
Inkling Books
InterVarsity Press
Judson Press
Life Cycle Books
Lift Every Voice
Lighthouse Publishing
NavPress
New Hope
On My Own Now
Our Sunday Visitor
Ravenhawk Books
Tate Publishing
WinePress
Word Alive

Yale Univ. Press
Zoë Life Publishing

SOCIOLOGY
(a) Baker Books

Aaron Book
ACW Press
American Binding
Blue Dolphin
Bondfire Books
Booklocker.com
Charisma House
Christian Writer's Ebook
Deep River Books
Eerdmans Pub., Wm. B.
Essence
Fairway Press
Faith Books & More
InterVarsity Press
Life Cycle Books
Lighthouse Publishing
On My Own Now
Tate Publishing
White Fire Publishing
WinePress
Word Alive
Zoë Life Publishing

SPIRITUAL GIFTS
(a) Baker Books
(a) B&H Publishing
(a) Kregel
(a) Nelson, Thomas

Aaron Book
ACW Press
Ambassador Books
American Binding
Blue Dolphin
Booklocker.com
Bridge Logos
Brown Books
Canticle Books
Charisma House
Christian Writer's Ebook
Church Growth Inst.
CLC Publications
Comfort Publishing
Creation House
CrossHouse

CrossLink Publishing
CSS Publishing
Deep River Books
Destiny Image (books)
Destiny Image (gifts)
Eerdmans Pub., Wm. B.
Essence
Fairway Press
Faith Books & More
Gospel Publishing
Grace Acres Press
Group Publishing
Guardian Angel
Halo Publishing Intl.
Harrison House
Hensley Publishing
Howard Books
INO Publishing
InterVarsity Press
Lift Every Voice
Lighthouse Publishing
Lutheran Univ. Press
Magnus Press
NavPress
New Hope
Pacific Press
Parson Place
Parsons Publishing
Salvation Publisher
Tate Publishing
Whitaker House
WinePress
Word Alive
Zoë Life Publishing

SPIRITUALITY
(a) Baker Books
(a) Ballantine
(a) Bethany House
(a) Doubleday Relig.
(a) FaithWords
(a) HarperOne
(a) Hay House
(a) Kregel
(a) Nelson, Thomas
(a) Tyndale House
(a) WaterBrook Press

Aaron Book
Abingdon Press

ACW Press
Ambassador Books
American Binding
Blue Dolphin
Bondfire Books
Booklocker.com
Bridge Logos
Brown Books
Canticle Books
Charisma House
Christian Heritage
Christian Writer's Ebook
CLC Publications
Comfort Publishing
Conari Press
Creation House
CrossLink Publishing
CSS Publishing
Deep River Books
Destiny Image (books)
Destiny Image (gifts)
Discovery House
Eerdmans Pub., Wm. B.
Essence
Fairway Press
Faith Books & More
Franciscan Media
Grace Acres Press
Guardian Angel
Halo Publishing Intl.
Howard Books
INO Publishing
InterVarsity Press
Kirk House
Lighthouse Publishing
Loyola Press
Lutheran Univ. Press
Magnus Press
NavPress
New Hope
On My Own Now
Pacific Press
Paragon House
Parsons Publishing
Pauline Books
Ravenhawk Books
Salt Works
Sunpenny Publishing
Tate Publishing
WinePress

Word Alive
Zoë Life Publishing

SPIRITUAL LIFE
(a) B&H Publishing
(a) Bethany House
(a) FaithWords
(a) HarperOne
(a) Kregel
(a) Nelson, Thomas
(a) WaterBrook Press

Aaron Book
Abingdon Press
ACW Press
Ambassador Books
American Binding
Barbour
Blue Dolphin
BMH Books
Bondfire Books
Booklocker.com
Bridge Logos
Brown Books
Canticle Books
Charisma House
Christian Writer's Ebook
Church Growth Inst.
CLC Publications
Comfort Publishing
Creation House
CrossHouse
CrossLink Publishing
CSS Publishing
Deep River Books
Destiny Image (books)
Eerdmans Pub., Wm. B.
Essence
Fairway Press
Faith Books & More
Grace Acres Press
Guardian Angel
Halo Publishing Intl.
Harrison House
Howard Books
Inheritance Press
INO Publishing
InterVarsity Press
JourneyForth/BJU
Judson Press

Lift Every Voice
Lighthouse Publishing
NavPress
New Hope
New Leaf
On My Own Now
Parsons Publishing
Pauline Books
Port Hole Public.
Randall House
Salvation Publisher
Tate Publishing
Wesleyan Publishing
Whitaker House
White Fire Publishing
WinePress
Word Alive
Zoë Life Publishing

SPIRITUAL WARFARE
(a) Baker Books
(a) B&H Publishing
(a) Nelson, Thomas

Aaron Book
ACW Press
American Binding
Blue Dolphin
Booklocker.com
Bridge Logos
Brown Books
Charisma House
Christian Writer's Ebook
CLC Publications
Comfort Publishing
Creation House CrossLink
    Publishing
Destiny Image (books)
Destiny Image (gifts)
Earthen Vessel
Eerdmans Pub., Wm. B.
Essence
Fairway Press
Faith Books & More
Grace Acres Press
Harrison House
Hensley Publishing
INO Publishing
Lighthouse Publishing
NavPress

New Hope
On My Own Now
Parson Place
Parsons Publishing
Salvation Publisher
Tate Publishing
VBC Publishing
Whitaker House
White Fire Publishing
WinePress
Word Alive
Zoë Life Publishing

SPORTS/RECREATION
(a) Baker Books
(a) Ballantine

Aaron Book
ACW Press
Ambassador Books
American Binding
Blue Dolphin
Booklocker.com
Brown Books
Charisma House
Christian Writer's Ebook
Cladach Publishing
Comfort Publishing
Deep River Books
Earthen Vessel
Essence
Fairway Press
Faith Books & More
Guardian Angel
Halo Publishing Intl.
Judson Press
Lighthouse Publishing
Ravenhawk Books
Reference Service
Sunpenny Publishing
Tate Publishing
WinePress
Word Alive
Zoë Life Publishing

STEWARDSHIP
(a) Baker Books
(a) Bethany House
(a) Kregel

Aaron Book
ACW Press

Ambassador Intl.
American Binding
Blue Dolphin
BMH Books
Booklocker.com
Brown Books
Christian Writer's Ebook
Church Growth Inst.
CLC Publications
Creation House
CrossLink Publishing
CSS Publishing
Deep River Books
Eerdmans Pub., Wm. B.
Essence
Fairway Press
Faith Books & More
Grace Acres Press
Group Publishing
Hensley Publishing
INO Publishing
InterVarsity Press
Judson Press
Kirk House
Lift Every Voice
Lighthouse Publishing
Lutheran Univ. Press
NavPress
New Hope
On My Own Now
Our Sunday Visitor
Pacific Press
Parson Place
Parsons Publishing
Randall House
Salvation Publisher
Tate Publishing
VBC Publishing
White Fire Publishing
WinePress
Word Alive
Zoë Life Publishing

THEOLOGY
(a) Baker Books
(a) Bethany House
(a) Cook, David C.
(a) Doubleday Relig.
(a) HarperOne
(a) Kregel

(a) Multnomah
(a) Nelson, Thomas
(a) Tyndale House

Aaron Book
Abingdon Press
ACW Press
Ambassador Intl.
American Binding
American Cath. Press
Blue Dolphin
BMH Books
Bondfire Books
Booklocker.com
Brown Books
Canticle Books
Christian Heritage
Christian Writer's Ebook
CLC Publications
Conciliar Press
Creation House
CrossLink Publishing
Crossway
CSS Publishing
Deep River Books
Earthen Vessel
Eerdmans Pub., Wm. B.
Essence
Fairway Press
Faith Books & More
Grace Acres Press
Inkling Books
INO Publishing
InterVarsity Press
Kirk House
Lift Every Voice
Lighthouse Publishing
Lutheran Univ. Press
Magnus Press
Meriwether
NavPress
Pacific Press
Randall House
Ravenhawk Books
Tate Publishing
Trinity Foundation
VBC Publishing
Wesleyan Publishing
White Fire Publishing
WinePress
Word Alive

Yale Univ. Press
Zoë Life Publishing
Zondervan

TIME MANAGEMENT
(a) Baker Books
(a) Cook, David C.
(a) Nelson, Thomas
Aaron Book
ACW Press
American Binding
Barbour
Blue Dolphin
Booklocker.com
Brown Books
Charisma House
Christian Writer's Ebook
CrossHouse
Cupola Press
DCTS Publishers
Deep River Books
Essence
Fairway Press
Faith Books & More
Grace Acres Press
Hensley Publishing
Judson Press
Kirk House
Lighthouse Publishing
NavPress
New Hope
On My Own Now
Salvation Publisher
Tate Publishing
VBC Publishing
WinePress
Word Alive
Zoë Life Publishing

TRACTS
Christian Writer's Ebook
Essence
Fruitbearer Pub.
Life Cycle Books
Trinity Foundation
Word Alive

TRAVEL
(a) Baker Books
(a) Ballantine

Aaron Book
ACW Press
American Binding
Booklocker.com
Brown Books
Christian Heritage
Christian Writer's Ebook
Cladach Publishing
Essence
Fairway Press
Faith Books & More
Lighthouse Publishing
New Leaf
Sunpenny Publishing
Tate Publishing
White Fire Publishers
WinePress
Word Alive
Zoë Life Publishing

TWEEN BOOKS
Aaron Book
ACW Press
Ambassador Books
Ambassador Intl.
American Binding
Barbour
Bondfire Books
Booklocker.com
Comfort Publishing
Eerdmans Pub., Wm. B.
Essence
Faith Books & More
Fruitbearer Pub.
Legacy Press
Lighthouse Publishing
Parsons Publishing
Pauline Books
Tate Publishing
WinePress
Zoë Life Publishing

WOMEN'S ISSUES
(a) Baker Academic
(a) Baker Books
(a) Ballantine
(a) B&H Publishing
(a) Bethany House
(a) Cook, David C.
(a) Doubleday Relig.

(a) FaithWords
(a) HarperOne
(a) Kregel
(a) Nelson, Thomas
Aaron Book
ACW Press
Adams Media
Ambassador Books
American Binding
AMG Publishers
Barbour
Blue Dolphin
BMH Books
Bondfire Books
Booklocker.com
Bridge Logos
Brown Books
Charisma House
Christian Writer's Ebook
Comfort Publishing
Creation House
CrossHouse
CrossLink Publishing
Crossway
Cupola Press
Deep River Books
Destiny Image (gifts)
Discovery House
Eerdmans Pub., Wm. B.
Essence
Fairway Press
Faith Books & More
Focus on the Family
Franciscan Media
Fruitbearer Pub.
Halo Publishing Intl.
Hensley Publishing
Howard Books
Inkling Books
INO Publishing
InterVarsity Press
JourneyForth/BJU
Judson Press
Kirk House
Langmarc
Life Cycle Books
Lift Every Voice
Lighthouse Publishing
Loyola Press

Moody Publishers
NavPress
Nelson, Thomas
New Hope
On My Own Now
Parson Place
Pauline Books
Port Hole Public.
Praeger Publishers
Ravenhawk Books
Reference Service
Sunpenny Publishing
Tate Publishing
VBC Publishing
Whitaker House
White Fire Publishing
WinePress
Word Alive
Zoë Life Publishing

WORLD ISSUES
(a) Baker Books
(a) Doubleday Relig.
(a) HarperOne
(a) Kregel
(a) Tyndale House

Aaron Book
ACW Press
American Binding
AMG Publishers
Ampelos Press
Blue Dolphin
Booklocker.com
Bridge Logos
Charisma House
Christian Writer's Ebook
Comfort Publishing
Creation House
CrossLink Publishing
Deep River Books
Eerdmans Pub., Wm. B.
Essence
Fairway Press
Faith Books & More
Halo Publishing Intl.
InterVarsity Press
Kirk House
Lift Every Voice
Lighthouse Publishing

NavPress
New Hope
Ravenhawk Books
Salt Works
Tate Publishing
VBC Publishing
White Fire Publishing
WinePress
Word Alive
Yale Univ. Press
Zoë Life Publishing

WORSHIP
(a) B&H Publishing
(a) Bethany House
(a) Cook, David C.
(a) Kregel
(a) Nelson, Thomas

Aaron Book
Abingdon Press
ACW Press
American Binding
Barbour
BMH Books
Bondfire Books
Booklocker.com
Bridge Logos
Charisma House
Christian Heritage
Christian Writer's Ebook
CLC Publications
Creation House
CrossLink Publishing
CSS Publishing
Deep River Books
Destiny Image (gifts)
Eerdmans Pub., Wm. B.
Essence
Fairway Press
Faith Books & More
Grace Acres Press
Group Publishing
Halo Publishing Intl.
Harrison House
InterVarsity Press
JourneyForth/BJU
Judson Press
Lift Every Voice
Lighthouse Publishing

Lutheran Univ. Press
NavPress
New Hope
Pacific Press
Parsons Publishing
Salt Works
Tate Publishing
VBC Publishing
WinePress
Word Alive

WORSHIP RESOURCES
(a) Baker Books
(a) B&H Publishing
(a) Kregel

Aaron Book
Abingdon Press
ACW Press
American Binding
American Cath. Press
Bondfire Books
Booklocker.com
Christian Writer's Ebook
CSS Publishing
DCTS Publishers
Deep River Books
Eerdmans Pub., Wm. B.
Essence
Fairway Press
Faith Books & More
Group Publishing
InterVarsity Press
Judson Press
Lighthouse Publishing
Lutheran Univ. Press
Meriwether
NavPress
Our Sunday Visitor
Parsons Publishing
Salt Works
Standard Publishing
Tate Publishing
WinePress
Word Alive
Zoë Life Publishing

WRITING HOW-TO
Aaron Book
American Binding

Bondfire Books
Booklocker.com
Christian Writer's
    Ebook
Deep River Books
Essence
Fairway Press
Faith Books & More
Lighthouse Publishing
Parson Place
Tate Publishing
WinePress
Word Alive
Zoë Life Publishing

YOUTH BOOKS (NONFICTION)

Note: Listing denotes books for 8- to 12-year-olds, junior highs, or senior highs. If all three, it will say "all." If no age group is listed, none was specified.

(a) Baker Books
(a) WaterBrook Press (All)

Aaron Book (8-12/Jr. High)
ACW Press (All)
Ambassador Books (All)

American Binding (Jr./Sr. High)
Barbour (8-12/Jr. High)
Bondfire Books
Booklocker.com (All)
Brown Books (All)
Christian Writer's Ebook (All)
Comfort Publishing (All)
Conciliar Press (8-12)
Contemporary Drama
Creation House (All)
CrossHouse (All)
Dawn Publications (Jr. High)
Deep River Books (All)
Eerdmans Pub., Wm. B. (All)
Essence (All)
Faith Books & More (All)
Focus on the Family (Sr. High)
Guardian Angel (8-12)
Halo Publishing Intl. (All)
INO Publishing
Legacy Press (8-12)
Life Cycle Books (8-12)
Lift Every Voice (All)
Lighthouse Publishing (All)
Meriwether (Jr./Sr. High)
Moody Publishers
NavPress (Sr. High)

New Leaf (All)
On My Own Now (Sr. High)
Pacific Press
Pauline Kids (8-12)
Ravenhawk Books (Jr./Sr. High)
Tate Publishing (All)
Warner Press (All)
WinePress (All)
Word Alive (All)
 Zoë Life Publishing

YOUTH PROGRAMS

(a) Baker Books
(a) Kregel

ACW Press
American Binding
Christian Writer's Ebook
Church Growth Inst.
Contemporary Drama
CrossLink Publishing
Fairway Press
Gospel Publishing
Group Publishing
Randall House Digital
Standard Publishing
Tate Publishing
Zoë Life Publishing

2

Alphabetical Listings of Book Publishers

If you do not find the publishers you are looking for, check the General Index. Check out any publisher thoroughly before signing a contract.

AARON BOOK PUBLISHING, 1104 Bristol Caverns Hwy., Bristol TN 37620. (423) 212-1208. E-mail: info@aaronbookpublishing.com. Website: www.AaronBookPublishing.com. Lidany Rouse, acq. ed. Professional self-publishing, print-on-demand. Book covers, formatting, editing, printing, and marketing products. 100% royalty from net sales. Considers simultaneous submissions. Hardcover, paperback, coffee-table books. Prefers mss by e-mail. Guidelines on website or by e-mail.
>   **Nonfiction/Fiction:** Query first; proposal/2-3 chapters; e-query.
>   **Special Needs:** Books of good content. Strong characters, great story line.
>   **Artwork:** Open to queries from freelance artists.
>   **Tips:** Open to almost any topic.

*ABINGDON PRESS, 201 Eighth Ave. S., PO Box 801, Nashville TN 37202. (615) 749-6000. Fax (615) 749-6512. E-mail: [first initial and last name]@umpublishing.org. Website: www.abingdon press.com. United Methodist Publishing House/Cokesbury. Editors: Mary C. Dean, ed-in-chief; Barbara Scott, fiction; Ron Kidd, study resources; Robert Ratcliff, professional and academic bks.; John Kutsko, dir. of acq.; Joseph A. Crowe, gen. interest bks. Books and church supplies directed primarily to a mainline religious market. Publishes 120 titles/yr.; hardcover, trade paperbacks. Receives 3,000 submissions annually. Less than 5% of books from first-time authors. Accepts mss through agents or authors. No reprints. Prefers 144 pgs. **Royalty 7.5% on retail.** Average first printing 3,500-4,000. Publication within 18 mos. No simultaneous submissions. Requires requested ms on disk. Responds in 2 mos. Prefers NRSV or a variety of which NRSV is one. Guidelines on website ("Submissions" at bottom of page); free catalog.
>   **Nonfiction:** Proposal/2 chapters; no phone/fax/e-query.
>   **Fiction:** Solicited or agented material only.
>   **Ethnic Books:** African American, Hispanic, Native American, Korean.
>   **Music:** Submit to Gary Alan Smith. See guidelines on website.
>   **Photos:** Accepts freelance photos for book covers.
>   **Tips:** "We develop and produce materials to help more people in more places come to know and love God through Jesus Christ and to choose to serve God and neighbor."
>   This publisher serviced by ChristianManuscriptSubmissions.com.

*ADAMS MEDIA CORP., 57 Littlefield St., Avon MA 02322. (508) 427-7100. Toll-free fax (800) 872-5628. Website: www.adamsmedia.com. Division of F + W Publications. Jill Alexander, sr. ed.; submit to Paula Munier. Publishes 250 titles/yr. Receives 6,500 submissions annually. 40% of books from first-time authors. Accepts mss through agents or authors. **Royalty; variable advance; or outright purchase.** Publication within 12-18 mos. Considers simultaneous submissions. Responds in 3 mos. to queries. No mss accepted by e-mail. Guidelines on website ("Submissions"); catalog for 9 x 12 SAE/5 stamps.
>   **Nonfiction:** Query first by mail; no phone/fax/e-query.
>   **Tips:** General publisher that does some inspirational books.

*AMBASSADOR BOOKS, INC., 997 Macarthur Blvd., Mahwah NJ 07430. Toll-free (800) 218-1903. (201) 825-7300. Toll-free fax (800) 836-3161. Fax (201) 825-8345. E-mail: info@paulistpress.com. Website: www.paulistpress.com. Catholic/Paulist Press. Gerry Goggins, adult ed. (ggoggins@paulist press.com); Jennifer Conlan, children's ed. (jconlan@paulistpress.com). Books of intellectual and spiritual excellence. Publishes 12 titles/yr.; hardcover, trade paperbacks. Receives 1,000 submissions annually. 50% of books from first-time authors. Accepts mss through agents or authors. No reprints. **Royalty 8-10% of net; advance $500-1,000.** Publication within 1 yr. Considers simultaneous submissions. Responds in 3-4 mos. Prefers NRSV. Guidelines by mail/e-mail/website ("Manuscript Submission"); free catalog (or on website).

Nonfiction: Query; no phone/fax/e-query.

Fiction: Query. Juvenile, young adult, adult; picture books & board books.

Photos/Artwork: Accepts freelance photos for book covers; open to queries from freelance artists.

Tips: "Our mission for adult books is to celebrate the spiritual dimension of this world by witnessing to the reality of the Way, the Truth, and the Life. For children, it is to foster the knowledge that they are precious to the Lord while encouraging a friendship with Him that will last a lifetime."

*AMBASSADOR INTERNATIONAL (formerly Ambassador-Emerald Intl.), 427 Wade Hampton Blvd., Greenville SC 29609. (864) 235-2434. Fax (864) 235-2491. E-mail: publisher@emeraldhouse.com. Website: www.ambassador-international.com. Sam Lowry, ed. Dedicated to spreading the gospel of Christ and empowering Christians through the written word. Publishes 30+ titles/yr.; hardcover, trade paperbacks, mass-market paperbacks, coffee-table books, digital. Receives 350-400 submissions annually. 65% of books from first-time authors. Accepts mss through agents or authors. Subsidy publishes 40-50%; no print-on-demand. No reprints. Prefers 30,000+ wds. or 100-250 pgs. **Royalty 10-18% of net; no advance.** Average first printing 2,000-3,000. Publication within 3 mos. Considers simultaneous submissions. Prefers requested ms by e-mail. Responds in up to 30 days. Prefers KJV, NIV, ESV, NKJV, NASB. Guidelines by mail/e-mail/website ("Get Published"/"submission guidelines" in text); free catalog.

Nonfiction: E-mail proposal/3 chapters; phone/fax/e-query OK.

Fiction: E-mail proposal/3 chapters; phone/fax/e-query OK. For adults.

Special Needs: Business, finance, biographies, novels, inspirational, devotional, topical, Bible studies.

Also Does: DVDs.

Photos/Artwork: Accepts freelance photos for book covers; open to queries from freelance artists.

Tips: "We're most open to a book which has a clearly defined market and the author's total commitment to the project. We do well with first-time authors. We have full international coverage. Many of our titles sell globally."

AMERICAN CATHOLIC PRESS, 16565 State St., South Holland IL 60473-2025. (708) 331-5485. Fax (708) 331-5484. E-mail: acp@acpress.org. Website: www.acpress.org or www.leafletmissal.com. Catholic worship resources. Father Michael Gilligan, ed. dir. Publishes 4 titles/yr.; hardcover. Receives 10 submissions annually. Reprints books. **Pays $25-100 for outright purchases only.** Average first printing 3,000. Publication within 1 yr. No simultaneous submissions. Responds in 2 mos. Prefers NAS. No guidelines; catalog for SASE.

Nonfiction: Query first; no phone/fax/e-query.

Tips: "We publish only materials on the Roman Catholic liturgy. Especially interested in new music for church services. No poetry or fiction."

*AMG PUBLISHERS/LIVING INK BOOKS, 6815 Shallowford Rd., Chattanooga TN 37421. Toll-free (800) 266-4977. (423) 894-6060. Toll-free fax (800) 265-6690. (423) 648-2244. E-mail: ricks@

amgpublishers.com, info@amgpublishers.com, or through website: www.amgpublishers.com. AMG International. Rick Steele, product development & acquisitions; Dr. Warren Baker, sr. ed. To provide biblically oriented books for reference, learning, and personal growth. Imprints: Living Ink Books; God and Country Press. Publishes 30-35 titles/yr.; hardcover, trade paperbacks, and oversized Bible studies. Receives 2,500 submissions annually. 30% of books from first-time authors. Accepts mss through agents or authors. Reprints books. Prefers 40,000-60,000 wds. or 176-224 pgs. **Royalty 10-16% of net; average advance $2,000.** Average first printing 3,500. Publication within 18 mos. Accepts simultaneous submissions. Prefers accepted ms by e-mail. Responds in 1-4 mos. Prefers KJV, NASB, NIV, NKJV, NLT. Guidelines by e-mail/website; catalog for 9 x 12 SAE/5 stamps.

Nonfiction: Query letter first; e-query preferred. "Looking for historical fiction and nonfiction for our God and Country Press imprint. Need more reference-type works; Bible studies 4-8 weeks in length; and YA fiction."

Fiction: Query letter first; e-query preferred. "Always looking for YA fantasy and historical fiction for adults."

Special Needs: Bible studies and reference—especially reference.

Also Does: Bible software, Bible audio cassettes, CD-ROMs.

Artwork: Open to queries from freelance artists.

Tips: "Most open to a book that is well thought out, clearly written, and finely edited. A professional proposal, following our specific guidelines, has the best chance of acceptance. Spend extra time in developing a good proposal. AMG is always looking for something new and different—with a niche. Write, and rewrite, and rewrite, and rewrite again."

This publisher serviced by ChristianManuscriptSubmissions.com.

*AVON INSPIRE, HarperCollins, 10 E. 53rd St., New York NY 10022. (212) 207-7000. Website: www.harpercollins.com. Cynthia DiTiberio, ed. Inspirational women's fiction. Publishes 8-10 titles/yr. Agented submissions only.

Fiction: Historical & contemporary; Amish.

*BAKER ACADEMIC, 6030 E. Fulton Rd., Ada MI 49301. (616) 676-9185. Fax (616) 676-9573. E-mail: submissions@bakeracademic.com. Website: www.bakeracademic.com. Imprint of Baker Publishing Group. Jim Kinney, ed. dir. Publishes religious academic books and professional books for students and church leaders. Publishes 50 titles/yr.; hardcover, trade paperbacks. 10% of books from first-time authors. Accepts mss through agents, submission services, or editor's personal contacts at writers' conferences. **Royalty; advance.** Publication within 1 yr. Guidelines on website ("Contact"/"Submit a Manuscript or Proposal"); catalog for 10 x 13 SAE/3 stamps.

Nonfiction: No unsolicited queries.

This publisher serviced by ChristianManuscriptSubmissions.com.

*BAKER BOOKS, 6030 E. Fulton Rd., Ada MI 49301. (616) 676-9185. Fax (616) 676-2315. Website: www.bakerbooks.com. Imprint of Baker Publishing Group. Ministry titles for the church. Publishes hardcover, trade paperbacks. No unsolicited proposals. Catalog for 10 x 13 SAE/3 stamps. Submit only through an agent, Authonomy.com, or ChristianManuscriptSubmissions.com.

*BALLANTINE PUBLISHING GROUP, 1745 Broadway, 18th Fl., New York NY 10019. (212) 782-9000. Website: www.randomhouse.com/BB. A Division of Random House. Submit to Religion Editor. General publisher that does a few religious books. Mss from agents only. No e-query. **Royalty 8-15%; variable advances.** Nonfiction & fiction. Guidelines on website; no catalog.

B&H PUBLISHING GROUP, 127—9th Ave. N., Nashville TN 37234-0115. E-mail: Manuscript Submission@lifeway.com. Website: www.bhpublishinggroup.com. Twitter: @BHpub. Facebook: www.facebook.com/bhpublishing. B&H Publishing Group, a division of LifeWay Christian Resources, is a team of mission-minded people with a passion for taking God's Word to the world. Because we believe Every Word Matters, we seek to provide innovative, intentional content that is grounded in biblical truth. Imprints: B&H Books, B&H Academic, Holman Bible Publishers, Holman Reference, Broadman ChurchSupplies, B&H Español. Publishes 90-100 titles/yr.; hardcover, trade paperback. Receives 3,000 submissions annually. 10% of books from first-time authors. Royalty on net; advance. Publication within 18 mos. Considers simultaneous submissions. Responds in 2-3 mos. Prefers HCSB. Guidelines by mail/e-mail.

Nonfiction: Query first; no phone/fax query.

Fiction: Query first; no phone/fax query.

Also Does: Licensing, Kindle Reader, some audio.

Blog: blog.bhpublishinggroup.com/

Tips: "Follow guidelines when submitting. Be informed that the market in general is very crowded with the book you might want to write. Do the research before submitting."

This publisher serviced by ChristianManuscriptSubmissions.com.

*BANTAM BOOKS. See Doubleday Religious on p. 74.

BARBOUR PUBLISHING INC., 1810 Barbour Dr., PO Box 719, Uhrichsville OH 44683. (740) 922-6045. Fax (740) 922-8065. Mission statement: To publish and distribute inspirational products offering exceptional value and biblical encouragement to the masses. E-mail: submissions@barbourbooks.com. Guidelines by website, www.barbourbooks.com (click on "Contact Us"/"How do I submit my manuscript for publishing?"). Accepts fiction proposals only through agents. Publishes 300+ titles/yr.; fiction, nonfiction, Bible reference, devotions, gift books, Christian classics, children's titles; hardcover, flexibound, trade paperbacks, mass market paperbacks. Considers simultaneous submissions & reprints.

*BETHANY HOUSE PUBLISHERS, 6030 E. Fulton Rd., Ada MI 49301. Website: www.bethanyhouse .com. Imprint of Baker Publishing Group. To help Christians apply biblical truth in all areas of life— whether through a well-told story, a challenging devotional, or the message of an illustrated children's book. Publishes 90-100 titles/yr.; hardcover, trade paperbacks. 2% of books from first-time authors. Accepts mss through agents only. Reprints on mass-market paperbacks. **Negotiable royalty on net; negotiable advance.** Publication within 1 yr. Considers simultaneous submissions. Responds in 3 mos. Guidelines on website ("Contact us"/"Submit a Manuscript or Proposal"). Catalog for 9 x 12 SAE/5 stamps.

Nonfiction: "Seeking well-planned and developed books in the following categories: personal growth, deeper-life spirituality, contemporary issues, women's issues, reference, applied theology, and inspirational."

Fiction: See website for current acquisitions needs.

Tips: "We do not accept unsolicited queries or proposals."

This publisher serviced by Authonomy.com and ChristianManuscriptSubmissions.com.

BLUE DOLPHIN PUBLISHING, INC., PO Box 8, Nevada City CA 95959. (530) 477-1503. Fax (530) 477-8342. E-mail: Bdolphin@bluedolphinpublishing.com. Website: www.bluedolphin publishing.com. Paul M. Clemens, pub. Imprints: Pelican Pond (fiction & poetry), Papillon Publishing (juvenile), and Symposium Publishing (nonfiction). Books that help people grow in their social and spiritual awareness. Publishes 20-24 titles/yr. (includes 10-12 print-on-demand). Receives 4,800 submissions annually. 90% of books from first-time authors. Prefers about 60,000 wds. or 200-300 pgs. **Royalty 10-15% of net; no advance.** Average first printing 300, then on demand. Publication within 10 mos. Considers simultaneous submissions. Requires requested ms on disk. Responds in 3-6 mos. Guidelines by e-mail/website (scroll down right side to "About Blue Dolphin"/"Guidance for Authors"); catalog for 8.5 x 11 SAE/2 stamps.

Nonfiction: Query or proposal/1 chapter; no phone/e-query. "Looking for books that will increase people's spiritual and social awareness. We will consider all topics."

Fiction: Query/2-pg. synopsis. Pelican Pond Imprint. For teens and adults; no children's board books or picture books.

Also Does: E-books.

Photos/Artwork: Accepts freelance photos for book covers; open to queries from freelance artists.

Tips: "Looking for mature writers whose focus is to help people lead better lives. Our authors are generally professionals who write for others—not just for themselves. We look for topics that would appeal to the general market, are interesting, different, and will aid in the growth and development of humanity. See website before submitting."

Note: This publisher also publishes books on a range of topics, including cross-cultural spirituality. They also may offer a co-publishing arrangement, not necessarily a royalty deal.

BMH BOOKS, PO Box 544, Winona Lake IN 46590. (574) 268-1122. Fax (574) 268-5384. E-mail: tdwhite@bmhbooks.com. Website: www.BMHbooks.com. Blog: www.fgbcworld-blog.com. Fellowship of Grace Brethren Churches. Terry White, ed./pub. Trinitarian theology; dispensational eschatology; emphasis on exegesis. Publishes 10-15 titles/yr.; hardcover, trade paperbacks. Receives 30 submissions annually. 50% of books from first-time authors. Accepts mss through agents or authors. Seldom reprints books. Prefers 50,000-75,000 wds. or 128-256 pgs. **Royalty 8-10% on retail; rarely pays an advance.** Average first printing 2,000. Publication within 1 yr. Prefers not to consider simultaneous submissions. Responds in 3 mos. Prefers KJV or NIV. Requires accepted mss by e-mail. Guidelines by mail/e-mail; free catalog.

Nonfiction: Proposal/2 chapters; no phone/fax query; e-query OK. "Most open to a small-group study book or text for Bible college/Bible institute."

Tips: "Most open to biblically based, timeless discipleship material."

BONDFIRE BOOKS, Parent co. Alive Communications, 7680 Goddard St, Ste 220, Colorado Springs CO 80920. (719) 260-7080. Fax: (719) 260-8223. E-mail: submissions@bondfirebooks.com. Website: www.bondfirebooks.com. Chief Kindler, ed. Bondfire Books is an e-publisher focused on kindling thought and action through Christian and inspirational content while maximizing digital prospects for authors. Publish 50+/yr. Receives 5,000 proposals/yr. 10% first-time authors. Accept books submitted by agents. Digital. Will reprint. Preferred book length 150,000 wds. Royalty 50% based on net. E-books 50%. No advance. Avg. time to publication 2 mos. Considers simultaneous submissions. Responds 2-4 wks. Catalog on website. Guidelines on website. Open to queries from freelance artists.

Nonfiction: proposal with 2 chap. E-mail queries. Require mss by e-mail.

Fiction: teens/adults. Query letter ONLY. Proposal with 2 chap.

Special Needs: Memoir, fiction, nonfiction, tie-ins to news events. News makers. Out of print with rts. reverted, in print works with available elec. rights.

Tips: "Publishers and agents are being much more selective with what they say yes to. And yet amidst increased competition, the cream always rises to the top. The great books get noticed and picked up." Contemporary fiction or big nonfiction book tied to a news maker. Primarily interested in working with authors with established platforms and audiences.

*BRIDGE LOGOS, 17750 N.W. 115th Ave., Bldg. 200, Ste. 220, Alachua FL 32615. (386) 462-2525. Fax (586) 462-2535. E-mail: editorial@bridgelogos.com or phildebrand@bridgelogos.com. Website: www.bridgelogos.com. Peggy Hildebrand, acq. ed. Publishes classics, books by Spirit-filled authors, and inspirational books that appeal to the general evangelical market. Imprint: Synergy. Publishes 40 titles/yr.; hardcover, trade paperbacks, mass-market paperbacks. Receives 200+ submissions annually. 30% of books from first-time authors. Accepts mss through agents or authors. Subsidy publishes to 5%; does very little print-on-demand. Reprints books. Prefers 250 pgs. **Royalty 10% on net; rarely pays $500 advance.** Average first printing 4,000-5,000. Publication within

6-12 mos. Considers simultaneous submissions. Responds in 6 wks. Prefers accepted mss by e-mail. Guidelines on website ("Information"/"Manuscript Submission"); free catalog.

Nonfiction: Proposal/3-5 chapters; no phone/fax query; e-query OK. "Most open to evangelism, spiritual growth, self-help, and education." Charges a $50 manuscript submission/evaluation fee.

Fiction: Proposal/3-5 chapters; no phone/fax query; e-query OK.

Special Needs: Reference, biography, current issues, controversial issues, church renewal, women's issues, and Bible commentary. Also teen, preteen, and kids' books.

Ethnic Books: African American & Hispanic.

Photos: Accepts freelance photos for book covers.

Tips: "Looking for well-written, timely books that are aimed at the needs of people and that glorify God. Have a great message, a well-written manuscript, and a specific plan and willingness to market your book. Looking for previously published authors with an active ministry who are experts on their subject."

BRP PUBLISHING GROUP, PO Box 822674, Vancouver WA 98682. (208) 352-0396. Fax (208) 246-3962. E-mail: publisher@barkingrainpress.org. Website: www.barkingrainpress.org. Ti Locke, ed. dir. Imprints: Barking Rain Press, Virtual Tales, Nitis Books. Publishes 12-15 bks./yr. Receives 100+ ms/yr. 60% first-time authors. Accepts bks. submitted by agents. Hardcover, trade paperbacks, digital, reprints. Prefers 20,000-100,000 wds. Royalty 50-60%. Advance for est. authors. Exclusively POD services & e-books. Publication within 12 mos. No simultaneous submissions. Responds 30-60 days. Catalog on website. Guidelines on website.

Fiction: Only book proposal w/4 chapters. Qtrly open submissions: Jan, Apr, Jul, Oct. Elec. submissions only. Sign up for reminder list on website.

Special Needs: Non-erotic romance, YA, speculative fiction.

Tips: Well written, good plot and story arc, no POV issues (head-hopping). Barking Rain Press is a non-profit publisher. Our mission is to help new authors and mid-list authors further their writing careers. Freelance openings posted on website.

CANTICLE BOOKS, PO Box 2666, Carlsbad CA 92018. (760) 806-3743. Fax (760) 806-3689. E-mail: magnuspress@aol.com. Website: www.magnuspress.com. Imprint of Magnus Press. Warren Angel, ed. dir. To publish biblical studies by Catholic authors that are written for the average person and that minister life to Christ's Church. Publishes 2 titles/yr.; trade paperbacks. Receives 60 submissions annually. 50% of books from first-time authors. Accepts mss through agents or authors. Reprints books. Prefers 105-300 pgs. **Royalty 6-12% on retail; no advance.** Average first printing 2,500. Publication within 1 yr. Considers simultaneous submissions. Accepts requested ms on disk. Responds in 1 mo. Guidelines by mail/e-mail/website ("Canticle Book Submissions"); free catalog.

Nonfiction: Query or proposal/3 chapters; fax query OK. "Looking for spirituality, thematic biblical studies, unique inspirational books."

Tips: "Our writers need solid knowledge of the Bible and a mature spirituality that reflects a profound relationship with Jesus Christ. Most open to well-researched, popularly written biblical studies geared to Catholics, or personal experience books that share/emphasize a person's relationship with Christ."

CHARISMA HOUSE (formerly Strang Book), 600 Rinehart Rd., Lake Mary FL 32746. (407) 333-0600. Fax (407) 333-7100. E-mail: creationhouse@charismamedia.com or charismahouse@charismamedia.com. Website: www.charismamedia.com. Communications. Submit to Acquisitions Assistant. To inspire and equip people to live a Spirit-led life and walk in the divine purpose for which they were called. This house has 8 imprints, which are listed with descriptions/details. Publishes 150 titles/yr.; hardcover, trade paperbacks, mass-market paperbacks. Receives 1,500 submissions annually. 65% of books from first-time authors. Prefers mss through agents. Reprints books.

Prefers 55,000 wds. **Royalty on net or outright purchase; advance.** Average first printing 7,500. Publication within 9 mos. Considers simultaneous submissions. Accepts requested ms on disk or on website. Responds in 6-10 wks. Guidelines by mail/e-mail/website (under "Submit Book Proposal"); free catalog.

Nonfiction: Proposal or complete ms; by mail or e-query OK; no phone query. Book proposal application on website. "Open to any books that are well written and glorify Jesus Christ."

Fiction: Proposal or complete ms; by mail or e-query OK; no phone query. Book proposal application on website. "For all ages. Fiction must have a biblical worldview and point the reader to Christ."

Photos: Accepts freelance photos for book covers.

Charisma House: Books on Christian living, mainly from a Charismatic/Pentecostal perspective. Topics: Christian living, work of the Holy Spirit, prophecy, prayer, Scripture, adventures in evangelism and missions, popular theology.

Siloam: Books about living in good health—body, mind, and spirit. Topics: alternative medicine; diet and nutrition; and physical, emotional, and psychological wellness. We prefer manuscripts from certified doctors, nutritionists, trainers, and other medical professionals. Proof of credentials may be required.

Frontline: Books on contemporary political and social issues from a Christian perspective.

Creation House: Copublishing imprint for a wide variety of Christian books. Author is required to buy a quantity of books from the first press run. This is not self-publishing or print-on-demand.

Realms: Christian fiction in the supernatural, speculative genre. Full-length adult novels, 80,000-120,000 wds. Will also consider historical or biblical fiction if supernatural element is substantial.

Excel: Publishes books that are targeted toward success in the workplace and businesses.

Casa Creación: Publishes and translates books into Spanish. (800) 987-8432. E-mail: casacreacion@.com. Website: www.casacreacion.com.

Publicaciones Casa: Publishes the same as Creation House and is for people who like to copublish in Spanish. Contact info same as Casa Creación.

This publisher serviced by ChristianManuscriptSubmissions.com.

THE CHARLES PRESS, PUBLISHERS, 230 N. 21st St., Ste. 202, Philadelphia PA 19103-1095. (215) 561-2786. E-mail: submissions@charlespresspub.com. Website: www.charlespresspub.com. Lauren Metzler, pub. (lauren@charlespresspub.com). Responds in 4-16 wks. Guidelines on website ("Book Proposal Submission Guidelines"); catalog.

Nonfiction: Submit a letter of inquiry first; no fax submissions.

*CHICKEN SOUP FOR THE SOUL BOOKS. See listing in Periodicals section.

*CHOSEN BOOKS, Division of Baker Publishing Group, 3985 Bradwater St., Fairfax VA 22031-3702. (703) 764-8250. E-mail: jcampbell@chosenbooks.com. Website: www.chosenbooks.com. Jane Campbell, editorial dir. Charismatic; Spirit-filled–life titles and some thematic narratives. No autobiographies. No unsolicited mss, but will respond to e-mail queries.

CHRISTIAN HERITAGE SOCIETY, Box 519, Baldwin Place NY 10505. Phone/fax (914) 962-3287. E-mail: gtkurian@aol.com. Website: www.encyclopediasociety.com. George Kurian, ed. Publishes 6 titles/yr.; hardcover, trade paperbacks. Receives 100 submissions annually. 50% of books from first-time authors. Prefers mss through agents. No subsidy. Reprints books. Prefers 120,000 wds. **Royalty 10-15% on net; no advance.** Average first printing 10,000. Publication within 1 yr. Considers simultaneous submissions. Responds in 3 mos. Guidelines by mail; free catalog.

Nonfiction: Query; e-query OK. "Looking for Christian history, reference books, memoirs, devotionals, and evangelism."

CHRISTIAN WRITER'S EBOOK NET, PO Box 446, Ft. Duchesne UT 84026. (435) 772-3429. E-mail: editor@writersebook.com or through website: www.writersebook.com. Nondenominational/ evangelical Christian. Linda Kay Stewart Whitsitt, ed-in-chief (linda@webtechdg.com); M. P. Whitsitt, asst. ed. (MP@webtechdg.com); Terry Gordon Whitsitt, asst. to ed. (terry@webtechdg.com). Gives first-time authors the opportunity to bring their God-given writing talent to the Christian market. Publishes 25 titles/yr. Receives 150 submissions annually. 95% of books from first-time authors. Accepts mss through agents or authors. Subsidy publishes 25%. Reprints books. Prefers 60+ pgs. **Royalty 35-50%; no advance.** E-books only for Kindle and other e-reader formats. Publication within 6 mos. Considers simultaneous submissions. Electronic queries and submissions only; mss need to be in electronic form (MS Word, WordPerfect, ASCII, etc.) to be published; send by e-mail (preferred). No mail submissions accepted without contact by e-mail first. Responds in 1-2 mos. Guidelines on website ("Publishing" on right side).

> **Nonfiction/Fiction:** E-query only. Any topic or genre.
> **Also Does:** Booklets, pamphlets, tracts. E-books.
> **Tips:** "Make sure your work is polished and ready for print. The books we publish are sold in our online store at Amazon and Ebay. If you are not sure what an e-book is, check out our website's FAQ page."

CHURCH GROWTH INSTITUTE, PO Box 7, Elkton MD 21922-0007. (434) 525-0022. Fax (434) 525-0608. E-mail: info@churchgrowth.org. Website: www.ChurchGrowth.org. Ephesians Four Ministries. Cindy G. Spear, product development dir. Providing practical tools for leadership, evangelism, and church growth. Publishes 3 titles/yr.; trade paperbacks/other. Receives 20 submissions annually. 7% of books from first-time authors. No mss through agents. Prefers 64-160 pgs. **Royalties vary; 6% on retail or outright purchase; no advance.** Average first printing 100. Publication within 1 yr. Considers simultaneous submissions. Responds in 3 mos. Requires requested ms on disk or by e-mail. Guidelines sent after query/outline is received by e-mail. No printed catalog; full product listing on website.

> **Nonfiction:** Query; no phone/fax query; e-query OK. "We prefer our writers to be experienced in what they write about."
> **Special Needs:** New or unique ministries (how-to). Self-discovery and evaluation tools, such as our Spiritual Gifts Inventory and Spiritual Growth Survey, Friendship Skills Assessment.
> **Photos:** Rarely use freelance photos.
> **Tips:** "Currently concentrating on own Team Ministry/Spiritual Gifts resources. Accept very few unsolicited submissions. Most open to ministry how-to manuals or audio albums (CDs/audiotapes and workbooks) for ministry leaders—something unique with a special niche. Must be practical and different from anything else on the same subject— or must be a topic/slant few others have published. May consider evaluation tools as mentioned above. No devotionals, life testimonies, commentaries, or studies on books of the Bible."

CLADACH PUBLISHING, PO Box 336144, Greeley CO 80633. (970) 371-9530. E-mail: staff@ cladach.com. Website: www.cladach.com. Independent, small Christian press. Catherine Lawton, pub. (cathyl@cladach.com). Seeks to influence those inside and outside the body of Christ by giving a voice to talented writers with a clear, articulate, and Christ-honoring vision. Categories: memoirs, fiction, relationships, God in creation. Publishes 2-3 titles/yr.; trade paperbacks and e-books. Receives 200 submissions annually. 60% of books from first-time authors. Accepts proposals through agents or authors. No subsidy, print-on-demand, or reprints. Prefers 160-256 pgs. **Royalty 7% on net; sometimes offers a small advance.** Average first printing 1,000. Publication within 1 yr. Considers simultaneous submissions. Responds in 3-6 mos. Prefers NIV, NRSV. Guidelines on website ("For Authors"); catalog online.

> **Nonfiction:** Query letter only first (we're very selective); e-query OK.

Fiction: Query letter only first (1-2 pgs.); e-query OK (copied into message). For adults. "Prefers gripping stories depicting inner struggles and real-life issues; well crafted. Interested in frontier fiction set in Colorado."

Tips: "We want writing that shows God active in our world and that helps readers experience His presence and power in their lives. Check out our website for current guidelines and published books to see whether your book is a fit for Cladach." Unsolicited mss are returned unopened.

*CLC PUBLICATIONS, PO Box 1449, Fort Washington PA 19034. (215) 542-1242. E-mail: sub missions@clcpublications.com. Website: www.clcpublications.com. CLC Ministries Intl. David Fessenden, mng. ed.; Becky English, assoc. ed. Books that reflect a passion for the topic and a depth of spirituality—a book that grows out of a fervent relationship with Christ. Publishes 12 titles/yr.; hardcover, trade paperbacks, mass-market paperbacks. Receives 200+ submissions annually. 80% of books from first-time authors. Accepts mss through agents or authors. Reprints books. Prefers under 60,000 wds. or under 300 pgs. **Royalty 10-12% of net; pays an advance.** Average first printing 3,000. Publication within 1 yr. Considers simultaneous submissions. Responds in 2-3 mos. Requires accepted mss on disk or by e-mail. Prefers NKJV. Guidelines by mail/e-mail/website (at top "Writers Guidelines"); catalog for 9 x 12 SAE/2 stamps.

Nonfiction: Query first; proposal/2-3 chapters; e-query OK. Books for the deeper life.

Special Needs: A fresh approach to deepening one's relationship with God.

Ethnic Books: African American.

This publisher serviced by ChristianManuscriptSubmissions.com.

COMFORT PUBLISHING, PO Box 6265, Concord NC 28027. (704) 782-2353. Fax (704) 782-2393. E-mail: khuddle@comfortpublishing.com. Website: www.comfortpublishing.com. Comfort Publishing Services, LLC. Pamilla S. Tolen, sr. vp.; Kristy Huddle, acq. mg. Submit to Kristy Huddle (khuddle@comfortpublishing.com). To promote Christian literature in a manner that is easy to read and understand, with a message that either teaches a principle or supports the truth of Christian faith. Nonfiction, self-help, true stories. Publishes 10 titles/yr.; hardcover, trade paperbacks, digital. Receives 3,000 submissions annually. 65% of books from first-time authors. Prefers mss through agents; will accept from authors. No subsidy or print-on-demand. No reprints. Prefers 75,000 wds. or 200 pgs. **Royalty 8-15% on retail; some advances; e-books 50% of net.** Average first printing 2,500. Publication within 12 mos. Considers simultaneous submissions. Responds in 18 mos. Accepts requested mss by e-mail. Guidelines by mail/e-mail/website ("Submission Guidelines"); digital catalog. Accepts freelance photos. Prefers NKJV.

Nonfiction: Proposal/3 chapters, or complete ms; e-query preferred.

Fiction: For teens & adults. Submit complete ms.

Special Needs: Adventure, romance, mystery romance, suspense, teen/YA fiction, adult.

Also Does: E-books.

Photos: Accepts freelance photos for book covers.

Tips: "Desire to break away from traditional Christian literature. Readers are looking for more modern stories that deal with current dilemmas. Through our books we want to provide entertainment but also present books that represent good moral judgment within the Christian experience."

CONARI PRESS, 665 Third St., Ste. 400, San Francisco CA 94107. E-mail: submissions@rwwbooks.com. Website: www.redwheelweiser.com. An imprint of Red Wheel/Weiser, LLC. Ms. Pat Bryce, acq. ed. Books on spirituality, personal growth, parenting, and social issues. Publishes 30 titles/yr. Responds in up to 3 mos. Guidelines and catalog on website ("Submission Guidelines"). Incomplete topical listings.

CONCILIAR PRESS, Ben Lomond CA. E-mail: khyde@conciliarmedia.com. Website: www.conciliar press.com. Antiochian Orthodox Christian Archdiocese of N.A. Katherine Hyde, acq. ed. Publishes

8-18 titles/yr. Receives 100 submissions annually. 20% of books from first-time authors. Accepts mss through agents or authors. Reprints books. **Royalty; no or small advance.** Average first printing 2,000. Accepts simultaneous submissions. E-mail submissions only. Responds in 1-3 mos. Prefers NKJV. Guidelines on website (scroll to bottom "Submissions"); catalog on website.

> **Nonfiction:** E-query only. Accepts Eastern Orthodox material from Eastern Orthodox authors only.
>
> **Children's Books:** E-query only. Send full manuscript for picture books under 2,000 wds. Accepts Eastern Orthodox material from Eastern Orthodox authors only.
>
> **Photos:** Accepts freelance photos for book covers.
>
> **Tips:** "Please explore our website before submitting and carefully follow posted guidelines. We accept only material by Eastern Orthodox Christians with specifically Orthodox content. We reserve the right not to respond to inappropriate submissions."

*CONCORDIA PUBLISHING HOUSE, 3558 S. Jefferson Ave., St. Louis MO 63118-3968. (314) 268-1080. E-mail: ed.engelbrecht@cph.org. Website: www.cph.org. Lutheran Church/Missouri Synod. Rev. Edward A. Engelbrecht, STM, sr. ed. Professional and academic books in biblical studies, 16th-century studies, historical theology, and theology and culture. Publication within 2 yrs. Responds in 8-12 wks. Guidelines on website (at bottom under "Service & Shopping Tools"/"Manuscript Submissions").

> **Nonfiction:** Proposal/sample chapters.
>
> **Tips:** "Freelance submissions are welcome. Prospective authors should consult the guidelines on the website for an author prospectus and submission guidelines."

CONTEMPORARY DRAMA SERVICE, Meriwether Publishing Co., 885 Elkton Dr., Colorado Springs CO 80907. E-mail: editor@meriwether.com. Website: www.meriwetherpublishing.com. Publishes Christian plays for mainline churches. Also supplemental textbooks on theatrical subjects. Prefers comedy but does publish some serious works. Accepts full-length or one-act plays—comedy or musical. General and Christian. Publishes 30 plays/yr. Responds in 4-6 wks. See the Meriwether Publishing listing or website for additional details ("Author's Corner" at top of list).

*DAVID C. COOK, 4050 Lee Vance View, Colorado Springs CO 80918. (719) 536-0100. Fax (719) 536-3269. Website: www.davidccook.com. Don Pape, publisher, print and media; Terry Behimer, ed. dir. and assoc. publisher; Ingrid Beck, mng. ed. Discipleship is foundational; everything we publish needs to move the reader one step closer to maturity in Christ. Brands: David C. Cook (for teachers or program leaders who want Bible-based discipleship resources; Bible and study resources for serious Bible students; books for Christian families seeking biblical answers to life problems; books to equip kids—birth to age 12—for life); and fiction (inspiring fiction for mature believers). Publishes 85 titles/yr.; hardcover, trade paperbacks. 10% of books from first-time authors. Requires mss through agents. Publication within 1-2 yrs. Considers simultaneous submissions. Responds in 3-6 mos. Prefers requested ms by e-mail. Prefers NIV. Guidelines by mail/e-mail/website ("Contact Information"/"Writers Guidelines" on left).

> **Nonfiction/Fiction:** Accepts submissions only through agents or on request of one of their editors at a writers' conference.
>
> This publisher serviced by ChristianManuscriptSubmissions.com.

CROSSLINK PUBLISHING, PO Box 1232, Rapid City SD 57709. Toll-free (800) 323-0853. Toll-free fax (800) 934-6762. E-mail: publisher@crosslink.org. Website: www.crosslink.org. Christian Church/Church of Christ. Rick Bates, dir. Focused on providing valuable resources to authors as well as bringing vibrant and helpful resources to the Christian community. Estab. 2008. Publishes 6-8 titles/yr.; trade paperbacks. Receives 20 submissions annually. 25% of books from first-time authors. Prefers mss through agents. No subsidy; does print-on-demand. No reprints. Prefers 200-300 pgs. **Royalty 10% of retail; no advance.** Average first printing 750. Publication within

3 mos. Considers simultaneous submissions. Responds in 7 days. Requires accepted mss by e-mail. Guidelines on website ("Publishing").

Nonfiction: Complete ms; e-query OK.

Special Needs: Devotionals and small group studies.

Photos/Artwork: Accepts freelance photos for book covers; open to queries from freelance artists.

Tips: "We are particularly interested in providing books that help Christians succeed in their daily walk (inspirational, devotional, small groups, etc.)."

CROSSWAY, 1300 Crescent St., Wheaton IL 60174. (630) 682-4300. Fax (630) 682-4785. E-mail: submissions@crossway.org. Website: www.crossway.org. A publishing ministry of Good News Publishers. Allan Fisher, sr. vp for book publishing; submit to Jill Carter, editorial administrator, or www.submissions.org. Publishes books that combine the truth of God's Word with a passion to live it out, with unique and compelling Christian content. Publishes 70 titles/yr.; hardcover, trade paperbacks. Receives 1,000 submissions annually. 1% of books from first-time authors. Accepts mss through agents or authors. No reprints. Prefers 25,000 wds. & up. **Royalty 10-21% of net; advance varies.** Average first printing 5,000-10,000. Publication within 18 mos. Considers simultaneous submissions. Responds in 6-8 wks. Prefers ESV. Guidelines on website; free catalog.

Nonfiction: Currently not accepting unsolicited submissions.

Also Does: Tracts (Good News Publishers).

This publisher serviced by ChristianManuscriptSubmissions.com.

**Recipient of five 2006 Silver Angel Awards from Excellence in Media.

CSS PUBLISHING GROUP INC., 5450 N. Dixie Hwy, Lima OH 45807-9559. (419) 227-1818. Fax (419) 228-9184. E-mail: david@csspub.com, or through website: www.csspub.com. Serves the needs of pastors, worship leaders, and parish program planners in the broad Christian mainline of the American church. Imprints: Fairway Press (subsidy—see separate listing); B.O.D. (Books On Demand); FaithWalk Books. Publishes 30-40 titles/yr.; trade paperbacks, digital. Receives 500-1,000 submissions annually. 50% of books from first-time authors. Subsidy publishes 50-60% through Fairway Press; does print-on-demand. Reprints books. Prefers 100-125 pgs. **No royalty or advance.** Average first printing 1,000. Publication within 12-24 mos. Considers simultaneous submissions. Responds in 3 wks. to 3 mos.; final decision within 12 mos. Requires requested ms on disk and in hard copy. Prefers NRSV. Guidelines by e-mail/website ("Contact Us"/"Submissions Guidelines"); no catalog.

Nonfiction: Query or proposal/3 chapters; phone/e-query OK; complete ms for short works. "Looking for pastoral resources for ministry; lectionary sermons. Our material is practical in nature."

Fiction: Complete ms. Easy-to-perform dramas and pageants for all age groups. "Our drama interest primarily includes Advent, Christmas, Epiphany, Lent, and Easter. We do not publish long plays." Subsidy-only for fiction.

Tips: "We're looking for authors who will help with the marketing of their books."

CUPOLA PRESS, 3280 Withers Avenue, Lafayette CA 94549. (925) 285-7754. Fax: (925) 256-6700. E-mail: info@cupolapress.com. Website: www.cupolapress.com. Gail Johnston, ed. Publishes 3 titles/yr. 50% by first-time authors. Does some POD. Publication in 1 year. Considers simultaneous submissions. Writer guidelines not available.

Nonfiction: Query letter only first. Query by e-mail. Inspirational nonfiction; how-to books with an enjoyable tone.

Tips: "Light reading for intentional living."

DAWN PUBLICATIONS, 12402 Bitney Springs Rd., Nevada City CA 95959. (530) 274-7775. Fax (530) 274-7778. E-mail: submission@dawnpub.com. Website: www.dawnpub.com. Glenn

Hovemann, acq. ed. Dedicated to inspiring in children a sense of appreciation for all of life on earth. Publishes 6 titles/yr.; hardcover, trade paperbacks. Receives 2,500 submissions annually. 35% of titles are by new authors. Accepts mss through agents or authors. No reprints. **Royalty on net; pays an advance.** Publication within 1-2 yrs. Considers simultaneous submissions. Responds in 2 mos. Guidelines/catalog on website ("Submissions").

> **Nonfiction:** Complete manuscript by mail or e-mail.
>
> **Artwork:** Open to queries from freelance artists (send sample c/o Muffy Weaver).
>
> **Tips:** "Most open to creative nonfiction. We look for nature awareness and appreciation titles that promote a relationship with the natural world and specific habitats, usually through inspiring treatment and nonfiction."

DESERT BREEZE PUBLISHING, E-mail: submissions@desertbreezepublishing.com. Website: www.desertbreezepublishing.com. Gail Delaney, ed. Goal is to publish exceptionally crafted and captivating romance novels in multiple genres. Accepts 50,000 wds. or over 100,000 wds. (prefers 75,000-100,000). No simultaneous submissions. Guidelines on website (click on "Submissions"); catalog online.

> **Fiction:** See guidelines. Now accepting women's fiction with either secondary or no romantic elements required.
>
> **Special Needs:** Seeking single-title works in all sub-genres. Will consider series. See guidelines for other specific genres.
>
> **Tips:** "If you have questions about the guidelines, e-mail us at submissionsquestions@desert breezepublishing.com."

DISCOVERY HOUSE PUBLISHERS, PO Box 3566, Grand Rapids MI 49501. Toll-free (800) 653-8333. (616) 942-9218. Fax (616) 974-2224. E-mail: dhptc@rbc.org. Website: www.dhp.org. RBC Ministries. Carol Holquist, pub.; submit to Manuscript Review Editor. Publishes nonfiction books that foster Christian growth and godliness. Publishes 12-18 titles/yr.; hardcover, trade paperbacks, mass-market paperbacks. Accepts mss through agents or authors. Reprints books. **Royalty 10-14% on net; no advance.** Publication within 12-18 mos. Considers simultaneous submissions. Prefers e-mail submissions. Responds in 4-6 wks. Guidelines by mail/e-mail/website (FAQ #4); free catalog.

> **Nonfiction:** Ms proposals preferred. If by e-mail, "Attn: Ms Review Editor" in subject line.
>
> This publisher serviced by ChristianManuscriptSubmissions.com.

*DOUBLEDAY RELIGIOUS PUBLISHING, 1745 Broadway, New York NY 10019. (212) 782-9000. Fax (212) 782-8338. E-mail: tmurphy@randomhouse.com. Website: www.randomhouse.com. Imprint of Random House, Inc. Trace Murphy, editorial dir. Imprints: Image, Galilee, New Jerusalem Bible, Three Leaves Press, Anchor Bible Commentaries, Anchor Bible Reference Library. Publishes 45-50 titles/yr.; hardcover, trade paperbacks. Receives 1,500 submissions annually. 10% of books from first-time authors. Requires mss through agents. Reprints books. **Royalty 7.5-15% on retail; pays an advance.** Average first printing varies. Publication within 8 mos. Considers simultaneous submissions. Responds in 4 mos. No disk. Guidelines on website ("About Random House"/"Manuscript Submissions"); catalog for 9 x 12 SASE/3 stamps.

> **Nonfiction:** Agented submissions only. Proposal/3 chapters; no phone query.
>
> **Fiction:** Religious fiction. Agented submissions only.
>
> **Ethnic Books:** African American; Hispanic.
>
> **Tips:** "Most open to a book that has a big and well-defined audience. Have a clear proposal, lucid thesis, and specified audience."
>
> This publisher serviced by ChristianManuscriptSubmissions.com.

DOVE INSPIRATIONAL PRESS, 1000 Burmaster St., Gretna LA 70053. (504) 368-1175. Fax (504) 368-1195. E-mail: editorial@pelicanpub.com. Website: www.pelicanpub.com. Nina Kooij, ed-in-chief. To publish books of quality and permanence that enrich the lives of those who read them.

Imprint of Pelican Publishing. Publishes 1 title/yr.; hardcover, trade paperbacks. Receives 250 submissions annually. No books from first-time authors. Accepts mss through agents or authors. Reprints books. Prefers 200+ pgs. **Royalty; some advances.** Publication within 9-18 mos. No simultaneous submissions. Responds in 1 mo. on queries. Requires accepted ms on disk. Prefers KJV. Guidelines on website ("About Us"/"Submissions").

Nonfiction: Proposal/2 chapters; no phone/fax/e-query.

Fiction: Children's picture books only.

Artwork: Open to queries from freelance artists.

EARTHEN VESSEL PUBLISHING, 9 Sunny Oaks Dr., San Raphael CA 94903. (415) 302-1199. Fax (415) 499-8199. E-mail: kentphilpott@comcast.net. Website: www.earthenvessel.net. Evangelical/Baptist. Kent & Katie Philpott, eds. Our goal is to preach Jesus Christ and Him crucified. Imprint: Siloam Springs Press. Publishes 3 titles/yr.; trade paperbacks. Receives 15 submissions annually. 50% of books from first-time authors. Prefers mss through agents; accepts through author. Reprints books. No subsidy or POD for now. Any length. **Royalty on retail price; no advance.** Average first printing varies. Publication within 6 mos. Considers simultaneous submissions. Accepted mss by disk or e-mail. Responds in 1 wk. to 1 mo. Guidelines on website; no catalog.

Nonfiction: Query first by phone or e-mail; proposal/1 chapter.

Fiction: Query first by phone or e-mail; proposal/1 chapter.

Special Needs: Books of a solid biblical nature, Christ centered, perhaps of a Reformed nature, but not limited to this theology. Special interest in awakenings and a special interest in pastors of small churches and their congregations.

Photos/Artwork: Accepts freelance photos for book covers; open to queries from freelance artists.

Tips: "Well-written and edited work is best. Not able to do major rewriting or editing. Lean toward, but not exclusively, Reformed thought. Our goal is to present the gospel to unbelievers and the Scriptures to believers. We are small and can do very little, but we look forward to working with the print-on-demand format."

*EERDMANS BOOKS FOR YOUNG READERS, 2140 Oak Industrial Dr. N.E., Grand Rapids MI 49505. Toll-free (800) 253-7521. (616) 459-4591. Fax (616) 459-6540. E-mail: youngreaders@eerdmans.com or info@eerdmans.com. Website: www.eerdmans.com/youngreaders. Wm. B. Eerdmans Publishing. Submit to Acquisitions Editor. Produces books for general trade, school, and library markets. Publishes 12-15 titles/yr.; hardcover, trade paperbacks. Receives 5,000 submissions annually. 3% of books from first-time authors. Prefers mss through agents. Age-appropriate length. **Royalty & advance vary.** Average first printing varies. Publication within 36 mos. No simultaneous submissions (mark "Exclusive" on envelope). Responds in 3 mos. Guidelines by mail/e-mail/website ("Submission Guidelines"); catalog for 9 x 12 SAE/4 stamps.

Fiction: Proposal/3 chapters for book length; complete ms for picture books. For children and teens. No e-mail or fax submissions.

Artwork: Please do not send illustrations with picture-book manuscripts unless you are a professional illustrator. When submitting artwork, send color copies, not originals. Send illustrations sample to Gayle Brown, art dir.

Tips: "Most open to thoughtful submissions that address needs in children's literature. We are not looking for Christmas stories at this time."

*WM. B. EERDMANS PUBLISHING CO., 2140 Oak Industrial Dr. N.E., Grand Rapids MI 49505. Toll-free (800) 253-7521. (616) 459-4591. Fax (616) 459-6540. E-mail: info@eerdmans.com. Website: www.eerdmans.com. Protestant/Academic/Theological. Jon Pott, ed-in-chief. Imprint: Eerdmans Books for Young Readers (see separate listing). Publishes 120-130 titles/yr.; hardcover, trade paperbacks. Receives 3,000-4,000 submissions annually. 10% of books from first-time authors. Accepts mss through agents or authors. Reprints books. **Royalty; occasional advance.** Average first printing 4,000. Publication within 1 yr. Considers simultaneous submissions. Responds in 4 wks. to query; several months for mss. Guidelines by mail/website (www.eerdmans.com/submit.htm); free catalog.

Nonfiction: Proposal/2-3 chapters; no fax/e-query. "Looking for religious approaches to contemporary issues, spiritual growth, scholarly works."

Fiction: Proposal/chapter; no fax/e-query. For all ages. "We are looking for adult novels with high literary merit."

Tips: "Most open to material with general appeal, but well-researched, cutting-edge material that bridges the gap between evangelical and mainline worlds. Please include e-mail and/or SASE for a response."

*FAITHWORDS/HACHETTE BOOK GROUP, 10 Cadillac Dr., Ste. 220, Brentwood TN 37027. (615) 221-0996, ext. 221. Fax (615) 221-0962. Website: www.faithwords.com. Hachette Book Group USA. Anne Horch, ed. Publishes 35 titles/yr.; hardcover, trade paperbacks, mass-market paperbacks. Few books from first-time authors. Requires mss through agents. Prefers 60,000-90,000 wds. **Royalty on retail; pays an advance.** Publication within 12 mos. Considers simultaneous submissions. Prefers proposals & accepted ms by e-mail. Guidelines on website ("Manuscript submissions" on right side).

Nonfiction: Proposal with table of contents & 3 chapters from agents only. No phone/fax query; e-query OK.

Fiction: For teens and adults. Proposal/3 chapters.

This publisher serviced by ChristianManuscriptSubmissions.com.

FOCUS ON THE FAMILY BOOK PUBLISHING AND RESOURCE DEVELOPMENT, (street address not required), Colorado Springs CO 80995. (719) 531-3400. Fax (719) 531-3448. E-mail through website: www.focusonthefamily.com. Exists to support the family; all our products are about topics pertaining to families. Publishes 30-40 titles/yr.; hardcover, trade paperbacks, mass-market paperbacks (rarely). 12% of books from first-time authors. Rarely reprints books. Length depends on genre. **Royalty or work-for-hire; advance varies.** Average first printing varies. Publication within 18 mos. No longer considers unsolicited submissions. Responds in 1-3 mos. Prefers NIV (but accepts 10 others). Guidelines by e-mail/website; no catalog.

Nonfiction: Query letter only through an agent or writers' conference contact with a Focus editor. "Most open to family advice topics. We look for excellent writing and topics that haven't been done to death—or that have a unique angle."

Fiction: Query letter only through an agent or writers' conference contact with a Focus editor. Stories must incorporate traditional family values or family issues; from 1900 to present day. Also does Mom Lit.

Artwork: Open to queries from freelance artists (but not for specific projects).

This publisher serviced by ChristianManuscriptSubmissions.com.

FRANCISCAN MEDIA (formerly St. Anthony Messenger Press) 28 West Liberty Street, Cincinnati OH 45202. Toll-free (800) 488-0488; (513) 241-5615. Fax (513) 241-0399. E-mail: samamin@FranciscanMedia.org. Websites: www.FranciscanMedia.org, www.Catalog.FranciscanMedia.org, www.AmericanCatholic.org. Director of Product Development for Franciscan Media Books: MCKendzia@FranciscanMedia.org. Directors of Product Development, Servant Books: Louise Paré (LPare@FranciscanMedia.org) and Claudia Volkman (CVolkman@FranciscanMedia.org). Managing Editor, Book Department: Katie Carroll (KCarroll@FranciscanMedia.org). Seeks to publish affordable resources for living a Catholic-Christian lifestyle. Imprints: Franciscan Media Books, Servant Books, Fischer Video Productions, Catholic Update Video, Franciscan Communications, Ikonographics (videos). Servant Books is dedicated to spreading the gospel of Jesus Christ, helping Catholics live in accordance with that gospel, and promoting renewal in the Church. Publishes on Christian living, the sacraments, Scripture, prayer, spirituality, popular apologetics, Church teaching, Mary, the saints, charismatic renewal, marriage and family life, and popular psychology. Catalog.FranciscanMedia.org /ServantBooks. Guidelines on website: www.AmericanCatholic.org. ("Contact Us"/"Writer's Guidelines"). Publishes 15-20 titles/yr; trade paperbacks (mostly). Receives 450 submissions annually. 5% of books from first-time authors. Accepts mss through agents or authors. Reprints books (seldom). Prefers 25,000-50,000 wds or 100-250 pgs. **Royalty 10-14% on net; advance $1,000-3,000.** Average first printing 4,000. Publication within 18 mos. No simultaneous submissions. Accepts requested mss by e-mail. Responds in 5-9 wks. Prefers NRSV. Catalog for 9 x 12 SAE/4 stamps. Nonfiction: proposal/outline/1-2 chapters; fax/e-query OK. Franciscan Media seeks manuscripts that inform and inspire adult Catholic Christians, that identify trends surfacing in the Catholic world, and that help Catholics and those who want to be Catholic understand their faith better. Publishes for those who want to connect to the world around them in the context of the Catholic faith and for those who minister to adult Catholics in the parish and in religious institutions and schools. Catalog.FranciscanMedia. org/FranciscanMediaBooks. Guidelines on website www.AmericanCatholic.org ("Contact Us"/"Writer's Guidelines"). Publishes 20-30 titles/yr.; trade paperbacks (mostly). Receives 450 submissions annually. 5% of books from first time authors. Accepts mss through agents or authors.

Nonfiction: proposal/outline/1-2 chapters; fax/e-query OK.

*GOSPEL LIGHT, 1957 Eastman Ave., Ventura CA 93003. Toll-free (800) 4-GOSPEL. (805) 644-9721, ext. 1223. Website: www.gospellight.com. Anita Griggs, ed. Accepts proposals for Sunday school and Vacation Bible School curriculum and related resources for children from birth through the preteen years; also teacher resources. Guidelines on website (scroll to bottom "Submissions").

Also Does: Sometimes has openings for readers of new curriculum projects. See website for how to apply.

Tips: "All our curriculum is written and field-tested by experienced teachers; most of our writers are on staff."

This publisher serviced by ChristianManuscriptSubmissions.com.

*GOSPEL PUBLISHING HOUSE, 1445 N. Boonville Ave., Springfield MO 65802. Toll-free (800) 641-4310. (417) 831-8000. E-mail: newproducts@gph.org. Website: www.gospelpublishing.com. Assemblies of God. Julie Horner, research & development dir. The majority of titles specifically address Pentecostal audiences in a variety of ministries in the local church. Publishes 5-10 titles/yr. Receives 250 submissions annually. 5% of books from first-time authors. Accepts mss through agents or authors. No reprints. **Royalty 5-10% of retail; no advance.** Average first printing 2,000. Publication within 1 yr. Considers simultaneous submissions. Responds in 4 mos. Requires accepted mss on disk or by e-mail. Guidelines on website (scroll to bottom "Writers Guides"); free catalog.

Nonfiction: Proposal/1 chapter; no phone query, e-query OK. "Looking for Holy Spirit; Pentecostal focus for pastors, local church lay leaders, and individuals; children's ministry programs and resources; small group resources."

Tips: "Most open to a new program or resource for small groups, children's ministry, compassion ministry, or evangelistic outreach, written by someone who is actively leading it at the local church."

GROUP PUBLISHING INC., Attn: Submissions, 1515 Cascade Ave., Loveland CO 80539-0481. Toll-free (800) 447-1070. (970) 292-4243. Fax (970) 622-4370. E-mail: PuorgBus@group.com. Website: www.group.com. Nondenominational. Kerri Loesche, contract & copyright administrator. Imprint: Group Books. To equip churches to help children, youth, and adults grow in their relationship with Jesus. Publishes 65 titles/yr.; trade paperbacks. Receives 1,000+ submissions annually. 5% of books from first-time authors. Accepts mss through agents or authors. Some subsidy. No reprints. Prefers 128-250 pgs. **Outright purchases of $25-3,000 or royalty of 8-10% of net; advance $3,000.** Average first printing 5,000. Publication within 12-18 mos. Considers simultaneous submissions. Responds in 6 mos. Requires requested ms in Word or by e-mail. Prefers NLT. Guidelines by mail (2 stamps)/e-mail/website; catalog.

Nonfiction: Query or proposal/2 chapters/intro/cover letter/SASE; no phone/fax query; e-query OK. "Looking for practical ministry tools for youth workers, C.E. directors, and teachers with an emphasis on active learning."

Artwork: Open to queries from freelance artists.

Tips: "Most open to a practical resource that will help church leaders change lives; innovative, active/interactive learning. Tell our readers something they don't already know, in a way that they've not seen before."

GUARDIAN ANGEL PUBLISHING INC., 12430 Tesson Ferry Rd., #186, St. Louis MO 63128. (314) 276-8482. E-mail: editorial_staff@guardianangelpublishing.com. Website: www.guardianangel publishing.com. Lynda S. Burch, pub. Goal is to inspire children to learn and grow and develop character skills to instill a Christian and healthy attitude of learning, caring, and sharing. Imprints: Wings of Faith, Angel to Angel, Angelic Harmony, Littlest Angels, Academic Wings, Guardian Angel Animals & Pets, Spanish Editions, Guardian Angel Health & Hygiene. Publishes 60-70 titles/yr.; trade paperbacks, some hardcover. Receives 600-800 submissions annually. 25% of books from first-time authors. No subsidy; does print-on-demand. Prefers 500-5,000 wds. or 32 pgs. **Royalty 30-50% on download; no advance.** Average first printing 50-100. Print books are wholesaled and distributed; e-books are sold through many distribution networks. Publication within 12-18 mos. No simultaneous submissions. Responds in 1 wk.-1 mo. Accepted mss by e-mail only. Guidelines on website ("Submissions" on left side); catalog as e-book PDF.

Nonfiction: Complete ms; no phone/fax query; e-query OK. "Looking for all kinds of kids' books."

Fiction: Complete ms; no phone/fax query; e-query OK.

Also Does: E-books.

Photos/Artwork: Accepts freelance photos for book covers; open to queries from freelance artists.

Contest: Sponsors children's writing contest for schools.

Tips: "Most open to books that teach children to read and love books; to learn or grow from books."

*GUIDEPOSTS BOOKS, 16 E. 34th St., 12th Fl., New York NY 10016-4397. (212) 251-8143. Website: www.guidepostsbooks.com. Guideposts Inc. Linda Raglan Cunningham, VP/ed-in-chief; Andrew Attaway, sr. acq. ed. Focuses on inspirational fiction, memoirs, story collections, devotionals, and faith-based true stories. Publishes 20 titles/yr.

This publisher serviced by ChristianManuscriptSubmissions.com.

HANNIBAL BOOKS, 313 S. 11th Street, Suite A, Garland TX 75040. Toll-free (800) 747-0738. Toll-free fax (888) 252-3022. E-mail: hannibalbooks@earthlink.net. Website: www.hannibalbooks.com. KLMK Communications Inc. Louis Moore, pub. Evangelical Christian publisher specializing in missions, marriage and family, critical issues, and Bible-study curriculum. Publishes 4-8 titles/yr.; trade paperbacks, mass-market paperbacks. Receives 300 submissions annually. 80% of books from first-time authors. Accepts mss from authors only. Some print-on-demand. Prefers 50,000-60,000 wds. **Royalty on net or outright purchase; no advance.** Average first printing 2,000-10,000. Publication within 3 mos. No simultaneous submissions. Responds in 1 mo. Prefers NIV. Guidelines on website ("Become an Author"/ "Writers Guidelines"); free catalog by mail.

Nonfiction: Book proposal/1-3 chapters; no phone/fax/e-query. "Looking for missionary, marriage restoration, homeschooling, and devotionals."

Fiction: Book proposal/1-3 chapters; accept e-mail inquiries as long as they are not impersonal, simultaneous submissions. Nothing we dislike more than seeing "Dear

Publisher" with (a) no indication in the letter or e-mail that the person has any familiarity with our company and (b) that gives every indication that the e-mail has been sent generically to dozens of publishers at the same time.

Tips: "We are looking for go-get-'em new authors with a passion to be published. Most open to missionary life and Bible studies. Obtain our guidelines and answer each question thoroughly."

HARBOURLIGHT BOOKS, PO Box 1738, Aztec NM 87410. E-mail: inquiry@harbourlightbooks.com. Website: www.pelicanbookgroup.com. Division of Pelican Ventures, LLC. Nicola Martinez, editor-in-chief. Christian fiction 25,000-80,000 wds. Limited-edition hardback, trade paperbacks, and e-book. **Royalty 40% on download; 7% on print. Pays nominal advance.** Accepts unagented submissions. Responds to queries in 30 days, full ms in 90 days. Considers reprints but accepts few. E-mail submissions only; see website for submission form and procedure.

Fiction: Query via submission form on website. Interested in series ideas.

*HARPERONE, 353 Sacramento St., #500, San Francisco CA 94111-3653. (415) 477-4400. Fax (415) 477-4444. E-mail: hcsanfrancisco@harpercollins.com. Website: www.harpercollins.com. Religious division of HarperCollins. Michael G. Maudlin, ed. dir. Strives to be the preeminent publisher of the most important books across the full spectrum of religion and spiritual literature, adding to the wealth of the world's wisdom by respecting all traditions and favoring none; emphasis on quality Christian spirituality and literary fiction. Publishes 75 titles/yr.; hardcover, trade paperbacks. Receives 10,000 submissions annually. 5% of books from first-time authors. Requires mss through agents. No reprints. Prefers 160-256 pgs. **Royalty 7.5-15% on retail; advance $20,000-100,000.** Average first printing 10,000. Publication within 18 mos. Considers simultaneous submissions. Responds in 3 mos. Requires requested ms on disk. Guidelines on website ("About Us"/"Manuscript Submissions"); catalog.

Nonfiction: Proposal/1 chapter; fax query OK.

Fiction: Complete ms; contemporary adult fiction, literary, fables & parables, spiritual.

Tips: "Agented proposals only."

*HARRISON HOUSE PUBLISHERS, Box 35035, Tulsa OK 74153. Toll-free (800) 888-4126. (918) 523-5400. E-mail: customerservice@harrisonhouse.com. Website: www.harrisonhouse.com. Evangelical/charismatic. Julie Lechlider, mng. ed. To challenge Christians to live victoriously, grow spiritually, and know God intimately. Publishes 20 titles/yr.; hardcover, trade paperbacks, mass-market paperbacks. 5% of books from first-time authors. No mss through agents. No reprints. **Royalty on net or retail; no advance.** Average first printing 5,000. Publication within 12-24 mos. Responds in 6 mos. Accepts requested ms by e-mail. No guidelines or catalog. Not currently accepting any proposals or manuscripts.

Nonfiction: Query first; then proposal/table of contents/1 chapter; no phone/fax query; e-query OK.

This publisher serviced by ChristianManuscriptSubmissions.com.

HAY HOUSE INC., PO Box 5100, Carlsbad CA 92018-5100. (760) 431-7695. E-mail: editorial@hayhouse.com. Website: www.hayhouse.com. Shannon Littrell, mg. ed.; Alex Freemon, submissions ed. Books to help heal the planet. Publishes 1 religious title/yr.; hardcover, trade paperbacks and e-books/print-on-demand paperbacks. Receives 50 religious submissions annually. 5% of books from first-time authors. Accepts mss through agents only. Prefers 70,000 wds. or 250 pgs. **Royalty.** Average first printing 5,000. Publication within 12-15 mos. Considers simultaneous submissions. Responds in 1-2 mos. Guidelines (www.hayhouse.com/guides.php).

Nonfiction: Proposal/3 chapters. "Looking for self-help/spiritual with a unique ecumenical angle."

Tips: "We are looking for books with a unique slant, ecumenical, but not overly religious. We want an open-minded approach." Includes a broad range of religious titles, including New Age.

HENSLEY PUBLISHING, 6116 E. 32nd St., Tulsa OK 74135. (918) 664-8520. Fax (918) 664-8562. E-mail: editorial@hensleypublishing.com. Website: www.hensleypublishing.com. Terri Kalfas, dir. of publishing. Goal is to get people studying the Bible instead of just reading books about the Bible; Bible study only. Publishes 5-10 titles/yr.; trade paperbacks. Receives 800 submissions annually. 50% of books from first-time authors. **Royalty on net; some outright purchases; no advance.** Average first printing varies. Publication within 12-18 mos. Considers simultaneous submissions. Requires requested ms in MAC format. Responds in 4 mos. Guidelines ("Writers' Corner") & catalog on website.

   Nonfiction: Query first, then proposal/first 3 chapters; no phone/fax query. "Looking for
   Bible studies of varying length for use by small or large groups, or individuals."

*HOWARD BOOKS, 216 Centreville Dr., Ste. 303, Brentwood TN 37027-3226. (615) 873-2080. E-mail through website: http://imprints.simonandschuster.biz.howard. Becky Nesbitt, vp & ed-in-chief; submit to Manuscript Review Committee. A division of Simon & Schuster Inc. Publishes 65 titles/yr.; hardcover, trade paperbacks. Receives 1,000 submissions annually. 5% of books from first-time authors. Prefers 200-250 pgs. **Negotiable royalty & advance.** Average first printing 10,000. Publication within 16 mos. Considers simultaneous submissions. Accepted ms by e-mail. Responds in 6-8 mos. No disk. Prefers NIV. Guidelines on website (click on "Author Resources"/"Manuscript Submission"); catalog.

   Nonfiction: Accepting queries by e-mail from agents only.
   Fiction: Proposal/3 chapters from agents only. Adult.
   Tips: "Our authors must first be Christ-centered in their lives and writing, then qualified to
   write on the subject of choice. Public name recognition is a plus. Authors who are also public
   speakers usually have a ready-made audience."
   This publisher serviced by ChristianManuscriptSubmissions.com.

*IDEALS PUBLICATIONS, 2630 Elm Hill Pike, Ste. 020, Nashville TN 37214. E-mail: pjay@guide posts.org. Website: www.idealsbooks.com. A Guideposts company. Peggy Schaefer, pub.; Melinda Rumbaugh, ed. Imprints: Ideals, Children's Books, Ideals Publications. Publishes 20 titles/yr. Receives 1,000 submissions annually. 5% from first-time authors. Ideals Children's 800-1,000 words. Average first printing 5,000. Publication within 12 months. Guidelines on website.

INHERITANCE PRESS, LLC, PO Box 950477, Lake Mary FL 32795. (407) 474-0483. E-mail: submissions@inheritancepress.com. Website: www.inheritancepress.com. Independent publisher. Monique Donahue, ed. **No advance.** Responds in 60 days. Guidelines on website ("Submissions"). Incomplete topical listings.

   Nonfiction: Proposal by mail or e-mail; no phone query.

INKLING BOOKS, 6528 Phinney Ave. N., Seattle WA 98103. (206) 365-1624. E-mail: editor@ inklingbooks.com. Website: www.InklingBooks.com. Michael W. Perry, pub. Publishes 6 titles/yr.; hardcover, trade paperbacks. No mss through agents. Reprints books. Prefers 150-400 pgs. **No advance.** Print-on-demand. Publication within 2 mos. No guidelines or catalog. Not currently accepting submissions.

INO PUBLISHING, Kemptville, Ontario, Canada. 613-258-9883. E-mail: eic@inopublishing@ gmail.com; www.darscorrections.com. Darlene Oakly, ed.; INO Image—Christian fiction and non-fiction/INO Source—Mainstream fiction; Publishes 5-6 titles/yr. 80% from first-time authors. Accept mss through agent; print-on-demand. Mass-market paperbacks, digital. Considers reprints. Prefers 50,000+ wds. **Royalty 10% based on net. 25% for e-books**. No advance. Publication in 12 months. Considers simultaneous submissions. Responds in 4-6 wks. Guidelines on website, e-mail, free with #10 SASE with 1st class stamp. Accepts freelance photos for covers. Particular interest in women's issues, parenting, and creation science.

Nonfiction: Query letter ONLY first. Proposal with 3 sample chp. E-mail queries only. Require MSS by e-mail.

Fiction: Query letter ONLY first. Accepts children's, teen, adult fiction.

Tips: Currently, Christian publishers are publishing Amish fiction, and most traditional Christian publishers require agented submissions. Writers and readers are trending towards science fiction, suspense, and speculative fiction. INO Publishing wants to look at manuscripts that particularly don't fall within the current publishing trends, and which fill this need for readers. Manuscripts should be as polished as possible before sending proposal. Stories need to have intriguing characters and plot, with a definite redemptive (good overcoming evil, learning from experience, and/or applying Scriptural teaching to everyday situations) ending. Looking for forward-thinking, life- and faith-challenging stories. INO Publishing combines traditional publishing with print-on-demand and e-publishing trends. INO provides proper editing, if needed, as well as author website, personal cover design and promotional materials, and marketing advice. Writers need to be involved in the promotional process and spearhead their own sales.

✗INTERVARSITY PRESS, Box 1400, Downers Grove IL 60515-1426. Receptionist: (630) 734-4000. Fax (630) 734-4200. E-mail: email@ivpress.com. Website: www.ivpress.com. InterVarsity Christian Fellowship. Andrew T. LePeau, ed. dir.; submit to General Book Editor or Academic Editor. IVP books are characterized by a thoughtful, biblical approach to the Christian life that transforms the hearts, souls, and minds of readers in the university, church, and the world, on topics ranging from spiritual disciplines to apologetics, to current issues, to theology. Imprints: IVP Academic (Gary Deddo, ed.), IVP Connect (Cindy Bunch, ed.), IVP Books (Al Hsu, ed.). Publishes 110-120 titles/yr.; hardcover, trade paperbacks, mass-market paperbacks. Receives 1,300 submissions annually. 15% of books from first-time authors. Accepts mss through agents or authors. Reprints books. Prefers 50,000 wds. or 200 pgs. **Negotiable royalty on retail or outright purchase; negotiable advance.** Average first printing 5,000. Publication within 12 mos. Considers simultaneous submissions. Responds in 3 mos. Prefers NIV, NRSV. Accepts e-mail submissions after acceptance. Guidelines on website (scroll to bottom "Submissions"); catalog for 9 x 12 SAE/5 stamps.

Nonfiction: Query only first, with detailed letter according to submissions guidelines, then proposal with 2 chapters; no phone/fax/e-query.

Ethnic Books: Especially looking for ethnic writers (African American, Hispanic, Asian American).

Also Does: Booklets, 5,000 wds.; e-books.

Blogs: www.ivpress.com/blogs/behindthebooks; www.ivpress.com/blogs/andyunedited; www.ivpress.com/blogs/addenda-errata.

Tips: "Most open to books written by pastors (though not collections of sermons) or other church staff, by professors, by leaders in Christian organizations. Authors need to bring resources for publicizing and selling their own books, such as a website, an organization they are part of that will promote their books, speaking engagements, well-known people they know personally who will endorse and promote their book, writing articles for national publication, etc."

This publisher serviced by ChristianManuscriptSubmissions.com.

*JOURNEYFORTH/BJU PRESS, 1700 Wade Hampton Blvd., Greenville SC 29614. (864) 370-1800, ext 4350. Fax (864) 298-0268. E-mail to: jb@bju.edu. Website: www.bjupress.com or www.journey forth.com. Nancy Lohr, acquisitions ed. Our goal is to publish engaging books for children with a biblical worldview as well as Bible studies and Christian-living titles for teens and adults. Publishes 8-12 titles/yr.; trade paperbacks. Receives 400 submissions annually (50 Christian living/350 youth novels). 10% of books from first-time authors. Accepts mss through agents or authors. **Royalty.** Average first printing varies. Publication within 12-18 mos. Considers simultaneous submissions but not multiple submissions. Accepts submissions by US mail or e-mail. Responds in 8-12 wks. Requires KJV. Guidelines online, by mail, or by e-mail; free catalog.

Nonfiction: Proposal/3-5 chapters; e-query OK.

Fiction: Proposal/5 chapters or complete ms. For children & teens. "Fiction must have a Christian worldview."

Artwork: Open to queries from freelance artists.

Tips: "The pre-college, homeschool market welcomes print-rich, well-written novels. No picture books, please, but compelling novels for early readers are always good for us, as are biographies on the lives of Christian heroes and statesmen. We focus on books for all ages that will help to both develop skill with the written word as well as discernment as a believer; we complement the educational goals of BJU Press, our K-12 textbook division."

JUDSON PRESS, PO Box 851, Valley Forge PA 19482-0851. Toll-free (800) 458-3766. Fax (610) 768-2107. E-mail: acquisitions@judsonpress.com. Website: www.judsonpress.com. American Baptist Churches USA/American Baptist Home Mission Societies. Rebecca Irwin-Diehl, ed. We are theologically moderate, historically Baptist, and in ministry to empower, enrich, and equip the disciples of Jesus and leaders in Christ's church. Publishes 12-15 titles/yr.; hardcover, trade paperbacks. Receives 800 submissions annually. 20% of books from first-time authors. Accepts mss through agents or authors. No subsidy; rarely does print-on-demand or reprints. Prefers 100-200 pgs. or 30,000-75,000 wds. **Royalty 10-15% on net; some work-for-hire agreements or outright purchases; occasional advance $300.** Average first printing 3,000. Publication within 18 mos. Considers simultaneous submissions. Requires accepted submissions on disk or by e-mail. Responds in 4-6 mos. Prefers NRSV. Guidelines on website (under "Contact Us"); catalog online.

Nonfiction: Query or proposal/2 chapters; e-query OK. Practical books for today's church and leaders.

Ethnic Books: African American & Hispanic.

Artwork: Open to queries from freelance artists.

Tips: "Most open to books that are unique, compelling, and practical. Theologically and socially we are a moderate publisher. And we like to see a detailed marketing plan from an author committed to partnering with us."

KIRK HOUSE PUBLISHERS, PO Box 390759, Minneapolis MN 55439. (952) 835-1828. Toll-free (888) 696-1828. Fax (952) 835-2613. E-mail: publisher@kirkhouse.com. Website: www.kirkhouse .com. Leonard Flachman, pub. Imprints: Lutheran University Press, Quill House Publishers. Publishes 10-15 titles/yr.; hardcover, trade paperbacks, coffee-table books. Receives hundreds of submissions annually. 95% of books from first-time authors. No mss through agents. No reprints. **Royalty 10-15% on net; no advance.** Average first printing 500-3,000. Publication within 6 mos. No simultaneous submissions. Initial inquiry only via e-mail. Requires hard copy and electronic submission. Responds in 2-3 wks. Guidelines by e-mail/website ("Submissions").

Nonfiction: Inquiries and author bio.

Tips: "Our catalog is eclectic; send a query. Our imprint, Quill House Publishers, accepts adult fiction."

*KREGEL PUBLICATIONS, PO Box 2607, Grand Rapids MI 49501-2607. (616) 451-4775. Fax (616) 451-9330. E-mail: kregelbooks@kregel.com. Website: www.kregelpublications.com. Blog: www.kregelpublications.blogspot.com. Evangelical/conservative. Dennis R. Hillman, pub.; Jim Weaver, academic & professional books ed.; submissions policy on website. To provide tools for ministry and Christian growth from a conservative, evangelical perspective. Imprints: Kregel Kidzone, Kregel Academic and Professional, Kregel Classics. Publishes 75 titles/yr.; hardcover, trade paperbacks. 20% of books from first-time authors. Prefers mss through agents. Reprints books. **Royalty 8-16% of net; some outright purchases; pays advances.** Average first printing 5,000. Publication within

12 mos. Considers simultaneous submissions. Responds in 4 mos. Guidelines by e-mail; catalog for 9 x 12 SAE/3 stamps. No longer reviewing unsolicited queries, proposals, or manuscripts, except through agents or ChristianManuscriptSubmissions.com.

Nonfiction: "Most open to contemporary issues or academic works."

Fiction: For all ages. "Looking for high-quality contemporary and Amish fiction with strong Christian themes and characters."

Tips: "We are very selective. Strong story lines with an evident spiritual emphasis are required." This publisher serviced by ChristianManuscriptSubmissions.com.

LANGMARC PUBLISHING, PO Box 90488, Austin TX 78709-0488. (512) 394-0989. Fax (512) 394-0829. E-mail: langmarc@booksails.com. Website: www.langmarc.com. Lutheran. Lois Qualben, pub. Focuses on spiritual growth of readers. Publishes 3-5 titles/yr.; hardcover, trade paperbacks. Receives 230 submissions annually. 60% of books from first-time authors. Accepts mss through agents or authors. No reprints. Prefers 150-300 pgs. **Royalty 10-14% on net; no advance.** Average first printing varies. Publication usually within 18 mos. Considers simultaneous submissions. Responds in 3 mos. Requires requested ms on disk. Prefers NIV. Guidelines on website ("Guidelines for Nonfiction Authors"); free catalog.

Nonfiction: Proposal/3 chapters; no phone query. "Most open to inspirational books."

*LEGACY PRESS, PO Box 261129, San Diego CA 92196. Toll-free (800) 323-7337. Toll-free fax (800) 331-0297. E-mail: editor@rainbowpublishers.com. Website: www.LegacyPressKids.com. Rainbow Publishers. Submit to Manuscript Submissions. Publishes nondenominational nonfiction and fiction for children in the evangelical Christian market. Publishes 15 titles/yr. Receives 250 submissions annually. 50% of books from first-time authors. Reprints books. Prefers 150 pgs. & up. Average first printing 5,000. Publication within 2 yrs. Considers simultaneous submissions. Prefers requested ms on disk. Responds in 2-8 wks. Prefers NIV. Guidelines (go to bottom "Submissions") & catalog on website.

Nonfiction: Proposal/3-5 chapters; no e-queries. "Looking for nonfiction for girls and boys ages 2-12."

Fiction: Proposal/3 chapters. For ages 2-12 only. Must include an additional component beyond fiction (e.g., devotional, Bible activities, etc.).

Special Needs: Nonfiction for ages 10-12, particularly Christian twists on current favorites, such as cooking, jewelry making, games, etc.

Artwork: Open to queries from freelance artists.

Tips: "All books must offer solid Bible teaching in a fun, meaningful way that appeals to kids. Research popular nonfiction for kids in the general market, then figure out how to present those fun ideas in ways that teach the Bible. As a smaller publisher, we seek to publish unique niche books that stand out in the market."

LIFE CYCLE BOOKS, 1085 Bellamy Rd N #20, Toronto ON M1H 3C7 Canada. (416) 690-5860. E-mail: paulb@lifecyclebooks.com. Website: www.lifecyclebooks.com. Paul Broughton, gen. mngr.; submit to Attention: The Editor. Canadian office: 1149 Bellamy Rd. N., Unit 20, Toronto ON M1H 1H7 Canada. Toll-free (866) 880-5860. Toll-free fax (866) 690-8532. Attn: The Editor. Specializes in pro-life material. Publishes 6 titles/yr.; trade paperbacks. Receives 100 submissions annually. No mss through agents. 50% of books from first-time authors. Reprints books. **Royalty 8-10% of net; outright purchase of brochure material, $250+; advance $250-1,000.** Subsidy publishes 10%. Publication within 1 yr. No simultaneous submissions. Responds in 3-5 wks. Catalog on website.

Nonfiction: Query or complete ms. "Our emphasis is on pro-life and pro-family titles."

Tips: "We are most involved in publishing leaflets of about 1,500 wds., and we welcome submissions of manuscripts of this length." No fiction or poetry.

*LIFT EVERY VOICE BOOKS, 820 N. LaSalle Blvd., Chicago IL 60610. (312) 329-2140. Fax (312) 329-4157. E-mail: lifteveryvoice@moody.edu. Website: www.lifteveryvoicebooks.com. African American imprint of Moody Publishers. Moody Bible Institute. Cynthia Ballenger, acq. ed. To publish culturally relevant books and promote other resources that will help millions of African Americans experience the power and amazement of a fresh encounter with Jesus Christ. Publishes 10 titles/yr. Receives 50-75 submissions annually. 98% of books from first-time authors. Accepts mss through agents or authors. No subsidy. Reprints books. Prefers minimum of 50,000 wds. or 250 pgs. **Royalty on retail; pays an advance.** Average first printing 5,000. Publication within 12 mos. Considers simultaneous submissions. Responds quarterly. Accepts requested ms by e-mail. Prefers KJV, NASB, NKJV. Guidelines by e-mail; free catalog.

> **Nonfiction:** Proposal/3 chapters; e-query OK.
> **Fiction:** Proposal/3 chapters; e-query OK. For all ages. Send for fiction writers' guidelines.
> **Special Needs**: Children's fiction, especially for boys; nonfiction & fiction for teen girls; also marriage books.
> **Ethnic Books**: African American imprint.
> **Photos:** Accepts freelance photos for book covers.
> **Tips:** "Looking for quality fiction and nonfiction. LEVB is looking for good, strong, and focused writing that is Christ-centered and speaks to the African American community."

LIGHTHOUSE PUBLISHING, 754 Roxholly Walk, Buford GA 30518. E-mail: info@lighthouse christianpublishing.com. Website: www.lighthousechristianpublishing.com. Nondenominational. Andy Overett, ed.; submit to Sylvia Charvet, sr. ed. To distribute a wide variety of Christian media to vast parts of the globe so people can hear about the gospel for free or very inexpensively (e-books, comics, movies, and online radio). Imprints: Lighthouse Publishing, Lighthouse Music Publishing. Publishes 30-40 titles/yr.; hardcover, trade paperbacks, mass-market paperbacks. Receives 100-150 submissions annually. 60% of books from first-time authors. Accepts mss through agents or authors. Subsidy publishes 35-40%. Does print-on-demand. Reprints books. Any length. Royalty on net; no advance. Publication within 6 to 8 mos. Considers simultaneous submissions. Prefers submissions by e-mail. Responds in 6-8 wks. Prefers NAS. Guidelines on website ("Submissions"); catalog $5.

> **Nonfiction:** Complete ms by e-mail only (info@lighthousechristianpublishing.com). Any topic. "Looking for children's books, Intelligent Design, and science."
> **Fiction:** Complete ms by e-mail only. Any genre, for all ages.
> **Ethnic Books:** Publishes books for almost all foreign-language markets.
> **Also Does:** Comics, animation on CD, music CDs, plans to do Christian computer games in the future. E-books.
> **Photos/Artwork:** Accepts freelance photos for book covers; open to queries from freelance artists.
> **Tips:** "Most open to children's books, comics, and graphic novels; scientific and academic works with a Christian perspective."

LIGHTHOUSE PUBLISHING OF THE CAROLINAS, 2333 Barton Oaks Dr., Raleigh NC. E-mail: lighthousepublishingcarolinas@gmail.com. Website: http://lighthousepublishingofthecarolinas.com. LPC is a traditional, royalty-paying publisher of e-books and print-on-demand (POD) paperbacks. Fiction, nonfiction, and niche devotional compilations. Unsolicited manuscripts returned unread.

LOVE INSPIRED (formerly Steeple Hill), 233 Broadway, Ste. 1001, New York NY 10279-0001. (212) 553-4200. Fax (212) 277-8969. E-mail: rachel_burkot@harlequin.ca. Website: www.harlequin.com. Harlequin Enterprises. Submit to any of the following: Joan Marlow Golan, exec. ed.; Melissa Endlich, sr. ed.; Emily Rodmell, asst. ed.; Rachel Burkot, ed. asst. Mass-market Christian romance novels. Imprints: Love Inspired, Love Inspired Historical, Love Inspired Suspense. Publishes 168 titles/yr.; mass-market paperbacks. Receives 500-1,000 submissions annually. 15% of books from first-time authors. Accepts mss through agents or authors. No reprints. Prefers 55,000-60,000 wds. **Royalty on retail; competitive advance.** Publication within 12-24 mos. Requires ms on disk/hard copy. Responds in 3 mos. Prefers KJV. Guidelines by mail/website; no catalog.

Fiction: Query letter or 3 chapters and up to 5-page synopsis; no phone/fax/e-query.

Tips: "We want character-driven romance with an author voice that inspires."

This publisher serviced by ChristianManuscriptSubmissions.com.

*LOYOLA PRESS, 3441 N. Ashland Ave., Chicago IL 60657. (773) 281-1818. Toll-free (800) 621-1008. Fax (773) 281-0152. E-mail: editorial@loyolapress.com. Website: www.loyolabooks.org. Catholic. Joseph Durepos, acq. ed. (durepos@loyolapress.com). Publishes in the Jesuit and Ignatian Spirituality tradition. Publishes 20-30 titles/yr.; hardcover, trade paperbacks. Receives 500 submissions annually. Accepts mss through agents or authors. Prefers 25,000-75,000 wds. or 150-300 pgs. **Standard royalty; reasonable advance.** Average first printing 7,500-10,000. Considers simultaneous submissions and first-time authors without agents. Responds in 10-12 wks. Prefers NRSV (Catholic Edition). Guidelines/catalog on website (under "Contact Us"/"Submissions").

Nonfiction: E-query first; proposal/sample chapters; no phone query.

Tips: "Looking for books and authors that help make Catholic faith relevant and offer practical tools for the well-lived spiritual life."

LUTHERAN UNIVERSITY PRESS, PO Box 390759, Minneapolis MN 55439. (952) 835-1828. Toll-free (888) 696-1828. Fax (952) 835-2613. E-mail: publisher@lutheranupress.org. Website: www.lutheranupress.org. Leonard Flachman, pub.; Karen Walhof, ed. Publishes 8-10 titles/yr.; hardcover, trade paperbacks, coffee-table books. Receives dozens of submissions annually. Subsidy publishes 25%. No print-on-demand or reprints. **Royalty 10-15% of net; no advance.** Average first printing 500-2,000. Publication within 6 mos. No simultaneous submissions. Responds in 3 wks. Guidelines by e-mail/website ("Submissions"); free catalog by mail.

Nonfiction: Proposal/sample chapters in electronic format.

Photos: Accepts freelance photos for book covers.

Tips: "We accept manuscripts only from faculty of Lutheran colleges, universities, seminaries, and Lutheran faculty from other institutions."

MAGNUS PRESS, PO Box 2666, Carlsbad CA 92018. (760) 806-3743. Fax (760) 806-3689. E-mail: magnuspres@aol.com. Website: www.magnuspress.com. Warren Angel, ed. dir. All books must reflect a strong belief in Christ, solid biblical understanding, and the author's ability to relate to the average person. Imprint: Canticle Books. Publishes 3 titles/yr.; trade paperbacks. Receives 60 submissions annually. 50% of books from first-time authors. Accepts mss through agents or authors. Reprints books. Prefers 105-300 pgs. **Graduated royalty on retail; no advance.** Average first printing 2,500. Publication within 1 yr. Considers simultaneous submissions. Accepts requested ms on disk. Responds in 1 mo. Guidelines by mail/e-mail/website ("Magnus Press Submissions"); free catalog by mail.

Nonfiction: Query or proposal/3 chapters; fax query OK. "Looking for spirituality, thematic biblical studies, unique inspirational/devotional books, e.g., *Adventures of an Alaskan Preacher*."

Tips: "Our writers need solid knowledge of the Bible and a mature spirituality that reflects a profound relationship with Jesus Christ. Most open to a popularly written biblical study that addresses a real concern/issue in the church at large today; or a unique inspirational book. Study the market; know what we do and don't publish."

MARCHER LORD PRESS, 8345 Pepperridge Dr., Colorado Springs CO 80920. (719) 266-8874. E-mail: Jeff@marcherlordpress.com. Website: www.marcherlordpress.com. Jeff Gerke, pub. Premier publisher of Christian speculative fiction—it's all they do. Publishes 6-8 titles/yr.; trade paperbacks. Receives 200 submissions annually. 70% of books from first-time authors. Accepts mss through agents or authors. No subsidy; does print-on-demand. No reprints. Prefers 65,000+ wds. **Author receives**

50% after development costs are recouped; advance. Publication within 6 mos. Considers simultaneous submissions. Responds in 9-18 mos. Guidelines/catalog on website ("Write for Us").
  Fiction: Submit only through acquisitions form on website.
  Special Needs: Full-length, Christian speculative fiction for an adult and older teen audience.
  Photos/Artwork: Accepts freelance photos for book covers; open to queries from freelance artists.
  Tips: "I'm most open to high fiction craftsmanship and a story that sweeps me away."

MERIWETHER PUBLISHING LTD./CONTEMPORARY DRAMA SERVICE, 885 Elkton Dr., Colorado Springs CO 80907. (719) 594-4422. Fax (719) 594-9916. E-mail: editor@meriwether.com. Website: www.meriwetherpublishing.com. Nondenominational. Arthur L. Zapel, exec. ed.; submit to Rhonda Wray, assoc. ed. Publishes 30-45 plays & books/yr. Primarily a publisher of plays for Christian and general markets; must be acceptable for use in a wide variety of Christian denominations. Imprint: Contemporary Drama Service. Publishes 3 bks./25 plays/yr. Receives 1,200 submissions annually (mostly plays). 75% of submissions from first-time authors. Accepts mss through agents or authors. No reprints. Prefers 225 pgs. **Royalty 10% of net or retail; no advance.** Average first printing of books 1,500-2,500, plays 500. Publication within 6 mos. Considers simultaneous submissions. No e-mail submissions. Responds in up to 3 mos. Any Bible version. Guidelines by mail/e-mail/website ("Writers Guidelines"); catalog for 9 x 12 SASE.
  Nonfiction: Table of contents/1 chapter; fax/e-query OK. "Looking for creative worship books, i.e., drama, using the arts in worship, how-to books with ideas for Christian education." Submit books to Meriwether.
  Fiction: Complete ms for plays. Plays only, for all ages. Always looking for Christmas and Easter plays (1 hr. maximum). Submit plays to Contemporary Drama.
  Special Needs: Religious drama—or religious plays—mainstream theology. We prefer plays that can be staged during a worship service.
  Tips: "Our books are on drama or any creative, artistic area that can be a part of worship. Writers should familiarize themselves with our catalog before submitting to ensure that their manuscript fits with the list we've already published." Contemporary Drama Service wants easy-to-stage comedies, skits, one-act plays, large-cast musicals, and full-length comedies for schools (junior high through college), and churches (including chancel dramas for Christmas and Easter). Most open to anything drama-related. "Study our catalog so you'll know what we publish and what would fit our list."

MOODY PUBLISHERS, 820 N. LaSalle Blvd., Chicago IL 60610. Fax (312) 329-2144. Email: acquisitions@moody.edu. Website: http://www.moodypublishers.com/. Imprints: Moody Publishers, Northfield Publishing, Lift Every Voice (African American). Moody Publishers exists to help our readers know, love, and serve Jesus Christ. Publishes 60-70 titles per year; hardcover, trade paperbacks, mass-market paperbacks, e-books. Receives 3,500 submissions annually; 10% of books from first-time authors. Does not accept unsolicited manuscripts in any category unless submitted via: literary agent; an author who has published with us; a Moody Bible Institute employee; a personal contact at a writers conference. **Royalty paid on net; advances begin at $500.** Average first printing 10,000. Publication within 1 year. Manuscripts submitted electronically. Responds in 1-2 mos. Prefers NAS, ESV, NKJV, NIV (1984). Guidelines (also on website at http://www.moodypublishers.com/pub_main.aspx?id=46381): Moody Publishers titles are designed to glorify God in content and style. Titles are selected for publication based upon fit with this goal, quality of writing, and potential for market success. Please do not call our offices with manuscript ideas. Rather, for submissions meeting the criteria detailed above, have your query sent to: Acquisitions Coordinator, Moody Publishers, 820 North LaSalle Blvd., Chicago, IL 60610. Responds in 1 month. Catalog for 9 x 12 SAE/$2.38 postage (mark "Media Mail").
  Nonfiction Categories & Audiences: Academic & Bible reference; spiritual growth; Millennials (18- to 30-year-olds); women; urban; family & relationships

Fiction: "We are looking for stories that glorify God both in content and style. Featured categories include mystery, contemporary, historical, young adult.
Ethnic Books: African American.
Tips: "Most open to books where the writer is a recognized expert with a platform to promote the book."
This publisher serviced by ChristianManuscriptSubmissions.com.

*MOPS INTERNATIONAL, 2370 S. Trenton Way, Denver CO 80231-3822. (303) 733-5353. Fax (303) 733-5770. E-mail: jblackmer@MOPS.org. Website: www.MOPS.org. Jean Blackmer, pub. mngr.; Carla Foote, dir. of media. Publishes books dealing with the needs and interests of mothers with young children, who may or may not be Christians. Publishes 2-3 titles/yr. Catalog on website.
   Nonfiction: Query or proposal/3 chapters; by mail, fax, or e-mail.
   Tips: "Review existing titles on our website to avoid duplication."

MOUNTAINVIEW PUBLISHING, 1284 Overlook Dr., Sierra Vista AZ 85635-5512. (520) 458-5602. Fax (520) 459-0162. E-mail: leeemory@earthlink.net. Website: www.trebleheartbooks.com. Christian division of Treble Heart Books. Ms. Lee Emory, ed./pub. Online Christian publisher; books never have to go out of print as long as they're being marketed and are selling. Imprints: Treble Heart (see separate listing), Sundowners, Whoodo Mysteries. Publishes 12-24 titles/yr; trade paperbacks. Receives 350 submissions annually. 70% of books from first-time authors. Accepts mss through agents or authors. No reprints. No word-length preference. **Royalty 35% of net on most sales; no advance.** Books are published electronically; average first printing 30-500. Publication usually within 1 yr. No simultaneous submissions (a 90-day exclusive is required on all submissions, plus a marketing plan). Responds in 90 days to submissions, 1-2 wks. to queries. Guidelines on website ("Submissions Guidelines" right side).
   Nonfiction: Send query (by e-mail) to: leeemory@earthlink.net. Submissions of full ms by invitation only. Excellent nonfiction, inspirational books are highly desired here.
   Fiction: Complete ms (by e-mail only). Genres: historical romances; contemporary romances; novellas; mainstream and traditional inspirations in most categories; also Christian mysteries, Christian horror, and Christian westerns, and some outstanding short stories.
   Photos: Accepts high-quality freelance photos for book covers.
   Tips: "All inspirational fiction should contain faith elements. Challenge the reader to think, to look at things through different eyes. Avoid point-of-view head hopping and clichés; avoid heavy-handed preaching. No dark angel stories, hardcore science fiction/fantasy, though will consider futuristic Christian works. Send consecutive chapters, not random. A well-developed marketing plan must accompany all submissions, and no submissions will be accepted for consideration unless guidelines are followed. Actively seeking more nonfiction at this time."

*MULTNOMAH BOOKS, 12265 Oracle Blvd., Ste. 200, Colorado Springs CO 80921. (719) 590-4999. Fax (719) 590-8977. E-mail: info@waterbrookmultnomah.com. Website: www.waterbrook multnomah.com. Part of WaterBrook Multnomah, a division of Random House Inc. Ken Petersen, VP/pub.dir. Imprint information listed below. Publishes 75 titles/yr.; hardcover, trade paperbacks. **Royalty on net; advance.** Multnomah is currently not accepting unsolicited manuscripts, proposals, or queries; no proposals for biographies, poetry, or children's books. Queries will be accepted through literary agents and at writers' conferences at which a Multnomah representative is present. Catalog on website.
   Multnomah Books: Christian living and popular theology books.
   Multnomah Fiction: Well-crafted fiction that uses truth to change lives.

NAVPRESS, 3820 N. 30th Street, Colorado Springs CO 80904. E-mail: editorial.submissions@ navpress.com. Website: www.navpress.com. Imprint: TH1NK. Publishes 45 titles/yr. Hardcover, trade paperbacks, digital. Reprints. **Royalties. ADVANCE.** Publication in 12-18 mos. Considers simultaneous submissions. Responds in 6-12 wks. Catalog free on request. Guidelines on website. Need books for TH1NK, 16- to 21-yr-olds, inc. Bible studies, nonfiction, YA fiction.

Nonfiction: proposal with 2-3 chap. E-mail queries OK. Require mss by e-mail.

Fiction: Teen/YA fiction. No adult at this time. Proposal with 2-3 sample chap.

Special Needs: Transforming, life-changing nonfiction and Bible studies, as well as YA fiction.

*THOMAS NELSON, FICTION, PO Box 141000, Nashville TN 37215. (615) 889-9000. Website: www.ThomasNelson.com. Thomas Nelson Inc. Ami McConnell, sr. acq. ed.; Amanda Bostic, acq. ed. Fiction from a Christian worldview. Publishes fewer than 70 titles/yr.; hardcover, trade paperbacks, mass-market paperbacks. Requires mss through agents; does not accept unsolicited manuscripts. Prefers 80,000-100,000 wds. **Royalty on net; pays an advance.** Publication within 12 mos. Accepts simultaneous submissions. Responds in about 60 days. No guidelines; free catalog by mail.

Fiction: Proposal/3 chapters. For teens and adults. Unsolicited queries are not considered and are not returned.

*THOMAS NELSON PUBLISHERS, PO Box 141000, Nashville TN 37214-1000. (615) 889-9000. Fax (615) 902-2745. Website: www.thomasnelson.com. Does not accept or review any unsolicited queries, proposals, or manuscripts.

This publisher serviced by ChristianManuscriptSubmissions.com.

*TOMMY NELSON. See Thomas Nelson Publishers above.

*NEW HOPE PUBLISHERS, Box 12065, Birmingham AL 35202-2065. (205) 991-8100. Fax (205) 991-4015. Website: www.newhopepublishers.com. Division of WMU. Imprints: New Hope Impact (missional community, social, personal-commitment, church-growth, and leadership issues); New Hope Arise (inspiring women, changing lives); New Hope Grow (Bible-study & teaching resources). Publishes 20-28 titles/yr.; hardcover, trade paperbacks. No unsolicited queries, proposals, or manuscripts.

This publisher serviced by ChristianManuscriptSubmissions.com.

*NEW LEAF PUBLISHING GROUP, PO Box 726, Green Forest AR 72638-0726. (870) 438-5288. Fax (870) 438-5120. E-mail: submissions@newleafpress.net or through website: www.nlpg.com. Craig Froman, acq. ed. The world's largest creation-based publisher. Imprints: New Leaf Press, Master Books, Attic Books. Publishes 25-30 titles/yr.; hardcover, trade paperbacks, occasionally high-end gift titles, digital. Receives 1,200 submissions annually. 15% of books from first-time authors. Accepts mss through agents or authors. No subsidy, print-on-demand, or reprints. No length preference. **Variable royalty on net; no advance.** Average first printing varies. Publication within 8 mos. Considers simultaneous submissions. Responds within 3 mos. Requires accepted ms on disk. Guidelines by mail/e-mail/website; free catalog by mail.

Nonfiction: Must complete Author's Proposal form; no phone/fax query; e-query OK. Accepts mss by e-mail. "Looking for books for the homeschool market, especially grades 1-8."

Fiction: Must complete Author Proposal Form. Query letter only first. Adult.

Special Needs: Stewardship of the earth; ancient man technology, inventions, etc.; educational products for grades K-6.

Contest: Master Books Scholarship Essay Contest; $3,000 college scholarship; www.newleaf publishinggroup.com/store/scholarship.htm.

Artwork: Open to queries from freelance artists.

Tips: "Accepts submissions only with Author's Proposal form available by e-mail or on our website."

*OAKTARA PUBLISHERS, PO Box 8, Waterford VA 20197. (540) 882-9062. Fax (540) 882-3719. E-mail: jnesbitt@oaktara.com or rtucker@oaktara.com. Website: www.oaktara.com. Jeff Nesbitt, mng. dir. (jnesbit@oaktara.com); Ramona Tucker, ed. dir. (rtucker@oaktara.com). To create opportunities for new, talented Christian writers and to promote leading-edge fiction by established

Christian authors; inspirational fiction only. Does print-on-demand. Reprints books. **Royalty; no advance.** Guidelines on website (scroll to bottom "Writers Guidelines").

Fiction: Submit by e-mail (attached file) in one Word file. For all ages.

ON MY OWN NOW MINISTRIES (formerly The Quilldriver), PO Box 573, Clarksville AR 72830. Phone/fax (479) 497-0321. E-mail: donna@onmyownnow.com. Website: www.onmyownnow.com. Donna Lee Schillinger, pub. Inspirational nonfiction directed at young adults (17-25). Imprint: Two-Faced Books. Publishes 3 titles/yr. Receives 12 submissions annually. 67% of books from first-time authors. No mss through agents. Would consider reprinting books. Prefers 200 pgs. **Royalties; $500 advance.** Average first printing 2,000. Publication within 18 mos. Considers simultaneous submissions. Responds in 8 wks. Prefers NIV. Guidelines by e-mail; catalog for #10 SAE/1 stamp.

Nonfiction: Query first; or proposal/2 chapters; e-query OK.

Tips: "Most open to books that are hip and biblically sound—must resonate with young adults."

*OUR SUNDAY VISITOR INC., 200 Noll Plaza, Huntington IN 46750-4303. (260) 356-8400. Toll-free (800) 348-2440. Fax (260) 356-8472. E-mail: booksed@osv.com. Website: www.osv.com. Catholic. Submit to Acquisitions Editor. To assist Catholics to be more aware and secure in their faith and capable of relating their faith to others. Publishes 30-40 titles/yr.; hardcover, trade paperbacks. Receives 500+ submissions annually. 10% of books from first-time authors. Prefers not to work through agents. Reprints books. **Royalty 10-12% of net; average advance $1,500.** Average first printing 5,000. Publication within 1-2 yrs. No simultaneous submissions. Responds in 3 mos. Requires requested ms on disk. Guidelines on website ("About Us"/"Writers Guidelines"); catalog for 9 x 12 SASE.

Nonfiction: Proposal/2 chapters; e-query OK. "Most open to devotional books (not first person), church history, heritage and saints, the parish, prayer, and family."

Also Does: Pamphlets, booklets.

Photos: Occasionally accepts freelance photos for book covers.

Tips: "All books published must relate to the Catholic Church; unique books aimed at our audience. Give as much background information as possible on author qualification, why the topic was chosen, and unique aspects of the project. Follow our guidelines. We are expanding our religious education product line and programs."

PACIFIC PRESS PUBLISHING ASSN., Box 5353, Nampa ID 83653-5353. (208) 465-2500. Fax (208) 465-2531. E-mail: booksubmissions@pacificpress.com. Website: www.pacificpress.com. Seventh-day Adventist. David Jarnes, book ed.; submit to Scott Cady, acq. ed. Books of interest and importance to Seventh-day Adventists and other Christians of all ages. Publishes 35-40 titles/yr.; hardcover, trade paperbacks. Receives 500 submissions annually. 5% of books from first-time authors. Accepts mss through agents or authors. No reprints. Prefers 50,000-130,000 wds. or 160-400 pgs. **Royalty 12-15% of net; advance $1,500.** Average first printing 5,000. Publication within 6 mos. Considers simultaneous submissions. Responds in 1 mo. Requires requested ms on disk or by e-mail. Guidelines at www.pacificpress.com/index/php?pgName=newsSubGuides; no catalog.

Nonfiction: Query only; e-query OK.

Fiction: Query only; almost none accepted; mainly biblical. Children's books: "Must be on a uniquely Seventh-day Adventist topic. No talking animals or fantasy."

Ethnic Books: Hispanic.

Also Does: Booklets.

Tips: "Most open to spirituality, inspirational, and Christian living. Our website has the most up-to-date information, including samples of recent publications. For more information, see www.adventistbookcenter.com. Do not send full manuscript unless we request it after reviewing your proposal."

PARAGON HOUSE, 1925 Oakcrest Ave., Ste. 7, St. Paul MN 55113-2619. (651) 644-3087. Fax (651) 644-0997. E-mail: submissions@paragonhouse.com. Website: www.paragonhouse.com.

Gordon Anderson, acq. ed. Serious nonfiction and texts with an emphasis on religion, philosophy, and society. Imprints: Omega, Vision of . . . . Publishes 12-15 titles/yr.; hardcover, trade paperbacks, e-books. Receives 1,200 submissions annually. 20% of books from first-time authors. Accepts mss through agents or author. Prefers average 250 pgs. **Royalty 7-10% of net; advance $1,000.** Average first printing 1,500-3,000. Publication within 12-18 mos. Considers few simultaneous submissions. Accepts e-mail submissions (attached file). Responds in 1-2 mos. Guidelines/catalog on website ("Help"/"Authors Guidelines" on left).

Nonfiction: Query; proposal/2-3 chapters or complete ms; no phone/fax query. Endorsements are helpful. "Looking for scholarly overviews of topics in religion and society; textbooks in philosophy; ecumenical subjects; and reference books."

PARSON PLACE PRESS LLC, PO Box 8277, Mobile AL 36689-0277. (251) 643-6985. E-mail: info@parsonplacepress.com. Website: www.parsonplacepress.com. Michael L. White, mng. ed. Devoted to giving both Christian authors and Christian readers a fair deal. Publishes 2-5 titles/yr.; hardcover, trade paperbacks, e-books. Receives 60 submissions annually. 80% of books from first-time authors. Accepts mss through agents or authors. Does print-on-demand. Reprints books. Prefers 100-200 pgs. **Royalty on net; no advance.** Average first printing 50. Publication within 3 mos. No simultaneous submissions. Responds in 4-6 wks. Requested mss by e-mail (attached file). Prefers NKJV or NASB. Guidelines on website ("Author Guidelines"); Electronic catalog on request.

Nonfiction: Proposal/2 chapters; e-query OK. Christian topic/content only.

Fiction: Proposal/2 chapters; e-query OK. For all ages.

Special Needs: In nonfiction: end-times prophecy, evangelism, and Bible studies. In fiction: mystery, romance, historical.

Photos/Artwork: Accepts freelance photos for book covers; open to queries from freelance artists.

Tips: "Most open to conservative, biblically based content that ministers to Christians. Write intelligently, clearly, sincerely, and engagingly."

PARSONS PUBLISHING HOUSE, PO Box 488, Stafford VA 22554. (850) 867-3061. Fax (540) 659-9043. E-mail: info@parsonspublishinghouse.com. Website: www.parsonspublishinghouse.com. Nondenominational. Diane Parsons, chief ed. Exists to partner with authors to release their voice into their world. Publishes 5 titles/yr.; hardcover, trade paperbacks. Receives 40 submissions annually. 85% of books from first-time authors. No mss through agents; accepts from authors. Reprints books. Prefers 120-160 pgs. **Royalty 10% on net; no advance.** Average first printing 300. Publication within 9 mos. Considers simultaneous submissions. Responds in 60 days. Prefers accepted mss by e-mail. Guidelines by e-mail/website ("Submissions"); no catalog.

Nonfiction: Query; e-query OK.

Fiction: Query; proposal/3 chapters; e-query OK. For teens & adults.

Ethnic Books: Hispanic.

Artwork: Open to queries from freelance artists.

Tips: "Most open to Christian living and worship."

PAULINE BOOKS & MEDIA, Daughters of St. Paul, 50 Saint Pauls Ave., Jamaica Plain MA 02130-3491. (617) 522-8911. E-mail: editorial@paulinemedia.com. Website: www.pauline.org. Catholic/Daughters of St. Paul. Christina Wegendt, FSP, and Sr. Sean Mayer, FSP, acq. eds. Submit to Brittany Schlorff, ed. asst. Responds to the hopes and needs of their readers with the Word of God and in the spirit of St. Paul, utilizing all available forms of media so others can find and develop faith in Jesus within the current culture. Publishes 20 titles/yr.; hardcover & trade paperbacks. Receives 350-400 submissions annually. 10% of books from first-time authors. Accepts mss through agents or authors. No subsidy or print-on-demand. Reprints books. Prefers 10,000-60,000 wds. **Royalty 5-10% on net; offers an advance.** Average first printing 4,000-10,000. Publication within 12 mos. Considers simultaneous submissions. Responds in 2-3 mos. Prefers requested ms by e-mail. Prefers NRSV. Guidelines by mail/e-mail/website (scroll to bottom "Manuscript Submissions"); free catalog by mail.

Nonfiction: Proposal/2 chapters; complete ms; e-query OK.

Fiction: Proposal/2 chapters; complete ms; e-query OK. For children only. "Looking for middle-reader chapter fiction with a Catholic worldview and values."

Special Needs: "Spirituality (prayer/holiness of life/seasonal titles), faith formation (religious instruction/catechesis), family life (marriage/parenting issues), biographies of the saints, prayer books. Of particular interest is our faith and culture line, which includes titles that show how Christ is present and may be more fully embraced and proclaimed within our media culture."

Tips: "Submissions are evaluated on adherence to gospel values, harmony with the Catholic tradition, relevance of topic, and quality of writing."

PAULINE KIDS, 50 St. Paul's Ave., Boston MA 02130. (617) 522-8911. Fax (617) 524-9805. E-mail: editorial@paulinemedia.com. Website: www.pauline.org. Pauline Books & Media/Catholic. Emily Beata Marsh, FSP, Christina M. Wegendt, FSP, and Jaymie Stuart Wolfe, eds.; submit to Brittany Schlorff, ed. asst. Seeks to provide wholesome and entertaining reading that can help children develop strong Christian values. Publishes 20-25 titles/yr.; hardcover, trade paperbacks. Receives 300-450 submissions annually. 10% of books from first-time authors. Accepts mss through agents or authors. Reprints books. **Royalty 5-10% on net; pays an advance.** Average first printing 4,000-5,000. Publication within 24 mos. Considers simultaneous submissions. Responds in 2-3 mos. Prefers accepted ms by e-mail. Prefers NRSV. Guidelines by mail/e-mail/website (scroll to bottom "Manuscript Submissions"); free catalog by mail.

Nonfiction/Fiction: Proposal/2 chapters for easy-to-read & middle-grade readers; complete ms for board and picture books; e-query OK.

Special Needs: Easy-to-read and middle-reader chapter fiction.

Photos/Artwork: Accepts freelance photos for book covers; open to queries from freelance artists.

PELICAN PUBLISHING CO. INC., 1000 Burmaster St., Gretna LA 70053. (504) 368-1175. Fax (504) 368-1195. E-mail: editorial@pelicanpub.com. Website: www.pelicanpub.com. Nina Kooij, ed-in-chief. To publish books of quality and permanence that enrich the lives of those who read them. Imprints: Firebird Press, Jackson Square Press, Dove Inspirational Press (see separate listing). Publishes 1 title/yr.; hardcover, trade paperbacks. Receives 250 submissions annually. No books from first-time authors. Accepts mss through agents or authors. Reprints books. Prefers 200+ pgs. **Royalty; pays some advances.** Publication within 9-18 mos. No simultaneous submissions. Responds in 1 mo. on queries. Requires accepted ms on disk. Prefers KJV. Guidelines on website ("About Us"/"Submissions").

Nonfiction: Proposal/2 chapters; no phone/fax/e-query. Children's picture books to 1,100 wds. (send complete ms); middle readers about Louisiana (ages 8-12) at least 25,000 wds.; cookbooks at least 200 recipes.

Fiction: Complete ms. Children's picture books only. For ages 5-8 only.

Artwork: Open to queries from freelance artists.

Tips: "On inspirational titles we need a high-profile author who already has an established speaking circuit so books can be sold at these appearances."

PORT YONDER PRESS, 6332—33rd Ave. Dr., Shellsburg IA 52332. (319) 436-3015. E-mail: contact@portyonderpress.com. Website: www.PortYonderPress.com. Chila Woychik, ed-in-chief. Imprint: SharksFinn. Crossover publisher of both Christian and general market books. Publishes 6-8 titles/yr. Receives 500 submissions annually. 30% of books from first-time authors. Accepts mss through agents or authors. Prefers 150-300 pgs. **Royalty 40-50% on net; small advance.** A traditional award-winning indie press using print-on-demand digital printing. Publication within 12-18 mos. No simultaneous queries or submissions. Accepts submissions only on first day of any month or at conferences where publisher/editor attends. Requires accepted mss by e-mail and hard copy. Responds in 2 mos. Guidelines on website (click on "Getting Published"). Not included in topical listings.

Poetry, Nonfiction & Fiction: Query only on first day of any month.

Tips: "Only the highest quality manuscripts will be accepted. Current needs: Crossover speculative fiction, mystery, spy thrillers, contemporary poetry, some western fiction, creative nonfiction, slipstream, and experimental. *Crossover—that which appeals to Christians and non-Christians alike. Our goal is to publish award-winning books of literary merit. Anything for our Christian imprints must be extremely non-preachy."

PRAEGER PUBLISHERS, 130 Cremona Dr., Santa Barbara CA 93117. (805) 968-1911. E-mail: achiffolo@abc-clio.com. Website: www.abc-clio.com. Imprint of ABC-CLIO. Michael Wilt, sr. acq. ed. Primary markets are public and university libraries worldwide; no trade distribution. Publishes 5-10 titles/yr. in religion; hardcover and e-book. Receives 100-120 submissions annually. Accepts mss through agents or authors. No subsidy or reprints. Prefers up to 100,000 wds. **Variable royalty on net; pays some advances.** Average first printing 750. Publication within 12-18 mos. Considers simultaneous submissions. Responds in 2-4 mos. Guidelines on website; catalog on website.

Nonfiction: Book proposal/1-3 chapters or all chapters available; e-query preferred.

Special Needs: Religion and society/culture; religious controversies/issues; paranormal; neuro-religion.

Ethnic Books: African American religion; Native American religion; Hispanic/Latino religion; Asian American religion.

Tips: "Most open to books on 'headline' issues and controversies; books on 'religion and culture' are needed; must be written for lay readership. No scholarly books. No self-help or how-to books. No scriptural studies or Bible scholarship. No fiction or poetry."

*RAINBOW PUBLISHERS, PO Box 261129, San Diego CA 92196. Toll-free (800) 323-7337. Toll-free fax (800) 331-0297. E-mail: editor@rainbowpublishers.com. Website: www.rainbow publishers.com. Tony Bonds, ed. Submit to The Editor. Publishes Bible-teaching, reproducible books for children's teachers. Publishes 20 titles/yr. Receives 250 submissions annually. 50% of books from first-time authors. Reprints books. Prefers 96 pgs. **Outright purchases $640 & up.** Average first printing 2,500. Publication within 2 yrs. Considers simultaneous submissions. Responds in 3 mos. No disk or e-mail submissions. Prefers NIV. Guidelines/catalog on website ("Submissions" at bottom).

Nonfiction: Proposal/2-5 chapters; no phone/e-query. "Looking for fun and easy ways to teach Bible concepts to kids, ages 2-12."

Special Needs: Creative puzzles and unique games.

Artwork: Open to queries from freelance artists.

Tips: "Visit your Christian bookstore or our website to see what we have already published. We have over 100 titles and do not like to repeat topics, so a proposal needs to be unique for us but not necessarily unique in the market. Most open to writing that appeals to teachers who work with kids and Bible activities that have been tried and tested on today's kids."

*RANDALL HOUSE DIGITAL, 114 Bush Rd., PO Box 17306, Nashville TN 37217. Toll-free (800) 877-7030. (615) 361-1221. Fax (615) 367-0535. E-mail through website: www.randallhouse.com. National Assn. of Free Will Baptists. Alan Clagg, dir. Produces curriculum-on-demand via the Internet, and electronic resources to supplement existing printed curriculum. Guidelines on website (click on "Contact Us"/"Book Proposal Guide").

Nonfiction: Query first; e-query OK.

Special Needs: Teacher-training material (personal or group), elective Bible studies for adults, children's curriculum (other than Sunday school), and elective materials for teens.

Also Does: Digital books.

Tips: "We are looking for writers with vision for worldwide ministry who would like to see their works help a greater section of the Body of Christ than served by the conventionally printed products."

*RANDALL HOUSE PUBLICATIONS, 114 Bush Rd., Nashville TN 37217. Toll-free (800) 877-7030. (615) 361-1221. Fax (615) 367-0535. E-mail: michelle.orr@randallhouse.com. Website: www.randallhouse.com. Free Will Baptist. Michelle Orr, sr. acq. ed. Publishes Sunday school and Christian education materials to make Christ known, from a conservative perspective. Publishes 10-15 titles/yr.; hardcover, trade paperbacks, digital. Receives 300-500 submissions annually. 40% of books from first-time authors. Accepts mss through agents or authors. No subsidy or reprints. Prefers 40,000 wds. **Royalty 12-18% on net; pays an advance.** Average first printing 5,000. Publication within 18 mos. Considers simultaneous submissions. Accepts requested mss by e-mail. Responds in 10-12 wks. Guidelines by e-mail/website ("Contact"/click on "Book Proposal Guide" in text); no catalog.

> **Nonfiction:** Query; e-query OK; proposal/2 chapters. Must fill out book proposal form they provide.
>
> **Artwork:** Open to queries from freelance artists (andrea.young@randallhouse.com).
>
> **Tips:** "We are expanding our book division with a conservative perspective. We have a very conservative view as a publisher."
>
> This publisher serviced by ChristianManuscriptSubmissions.com.

RAVENHAWK BOOKS, 7739 E. Broadway Blvd., #95, Tucson AZ 85710. E-mail: ravenhawk6dof@yahoo.com. Website: www.6dofsolutions.com. Blog: see website. The 6DOF Group. Karl Lasky, pub.; Shelly Geraci, submissions ed. Publishes variable number of titles/yr.; hardcover, trade paperbacks. Receives 1,000-1,500 submissions annually. 70% of books from first-time authors. Print-on-demand. Reprints books. **Royalty 40-50% on gross profits; no advance.** Average first printing 2,500. Publication in up to 18 mos. Considers simultaneous submissions. Responds in 6 wks., if interested. Catalog on website.

> **Nonfiction:** Query first; e-query OK. "Looking for profitable books from talented writers."
>
> **Fiction:** Query first. For all ages. Unsolicited full mss returned unopened.
>
> **Special Needs:** Looking for books from young authors, 16-22 years old.
>
> **Photos/Artwork:** Accepts freelance photos for book covers; open to queries from freelance artists.
>
> **Tips:** "Most open to crisp, creative, entertaining writing that also informs and educates. Writing, as any creative art, is a gift from God. Not everyone has the innate talent to do it well. We are author-oriented. We don't play games with the numbers."

REFERENCE SERVICE PRESS, 5000 Windplay Dr., Ste. 4, El Dorado Hills CA 95762. (916) 939-9620. Fax (916) 939-9626. E-mail: info@rspfunding.com. Website: www.rspfunding.com. R. David Weber, ed. Books related to financial aid and Christian higher education. Publishes 1 title/yr.; hardcover, trade paperbacks. Receives 3-5 submissions annually. Most books from first-time authors. No reprints. **Royalty 10% of net; usually no advance.** Publication within 5 mos. May consider simultaneous submissions. No guidelines; free catalog for 2 stamps.

> **Nonfiction:** Proposal/several chapters.
>
> **Special Needs:** Financial aid directories for Christian college students.

*REVELL BOOKS, Fleming H. Revell, Box 6287, Grand Rapids MI 49516. (616) 676-9185. Fax (616) 676-2315. Website: www.revellbooks.com. Imprint of Baker Publishing Group. Publishes inspirational fiction and nonfiction for the broadest Christian market. Catalog on website. No unsolicited mss. Submit only through an agent, Authonomy.com, or ChristianManuscriptSubmissions.com.

*STANDARD PUBLISHING, 8805 Governor's Hill Dr., Ste. 400, Cincinnati OH 45249. (513) 931-4050. Fax (513) 931-0950. Website: www.standardpub.com. CFM Religion Publishing Group LLC. Provides true-to-the-Bible resources that inspire, educate, and motivate Christians to a growing relationship with Jesus Christ. Accepts mss through agents or authors. Hardcover & trade paperbacks. No reprints. **Royalty or outright purchase; advance.** No simultaneous submissions. Responds in 3-6 mos. Prefers NIV/KJV. Guidelines on website (www.standardpub.com/writers).

> **Nonfiction:** Query only; e-query OK.
> **Fiction:** Query only; e-query OK. Children's picture or board books; juvenile novels.
> **Special Needs:** Adult and youth ministry resources; children's ministry resources.
> This publisher serviced by ChristianManuscriptSubmissions.com.

ST. ANTHONY MESSENGER PRESS (see FRANCISCAN MEDIA)

*SUMMERSIDE PRESS/LOVE FINDS YOU, 11024 Quebec Cir., Bloomington MN 55438. (612) 321-1015. E-mail: info@summersidepress.com. Website: www.summersidepress.com. Rachel Meisel, fiction ed. Inspirational romance fiction series. Accepts mss through agents only. Publishes 12 titles/yr. Prefers 80,000 wds. or 320 pgs. Guidelines on website ("Submissions").

> **Fiction:** Send a paragraph overview, plus a 2-3 page synopsis by e-mail (attached file).
> **Tips:** "This series features inspirational romance novels set in actual cities and towns across the US."

SUNPENNY PUBLISHING, 10 Aspen Close, Harriseahead Staffordshire ST7 4HD, United Kingdom. E-mail: writers@sunpenny.com. Website: www.sunpenny.com. Jo Holloway, ed. Publishes 3-5 titles/yr.; hardcover, trade paperbacks, mass-market paperbacks, electronic originals. 50% of books from first-time authors. Accepts mss through agents or authors. **Royalty 15% of margin.** Considers simultaneous submissions. Responds in 1-2 wks. to queries; 1-2 mos. to proposals; 2-3 mos. to manuscripts. Guidelines ("Submissions") & catalog on website.

> **Nonfiction:** Query, proposal, or complete ms. Christian/inspirational books.
> **Fiction:** Query, proposal, or complete ms. Christian/inspirational books.
> **Photos/Artwork:** Accepts freelance photos for book covers; open to queries from freelance artists.

THE TRINITY FOUNDATION, PO Box 68, Unicoi TN 37692. (423) 743-0199. Fax (423) 743-2005. E-mail: tjtrinityfound@aol.com. Website: www.trinityfoundation.org. Thomas W. Juodaitis, ed. To promote the logical system of truth found in the Bible. Publishes 5 titles/yr.; hardcover, trade paperbacks. Receives 3 submissions annually. No books from first-time authors. No mss through agents. Reprints books. Prefers 200 pgs. **Outright purchases up to $1,500; free books; no advance.** Average first printing 2,000. Publication within 9 mos. No simultaneous submissions. Requires requested ms in electronic editable format. Responds in 2-3 mos. No guidelines; catalog on website.

> **Nonfiction:** Query letter only. Open to Calvinist/Clarkian books, Christian philosophy, economics, and politics.
> **Also Does:** Pamphlets, booklets, tracts.
> **Photos:** Accepts freelance photos for book covers.
> **Tips:** "Most open to doctrinal books that conform to the Westminster Confession of Faith; nonfiction, biblical, and well-reasoned books, theologically sound, clearly written, and well organized."

*TYNDALE ESPAÑOL, 351 Executive Dr., Carol Stream IL 60188. (630) 784-5272. Fax (630) 344-0943. E-mail: andresschwartz@tyndale.com. Website: www.tyndale.com. Andres Schwartz, dir. Spanish division of Tyndale House Publishers.

TYNDALE HOUSE PUBLISHERS, INC. 351 Executive Dr., Carol Stream IL 60188. Toll-free (800) 323-9400. (630) 668-8300. Toll-free fax (800) 684-0247. E-mail through website: www.tyndale.com. Submit to Manuscript Review Committee. Practical Christian books for home and family. Imprints: Tyndale Español (Spanish imprint). Publishes 150-200 titles/yr.; hardcover, trade paperbacks. 5% of books from first-time authors. Requires mss through agents. Average first printing 5,000-10,000. Publication within 9 mos. Considers simultaneous submissions. Responds in 3-6 mos. Prefers NLT. No unsolicited mss. Guidelines/catalog on website (under "Site Map"/"Authors"/"Manuscript Policy").

> **Nonfiction:** Query from agents or published authors only; no phone/fax query. No unsolicited mss (they will not be acknowledged or returned).
>
> **Fiction:** "We accept queries only from agents, Tyndale authors, authors known to us from other publishers, or other people in the publishing industry. Novels 75,000-100,000 wds. All must have an evangelical Christian message."
>
> **Also Does:** E-books.
>
> This publisher serviced by ChristianManuscriptSubmissions.com.

VBC PUBLISHING, PO Box 9101, Vallejo CA 94591. (707) 315-1219. Fax (707) 648-2169. E-mail: akgordon1991@att.net. Vallejo Bible College. Kevin Gordon, pres. To glorify the Lord through Christian literature; to provide the Christian community with material to aid them in their personal studies and to help in their life and ministry. New publisher; plans 1-5 titles/yr.; hardcover, trade paperbacks. Receives 10 submissions annually. Plans to publish 50% of books from first-time authors. Accepts mss through agents or authors. Print-on-demand publisher. No reprints. Prefers 100+ pgs. **Royalty 8-12% on net; no advance.** Publication within 8 mos. Considers simultaneous submissions. Responds in 2-6 wks. Accepted mss on disk. Prefers KJV, NKJV, NASB, NIV. Guidelines by mail; no catalog.

> **Nonfiction:** Proposal/2 chapters or complete ms; phone/e-query OK; no fax query.
>
> **Special Needs:** Biblical theology, Bible study, and Christian living.
>
> **Artwork:** Open to queries from freelance artists.
>
> **Tips:** "Most open to doctrinally sound and relevant manuscripts. Have a well-written manuscript and a plan to market your book. Follow guidelines when submitting and trust in the Lord!"

THE VISION FORUM, 4719 Blanco Rd., San Antonio TX 78212. (210) 340-5250. Fax (210) 340-8577. Website: www.visionforum.com. Douglas W. Phillips, pres. Dedicated to the restoration of the biblical family. Historical fiction, practical Christian living.

WARNER PRESS INC., 1201 E. 5th St., Anderson IN 46012. Fax (765) 640-8005. E-mail: rfogle@warnerpress.org. Website: www.warnerpress.org. Church of God. Karen Rhodes, sr. ed.; submit to Robin Fogle, asst. product ed. Committed to excellence in developing and marketing products and services based on scriptural truths to energize, educate, nurture, inspire, and unite the whole people of God. Hardcover, paperback, and e-books. Receives 100+ submissions annually. Rarely accepts mss through agents. No subsidy. No reprints. Not presently publishing kids' picture books. 250-350 pgs. for teen books. **Royalty & advance based on the author and type of book.** Publication within 12 mos. Considers simultaneous submissions. Responds in 6-8 wks. Prefers KJV or NIV. Guidelines on website (scroll to bottom "Submissions Guidelines"); no catalog.

> **Nonfiction:** Complete ms; fax/e-query OK. Accepts e-mail submissions.
>
> **Fiction:** Query first, then complete ms; fax/e-query OK. Accepts e-mail submissions. Also producing chapter books (120-150 pages) for ages 8-12. "We want our books to be biblically sound with a nondenominational viewpoint."
>
> **Artwork:** Send to Curtis Corzine, Creative Art Director (curtis@warnerpress.org).
>
> **Tips:** "We primarily create books for ages 6-10 (picture books) and 8-12 (fantasy fiction). We are looking for books that are not preachy but do contain a biblical or moral foundation. Well-written, creative books by writers who have done their market research. To see other products we produce, visit our website."

*WATERBROOK PRESS, 12265 Oracle Blvd., Ste. 200, Colorado Springs CO 80921. (719) 590-4999. Fax (719) 590-8977. E-mail: info@waterbrookmultnomah.com. Website: www.waterbrook multnomah.com. Part of WaterBrook Multnomah, a division of Random House Inc. Ken Petersen, VP/ed-in-chief; Laura Barker, ed. dir. Publishes 75 titles/yr.; hardcover, trade paperbacks. **Royalty on net; advance.** WaterBrook is currently not accepting unsolicited manuscripts, proposals, or queries; no proposals for biographies or poetry. Queries will be accepted though literary agents and at writers' conferences at which a WaterBrook representative is present. Catalog on website.

> **Nonfiction/Fiction:** Agented submissions only.

WATERSHED BOOKS, PO Box 1738, Aztec NM 87410. E-mail: customer@pelicanbookgroup.com. Website: www.pelicanbookgroup.com. Division of Pelican Ventures, LLC. Nicola Martinez, editor-in-chief. Christian fiction 25,000-60,000 wds. Limited-edition hardback, trade paperbacks, and e-book. **Royalty 40% on download; 7% on print.** Pays nominal advance. Accepts unagented submissions. Responds to queries in 30 days, full ms in 90 days. Considers reprints but accepts few. E-mail submissions only; see website for submission form and procedure.

> **Fiction:** Query via submission form on website. Interested in series ideas. Submissions must be Young Adult fiction that features young adult characters.

*WESLEYAN PUBLISHING HOUSE, PO Box 50434, Indianapolis IN 46250-0434. (317) 774-7900. E-mail: wph@wesleyan.org. Website: www.wesleyan.org/wph. The Wesleyan Church. Attn: Editorial Director. Communicates the life-transforming message of holiness to the world. Publishes 30 titles/yr.; hardcover, trade paperbacks. Receives 150 submissions annually. 25% of books from first-time authors. Accepts mss through agents or authors. No reprints. Prefers 25,000-40,000 wds. **Royalty and advance.** Average first printing 4,000. Publication within 9-12 mos. Considers simultaneous submissions. Prefers ms by e-mail (submissions@wesleyan.org). Responds within 60-90 days. Prefers NIV. Guidelines by e-mail/website (www.wesleyan.org/wg). Free online catalog.

> **Nonfiction:** Proposal/3-5 chapters; no phone/fax/e-query. "Looking for books that help Christians understand the faith and apply it to their lives."
> This publisher serviced by ChristianManuscriptSubmissions.com.

*WHITAKER HOUSE, 1030 Hunt Valley Cir., New Kensington PA 15068. (724) 334-7000. (724) 334-1200. E-mail: publisher@whitakerhouse.com. Website: www.whitakerhouse.com. Whitaker Corp. Tom Cox, sr. ed. To advance God's Kingdom by providing biblically based products that proclaim the power of the gospel and minister to the spiritual needs of people around the world. Publishes 30-40 titles/yr.; hardcover, trade paperbacks, mass-market paperbacks. Receives 500 submissions annually. 15% of books from first-time authors. Accepts mss through agents or authors. No subsidy, print-on-demand, or reprints. Prefers 50,000 wds. **Royalty 6-15% on net; some variable advances.** Average first printing 5,000. Publication within 10 mos. Considers simultaneous submissions. Prefers accepted ms by e-mail. Responds in 4 mos. Prefers NIV. Guidelines on website ("Submissions Guidelines" center); no catalog.

> **Nonfiction/Fiction:** Query only first; no phone/fax query; e-query OK.
> **Special Needs:** Charismatic nonfiction, Christian historical romance, Amish romance, Christian African American romance.
> **Ethnic Books:** Spanish translations of current English titles.
> **Tips:** "Looking for quality nonfiction and fiction by authors with a national marketing platform. Most open to high-quality, well-thought-out, compelling pieces of work. Review the guidelines and submit details as thoroughly as possible for publication consideration."

WHITE FIRE PUBLISHING, (866) 245-2211. Fax: (410) 571-0292. E-mail info@whitefire-publishing.com. Website: www.whitefire-publishing.com. Roseanna White, ed. Publishes 4-10 titles/yr. Receives 100 submissions annually. 60% of books from first-time authors. Prefers mss through agents. Prefers 60,000-150,000 wds. Publishes trade paperbacks and digital. **Royalty 10-15%. Pay**

for e-books 50% on net. Offers advance. Average first run 1,000. Publication in 6-12 months. Accepts simultaneous submissions. Responds to proposals within 3 months. Guidelines on website.

> **Nonfiction:** Query letter only first. Query by e-mail. Narrative nonfiction. Must meet our motto of "Where Spirit Meets the Page." Send to Wendy Chorot, Non-Fiction Editor at w.chorot@whitefire-publishing.com.
>
> **Fiction:** Query letter only first. Query by e-mail. Accepts fiction for teens and adults. Likes historical, especially with exotic settings and with romance threads.
>
> **Tips:** "Where Spirit Meets the Page." Looking for unique voices and settings others shy away from. Fiction editors Dina Sleiman, d.sleiman@whitefire-publishing.com, and Roseanna White, r.white@whitefire-publishing.com.

WHITE ROSE PUBLISHING, PO Box 1738, Aztec NM 87410. E-mail: customer@pelicanbookgroup.com. Website: www.pelicanbookgroup.com. A division of Pelican Ventures, LLC. Nicola Martinez, ed.-in-chief. Christian romance 10,000-80,000 wds. Limited-edition hardback, trade paperbacks, and e-book. **Royalty 40% on download; 7% on print. Pays nominal advance.** Accepts unagented submissions. Responds to queries in 30 days, full ms in 90 days. Considers reprints but accepts few. E-mail submissions only; see website for submission form and procedure.

> **Fiction:** Query via submission form on website. Interested in series ideas. Submissions must be Christian romance.

WRITE NOW PUBLICATIONS, PO Box 110390, Nashville TN 37222. Toll-free (800) 21-WRITE. E-mail: RegAForder@aol.com. Website: www.writenowpublications.com. Reg A. Forder, exec. ed. To train and develop quality Christian writers; books on writing and speaking for writers and speakers. Royalty division of ACW Press. Publishes 1-2 titles/yr.; trade paperbacks. Receives 6 submissions annually. 0% from first-time authors. Accepts mss through agents or authors. Reprints books. **Royalty 10% of net.** Average first printing 2,000. Publication within 12 mos. Considers simultaneous submissions. Requires requested ms on disk. No guidelines/catalog.

> **Nonfiction:** Writing how-to only. Query letter only; e-query OK.

YALE UNIVERSITY PRESS, PO Box 209040, New Haven CT 06518-9040. (203) 432-6807. Fax (203) 436-1064. E-mail: jennifer.banks@yale.edu. Website: www.yalepress.yale.edu. Jennifer Banks, ed. Publishes scholarly and general-interest books, including religion. Publishes 15 religious titles/yr.; hardcover, trade paperbacks. Receives 1,000 submissions annually. 10% of books from first-time authors. Accepts mss through agents or authors. **Royalty from 0% to standard trade royalties; advance $0-100,000.** Publication within 1 yr. Considers simultaneous submissions. Requires requested ms on hard copy; no e-mail submissions. Responds in 2 mos. Guidelines/catalog on website (www.yalebooks.com).

> **Nonfiction:** Query or proposal/sample chapters; fax query OK; no e-query. "Excellent and salable scholarly books."
>
> **Contest:** Yale Series of Younger Poets competition. Open to poets under 40 who have not had a book of poetry published. Submit manuscripts of 48-64 pgs. by November 15. Entry fee $20. Send SASE for guidelines (also on website). Send complete manuscript.

*ZONDERKIDZ, 5300 Patterson S.E., Grand Rapids MI 49530-0002. (616) 698-6900. Fax (616) 698-3578. E-mail: zpub@zondervan.com. Website: www.zonderkidz.com. Zondervan/ HarperCollins. Children's book line of Zondervan; ages 12 & under. Not currently accepting proposals.

> This publisher serviced by ChristianManuscriptSubmissions.com.

*ZONDERVAN, General Trade Books; Academic and Professional Books, 5300 Patterson S.E., Grand Rapids MI 49530-0002. (616) 698-6900. Manuscript submission line: (616) 698-3447. E-mail through website: www.zondervan.com. HarperCollins Publishers. Mission is to be the leading Christian communications company meeting the needs of people with resources that glorify Jesus

Christ and promote biblical principles. Publishes 120 trade titles/yr.; hardcover, trade paperbacks, mass-market paperbacks. Few books from first-time authors. Accepts mss through agents or authors. No subsidy or reprints. **Royalty 12-14% of net; variable advance.** Publication within 12-18 mos. Considers simultaneous submissions. Requires requested ms by e-mail. Prefers NIV. Guidelines on website (under "About Us"/"Manuscript Submissions"); catalog online.

Nonfiction: Submissions only by e-mail and only certain types of mss. See website for e-mail address and submission guidelines.

Fiction: No fiction at this time; refer to website for updates.

Special Needs: Currently accepting unsolicited book proposals in academic, reference, or ministry resources only (see guidelines).

Children's Lines: ZonderKidz and Faithgirlz (not currently accepting new products).

Ethnic Books: Vida Publishers division: Spanish and Portuguese.

Tips: "Almost no unsolicited manuscripts are published. Book proposals should be single-spaced with one-inch margins on all sides."

This publisher serviced by ChristianManuscriptSubmissions.com.

3

Subsidy Publishers

A subsidy publisher requires that the author pay for any part of the publishing costs. They may call themselves by a variety of names, such as book packager, cooperative publisher, self-publisher, or simply someone who helps authors get their books printed. Print-on-demand (POD) businesses print books in quantities as low as one at a time and usually much faster than traditional publishers. Custom publishers develop new authors to eventually work with royalty publishers.

To my knowledge the following subsidy publishers are legitimate (as opposed to simply being out to take your money and offering little in return), but I cannot guarantee that. Any time you pay for any part of the production of your book, you are entering into a nontraditional relationship. Some subsidy publishers do some royalty publishing, so you could approach them as a royalty publisher. They are likely to offer you a subsidy deal, so if you are interested only in a royalty arrangement, indicate that in your cover letter.

Some subsidy publishers will publish any book, as long as the author is willing to pay for it. Others are as selective about what they publish as a royalty publisher would be. As subsidy publishers become more selective, the professional quality of subsidy books is improving.

It has been my experience that for every complaint I get about a publisher, several other authors sing the praises of the same publisher. All I can do is give a brief overview of what to expect from a subsidy publisher and what terms should raise a red flag.

If you are unsuccessful placing your book with a royalty publisher but feel strongly about seeing it published, a subsidy publisher can make printing your book easier and often less expensive than doing it yourself.

Get more than one bid to determine whether the terms you are being offered are competitive. A legitimate subsidy publisher will provide a list of former clients as references. Get a catalog of the publisher's books to check the quality of their work, the bindings, etc. See if their books are available through Amazon.com or similar online services. (Some Christian or general bookstores will not carry a self-published book.) Get answers before committing yourself. Also have someone in the book publishing industry review your contract before you sign it. Some experts listed in the Editorial Services section of this book review contracts. The listings below include printers who could help you complete the printing process yourself.

The more copies of a book printed, the lower the cost per copy. But never let a publisher talk you into more copies than you think is reasonable. Also, some subsidy publishers will do as much promotion as a royalty publisher; others do none at all. If the publisher is not doing promotion and you don't have any means of distribution, you may prefer print-on-demand so you don't end up with a garage full of books you can't sell.

Definitions of different types of publishers:

Commercial/Mainstream/Traditional Publisher: One who takes all the risks and pays all the costs of producing and promoting your book (see previous book section).

Vanity Publisher: Prints at the author's expense. Will print any book the author is willing to pay for. May offer marketing help, warehousing, editing, or promotion of some sort at the author's expense.

Subsidy Publisher: Shares the cost of printing and binding a book. Often more selective, but the completed books belong to the publisher, not the author. Author may buy books from the publisher and may also collect a royalty for books the publisher sells.

Self-Publishing: Author pays all the costs of publishing the book and is responsible for all the marketing, distribution, promotion, etc. Author may select a service package that defines the cost and services. The books belong to the author and he/she keeps all the income from sales. Following this section I include the names and addresses of Christian book distributors. Some will consider distributing a subsidy-published book. You may want to contact them to determine their interest before you sign a contract with a subsidy publisher. For more help on self-publishing, go to: www.bookmarket.com/index.html.

(*) before a listing indicates unconfirmed information or no information update.

---

*ACW PRESS, American Christian Writers, PO Box 110390, Nashville TN 37222. Toll-free (800) 21-WRITE. E-mail: Jim@JamesWatkins.com. Website: www.acwpress.com. Reg A. Forder, owner; Jim Watkins, editorial advisor. A self-publishing book packager. Imprint: Write Now Publications (see separate listing). Publishes 40 titles/yr.; hardcover, trade paperbacks, mass-market paperbacks, coffee-table books. Reprints books. SUBSIDY PUBLISHES 95%; does print-on-demand. Average first printing 2,500. Publication within 4-6 mos. Responds in 48-72 hrs. Request for estimate form available on website. Not in topical listings; will consider any nonfiction or fiction topic. Guidelines by e-mail/website.

Nonfiction/Fiction: All types considered.

Tips: "We offer a high-quality publishing alternative to help Christian authors get their material into print. High standards, high quality. If authors have a built-in audience, they have the best chance to make self-publishing a success." Has a marketing program available to authors. This publisher serviced by ChristianManuscriptSubmissions.com.

AMERICAN BINDING & PUBLISHING CO., PO Box 60049, Corpus Christi TX 78466-0049. Toll-free (800) 863-3708. (361) 658-4221. E-mail: rmagner@grandecom.net. Website: www.american bindingpublishing.com. Rose Magner, pub. E-book publishing. Downloads only.

AMPELOS PRESS, 951 Anders Rd., Lansdale PA 19446. Phone/fax (484) 991-8581. E-mail: mbagnull@aol.com. Website: www.writehisanswer.com. Marlene Bagnull, LittD, pub./ed. Services (depending on what is needed) include critiquing, editing, proofreading, typesetting, and cover design. Publishes 1-3 titles/yr. SUBSIDY PUBLISHES 100%. Query only. Not included in topical listings (see Tips).

Special Needs: Books about missions and meeting the needs of children both at home and abroad.

Tips: "Our vision statement reads: 'Strongly, unashamedly, uncompromisingly Christ-centered. Exalting the name of Jesus Christ. Seeking to teach His ways through holding up the Word of God as the Standard.' (*Ampelos* is the Greek word for 'vine' in John 15:5.)"

*BELIEVERSPRESS, 6820 W. 115th St., Bloomington MN 55438. Toll-free (866) 794-8774. E-mail: info@believerspress.com. Website: www.believerspress.com. A division of Bethany Press International. Submit through website. Funds global missions training with proceeds. Provides authors with a Christian team of A-list industry professionals to help them achieve their publishing goals. Offers professional packages and a la carte services to fit every budget. Authors are in full control and pay only for services they need. All work is work-for-hire. Includes editorial, typesetting, cover design, digital/conventional book printing and production, e-books, POD, distribution to trade, marketing/publicity, author e-store book sales, social media, and blog articles by industry professionals.

BIOGRAPHICAL PUBLISHING CO., 95 Sycamore Dr., Prospect CT 06712-1493. (203) 758-3661. Fax (305) 768-0261. E-mail: biopub@aol.com. Website: www.biopub.co.cc. John R. Guevin, ed. Provides services to get books published and to help market and sell them. Publishes 1-4 religious titles/yr.; hardcover, trade paperbacks, digital. Receives 200 submissions annually. 75% of books from first-time authors. Accepts mss through agents. No print-on-demand. Reprints books. Prefers 50-500 pgs. **Author receives 95% of sales amount after expenses; no advance.** Average first printing 100-1,000. Publication within 2 mos. Considers simultaneous submissions. Responds in 1 wk. Guidelines by mail/e-mail/website; free catalog.

Nonfiction: Query letter only first. Most open to topical issues.

Fiction: Query letter only first. Any genre.

Photos/Artwork: Accepts freelance photos for book covers; open to queries from freelance artists.

BOOKLOCKER.COM INC., 5726 Cortez Road W. #349, Bradenton, FL 34210. (305) 768-0261. fax: (305) 768-0261. E-mail: angela@booklocker.com. Website: www.booklocker.com. Angela Hoy, pub. We seek unique, eclectic, and different manuscripts. Publishes 400 titles/yr.; hardcover, trade paperbacks, e-books. 70% of books from first-time authors. No mss through agents. SUBSIDY PUBLISHES 100%; does print-on-demand. Reprints books. Prefers 48-1050 pgs.; less for children's books. **Royalty 35% on retail (15% on wholesale orders; 35% on booklocker.com orders; 50-70% for e-books); no advance.** Publication within 4-6 wks. Considers simultaneous submissions. Responds in less than a week. Bible version is author's choice. Guidelines on website; no catalog.

Nonfiction: Complete ms; e-query OK. "We're open to all unique ideas."

Fiction: Complete ms; e-query OK. All genres for all ages.

Ethnic Books: Publishes for all ethnic groups.

Photos/Artwork: Uses stock photos or author-supplied photos/artwork.

Contest: The WritersWeekly.com 24-Hour Short Story Contest is held quarterly.

BROWN BOOKS PUBLISHING GROUP, 16250 Knoll Trail Dr. Ste. 205, Dallas TX 75248. (972) 381-0009. Fax (972) 248-4336. E-mail: publishing@brownbooks.com. Website: www.brownbooks .com. Publishes books in the areas of self-help, religion/inspirational, relationships, business, mind/body/spirit, and women's issues; we build relationships with our authors. Imprints: Personal Profiles, The P3 Press. Publishes 150 titles/yr.; hardcover, trade paperbacks, coffee-table books. Receives 4,000 submissions annually. 70% of books from first-time authors. No mss through agents. SUBSIDY PUBLISHES 100% through Personal Profiles & P3 imprints. **Royalty 100% of retail; no advance.** Authors retain rights to their work. Average first printing 3,000-5,000. Publication in 6 mos. Accepts simultaneous submissions. Responds in 2 wks. Requires mss on disk or by e-mail. Responds in 2 wks. Guidelines on website.

Nonfiction: Complete ms; phone/e-query preferred.

Fiction: Complete ms; phone/e-query OK. For all ages.

Tips: "We publish all genres with an emphasis on business, self-help, children's, and general Christian topics."

*CHRISTIAN SMALL PUBLISHERS ASSOCIATION (CSPA), P.O. Box 481022, Charlotte NC 28269. (704) 277-7194. CSPA is an organization for small publishers producing materials for the Christian marketplace. We help small publishers (including those who self-publish) market their books.

CREATION HOUSE, 600 Rinehart Rd., Lake Mary FL 32746-4872. (407) 333-0600. Fax (407) 333-7100. E-mail: creationhouse@charismamedia.com. Website: www.creationhouse.com. Charisma Media. Submit to Acquisitions Editor. To inspire and equip people to live a Spirit-led life and to walk in the divine purpose for which they were created. Publishes 125 titles/yr.; hardcover, trade paperbacks, mass-market paperbacks, coffee-table books. Receives 1,500 submissions annually. 80% of books from first-time authors. Accepts mss through agents. Reprints books. Prefers 25,000+ wds. or 100-200 pgs. **Royalty 12-15% of net; no advance.** Average first printing 2,000. Publication within 2-4 mos. Considers simultaneous submissions. Responds in 10-12 wks. Open to submissions on disk or by e-mail. Guidelines by mail/e-mail; free catalog.

Nonfiction: Proposal/complete ms; no phone/fax query; e-query OK. "Open to any books that are well written and glorify Jesus Christ."

Fiction: Proposal/complete ms; no phone/fax query; e-query OK. For all ages. "Fiction must have a biblical worldview and point the reader to Christ."

Photos: Accepts freelance photos for book covers.

Tips: "We use the term co-publishing to describe a hybrid between conventional royalty publishing and self- or subsidy publishing, utilizing the best of both worlds. We produce a high-quality book for our own inventory, market it, distribute it, and pay the author a royalty on every copy sold. In return, the author agrees to buy, at a deep discount, a portion of the first print run."

CREDO HOUSE PUBLISHERS, 3148 Plainfield Ave. NE, Ste. 111, Grand Rapids MI 49525-3285. (616) 363-2686. E-mail: connect@credocommunications.net. Website: www.credocommunications .net. A division of Credo Communications LLC. Timothy J. Beals, pres. Works with Christian ministry leaders and organizations to develop life-changing books, Bible-related products, and other Christian resources. CUSTOM PUBLISHER. Publishes 6-12 titles/yr. Publication within 60-90 days. Average first printing 2,500. Guidelines on website. Not included in topical listings.

Nonfiction/Fiction: Complete online author survey.

CROSSHOUSE PUBLISHING, 2844 S FM 549, Suite A, Rockwall TX 75032. Toll-free (877) 212-0933. Fax (877) 212-0933. E-mail: sales@crosshousepublishing.org or through website: www.crosshouse publishing.org. Self-publishing branch of KLMK Communications. Dr. Katie Welch, pub. To achieve excellence in Christian self-publishing without sacrificing personal interest and care for customers. Publishes hardcover, trade paperbacks. No mss through agents. SUBSIDY PUBLISHER. **Royalty 25% on net; no advance.** Publication within 3 mos. Guidelines on website (under "Downloads").

Nonfiction/Fiction: Accepts fiction for all ages.

Photos: Accepts freelance photos for book covers.

Tips: "We provide authors the opportunity to have their books distributed through a wide array of Christian and general bookstores. We aspire to offer the marketplace superior Christian literature that will impact readers' lives."

DCTS PUBLISHING, PO Box 40276, Santa Barbara CA 93140. (805) 570-3168. E-mail: dennis@ dctspub.com. Website: www.dctspub.com. "For authors who want quality low-cost publishing, we will partner with you in producing a fantastic marketable book that will sell anywhere in the world. Please contact me for more details." Dennis Stephen Hamilton, ed. Books are designed to enrich the mind, encourage the heart, and empower the spirit. Publishes 5 titles/yr. Receives 25 submissions annually. 35% of books from first-time authors. No mss through agents. SUBSIDY PUBLISHES 70%. No reprints. Prefers 100-300 pgs. **Royalty 17% of retail; no advance.** Average first printing 3,500. Publication within 6-8 mos. No simultaneous submissions. Prefers KJV. Guidelines by mail; free catalog/brochure.

Nonfiction: Query or proposal/2-3 chapters; e-query OK.

DEEP RIVER BOOKS (formerly VMI Publishers), 26306 Metolius Meadows Dr., Camp Sherman OR 97730. E-mail: bill@deepriverbooks.com, nancie@deepriverbooks.com. Website: www.deepriver books.com. Bill and Nancie Carmichael, pubs. Partnering with new authors. Publishes 35 titles/yr.; hardback, trade paperbacks, coffee-table books. Receives hundreds of submissions annually. 90% of books from first-time authors. Accepts mss through agents. No reprints. Prefers 45,000+ wds. or 192-400 pgs. **Royalty 12-18% of net; no advance.** CUSTOM PUBLISHER; see website for details. Average first printing 2,500+. Publication within 9-12 mos. Considers simultaneous submissions. Requires accepted ms by e-mail. Responds in 2 mos. Guidelines on website.

Nonfiction: Query first by e-mail only; proposal/2-3 chapters.

Fiction: Query first by e-mail only; proposal/2-3 chapters. For all ages. "Anything Christian or inspirational that is well written, especially from new authors."

Tips: "Go to our website first, and read how we partner with new authors. Then, if you feel Deep River Books would be a good fit for you, e-mail your proposal."
This publisher serviced by ChristianManuscriptSubmissions.com.

DESTINY IMAGE PUBLISHERS, PO Box 310, Shippensburg PA 17257. Toll-free (800) 722-6774. (717) 532-3040. Fax (717) 532-9291. E-mail: rrr@destinyimage.com or through website: www .destinyimage.com. Ronda Ranalli, ed. mngr. To help people grow deeper in their relationship with God and others. Imprints: Destiny Image Fiction, Destiny Image Dark Matter. Publishes 120 titles/yr. Receives 800-900 submissions annually. 10% of books from first-time authors. Accepts mss through agents or authors. Reprints books. Prefers 40,000-60,000 wds. **Royalty 10-15% on net; no advance.** Average first printing 10,000. Publication within 12 mos. Considers simultaneous submissions. Send unsolicited mss via their online Manuscript Submission Form. Responds in up to 6 mos. Guidelines on website; free catalog.

Nonfiction: Query or proposal/chapters; no e-query. Charges a $25 fee for unsolicited manuscripts (enclose with submission).

Fiction: Proposal/1-2 chapters. Adult.

Tips: "Most open to books on the deeper life, or of charismatic interest."

ESSENCE PUBLISHING CO. INC., 20 Hanna Ct., Belleville ON K8P 5J2, Canada. Toll-free (800) 238-6376, ext. 7110. (613) 962-2360. Fax (613) 962-3055. E-mail: info@essence-publishing.com. Website: www.essence-publishing.com. David Visser, mng. ed.; Sherrill Brunton, publishing mgr., (s.brunton@essence-publishing.com). Provides affordable, short-run book publishing to mainly the Christian community; dedicated to furthering the work of Christ through the written word. Imprints: Essence Publishing, Guardian Books, Epic Press. Epic Press is reserved for non-Christian books such as biographies, cookbooks, text books, history books, etc.). Publishes 100-150+ titles/yr.; hardcover, trade paperbacks, mass-market paperbacks, coffee-table books. Receives 250+ submissions annually. 75% of books from first-time authors. Accepts mss from agents or authors. SUBSIDY PUBLISHES 100%. Does print-on-demand. Reprints books. Any length. Completes books in other languages. **Royalty. 50% from bookstore and e-books, no advance.** Average first printing 500-1,000. Publication within 3 mos. Considers simultaneous submissions. Responds in 2 wks. Prefers requested ms on disk or by e-mail. Bible version is author's choice. Free publishing guide by mail/e-mail; catalog online (www.essencebookstore.com); and international distribution available. E-books available with listings on Kindle and Apple.

Nonfiction: Complete ms; phone/fax/e-query OK. Accepts all topics.

Fiction: Complete ms. All genres for all ages. Including full-color children's picture books.

Also Does: Pamphlets, booklets, tracts, and posters.

Photos/Artwork: Accepts freelance photos for book covers; open to queries from freelance artists.

FAIRWAY PRESS, subsidy division for CSS Publishing Company, 5450 N. Dixie Hwy., Lima OH 45807-9559. Toll-free (800) 241-4056. (419) 227-1818. E-mail: david@csspub.com or through website: www.fairwaypress.com. David Runk, ed. (david@csspub.com); submit to Attn: Sales Representative. Imprint: Express Press. Publishes 30-50 titles/yr. Receives 200-300 submissions annually. 80% of books from first-time authors. Reprints books. SUBSIDY PUBLISHES 100%. **Royalty to 50%; no advance.** Average first printing 500-1,000. Publication within 6-9 mos. Considers simultaneous submissions. Responds in up to 1 mo. Prefers requested ms on disk; no e-mail submissions. Prefers NRSV. Guidelines on website ("Submit Your Manuscript"); catalog for 9 x 12 SAE.

Nonfiction: Complete ms; phone/fax/e-query OK. All types. "Looking for manuscripts with a Christian theme, and seasonal material."

Fiction: Complete ms. For adults, teens, or children; all types. No longer producing anything in full color or with four-color illustrations.

FAITH BOOKS & MORE, 3255 Lawrenceville-Suwanee Rd., Ste. P250, Suwanee GA 30024. (678) 232-6156. E-mail: publishing@faithbooksandmore.com. Website: www.faithbooksandmore.com. 100% custom publishing. Nicole Smith, mng. ed. Imprints: Faith Books & More; Friends of Faith, Corporate Connoisseur, or custom imprint for author branding. Publishes 100 titles/yr; hardcover, trade paperbacks, and e-books. Receives 200 submissions annually. 90% of books from first-time authors. Accepts mss through agents or authors. SUBSIDY PUBLISHES 50%; does print-on-demand and offset. Reprints books. Any length; no less than 4 pages. **Royalty; no advance.** Publication within 2 mos. Considers simultaneous submissions. Responds in 1 mo. Prefers NKJV or NIV. Guidelines by e-mail/website; no catalog.

Nonfiction: Complete ms; phone/e-query OK. Any topic.

Fiction: Complete ms; phone/e-query OK. Any genre, for all ages.

Photos/Artwork: Accepts freelance photos for book covers; considers queries from freelance artists.

FRUITBEARER PUBLISHING LLC, PO Box 777, Georgetown DE 19947. (302) 856-6649. Fax (302) 856-7742. E-mail: cfa@candyabbott.com or through website: www.fruitbearer.com. Candy Abbott, mng. partner. Offers editing services and advice for self-publishers. Publishes 5-10 titles/yr.; hardcover, picture books. Receives 10-20 submissions annually. 90% of books from first-time authors. SUBSIDY PUBLISHES 100%. No reprints. Average first printing 500-5,000. Publication within 1-6 mos. Responds in 3 mos. Guidelines by mail/e-mail; brochure for #10 SAE/1 stamp.

Nonfiction: Proposal/2 chapters; phone/fax/e-query OK.

Fiction: For all ages.

Also Does: Pamphlets, booklets, tracts.

Photos: Accepts freelance photos for book covers.

Tips: "Accepting limited submissions."

GRACE ACRES PRESS, PO Box 22, Larkspur CO 80118. (303) 681-9995. Fax (303) 681-9996. E-mail: info@GraceAcresPress.com. Website: www.GraceAcresPress.com. Grace Acres, Inc. Anne R. Fenske, ed./pub. A conservative publisher with an emphasis on dispensational theology. Publishes 4-6 titles/yr.; hardcover, trade paperbacks, digital. Receives 50-100 submissions annually. 80-90% of books from first-time authors. Accepts mss through agents or authors. SUBSIDY PUBLISHER. Reprints books. **Royalty 10-15% on net; no advance.** Average first printing 1,500-2,500. Publication within 6 mos. Considers simultaneous submissions. Responds in 3 mos. Guidelines by e-mail; free catalog.

Nonfiction: Query first; e-query OK. Requires accepted mss on disk.

Artwork: Open to queries from freelance artists.

Tips: "Most open to a book with a built-in audience/buyer; i.e., speaker, textbook."

HALO PUBLISHING INTL., 1031 Cherry Spring, AP #726, Houston TX 77038. (877) 705-9647. E-mail: contact@halopublishing.com. Website: www.halopublishing.com. www.facebook.com /HaloPublishing. Twitter: @halopublishing. V. S. Grenier, chief ed. Publishes unique subject matter. Publishes 75-100 titles/yr.; hardcover, trade paperbacks. Receives 600-1,000 submissions annually. 99% of books from first-time authors. **Royalty 95%; no advance.** Publication within 2 mos. Considers simultaneous submissions. Responds in 1 mo. Guidelines by e-mail/website; no catalog.

Nonfiction: Proposal/3 chapters; phone/e-query OK.

Fiction: Proposal/3 chapters; phone/e-query OK. For all ages.

Special Needs: Educational books.

Artwork: Open to queries from freelance artists.

MARKETINGNEWAUTHORS.COM, 2910 E. Eisenhower Pkwy., Ann Arbor MI 48108. Toll-free (800) 431-1579. (734) 975-0028. Fax (734) 973-9475. E-mail: info@marketingnewauthors.com or MarketingNewAuth@aol.com. Website: www.MarketingNewAuthors.com. Imprint of Robbie Dean Press. To primarily serve authors who wish to self-publish. Dr. Fairy C. Hayes-Scott, owner. 100% of books from first-time authors. Accepts mss through agents. SUBSIDY PUBLISHES 100%. Reprints books. Length flexible. Publication within 6 mos. Considers simultaneous submissions. Responds in 2-6 wks. Guidelines by e-mail/website (under "Self-Publishing with MANA"). Offers 7 different marketing plans; see website.

PORT HOLE PUBLICATIONS, 179 Laurel St., Florence OR 97439. (541) 902-9091. E-mail: info@ ellentraylor.com. Website: www.portholepublications.com. Ellen Traylor, ed./pub. A COOPERATIVE PUBLISHER requiring a financial investment on the part of the author, along with a standard contract and optional marketing package.

Nonfiction/Fiction: Query first.

Tips: "We are open to publishing family-friendly and/or Christian content books of any length or genre. We are especially open to thought-provoking books on being a Christian in this difficult world, terrific fiction, Christian philosophy, short-story collections, and poetry (no sermons, please)."

THE SALT WORKS, P.O. Box 37, Roseville CA 95678. (916) 784-0500. Fax (916) 773-7421. E-mail: books@publishersdesign.com. Website: www.publishersdesign.com. Division of Publishers Design Group Inc. Robert Brekke, pub.; submit to Project Manager. Seeks to demonstrate through books that God is sovereign, just, and merciful in all he does. Imprint: Salty's Books (children's—see separate listing), PDG, Humpback Books. Publishes 7-10 titles/yr.; hard cover, trade paperbacks, coffee-table books. Receives 100+ submissions annually. 90% of Christian books from first-time authors. No mss through agents. SUBSIDY PUBLISHES 95%. Offset and print-on-demand. Reprints books. Prefers 95,000-150,000 wds. **Rarely pays royalty of 7-12% on net; occasional advance.** Average first printing 1,500-5,000. Publication within 4-12 mos. Considers simultaneous submissions. Responds within 45 days. Prefers ESV/NASB/NKJV/NIV (in that order). Prospects must study publisher's web site labeled "Custom Publishing" along with all five case studies before contacting. After preliminary screening, prospect will be sent a Project Questionnaire and a Project Assessment will be performed for projects with strong concepts.

Nonfiction: E-query only first; after query & phone meeting, send proposal. Unsolicited mss returned unopened.

Fiction: E-query only first; after query & phone meeting, send proposal. Unsolicited mss returned unopened. For adults and children. "Looking for titles that help believers in exploring and facing common issues surrounding God's sovereignty, his grace and forgiveness, their own sin and idolatry, and the areas where pop culture has influenced the church. Characters are blatantly human."

Special Needs: Looking for titles that communicate a biblical Christian worldview without promoting overly simplistic, idealistic, or theoretical solutions to life's biggest questions; books that honestly show no timidity in addressing our humanness. Looking for manuscripts that demonstrate that society's problems are rooted in the personal and spiritual, not in the political, educational, moral, and financial realms.

Also Does: Board games and other specialty products: fitness products, art projects and products, interactive projects for children. Specializes in projects designed to build a person or organization into a brand in the marketplace. See publisher's "MarketByPublishing.com" division for details.

Photos/Artwork: Rarely accepts freelance photos for book covers; open to queries from freelance artists.

Tips: "Most open to books that look at the Christian experience through a realistic biblical and Reformed perspective. Books that address the Christian's real problems as a 'heart' problem—not a theological problem; not from a victim mind-set, not a mental or logical one; not from a perspective of merely needing another program, pep talk, or the latest rehash of formulas for victorious living. Books that show the author understands that unless God changes the heart and brings a person to repentance, there are no real and lasting answers."

This publisher serviced by ChristianManuscriptSubmissions.com.

SALVATION PUBLISHER AND MARKETING GROUP, PO Box 40860, Santa Barbara CA 93140. (805) 682-0316. Fax (call first). E-mail: opalmaedailey@aol.com. Wisdom Today Ministries. Opal Mae Dailey, ed-in-chief. We encourage, inspire, and educate; author has the choice to be involved as much or little as desired—which gives the opportunity to control income; personal coaching and collective marketing available. Publishes 5-7 titles/yr.; hardcover, trade paperbacks, mass-market paperbacks. 60% of books from first-time authors. No mss through agents. SUBSIDY PUBLISHES 80%; does print-on-demand. Reprints books. Prefers 96-224 pgs. Average first printing 1,000. Publication within 3-4 mos. No simultaneous submissions. Accepts requested ms on disk or by e-mail (not attachments). Responds in 1 mo. Prefers KJV. Guidelines (also by e-mail).

Nonfiction: Query only first; phone/fax/e-query OK.

Tips: "Turning taped messages into book form for pastors is a specialty of ours. We do not accept any manuscript that we would be ashamed to put our name on."

STONEHOUSE INK, (208) 514-6631. E-mail: stonehousepress@hotmail.com. Website: www .stonehouseink.net. Clean-fiction imprint of Ampelon Press (www.ampelonpublishing.com). Aaron Patterson, ed./pub. Specializing in thrillers, mystery, young adult, paranormal, and out-of-print titles. Find on Facebook and Twitter @StoneHouseInk.

STRONG TOWER PUBLISHING, PO Box 973, Milesburg PA 16853. E-mail: strongtowerpubs@aol .com. Website: www.strongtowerpublishing.com. Heidi L. Nigro, pub. Specializes in eschatology and books that challenge readers to think more deeply about their faith and scriptural truths; must be biblically responsible, doctrinally defensible, and consistent with their statement of faith. Publishes 1-2 titles/yr.; trade paperbacks. 50% of books from first-time authors. No mss through agents. Reprints books. PRINT-ON-DEMAND 100%. **Royalty 25% of net; no advance.** Average first printing 50. Publication within 3-4 mos. Guidelines/information/prices on website.

Nonfiction: Query. Eschatology.

Tips: "We recommend that all first-time authors have their manuscripts professionally edited. We will consider putting first-time authors into print, but by invitation only. That invitation comes only after the manuscript has been thoroughly evaluated and we have discussed the pros and cons of our unique on-demand publishing model with the author."

TATE PUBLISHING & ENTERPRISES LLC, Tate Publishing Bldg., 127 E. Trade Center Ter., Mustang OK 73064-4421. Toll-free (888) 361-9473. Fax (405) 376-4401. E-mail: publish@tatepublishing .com. Website: www.tatepublishing.com. Dr. Richard Tate, founder and chairman of the board. Owns and operates their own, state-of-the-art printing plant facility. Publishes 120 titles/yr.; hardcover, trade paperbacks, mass-market paperbacks. Receives 60,000-75,000 unsolicited contacts annually. 60% of books from first-time authors. Accepts mss through agents. SUBSIDY LIKELY. First-time authors may be asked to contribute $3,990 if they need marketing and a publicist. The retainer is refunded to the author once the book sells 1,000 copies. No print-on-demand. Accepts reprints. Prefers 115,000 wds. **Royalty 15-40% of net; negotiable author cash advances if the author meets minimum requirements.** Average first printing 5,000. Publication within 4-6 mos. Considers simultaneous submissions. Responds in 3-6 wks. Accepts submissions by e-mail or US mail. Any Bible version. Guidelines by mail/e-mail/website; free catalog.

Nonfiction: Proposal with synopsis & any number of chapters, or complete ms; phone/fax/e-query OK. Any topic. "Looking for books that sell."

Fiction: Proposal with synopsis & any number of chapters or complete ms; phone/fax/ e-query OK. For all ages. Any genre.

Ethnic Books: For all ethnic markets.

Artwork: Has 31 full-time artists on staff; open to queries from freelance artists.

Tips: "We invest resources in every work we accept, and accept first-time authors."

TRUTH BOOK PUBLISHERS, 824 Bills Rd., Franklin IL 62638. (217) 675-2191. (217) 675-2050. E-mail: truthbookpublishers@yahoo.com. Website: www.truthbookpublishers.com. JaNell Lyle, ed. Publishes 75 titles/yr. Receives 100 submissions annually. 75% of books from first-time authors. Accepts mss through agents. Prefers 360 pgs. Average first run 100–500. Publication within 2 mo. Responds within 2 weeks. Guidelines by e-mail/website.

Nonfiction: Send book proposal with 3 sample chapters.

Fiction: Send book proposal with 3 sample chapters.

Tips: "We are missionary minded and desire to help the body of Christ mature."

*WESTBOW PRESS, 1663 Liberty Dr., Bloomington IN 47403. Toll-free (866) 928-1240. Website: www.westbowpress.com. Subsidy division of Thomas Nelson Publishers. Kevin A. Gray, news media contact. Estab. 2009. Does print-on-demand and digital formats. Fill out online form to receive information on their publishing program. Guidelines on website (click on "FAQ").

WINEPRESS PUBLISHING, PO Box 428, 1730 Railroad St., Enumclaw WA 98022. Toll-free (800) 326-4674. (360) 802-9758. Fax (360) 802-9992. E-mail: acquisitions@winepresspublishing.com. Website: www.winepresspublishing.com. Blog: www.winepressofwords.com. The WinePress Group. Submit via website, or call acquisitions department. To ensure the highest quality and service, WP uses custom online software that allows you to track your book project from beginning to end. Imprints: WinePress Publishing, WinePress Kids (children's books), Annotation Press (general market, family friendly), UpWrite Books (writers resources), and WinePress POD. Publishes 200-300 titles/yr.; hardcover, trade paperbacks, mass-market paperbacks, coffee-table books. Receives 700+ submissions annually. 70% of books from first-time authors. Accepts mss through agents. BOOK PACKAGER/CUSTOM PUBLISHER 100%. Reprints books. Lengths range from 1,000-150,000 wds. or 16-1,300 pgs. **Author pays production costs, keeps all profit from sales.** Average first printing 2,500 (1,000 min.). Publication in 6-9 mos. Considers simultaneous submissions. Responds in 48 hrs. Accepts requested ms by email, hardcopy, or disk. Any Bible version. Guidelines by e-mail or on website; free catalog.

Nonfiction: Complete ms; e-query OK. Publishes all family-friendly, biblically oriented topics.

Fiction: Complete ms. Publishes all family-friendly, biblically oriented material and genres. For all ages.

Print-On-Demand: "WinePress POD benefits from full distribution and a bookstore return service as POD is handled with the same high quality editorial and design standards as offset printing. Easy upgrade to offset print runs available."

Also Does: Audiobooks, e-books, multimedia, website design & hosting, blogs, DVD production, CD/book packages, manuals, genuine-leather Bibles, full-color children's books, board books, full publicity and marketing campaigns, book trailers, marketing consultation, blog and social network consultations, and advertising campaigns.

Photos/Artwork: Accepts copyright-free photos and artwork.

Tips: "WinePress has offered definitive publishing solutions since 1991. We partner with authors through a wide range of services provided by our in-house departments, including production, design, video, multimedia, Internet, publicity, promotions, warehousing fulfillment, and distribution departments. To ensure the highest quality, everything is coordinated by our unique online Co-C.A.P.T.A.I.N. software and friendly staff. We do not accept all manuscripts for publication and advise potential authors to first review our doctrinal standards on our website. Free tips and guides are available at our blog: www.winepressof words.com."

This publisher serviced by ChristianManuscriptSubmissions.com.

***WORD ALIVE PRESS,** 131 Cordite Rd., Winnipeg MB R3W 1S1, Canada. Toll-free (866) 967-3782. (204) 777-7100. Toll-free fax (800) 352-9272. (204) 669-0947. E-mail: publishing@wordalive press.ca. Website: www.wordalivepress.ca. C. Schmidt, publishing consultant. SUBSIDY PUBLISHER. Offset printing, print-on-demand, editing services, sales, marketing and distribution services, website development, professional custom cover design, Adobe and Kindle e-books, audio-books, and MP3 book files. Guidelines and price list available. Request their "Free Guide to Publishing" brochure from their website.

Nonfiction/Fiction: All genres. Fiction for all ages.

ZOË LIFE PUBLISHING, 9282 General Dr., Suite 150, Plymouth MI 48170. (734) 254-1043. Fax (734) 254-1063. E-mail: info@zoelifepub.com. Website: www.zoelifepub.com. Zoë Life Industries LLC. Sabrina Adams, ed. Books that help people live better, more productive lives while growing closer to God. Imprints: Pen of a Ready Writer, Titus, Business Builders. Publishes 40 titles/yr.; hardcover, trade paperbacks, mass-market paperbacks, coffee-table books, digital. 50+% of books from first-time authors. Accepts mss through authors or agents. SUBSIDY PUBLISHES 50%; no print-on-demand or reprints. Length open. **Royalty 10-25% of net; usually no advance.** Average first printing 3,000. Publication within 12 mos. Responds in 21-40 days. Open on Bible version. Guidelines by e-mail/website; free catalog.

Nonfiction: Proposal/ 3 chapters + final chapter; phone/fax/e-query OK.

Fiction: Proposal/ 3 chapters + final chapter; phone/fax/e-query OK. For all ages; all genres. Complete mss for picture books.

Special Needs: Children's books, tweens, women's issues, Bible studies, and Christian living.

Photos: Accepts freelance photos for book covers.

4

Distributors

CHRISTIAN BOOK/MUSIC/GIFT DISTRIBUTORS

*AMAZON ADVANTAGE PROGRAM, Go to Amazon.com, scroll down to "Features & Services," click on "Selling with Amazon," and on the drop-down menu, click on "Advantage Program" in left-hand column. This is the site to contact if you want Amazon to distribute your book.

B. BROUGHTON CO., LTD., 322 Consumers Rd., North York ON M2J 1P8, Canada. Toll-free (800) 268-4449 (Canada only). (416) 690-4777. Fax (416) 690-5357. E-mail: sales@bbroughton.com. Website: www.bbroughton.com. Brian Broughton, owner. Canadian distributor. Distributes books, DVDs, gifts, greeting cards. Does not distribute self-published books.

*CBA MAILING LISTS OF CHRISTIAN BOOKSTORES, 9240 Explorer Dr., Ste. 200, Colorado Springs CO 80920. (719) 265-9895. Fax (719) 272-3510. E-mail: info@cbaonline.org. Website: www.cbaonline.org. Contact: info@cbaonline.org. Available for rental. Three different lists available, including nonmember stores, 4,700 addresses ($249); member stores, 1,275 addresses ($599); or a combined list of all stores, 5,800 addresses ($699). Prices and numbers available subject to change. Call toll-free (800) 252-1950 for full details.

*CHRISTIAN BOOK DISTRIBUTORS, PO Box 7000, Peabody MA 01961-7000. Toll-free (800) 247-4784. (978) 977-5000. Fax (978) 977-5010. E-mail through website: www.christianbooks.com. Does not distribute self-published books.

QUALITY BOOKS, 1003 W. Pines Rd., Oregon IL 61061. Toll-free (800) 323-4241. (815) 732-4450. Fax (815) 732-4499. E-mail: publisher.relations@quality-books.com. Website: www.qualitybooks .com. Distributes small press books, audios, DVDs, CD-ROMs, and Blu-ray to public libraries. Distributes self-published books; asks for 1 copy of your book.

WORD ALIVE, INC., 131 Cordite Rd., Winnipeg MB R3W 1S1, Canada. Toll-free (800) 665-1468. (204) 667-1400. Toll-free fax (800) 352-9272. (204) 669-0947. E-mail: orderdesk@wordalive.ca. Website: www.wordalive.ca. Distributor of Christian books and products into the Canadian market. Contact: Rosa Peters. Contact by e-mail.

PART 2
Periodical Publishers

5

Topical Listings of Periodicals

Study the periodicals in the primary/alphabetical listings (as well as their writer's guidelines and sample copies) and select the most likely targets for the piece you are writing.

Most ideas can be written for more than one periodical if you slant them to the needs of different audiences. Have a target periodical and audience in mind before you start writing. Each topic is divided by age group/audience.

If the magazine requires a query letter, write that first, and then follow their suggestions if they give you a go-ahead to write the article.

APOLOGETICS
ADULT/GENERAL
Bible Advocate
Brink Magazine
CBN.com
Christianity Today
Christian Online
Christian Ranchman
Christian Research
Christian Standard
Columbia
Live
Lookout
Manna
Movieguide
On Mission
Our Sunday Visitor
Perspectives
Priscilla Papers
Seek

CHILDREN
SHINE brightly

DAILY DEVOTIONALS
Brink Magazine
Penned from the Heart

MISSIONS
Studio

PASTORS/LEADERS
Christian Century
Enrichment
Small Groups.com

TEEN/YOUNG ADULT
Boundless Webzine
Young Salvationist

ARTS/ENTERTAINMENT
ADULT/GENERAL
Genuine Motivation
Guide

CHILDREN
Guide

PASTORS/LEADERS
Brink Magazine

TEEN/YOUNG ADULT
Genuine Motivation
Single! Young
   Christian Woman
Susie

WOMEN
Single! Young Christian Woman

BEAUTY/FASHION
ADULT/GENERAL
Genuine Motivation
Guide

CHILDREN
Guide

TEEN/YOUNG ADULT
Genuine Motivation
Single! Young
   Christian Woman
Susie

WOMEN
Single! Young Christian Woman

BIBLE STUDIES
ADULT/GENERAL
CBN.com
Christian Online
Christian Ranchman
Christian Research
Christian Standard
Church Herald
   & Holiness
Columbia
Eternal Ink
Gem
Kyria
Mature Years
Our Sunday Visitor
Perspectives
Priscilla Papers
Seek
War Cry

CHILDREN
SHINE brightly

CHRISTIAN EDUCATION/ LIBRARY
Group

PASTORS/LEADERS
Sharing the Practice
SmallGroups.com

WOMEN
Virtuous Woman

BOOK EXCERPTS
ADULT/GENERAL
CBN.com
Charisma
Chicken Soup Books
Christianity Today
Christian Retailing
Columbia
Genuine Motivation
Indian Life
Power for Living
Priscilla Papers

PASTORS/LEADERS
Christian Century
Ministry Today

TEEN/YOUNG ADULT
Boundless Webzine
Genuine Motivation
Single! Young Christian Woman

WOMEN
Share
Single! Young Christian Woman
Virtuous Woman

WRITERS
Freelance Writer's Report
Writer

BOOK REVIEWS
ADULT/GENERAL
America
Brink Magazine
CBN.com
Charisma
Christian Courier/Canada
Christianity Today
Christian Journal
Christian Ranchman
Christian Research
Christian Retailing
Eternal Ink
Faith Today
Genuine Motivation
Home Times
Indian Life
Movieguide
Our Sunday Visitor
Prairie Messenger
Priscilla Papers

Studio
Testimony
Time of Singing
Weavings

CHILDREN
SHINE brightly

CHRISTIAN EDUCATION/ LIBRARY
Church Libraries
Group

MISSIONS
Operation Reveille

PASTORS/LEADERS
Christian Century
Diocesan Dialogue
Enrichment
Leadership
Ministry Today
Sharing the Practice

TEEN/YOUNG ADULT
Boundless Webzine
Genuine Motivation
Single! Young Christian Woman

WOMEN
Dabbling Mum
Glory & Strength
Share
Single! Young Christian Woman
Virtuous Woman

WRITERS
Adv. Christian Writer
Christian Communicator
Fellowscript
Writer

CANADIAN/FOREIGN MARKETS
ADULT/GENERAL
Canada Lutheran
Canadian Lutheran
Christian Courier/Canada
Creation
Faith Today
Indian Life
Messenger
Prairie Messenger

Studio
Testimony

DAILY DEVOTIONALS
Rejoice!

WRITERS
Fellowscript

CELEBRITY PIECES
ADULT/GENERAL
American Tract
Angels on Earth
Brink Magazine
CBN.com
Christian Journal
Christian Online
Christian Ranchman
Genuine Motivation
Guideposts
Home Times
Indian Life
Kindred Spirit
Movieguide
Our Sunday Visitor
Power for Living
Priority!
War Cry

CHILDREN
SHINE brightly

PASTORS/LEADERS
Ministry Today

TEEN/YOUNG ADULT
Genuine Motivation
Single! Young Christian Woman
Young Salvationist

WOMEN
Single! Young Christian Woman
Virtuous Woman

WRITERS
Writer's Chronicle

CHRISTIAN BUSINESS
ADULT/GENERAL
Angels on Earth
Brink Magazine
CBA Retailers
CBN.com

Christian Courier/Canada
Christian News NW
Christian Online
Christian Ranchman
Christian Retailing
Faith Today
Gem
Genuine Motivation
Guideposts
Home Times
Lookout
Manna
Our Sunday Visitor
Power for Living
War Cry

PASTORS/LEADERS
InSite

TEEN/YOUNG ADULT
Boundless Webzine
Genuine Motivation
Single! Young
    Christian Woman

WOMEN
Dabbling Mum
Single! Young Christian Woman
Virtuous Woman

CHRISTIAN EDUCATION
ADULT/GENERAL
America
Christian Courier/Canada
Christian Examiner
Christian Home & School
Christianity Today
Christian News NW
Christian Online
Christian Ranchman
Christian Retailing
Christian Standard
Columbia
Eternal Ink
Faith Today
Gem
Genuine Motivation
Guide
Home Times
Live
Lookout

Manna
Movieguide
Our Sunday Visitor
Penned from the Heart
Perspectives
Presbyterians Today
Seek
Testimony
War Cry

CHILDREN
Guide
JuniorWay

CHRISTIAN EDUCATION/
LIBRARY
Group

PASTORS/LEADERS
Christian Century
Enrichment
Ministry Today
SmallGroups.com

TEEN/YOUNG ADULT
Boundless Webzine
Genuine Motivation

WOMEN
Right to the Heart
Share

CHRISTIAN LIVING
ADULT/GENERAL
America
American Tract
Angels on Earth
Bible Advocate
Brink Magazine
Canada Lutheran
Catholic New York
CBN.com
Charisma
Chicken Soup Books
Christian Courier/Canada
Christian Examiner
Christian Home & School
Christianity Today
Christian Journal
Christian Online
Christian Quarterly
Christian Ranchman

Christian Research
Christian Standard
Church Herald
   & Holiness
Columbia
Eternal Ink
Faith Today
Fit Christian
Gem
Gems of Truth
Genuine Motivation
Good News
Guide
Guideposts
Home Times
Indian Life
Keys to Living
Kyria
Leaves
Light & Life
Live
Lookout
Lutheran Digest
Manna
Mature Living
Mature Years
Men of the Cross
Our Sunday Visitor
Penned from the Heart
Pentecostal Evangel
Perspectives
Power for Living
Presbyterians Today
Seek
Storyteller
SW Kansas Faith
Testimony
Vision
Vista
War Cry

CHILDREN
Focus/Clubhouse Jr.
Guide
JuniorWay
Partners
Pockets

CHRISTIAN EDUCATION/
LIBRARY
Group

DAILY DEVOTIONALS
Brink Magazine
Penned from the Heart

PASTORS/LEADERS
Christian Century

TEEN/YOUNG ADULT
Boundless Webzine
Genuine Motivation
Single! Young Christian Woman
Young Salvationist

WOMEN
Glory & Strength
MomSense
P31 Woman
Right to the Heart
Share
Single! Young Christian Woman
Virtuous Woman
Women of the Cross

CHURCH GROWTH
ADULT/GENERAL
America
Christian Examiner
Christian News NW
Christian Online
Christian Quarterly
Christian Standard
Columbia
Gem
Genuine Motivation
Good News
Live
Lookout
Our Sunday Visitor
Penned from the Heart
Presbyterians Today
Seek
Testimony

CHRISTIAN EDUCATION/
LIBRARY
Group

MISSIONS
Operation Reveille

PASTORS/LEADERS
Christian Century
Enrichment

Growth Points
Leadership
Ministry Today
Sharing the Practice

TEEN/YOUNG ADULT
Genuine Motivation
Single! Young
    Christian Woman

WOMEN
Share
Single! Young
    Christian Woman

CHURCH HISTORY
ADULT/GENERAL
America
CBN.com
Christian Online
Christian Standard
Columbia
Faith Today
Genuine Motivation
Guide
Lookout
Movieguide
Our Sunday Visitor
Presbyterians Today
Priscilla Papers

CHRISTIAN EDUCATION/
LIBRARY
Group

DAILY DEVOTIONALS
Penned from the Heart

MISSIONS
Operation Reveille

PASTORS/LEADERS
Christian Century
Enrichment
Leadership
Sharing the Practice

TEEN/YOUNG ADULT
Boundless Webzine
Genuine Motivation

WOMEN
Share

CHURCH LIFE
ADULT/GENERAL
America
Bible Advocate
Canada Lutheran
CBN.com
Christian Home
    & School
Christianity Today
Christian Journal
Christian News NW
Christian Online
Christian Standard
Columbia
Eternal Ink
Faith Today
Gem
Good News
Home Times
Leaves
Light & Life
Live
Lookout
Our Sunday Visitor
Penned from the Heart
Pentecostal Evangel
Presbyterians Today
Priscilla Papers
Seek
Testimony
War Cry

CHRISTIAN EDUCATION/
LIBRARY
Group

DAILY DEVOTIONALS
Penned from the Heart

PASTORS/LEADERS
Christian Century
Enrichment
Leadership
Ministry Today
Parish Liturgy
Priest
Sharing the Practice

TEEN/YOUNG ADULT
Boundless Webzine

WOMEN
Share

CHURCH MANAGEMENT
ADULT/GENERAL
America
Canada Lutheran
Christian News NW
Christian Online
Christian Standard
Faith Today
Gem
Lookout
Our Sunday Visitor
Priscilla Papers

CHRISTIAN EDUCATION/ LIBRARY
Group

DAILY DEVOTIONALS
Penned from the Heart

PASTORS/LEADERS
Enrichment
Growth Points
Leadership
Ministry Today
Sharing the Practice

WOMEN
Share

CHURCH OUTREACH
ADULT/GENERAL
America
Bible Advocate
Canada Lutheran
CBN.com
Christian Home & School
Christian News NW
Christian Online
Christian Research
Christian Standard
Columbia
Eternal Ink
Faith Today
Gem
Good News
Home Times
Light & Life
Lookout
On Mission
Our Sunday Visitor
Presbyterians Today

Priority!
Priscilla Papers
Seek
Testimony

CHRISTIAN EDUCATION/ LIBRARY
Group

PASTORS/LEADERS
Christian Century
Enrichment
Growth Points
Leadership
Ministry Today
Sharing the Practice
Small Groups.com

WOMEN
Share

CHURCH TRADITIONS
ADULT/GENERAL
America
Brink Magazine
Canada Lutheran
CBN.com
Christian Examiner
Christian Online
Christian Research
Christian Standard
Columbia
Eternal Ink
Faith Today
Gem
Light & Life
Our Sunday Visitor
Perspectives
Presbyterians Today
Priscilla Papers
Testimony

CHRISTIAN EDUCATION/ LIBRARY
Group

DAILY DEVOTIONALS
Penned from the Heart

PASTORS/LEADERS
Christian Century
Leadership
Ministry Today

Parish Liturgy
Sharing the Practice

WOMEN
Share

CONTROVERSIAL ISSUES
ADULT/GENERAL
American Tract
Bible Advocate
Brink Magazine
Canada Lutheran
CBN.com
Christian Courier/Canada
Christian Examiner
Christian Home & School
Christianity Today
Christian Online
Christian Standard
Columbia
Eternal Ink
Faith Today
Genuine Motivation
Good News
Home Times
Indian Life
Light & Life
Live
Lookout
Manna
Movieguide
Now What?
Our Sunday Visitor
Perspectives
Prairie Messenger
Priscilla Papers
War Cry

CHILDREN
Skipping Stones

CHRISTIAN EDUCATION/ LIBRARY
Group

MISSIONS
Operation Reveille

PASTORS/LEADERS
Christian Century
Enrichment
InSite
Ministry Today

TEEN/YOUNG ADULT
Boundless Webzine
Genuine Motivation
Single! Young Christian Woman
Young Salvationist

WOMEN
Glory & Strength
Single! Young Christian Woman

CRAFTS
ADULT/GENERAL
Christian Online
Guide
Indian Life
Mature Living

CHILDREN
Focus/Clubhouse
Focus/Clubhouse Jr.
Guide
JuniorWay
Pockets
SHINE brightly

WOMEN
MomSense
P31 Woman
Virtuous Woman

CREATION SCIENCE
ADULT/GENERAL
Answers Magazine
Bible Advocate
CBN.com
Christian Courier/Canada
Christian Examiner
Christian Research
Creation Illust.
Guide
Home Times
Indian Life
Light & Life
Live
Lookout
War Cry

CHILDREN
Guide

TEEN/YOUNG ADULT
Boundless Webzine
Young Salvationist

CULTS/OCCULT
ADULT/GENERAL
American Tract
Bible Advocate
CBN.com
Christian Examiner
Christian Research
Guide
Light & Life
Lookout
Now What?

CHILDREN
Guide

PASTORS/LEADERS
Ministry Today

TEEN/YOUNG ADULT
Boundless Webzine
Young Salvationist

CURRENT/SOCIAL ISSUES
ADULT/GENERAL
American Tract
Bible Advocate
Brink Magazine
Canada Lutheran
Catholic New York
CBN.com
Christian Courier/Canada
Christian Examiner
Christian Home & School
Christianity Today
Christian Journal
Christian Online
Christian Ranchman
Christian Research
Christian Standard
Columbia
Faith Today
Gem
Genuine Motivation
Good News
Guide
Home Times
Indian Life
Light & Life
Live
Lookout
Manna
Movieguide

Now What?
Our Sunday Visitor
Perspectives
Prairie Messenger
Priority!
Priscilla Papers
Seek
Storyteller
War Cry

CHILDREN
Guide
JuniorWay
SHINE brightly
Skipping Stones

CHRISTIAN EDUCATION/ DAILY DEVOTIONALS
Brink Magazine
Penned from the Heart

MISSIONS
Operation Reveille

PASTORS/LEADERS
Christian Century
Enrichment
InSite
Leadership
Ministry Today

TEEN/YOUNG ADULT
Boundless Webzine
Genuine Motivation
Single! Young Christian Woman
Young Salvationist

WOMEN
Glory & Strength
Single! Young Christian Woman
Virtuous Woman

DEATH/DYING
ADULT/GENERAL
America
American Tract
Bible Advocate
Brink Magazine
CBN.com
Chicken Soup Books
Christianity Today
Christian Online
Christian Quarterly

Christian Ranchman
Columbia
Gem
Genuine Motivation
Guide
Guideposts
Indian Life
Light & Life
Live
Lookout
Now What?
Our Sunday Visitor
Prairie Messenger
Presbyterians Today
Seek
Storyteller
Testimony
War Cry

CHILDREN
Guide
Skipping Stones

DAILY DEVOTIONALS
Penned from the Heart

PASTORS/LEADERS
Christian Century
Enrichment
InSite
Leadership
Sharing the Practice

TEEN/YOUNG ADULT
Boundless Webzine
Genuine Motivation
Single! Young Christian Woman

WOMEN
Glory & Strength
Single! Young Christian Woman
Virtuous Woman

DEPRESSION
ADULT/GENERAL
Bible Advocate
Genuine Motivation
Now What?

WOMEN
Brink Magazine
Glory & Strength
Single! Young Christian Woman

DEVOTIONALS/ MEDITATIONS
ADULT/GENERAL
America
CBN.com
Chicken Soup Books
Christian Home & School
Christian Journal
Christian Online
Christian Quarterly
Christian Ranchman
Columbia
Eternal Ink
Gem
Genuine Motivation
Good News
Keys to Living
Kyria
Leaves
Live
Lutheran Digest
Mature Living
Penned from the Heart
Pentecostal Evangel
Perspectives
Vision
War Cry
Weavings
WorshipMinistryDevotions.com

CHILDREN
Keys for Kids
Pockets

CHRISTIAN EDUCATION/ LIBRARY
Group

DAILY DEVOTIONALS
Brink Magazine
Christian Devotions
Daily Dev. for Deaf
Light from the Word
Penned from the Heart
Quiet Hour
Rejoice!
Secret Place
Upper Room
Word in Season

PASTORS/LEADERS
Ministry Today

TEEN/YOUNG ADULT
Single! Young Christian Woman
Take Five Plus

WOMEN
Dabbling Mum
Glory & Strength
Single! Young Christian Woman
Virtuous Woman

WRITERS
Fellowscript

DISCIPLESHIP
ADULT/GENERAL
Bible Advocate
Canada Lutheran
CBN.com
Christian Journal
Christian Online
Christian Ranchman
Christian Research
Christian Standard
Columbia
Eternal Ink
Faith Today
Gem
Genuine Motivation
Good News
Guide
Kyria
Light & Life
Live
Lookout
Manna
Men of the Cross
Movieguide
Penned from the Heart
Perspectives
Seek
War Cry

CHILDREN
Guide
SHINE brightly

CHRISTIAN EDUCATION/ LIBRARY
Group

DAILY DEVOTIONALS
Brink Magazine
Penned from the Heart

PASTORS/LEADERS
Christian Century
Enrichment
Growth Points
InSite
Leadership
SmallGroups.com

TEEN/YOUNG ADULT
Boundless Webzine
Single! Young Christian Woman
Young Salvationist

WOMEN
Glory & Strength
P31 Woman
Single! Young Christian Woman
Virtuous Woman
Women of the Cross

DIVORCE
ADULT/GENERAL
American Tract
Angels on Earth
Bible Advocate
CBN.com
Christian Examiner
Christian Online
Christian Quarterly
Christian Ranchman
Columbia
Gem
Guide
Guideposts
Home Times
Kyria
Light & Life
Live
Lookout
Manna
Our Sunday Visitor
Perspectives
Priscilla Papers
Seek
Storyteller
War Cry

CHILDREN
Guide

PASTORS/LEADERS
Christian Century

TEEN/YOUNG ADULT
Young Salvationist

WOMEN
Glory & Strength

DOCTRINAL
ADULT/GENERAL
Bible Advocate
CBN.com
Christian Online
Christian Research
Christian Standard
Guide
Movieguide
Our Sunday Visitor
Perspectives
Priscilla Papers

CHILDREN
Guide

PASTORS/LEADERS
Sharing the Practice

DVD REVIEWS
ADULT/GENERAL
Genuine Motivation

WOMEN
Brink Magazine
Glory & Strength
Single! Young Christian Woman

ECONOMICS
ADULT/GENERAL
America
CBA Retailers
CBN.com
Christian Online
Christian Ranchman
Christian Retailing
Genuine Motivation
Home Times
Light & Life
Live
Movieguide
Our Sunday Visitor
Perspectives

TEEN/YOUNG ADULT
Boundless Webzine
Single! Young Christian Woman

WOMEN
Single! Young Christian Woman

ENCOURAGEMENT
ADULT/GENERAL
Bible Advocate
Bridal Guides
Brink Magazine
CBN.com
Christian Home & School
Christian Journal
Christian Online
Christian Quarterly
Christian Ranchman
Christian Standard
Gems of Truth
Genuine Motivation
Home Times
Indian Life
Keys to Living
Kyria
Leaves
Light & Life
Live
Lookout
Lutheran Digest
Manna
Mature Living
Men of the Cross
Penned from the Heart
Seek
Storyteller
Vision
Vista

CHILDREN
SHINE brightly
Skipping Stones

DAILY DEVOTIONALS
Brink Magazine
Penned from the Heart

TEEN/YOUNG ADULT
Boundless Webzine
Genuine Motivation
Single! Young Christian Woman
Young Salvationist

WOMEN
Glory & Strength
P31 Woman

Single! Young Christian Woman
Virtuous Woman
Women of the Cross

WRITERS
Christian Communicator
Fellowscript

ENVIRONMENTAL ISSUES
ADULT/GENERAL
America
Bible Advocate
Brink Magazine
Christian Courier/Canada
Christian Online
Creation Illust.
Faith Today
Genuine Motivation
Guide
Light & Life
Lookout
Our Sunday Visitor
Perspectives
Prairie Messenger
Seek
War Cry

CHILDREN
Guide
Pockets
SHINE brightly
Skipping Stones
PASTORS/LEADERS
    Christian Century
InSite

TEEN/YOUNG ADULT
Boundless Webzine
Single! Young Christian Woman
Young Salvationist

WOMEN
Share
Single! Young Christian Woman

ESSAYS
ADULT/GENERAL
America
Chicken Soup Books
Christian Courier/Canada
Christianity Today
Christian Online

Columbia
Faith Today
Gem
Genuine Motivation
Lutheran Digest
Our Sunday Visitor
Seek
Storyteller
War Cry

CHILDREN
Skipping Stones

PASTORS/LEADERS
Christian Century
Priest

TEEN/YOUNG ADULT
Genuine Motivation
Single! Young Christian Woman

WOMEN
Dabbling Mum
Single! Young Christian Woman

WRITERS
Adv. Christian Writer
Christian Communicator
Writer
Writer's Chronicle
Writer's Digest

ETHICS
ADULT/GENERAL
America
Angels on Earth
Brink Magazine
CBN.com
Christian Courier/Canada
Christian Examiner
Christian Online
Christian Ranchman
Christian Research
Christian Standard
Columbia
Faith Today
Genuine Motivation
Light & Life
Live
Lookout
Manna
Movieguide

Our Sunday Visitor
Perspectives
Prairie Messenger
Priscilla Papers
Seek
War Cry

CHILDREN
Skipping Stones

DAILY DEVOTIONALS
Brink Magazine
Penned from the Heart

PASTORS/LEADERS
Christian Century
Enrichment
Ministry Today
Sharing the Practice

TEEN/YOUNG ADULT
Boundless Webzine
Genuine Motivation
Single! Young Christian Woman
Young Salvationist

WOMEN
Single! Young Christian Woman

ETHNIC/CULTURAL PIECES
ADULT/GENERAL
America
Brink Magazine
Canada Lutheran
CBA Retailers
CBN.com
Christian Courier/Canada
Christian Home & School
Christian Online
Columbia
Faith Today
Gem
Genuine Motivation
Good News
Guide
Indian Life
Light & Life
Live
Lookout
Manna
Movieguide

Our Sunday Visitor
Penned from the Heart
Prairie Messenger
Priscilla Papers
Seek
War Cry

CHILDREN
Guide
Skipping Stones

DAILY DEVOTIONALS
Brink Magazine
Penned from the Heart

MISSIONS
Operation Reveille

PASTORS/LEADERS
Christian Century
Enrichment
Ministry Today

TEEN/YOUNG ADULT
Boundless Webzine
Genuine Motivation
Single! Young Christian Woman
Young Salvationist

WOMEN
Single! Young Christian Woman

**EVANGELISM/
WITNESSING**
ADULT/GENERAL
America
American Tract
Bible Advocate
Brink Magazine
CBN.com
Christian Home & School
Christianity Today
Christian Online
Christian Ranchman
Christian Research
Christian Standard
Columbia
Faith Today
Gem
Genuine Motivation
Good News
Guide
Leaves

Light & Life
Live
Lookout
Manna
On Mission
Our Sunday Visitor
Penned from the Heart
Power for Living
Priority!
Seek
Testimony
War Cry

CHILDREN
Focus/Clubhouse Jr.
Guide
JuniorWay

*CHRISTIAN EDUCATION/
LIBRARY*
Group

DAILY DEVOTIONALS
Brink Magazine
Penned from the Heart

MISSIONS
Operation Reveille

PASTORS/LEADERS
Cook Partners
Enrichment
Growth Points
Leadership
Ministry Today
SmallGroups.com

TEEN/YOUNG ADULT
Boundless Webzine
Genuine Motivation
Single! Young Christian Woman
Young Salvationist

WOMEN
P31 Woman
Share
Single! Young Christian Woman

EXEGESIS
ADULT/GENERAL
Bible Advocate
CBN.com
Christian Ranchman
Christian Standard

Our Sunday Visitor
Perspectives
Priscilla Papers

PASTORS/LEADERS
Enrichment

TEEN/YOUNG ADULT
Boundless Webzine

FAITH
ADULT/GENERAL
America
Believers Bay
Bible Advocate
Brink Magazine
Canada Lutheran
CBN.com
Christian Courier/Canada
Christian Home & School
Christianity Today
Christian Journal
Christian Online
Christian Quarterly
Christian Research
Christian Retailing
Christian Standard
Church Herald & Holiness
Columbia
Eternal Ink
Gem
Genuine Motivation
Guide
Home Times
Indian Life
Kyria
Light & Life
Live
Lookout
Lutheran Digest
Manna
Now What?
Our Sunday Visitor
Penned from the Heart
Prairie Messenger
Priscilla Papers
Seek
SW Kansas Faith
Testimony
Vista
Weavings

CHILDREN
Focus/Clubhouse Jr.
Guide
JuniorWay
SHINE brightly

**CHRISTIAN EDUCATION/
LIBRARY**
Group

DAILY DEVOTIONALS
Brink Magazine
Penned from the Heart

PASTORS/LEADERS
Ministry Today
Plugged In
SmallGroups.com

TEEN/YOUNG ADULT
Boundless Webzine
Genuine Motivation
Single! Young Christian Woman
Young Salvationist

WOMEN
Glory & Strength
P31 Woman
Single! Young Christian Woman
Virtuous Woman
Women of the Cross

FAMILY LIFE
ADULT/GENERAL
America
Angels on Earth
Believers Bay
Brink Magazine
Canada Lutheran
CBN.com
Chicken Soup Books
Christian Courier/Canada
Christian Home & School
Christian Journal
Christian Online
Christian Quarterly
Christian Ranchman
Church Herald & Holiness
Columbia
Eternal Ink
Gem
Guide
Guideposts

Home Times
Indian Life
Keys to Living
Kyria
Live
Lookout
Lutheran Digest
Manna
Mature Years
Men of the Cross
Our Sunday Visitor
Penned from the Heart
Pentecostal Evangel
Power for Living
Prairie Messenger
Priscilla Papers
Seek
Storyteller
SW Kansas Faith
Testimony
Thriving Family
Vision
Vista
War Cry

CHILDREN
Focus/Clubhouse
Focus/Clubhouse Jr.
Guide
JuniorWay
Pockets

**CHRISTIAN EDUCATION/
LIBRARY**
Group

DAILY DEVOTIONALS
Penned from the Heart

PASTORS/LEADERS
Enrichment
InSite
Ministry Today

TEEN/YOUNG ADULT
Young Salvationist

WOMEN
Dabbling Mum
Glory & Strength
MomSense
P31 Woman
Share

Virtuous Woman
Women of the Cross

FEATURE ARTICLES
ADULT/GENERAL
Bible Advocate
Canada Lutheran
Columbia
Faith Today

**CHRISTIAN EDUCATION/
LIBRARY**
Seek

WOMEN
Brink Magazine
Glory & Strength

FILLERS: ANECDOTES
ADULT/GENERAL
Angels on Earth
Bridal Guides
Christian Journal
Christian Quarterly
Christian Ranchman
Church Herald & Holiness
Eternal Ink
Gem
Home Times
Lutheran Digest
Manna
Movieguide
Pentecostal Evangel
Vista
War Cry

CHILDREN
Skipping Stones

PASTORS/LEADERS
Enrichment
Leadership
Sharing the Practice

TEEN/YOUNG ADULT
Genuine Motivation
Single! Young
    Christian Woman
Young Salvationist

WOMEN
Glory & Strength
Right to the Heart

Single! Young
   Christian Woman
Virtuous Woman

WRITERS
Fellowscript
New Writer's Mag.

FILLERS: CARTOONS
ADULT/GENERAL
American Tract
Angels on Earth
Bridal Guides
Christian Journal
Christian Quarterly
Christian Ranchman
Gem
Guide
Home Times
Lutheran Digest
Mature Years
Movieguide
Power for Living
Presbyterians Today
Storyteller

CHILDREN
Guide
SHINE brightly
Skipping Stones

CHRISTIAN EDUCATION/
LIBRARY
Group

PASTORS/LEADERS
Christian Century
Diocesan Dialogue
Enrichment
Leadership
Priest
Sharing the Practice
SmallGroups.com

TEEN/YOUNG ADULT
Young Salvationist

WOMEN
Glory & Strength

WRITERS
New Writer's Mag.
Writer

FILLERS: FACTS
ADULT/GENERAL
Bridal Guides
Christian Ranchman
Gem
Home Times
Lutheran Digest
Movieguide
Pentecostal Evangel
Vista

MISSIONS
Boundless Webzine
Operation Reveille

PASTORS/LEADERS
Enrichment

TEEN/YOUNG ADULT
Young Salvationist

WOMEN
Glory & Strength
Virtuous Woman

WRITERS
New Writer's Mag.

FILLERS: GAMES
ADULT/GENERAL
Christian Ranchman
Gem
Guide
Movieguide

CHILDREN
Guide
Pockets
SHINE brightly

CHRISTIAN EDUCATION/
LIBRARY
Group

TEEN/YOUNG ADULT
Young Salvationist

FILLERS: IDEAS
ADULT/GENERAL
Bridal Guides
Christian Home
   & School
Christian Quarterly
Christian Ranchman

Gem
Home Times
Manna
Movieguide
Seek

CHRISTIAN EDUCATION/
LIBRARY
Group

PASTORS/LEADERS
Small Groups.com

WOMEN
P31 Woman
Right to the Heart
Virtuous Woman

FILLERS: JOKES
ADULT/GENERAL
Christian Journal
Christian Ranchman
Eternal Ink
Gem
Home Times
Lutheran Digest
Mature Years
Movieguide

PASTORS/LEADERS
Sharing the Practice

WOMEN
Virtuous Woman

FILLERS: KID QUOTES
ADULT/GENERAL
Bridal Guides
Christian Journal
Eternal Ink
Home Times
Indian Life
Movieguide

FILLERS: NEWSBREAKS
ADULT/GENERAL
Christian Journal
Christian Ranchman
Gem
Home Times
Movieguide
Vista

MISSIONS
Operation Reveille

WRITERS
New Writer's Mag.

FILLERS: PARTY IDEAS
ADULT/GENERAL
Bridal Guides
Christian Ranchman
Manna
Movieguide

WOMEN
P31 Woman
Right to the Heart
Virtuous Woman

FILLERS: PRAYERS
ADULT/GENERAL
Angels on Earth
Bridal Guides
Christian Journal
Christian Online
Christian Ranchman
Eternal Ink
Gem
Home Times
Mature Years
Movieguide
Vista

CHILDREN
SHINE brightly

DAILY DEVOTIONALS
Word in Season

TEEN/YOUNG ADULT
Young Salvationist

WOMEN
Glory & Strength
Right to the Heart
Virtuous Woman

FILLERS: PROSE
ADULT/GENERAL
Bible Advocate
Bridal Guides
Christian Online
Christian Ranchman
Eternal Ink

Gem
Movieguide
Pentecostal Evangel

CHILDREN
Partners

WRITERS
Freelance Writer's
   Report
Writer

FILLERS: QUIZZES
ADULT/GENERAL
Bridal Guides
Christian Online
Christian Ranchman
Church Herald
   & Holiness
Gem
Guide
Movieguide

CHILDREN
Focus/Clubhouse
Guide
Partners
SHINE brightly
Skipping Stones

**CHRISTIAN EDUCATION/
LIBRARY**
Ministry Today

TEEN/YOUNG ADULT
Young Salvationist

WOMEN
Virtuous Woman

FILLERS: QUOTES
ADULT/GENERAL
Bridal Guides
Christian Journal
Christian Quarterly
Christian Ranchman
Gem
Home Times
Indian Life
Movieguide
Seek
Storyteller
Vista

CHILDREN
Partners
Skipping Stones

WOMEN
Glory & Strength
Right to the Heart

WRITERS
Fellowscript

FILLERS: SHORT HUMOR
ADULT/GENERAL
Angels on Earth
Bridal Guides
Christian Journal
Christian Online
Christian Quarterly
Christian Ranchman
Eternal Ink
Gem
Home Times
Indian Life
Lutheran Digest
Manna
Mature Living
Movieguide
Presbyterians Today
Seek

CHILDREN
SHINE brightly

PASTORS/LEADERS
Enrichment
Leadership
Sharing the Practice

TEEN/YOUNG ADULT
Young Salvationist

WOMEN
Glory & Strength

WRITERS
Christian Communicator
Fellowscript
New Writer's Mag.

FILLERS: TIPS
ADULT/GENERAL
Bridal Guides
Christian Ranchman

Home Times
Manna
Movieguide
Storyteller

PASTORS/LEADERS
Enrichment

WOMEN
Glory & Strength
MomSense
Virtuous Woman

WRITERS
Fellowscript
Freelance Writer's
    Report

FILLERS: WORD PUZZLES
ADULT/GENERAL
Bridal Guides
Christian Journal
Christian Quarterly
Christian Ranchman
Gem
Guide
Mature Years
Movieguide
Power for Living

CHILDREN
Focus/Clubhouse
Guide
Partners
Pockets
SHINE brightly
Skipping Stones

TEEN/YOUNG ADULT
Young Salvationist

FOOD/RECIPES
ADULT/GENERAL
Bridal Guides
CBN.com
Christian Online
Christian Quarterly
Indian Life
Mature Living

CHILDREN
Focus/Clubhouse
Focus/Clubhouse Jr.

Pockets
SHINE brightly

TEEN/YOUNG ADULT
Boundless Webzine

WOMEN
Dabbling Mum
Glory & Strength
Virtuous Woman

GRANDPARENTING
ADULT/GENERAL
Christian Standard
Columbia
Seek

WOMEN
Brink Magazine
Glory & Strength

HEALING
ADULT/GENERAL
America
Angels on Earth
CBN.com
Christian Home & School
Christian Online
Christian Quarterly
Christian Ranchman
Gem
Good News
Guideposts
Home Times
Light & Life
Live
Our Sunday Visitor
Perspectives
Seek
Testimony

CHILDREN
Skipping Stones

DAILY DEVOTIONALS
Penned from the Heart

TEEN/YOUNG ADULT
Boundless Webzine

WOMEN
Glory & Strength
Share
Virtuous Woman

HEALTH
ADULT/GENERAL
Angels on Earth
Brink Magazine
CBN.com
Christian Courier/Canada
Christian Home & School
Christian Online
Christian Quarterly
Christian Ranchman
Fit Christian
Genuine Motivation
Guide
Guideposts
Home Times
Light & Life
Live
Lookout
Mature Years
Our Sunday Visitor
Penned from the Heart
Pentecostal Evangel
Testimony
Vista
War Cry

CHILDREN
Guide
Skipping Stones

DAILY DEVOTIONALS
Penned from the Heart

PASTORS/LEADERS
Christian Century
InSite

TEEN/YOUNG ADULT
Boundless Webzine
Genuine Motivation
Single! Young Christian Woman

WOMEN
Dabbling Mum
Glory & Strength
Share
Single! Young Christian Woman
Virtuous Woman

HISTORICAL
ADULT/GENERAL
Angels on Earth
Capper's

CBN.com
Christian Courier/Canada
Christian Online
Columbia
Faith Today
Guide
Home Times
Indian Life
Light & Life
Lutheran Digest
Our Sunday Visitor
Perspectives
Power for Living
Priscilla Papers
Storyteller

CHILDREN
Focus/Clubhouse Jr.
Guide

PASTORS/LEADERS
Leadership
Ministry Today
Priest

TEEN/YOUNG ADULT
Boundless Webzine

HOLIDAY/SEASONAL
ADULT/GENERAL
American Tract
Angels on Earth
Brink Magazine
Capper's
Catholic New York
CBN.com
Chicken Soup Books
Christian Courier/Canada
Christian Home & School
Christian Journal
Christian Online
Christian Retailing
Columbia
Eternal Ink
Gem
Gems of Truth
Genuine Motivation
Guide
Guideposts
Home Times
Light & Life

Live
Lookout
Manna
Mature Living
Mature Years
On Mission
Our Sunday Visitor
Penned from the Heart
Power for Living
Prairie Messenger
Seek
Vista
War Cry

CHILDREN
Focus/Clubhouse
Focus/Clubhouse Jr.
Guide
JuniorWay
Pockets
SHINE brightly
Skipping Stones

CHRISTIAN EDUCATION/ LIBRARY
Group

DAILY DEVOTIONALS
Brink Magazine
Penned from the Heart

TEEN/YOUNG ADULT
Boundless Webzine
Genuine Motivation
Single! Young
      Christian Woman
Young Salvationist

WOMEN
Glory & Strength
P31 Woman
Virtuous Woman

HOLY SPIRIT
ADULT/GENERAL
Columbia
Genuine Motivation
Kyria
Single! Young
      Christian Woman

PASTORS/LEADERS
Brink Magazine

HOMESCHOOLING
ADULT/GENERAL
Columbia
Guide
Home Times
Our Sunday Visitor

CHILDREN
Guide
Skipping Stones

TEEN/YOUNG ADULT
Boundless Webzine

WOMEN
Virtuous Woman

HOMILETICS
ADULT/GENERAL
CBN.com
Christian Ranchman
Columbia
Perspectives
Priscilla Papers
Testimony

PASTORS/LEADERS
Christian Century
Enrichment
Preaching
Priest

HOW-TO
ADULT/GENERAL
Bridal Guides
Brink Magazine
Canada Lutheran
CBA Retailers
CBN.com
Christian Online
Christian Retailing
Faith Today
Home Times
Live
On Mission
Presbyterians Today
Testimony
Vista

CHRISTIAN EDUCATION/ LIBRARY
Church Libraries
Group

PASTORS/LEADERS
Ministry Today
Newsletter Newsletter

WOMEN
Dabbling Mum
Virtuous Woman

WRITERS
Adv. Christian Writer
Fellowscript
Freelance Writer's Report
Poets & Writers
Writer's Digest

HOW-TO ACTIVITIES (JUV.)
ADULT/GENERAL
Christian Home & School
Christian Online
Keys to Living
On Mission

CHILDREN
Focus/Clubhouse
Focus/Clubhouse Jr.
Guide
JuniorWay
Pockets
SHINE brightly

CHRISTIAN EDUCATION/ LIBRARY
Group

HUMOR
ADULT/GENERAL
American Tract
Angels on Earth
Brink Magazine
CBN.com
Chicken Soup Books
Christian Courier/Canada
Christian Home & School
Christianity Today
Christian Journal
Christian Online
Christian Quarterly
Christian Ranchman
Eternal Ink
Gem
Genuine Motivation

Guide
Home Times
Indian Life
Lookout
Manna
Mature Living
Our Sunday Visitor
Penned from the Heart
Seek
Storyteller
Testimony
Thriving Family
Vista
War Cry
Weavings

CHILDREN
Focus/Clubhouse Jr.
Guide
SHINE brightly

DAILY DEVOTIONALS
Penned from the Heart

PASTORS/LEADERS
Enrichment
Leadership
Priest

TEEN/YOUNG ADULT
Boundless Webzine
Genuine Motivation
Single! Young Christian Woman
Young Salvationist

WOMEN
Glory & Strength
MomSense
Single! Young Christian Woman

WRITERS
Christian Communicator
New Writer's Mag.

INNER LIFE
ADULT/GENERAL
Canada Lutheran
CBN.com
Christian Journal
Christian Ranchman
Genuine Motivation
Kyria
Light & Life

Live
Mature Years
Our Sunday Visitor
Penned from the Heart
Presbyterians Today
Seek
Testimony
Weavings

TEEN/YOUNG ADULT
Boundless Webzine
Single! Young Christian Woman
Young Salvationist

WOMEN
Glory & Strength
Single! Young Christian Woman

INSPIRATIONAL
ADULT/GENERAL
Angels on Earth
Bridal Guides
Brink Magazine
Capper's
CBN.com
Chicken Soup Books
Christian Home & School
Christian Journal
Christian Online
Christian Quarterly
Christian Ranchman
Columbia
Eternal Ink
Gem
Genuine Motivation
Good News
Guideposts
Home Times
Indian Life
Keys to Living
Leaves
Live
Lookout
Lutheran Digest
Mature Living
Partners
Penned from the Heart
Power for Living
Prairie Messenger
Presbyterians Today
Priority!

Seek
Storyteller
SW Kansas Faith
Testimony
Vista
War Cry

CHILDREN
Partners
SHINE brightly

DAILY DEVOTIONALS
Brink Magazine
Penned from the Heart
Rejoice!

MISSIONS
Operation Reveille

PASTORS/LEADERS
Ministry Today
Priest

TEEN/YOUNG ADULT
Boundless Webzine
Genuine Motivation
Single! Young Christian Woman
Young Salvationist

WOMEN
Glory & Strength
MomSense
P31 Woman
Right to the Heart
Share
Single! Young Christian Woman
Virtuous Woman

WRITERS
Writer's Digest

INTERVIEWS/PROFILES
ADULT/GENERAL
American Tract
Brink Magazine
Catholic New York
CBN.com
Charisma
Christianity Today
Christian Online
Christian Ranchman
Columbia
Eternal Ink
Faith Today

Gem
Good News
Guideposts
Home Times
Indian Life
Kindred Spirit
Light & Life
Lookout
Manna
On Mission
Our Sunday Visitor
Power for Living
Priority!
Testimony
War Cry
Weavings

CHILDREN
Pockets
SHINE brightly
Skipping Stones

CHRISTIAN EDUCATION/ LIBRARY
Church Libraries

MISSIONS
Operation Reveille

PASTORS/LEADERS
Christian Century
Enrichment
InSite
Ministry Today
Priest

TEEN/YOUNG ADULT
Boundless Webzine
Young Salvationist

WOMEN
Glory & Strength
Virtuous Woman

WRITERS
Adv. Christian Writer
Christian Communicator
Fellowscript
New Writer's Mag.
Poets & Writers
Writer
Writer's Chronicle
Writer's Digest

LEADERSHIP
ADULT/GENERAL
Angels on Earth
CBN.com
Christian Courier/Canada
Christian Home & School
Christian Retailing
Christian Standard
Columbia
Faith Today
Gem
Good News
Kyria
Light & Life
Lookout
Manna
Men of the Cross
Our Sunday Visitor
Priscilla Papers
Testimony
Vista

CHRISTIAN EDUCATION/ LIBRARY
Group

PASTORS/LEADERS
Christian Century
Enrichment
Growth Points
InSite
Leadership
Ministry Today
Plugged In
SmallGroups.com

TEEN/YOUNG ADULT
Boundless Webzine

WOMEN
Right to the Heart
Share
Women of the Cross

LIFESTYLE ARTICLES
ADULT/GENERAL
Brink Magazine
Canada Lutheran
CBN.com
Christian Journal
Christian Ranchman
Faith Today

Fit Christian
Genuine Motivation
Home Times
Light & Life
Live
Lookout
Manna
Mature Living
Our Sunday Visitor
Priority!
Seek
Share

TEEN/YOUNG ADULT
Boundless Webzine
Genuine Motivation
Single! Young Christian Woman

WOMEN
Glory & Strength
Single! Young Christian Woman

LITURGICAL
ADULT/GENERAL
Columbia
Our Sunday Visitor
Perspectives
Prairie Messenger
Testimony

PASTORS/LEADERS
Christian Century
Diocesan Dialogue
Parish Liturgy

MARRIAGE
ADULT/GENERAL
Angels on Earth
Bible Advocate
Bridal Guides
Brink Magazine
CBN.com
Christian Courier/Canada
Christian Examiner
Christian Home & School
Christian Journal
Christian Online
Christian Quarterly
Christian Ranchman
Christian Research
Christian Standard

Church Herald & Holiness
Columbia
Gem
Guideposts
Home Times
Indian Life
Kyria
Light & Life
Live
Lookout
Manna
Mature Living
Men of the Cross
Our Sunday Visitor
Penned from the Heart
Perspectives
Prairie Messenger
Priscilla Papers
Seek
Testimony
Thriving Family
Vista
War Cry

DAILY DEVOTIONALS
Penned from the Heart

PASTORS/LEADERS
Christian Century
Ministry Today
SmallGroups.com

TEEN/YOUNG ADULT
Boundless Webzine
Genuine Motivation

WOMEN
Dabbling Mum
Glory & Strength
MomSense
P31 Woman
Virtuous Woman
Women of the Cross

MEN'S ISSUES
ADULT/GENERAL
Brink Magazine
CBN.com
Chicken Soup Books
Christian Examiner
Christian Journal
Christian News NW

Christian Online
Christian Quarterly
Christian Ranchman
Columbia
Gem
Genuine Motivation
Home Times
Indian Life
Light & Life
Live
Lookout
Manna
Men of the Cross
Our Sunday Visitor
Penned from the Heart
Perspectives
Priscilla Papers
Testimony

PASTORS/LEADERS
SmallGroups.com

TEEN/YOUNG ADULT
Boundless Webzine

MIRACLES
ADULT/GENERAL
Angels on Earth
CBN.com
Chicken Soup Books
Christian Home & School
Christianity Today
Christian Online
Christian Quarterly
Christian Ranchman
Christian Standard
Columbia
Gem
Genuine Motivation
Good News
Guide
Guideposts
Home Times
Light & Life
Live
Lookout
Now What?
Our Sunday Visitor
Penned from the Heart
Perspectives
Power for Living

Priority!
Priscilla Papers
Seek
Storyteller
Testimony

CHILDREN
Guide

DAILY DEVOTIONALS
Penned from the Heart

PASTORS/LEADERS
Ministry Today

TEEN/YOUNG ADULT
Boundless Webzine
Genuine Motivation
Single! Young Christian Woman
Young Salvationist

WOMEN
Glory & Strength
Single! Young Christian Woman

MISSIONS
ADULT/GENERAL
Brink Magazine
Canada Lutheran
Christian Home & School
Christian Ranchman
Church Herald & Holiness
Columbia
Faith Today
Genuine Motivation
Guide
Live
On Mission
Our Sunday Visitor

CHILDREN
Guide

DAILY DEVOTIONALS
Brink Magazine

MISSIONS
Operation Reveille

PASTORS/LEADERS
Enrichment

TEEN/YOUNG ADULT
Genuine Motivation
Single! Young Christian Woman

WOMEN
Single! Young Christian Woman

MONEY MANAGEMENT
ADULT/GENERAL
Bridal Guides
Brink Magazine
CBA Retailers
CBN.com
Christian Journal
Christian Online
Christian Quarterly
Christian Ranchman
Gem
Genuine Motivation
Home Times
Live
Lookout
Manna
Mature Years
Our Sunday Visitor
Penned from the Heart
Testimony
War Cry

CHILDREN
SHINE brightly

DAILY DEVOTIONALS
Penned from the Heart

PASTORS/LEADERS
Enrichment
SmallGroups.com

TEEN/YOUNG ADULT
Boundless Webzine
Genuine Motivation
Single! Young Christian Woman

WOMEN
Glory & Strength
Single! Young Christian Woman
Virtuous Woman

MOVIE REVIEWS
ADULT/GENERAL
CBN.com
Christian Journal
Genuine Motivation
Home Times
Movieguide
Our Sunday Visitor

Perspectives
Prairie Messenger

TEEN/YOUNG ADULT
Genuine Motivation
Single! Young Christian Woman

WOMEN
Glory & Strength
Single! Young Christian Woman
Virtuous Woman

MUSIC REVIEWS
ADULT/GENERAL
CBN.com
Charisma
Christian Journal
Christian Retailing
Faith Today
Genuine Motivation
Movieguide
Our Sunday Visitor
Prairie Messenger
Presbyterians Today
Testimony

CHRISTIAN EDUCATION/
LIBRARY
Church Libraries

PASTORS/LEADERS
Christian Century
Ministry Today
Parish Liturgy

TEEN/YOUNG ADULT
Genuine Motivation
Single! Young Christian Woman

WOMEN
Glory & Strength
Single! Young Christian Woman
Virtuous Woman

NATURE
ADULT/GENERAL
Brink Magazine
CBN.com
Christian Courier/Canada
Creation
Creation Illust.
Gem
Guide

Keys to Living
Lutheran Digest
Our Sunday Visitor
Partners
Penned from the Heart
Seek
Storyteller
Testimony

CHILDREN
Focus/Clubhouse Jr.
Guide
Partners
SHINE brightly
Skipping Stones

TEEN/YOUNG ADULT
Boundless Webzine
Genuine Motivation
Single! Young Christian Woman

WOMEN
Single! Young Christian Woman
Virtuous Woman

NEWS FEATURES
ADULT/GENERAL
Catholic New York
CBN.com
Charisma
Christian Examiner
Christian News NW
Christian Ranchman
Christian Research
Christian Retailing
Faith Today
Genuine Motivation
Home Times
Indian Life
Manna
Movieguide
Our Sunday Visitor
Partners
Priority!
Testimony
War Cry

CHILDREN
Partners
Pockets

MISSIONS
Operation Reveille

PASTORS/LEADERS
Christian Century
Ministry Today

TEEN/YOUNG ADULT
Genuine Motivation
Single! Young Christian Woman

WOMEN
Single! Young Christian Woman

WRITERS
Poets & Writers

NEWSPAPERS/TABLOIDS
Catholic New York
Christian Courier/Canada
Christian Examiner
Christian Journal
Christian News NW
Christian Ranchman
Home Times
Indian Life
Manna
Our Sunday Visitor
Prairie Messenger
SW Kansas Faith

NOSTALGIA
ADULT/GENERAL
Home Times
Lutheran Digest
Mature Living
Seek
Storyteller
Testimony

PASTORS/LEADERS
Priest

WOMEN
Glory & Strength

ONLINE PUBLICATIONS
ADULT/GENERAL
America
Answers Magazine
Believers Bay
Brink Magazine
CBN.com
Charisma
Christian Examiner
Christianity Today

Christian Journal
Christian Online
Christian Standard
Columbia
Eternal Ink
Faith Today
Kyria
Lookout
Manna
Men of the Cross
Now What?
On Mission
Pentecostal Evangel
Perspectives
Priority!
Testimony

CHILDREN
Focus/Clubhouse
Focus/Clubhouse Jr.
Keys for Kids
Kids' Ark

MISSIONS
Operation Reveille

PASTORS/LEADERS
Cook Partners
InSite
Leadership
Newsletter Newsletter
Preaching
SmallGroups.com

TEEN/YOUNG ADULT
Boundless Webzine
Young Salvationist

WOMEN
Dabbling Mum
Glory & Strength
Right to the Heart
Virtuous Woman
Women of the Cross

WRITERS
Freelance Writer's Report

OPINION PIECES
ADULT/GENERAL
Brink Magazine
Catholic New York
CBN.com

Christian Courier/Canada
Christian Examiner
Christianity Today
Christian News NW
Christian Research
Home Times
Indian Life
Lookout
Movieguide
Our Sunday Visitor
Perspectives
Prairie Messenger
Testimony

CHILDREN
Skipping Stones

**CHRISTIAN EDUCATION/
LIBRARY**
Group

MISSIONS
Operation Reveille

PASTORS/LEADERS
Ministry Today
Priest

WRITERS
Adv. Christian Writer
New Writer's Mag.

PARENTING
ADULT/GENERAL
American Tract
Angels on Earth
Canada Lutheran
CBN.com
Chicken Soup Books
Christian Courier/
    Canada
Christian Home & School
Christian Quarterly
Christian Ranchman
Christian Research
Columbia
Gem
Home Times
Indian Life
Light & Life
Live
Lookout
Manna

Movieguide
Our Sunday Visitor
Penned from the Heart
Pentecostal Evangel
Power for Living
Prairie Messenger
Seek
SW Kansas Faith
Testimony
Thriving Family
Vista
War Cry

DAILY DEVOTIONALS
Penned from the Heart

PASTORS/LEADERS
Plugged In

WOMEN
Dabbling Mum
Glory & Strength
MomSense
P31 Woman
Virtuous Woman

PASTORS' HELPS
PASTORS/LEADERS
Christian Century
Cook Partners
Diocesan Dialogue
Enrichment
Growth Points
InSite
Leadership
Ministry Today
Newsletter Newsletter
Parish Liturgy
Plugged In
Preaching
Sharing the Practice
SmallGroups.com

PEACE ISSUES
ADULT/GENERAL
CBN.com
Columbia
Genuine Motivation
Lookout
Our Sunday Visitor
Penned from the Heart
Perspectives

Seek
Testimony

CHILDREN
Pockets
Skipping Stones

PASTORS/LEADERS
Christian Century

TEEN/YOUNG ADULT
Genuine Motivation
Single! Young Christian Woman

WOMEN
Single! Young Christian Woman

PERSONAL EXPERIENCE
ADULT/GENERAL
Angels on Earth
Bible Advocate
Bridal Guides
Brink Magazine
Catholic New York
CBN.com
Chicken Soup Books
Christian Courier/Canada
Christianity Today
Christian Journal
Christian Online
Christian Quarterly
Columbia
Gem
Genuine Motivation
Guide
Guideposts
Home Times
Keys to Living
Kyria
Leaves
Light & Life
Live
Lookout
Mature Living
Now What?
On Mission
Partners
Penned from the Heart
Power for Living
Seek
Storyteller
Testimony

Vision
War Cry

CHILDREN
Guide
Partners
Skipping Stones

CHRISTIAN EDUCATION/ LIBRARY
Group

DAILY DEVOTIONALS
Penned from the Heart
Rejoice!

PASTORS/LEADERS
Priest

TEEN/YOUNG ADULT
Boundless Webzine
Genuine Motivation
Single! Young Christian
    Woman
Young Salvationist

WOMEN
Glory & Strength
MomSense
Single! Young Christian Woman
Virtuous Woman

WRITERS
New Writer's Mag.

PERSONAL GROWTH
ADULT/GENERAL
Bible Advocate
CBN.com
Christian Courier/Canada
Christian Journal
Christian Online
Christian Quarterly
Christian Ranchman
Columbia
Gem
Genuine Motivation
Guide
Home Times
Indian Life
Keys to Living
Kyria
Leaves
Light & Life

Live
Lookout
Lutheran Digest
Manna
Mature Living
Mature Years
Now What?
Penned from the Heart
Prairie Messenger
Seek
Share
Testimony
War Cry

CHILDREN
Guide
Skipping Stones

DAILY DEVOTIONALS
Penned from the Heart

PASTORS/LEADERS
Ministry Today

TEEN/YOUNG ADULT
Boundless Webzine
Genuine Motivation
Single! Young Christian Woman
Young Salvationist

WOMEN
Dabbling Mum
Glory & Strength
MomSense
P31 Woman
Single! Young Christian
    Woman
Virtuous Woman

PHOTO ESSAYS
ADULT/GENERAL
Genuine Motivation
Our Sunday Visitor
Priority!

CHILDREN
Skipping Stones

PASTORS/LEADERS
Priest

TEEN/YOUNG ADULT
Genuine Motivation
Single! Young Christian Woman

WOMEN
Single! Young Christian
    Woman

PHOTOGRAPHS
Note: "Reprint" indicators (R) have been deleted from this section and "B" for black & white glossy prints or "C" for color transparencies inserted. An asterisk (*) before a listing indicates they buy photos with articles only.

ADULT/GENERAL
American Tract
Bible Advocate—C
*Bridal Guides—B/C
Canada Lutheran—B
Catholic New York—B
CBA Retailers—C
*Charisma—C
*Christian Courier/
    Canada—B
*Christian Examiner—C
Christian Home & School—C
*Christianity Today—C
*Christian Online
Christian Retailing—C
*Christian Standard—B/C
*Guideposts—B/C
*Home Times—B/C
Indian Life—B/C
Leaves—B/C
Light & Life—B/C
*Live—B/C
*Lookout—B/C
*Manna—C
*Mature Living
*Mature Years—C
On Mission—B/C
Our Sunday Visitor—B/C
Pentecostal Evangel—B/C
*Perspectives—B
Power for Living—B
*Presbyterians Today—B/C
*Seek—C
*Storyteller—B
*Testimony—B/C
Vision—B/C
*War Cry—B/C

CHILDREN
*Focus/Clubhouse—C
*Focus/Clubhouse Jr.—C
*Pockets—C
SHINE brightly—C
Skipping Stones

CHRISTIAN EDUCATION/ LIBRARY
*Church Libraries—B/C

DAILY DEVOTIONALS
Secret Place—B
Upper Room

MISSIONS
Operation Reveille—B/C

PASTORS/LEADERS
Christian Century—B/C
*InSite—C
*Leadership—B
Priest

TEEN/YOUNG ADULT
Take Five Plus—B/C

WOMEN
Glory & Strength
Right to the Heart

WRITERS
Best New Writing—C
*New Writer's Mag.
*Poets & Writers
*Writer's Chronicle—B
*Writer's Digest—B

POETRY
ADULT/GENERAL
America
Bible Advocate
Bridal Guides
Christian Courier/Canada
Christian Journal
Christian Research
Creation Illust.
Eternal Ink
Gem
Home Times
Indian Life
Keys to Living
Leaves
Light & Life

Live
Lutheran Digest
Mature Living
Mature Years
Men of the Cross
Penned from the Heart
Perspectives
Prairie Messenger
Priscilla Papers
Relief Journal
Storyteller
Studio
Testimony
Time of Singing
Vision
Weavings

CHILDREN
Focus/Clubhouse Jr.
Partners
Pockets
SHINE brightly
Skipping Stones

DAILY DEVOTIONALS
Christian Devotions
God's Word for Today
Penned from the Heart
Secret Place

PASTORS/LEADERS
Christian Century
Sharing the Practice

TEEN/YOUNG ADULT
Take Five Plus
Young Salvationist

WOMEN
Glory & Strength
MomSense
Virtuous Woman

WRITERS
Best New Writing
Christian Communicator
New Writer's Mag.
Writer's Digest

POLITICS
ADULT/GENERAL
Brink Magazine
CBN.com

Christian Courier/Canada
Christian Examiner
Christianity Today
Faith Today
Home Times
Light & Life
Movieguide
Our Sunday Visitor
Perspectives
Testimony

PASTORS/LEADERS
Christian Century

TEEN/YOUNG ADULT
Boundless Webzine

PRAISE
ADULT/GENERAL
Genuine Motivation
Kyria

WOMEN
Brink Magazine
Glory & Strength
Single! Young Christian Woman

PRAYER
ADULT/GENERAL
Angels on Earth
Believers Bay
Bible Advocate
Brink Magazine
CBN.com
Christian Home & School
Christianity Today
Christian Journal
Christian Online
Christian Quarterly
Christian Ranchman
Christian Research
Christian Standard
Columbia
Gem
Genuine Motivation
Good News
Guide
Home Times
Kyria
Leaves
Light & Life
Live

Lookout
Lutheran Digest
Manna
Mature Years
Our Sunday Visitor
Penned from the Heart
Pentecostal Evangel
Perspectives
Presbyterians Today
Priority!
Seek
Testimony
War Cry

CHILDREN
Guide

CHRISTIAN EDUCATION/
LIBRARY
Group

DAILY DEVOTIONALS
Brink Magazine
Penned from the Heart

PASTORS/LEADERS
Diocesan Dialogue
Leadership
Ministry Today
SmallGroups.com

TEEN/YOUNG ADULT
Boundless Webzine
Single! Young Christian Woman
Young Salvationist

WOMEN
Glory & Strength
P31 Woman
Right to the Heart
Single! Young Christian
    Woman
Virtuous Woman

PROPHECY
ADULT/GENERAL
Believers Bay
Bible Advocate
CBN.com
Christian Online
Christian Quarterly
Christian Research
Light & Life

Live
Our Sunday Visitor
Testimony

PASTORS/LEADERS
Ministry Today

TEEN/YOUNG ADULT
Young Salvationist

PSYCHOLOGY
ADULT/GENERAL
CBN.com
Christian Courier/Canada
Christian Online
Gem
Light & Life
Our Sunday Visitor
Testimony

WOMEN
Glory & Strength

RACISM
ADULT/GENERAL
Brink Magazine
CBN.com
Christianity Today
Columbia
Faith Today
Genuine Motivation
Guide
Light & Life
Live Lookout
Manna
Our Sunday Visitor
Perspectives
Priscilla Papers
Testimony

CHILDREN
Guide
Skipping Stones

PASTORS/LEADERS
Ministry Today

TEEN/YOUNG ADULT
Boundless Webzine
Genuine Motivation
Single! Young Christian
    Woman
Young Salvationist

WOMEN
Single! Young Christian Woman

RECOVERY
ADULT/GENERAL
Bible Advocate
CBN.com
Christian Journal
Home Times
Kyria
Light & Life
Live
Lookout
Manna
Our Sunday Visitor
Priority!
Seek

PASTORS/LEADERS
Ministry Today

TEEN/YOUNG ADULT
Boundless Webzine

WOMEN
Glory & Strength
Right to the Heart

RELATIONSHIPS
ADULT/GENERAL
Angels on Earth
Bridal Guides
Brink Magazine
Canada Lutheran
CBN.com
Chicken Soup Books
Christian Home & School
Christian Journal
Christian Online
Christian Quarterly
Christian Ranchman
Eternal Ink
Faith Today
Gem
Gems of Truth
Genuine Motivation
Guideposts
Home Times
Keys to Living
Kyria
Light & Life

Live
Lookout
Manna
Mature Years
Men of the Cross
Our Sunday Visitor
Penned from the Heart
Pentecostal Evangel
Perspectives
Priscilla Papers
Seek
Storyteller
Testimony
Vision
Vista
War Cry

CHILDREN
SHINE brightly
Skipping Stones

CHRISTIAN EDUCATION/ LIBRARY
Group

PASTORS/LEADERS
Leadership
SmallGroups.com

TEEN/YOUNG ADULT
Boundless Webzine
Genuine Motivation
Single! Young Christian Woman
Young Salvationist

WOMEN
Dabbling Mum
Glory & Strength
MomSense
P31 Woman
Single! Young Christian Woman
Virtuous Woman

RELIGIOUS FREEDOM
ADULT/GENERAL
Brink Magazine
CBN.com
Christian Examiner
Christian Home & School
Christianity Today
Christian Online
Christian Ranchman
Columbia

Faith Today
Gem
Genuine Motivation
Guide
Home Times
Light & Life
Live
Lookout
Manna
Our Sunday Visitor
Perspectives
Prairie Messenger
Seek
Testimony

CHILDREN
Guide
Skipping Stones

MISSIONS
Operation Reveille

PASTORS/LEADERS
Christian Century

TEEN/YOUNG ADULT
Boundless Webzine
Genuine Motivation
Single! Young Christian Woman

WOMEN
Single! Young Christian Woman

RELIGIOUS TOLERANCE
ADULT/GENERAL
Brink Magazine
CBN.com
Christian Examiner
Christian Home & School
Christianity Today
Christian Online
Columbia
Faith Today
Genuine Motivation
Light & Life
Live
Lookout
Manna
Our Sunday Visitor
Perspectives
Prairie Messenger
Seek
Testimony

CHILDREN
Skipping Stones

MISSIONS
Operation Reveille

PASTORS/LEADERS
Christian Century

TEEN/YOUNG ADULT
Boundless Webzine
Genuine Motivation
Single! Young Christian Woman

WOMEN
Single! Young Christian Woman

REVIVAL
ADULT/GENERAL
Bible Advocate
CBN.com
Christian Home & School
Christian Quarterly
Christian Ranchman
Columbia
Home Times
Light & Life
Live
Lookout
Manna

PASTORS/LEADERS
Ministry Today

TEEN/YOUNG ADULT
Boundless Webzine

SALVATION TESTIMONIES
ADULT/GENERAL
American Tract
Believers Bay
CBN.com
Christian Home & School
Christian Journal
Christian Online
Christian Quarterly
Christian Ranchman
Christian Research
Columbia
Gem
Guide
Guideposts
Home Times

Leaves
Light & Life
Live
Now What?
On Mission
Power for Living
Priority!
Seek
Testimony
War Cry

CHILDREN
Guide

CHRISTIAN EDUCATION/
LIBRARY
Group

TEEN/YOUNG ADULT
Boundless Webzine

SCIENCE
ADULT/GENERAL
Answers Magazine
CBN.com
Christian Courier/
    Canada
Creation
Creation Illust.
Faith Today
Guide
Home Times
Light & Life
Our Sunday Visitor
Perspectives
Testimony

CHILDREN
Guide
Skipping Stones

SELF-HELP
ADULT/GENERAL
CBN.com
Home Times
Light & Life
Lookout
Manna
Men of the Cross
Seek
Testimony

CHILDREN
Skipping Stones

WOMEN
Glory & Strength
Women of the Cross

SENIOR ADULT ISSUES
ADULT/GENERAL
Angels on Earth
CBN.com
Christian Quarterly
Christian Ranchman
Christian Standard
Columbia
Faith Today
Gem
Home Times
Light & Life
Live
Mature Living
Mature Years
Our Sunday Visitor
Penned from the Heart
Power for Living
Seek
Testimony
War Cry

DAILY DEVOTIONALS
Penned from the Heart

PASTORS/LEADERS
Diocesan Dialogue

SERMONS
ADULT/GENERAL
Testimony
Weavings

PASTORS/LEADERS
Ministry Today
Preaching
Sharing the Practice

SHORT STORY: ADULT/
GENERAL
Best New Writing
CBN.com
New Writer's Mag.
Perspectives
Seek

SHORT STORY: ADULT/
RELIGIOUS
Angels on Earth
Bridal Guides
CBN.com
Christian Century
Christian Courier/
    Canada
Christian Home
    & School
Christian Journal
Christian Online
Christian Ranchman
Christian Research
Gem
Gems of Truth
Glory & Strength
Home Times
Indian Life
Live
On Mission
Perspectives
Relief Journal
Seek
Studio
Testimony
Vision
Vista

SHORT STORY:
ADVENTURE
ADULT
Angels on Earth
Best New Writing
CBN.com
Gem
Indian Life
Partners
Storyteller
Studio
Vision
Weavings

CHILDREN
Eternal Ink
Focus/Clubhouse Jr.
Kids' Ark
Partners
SHINE brightly
Skipping Stones

TEEN/YOUNG ADULT
Partners
SHINE brightly
Storyteller

SHORT STORY: ALLEGORY
ADULT
CBN.com
Christian Journal
Gem
Glory & Strength
Home Times
Indian Life
Men of the Cross
Studio
Vision
Women of the Cross

TEEN/YOUNG ADULT
Home Times

SHORT STORY: BIBLICAL
ADULT
CBN.com
Christian Journal
Christian Online
Christian Ranchman
Gem
Kindred Spirit
Seek
Studio
Vista

CHILDREN
Christian Ranchman
Eternal Ink
Focus/Clubhouse
Pockets

TEEN/YOUNG ADULT
Christian Ranchman
Home Times

SHORT STORY: CONTEMPORARY
ADULT
Angels on Earth
CBN.com
Christian Century
Christian Courier/
   Canada

Christian Home
   & School
Gem
Indian Life
Mature Living
New Writer's Mag.
Partners
Perspectives
Relief Journal
Seek
Storyteller
Studio
Vision

CHILDREN
Focus/Clubhouse
Focus/Clubhouse Jr.
Kids' Ark
Partners
Pockets
SHINE brightly

TEEN/YOUNG ADULT
Home Times
Partners
Storyteller

SHORT STORY: ETHNIC
ADULT
Gem
Indian Life
Relief Journal
Seek
Studio

CHILDREN
Focus/Clubhouse
Kids' Ark
Skipping Stones

TEEN/YOUNG ADULT
SHINE brightly

SHORT STORY: FANTASY
ADULT
Gem
Storyteller
Studio

CHILDREN
Focus/Clubhouse
SHINE brightly

TEEN/YOUNG ADULT
SHINE brightly
Storyteller

SHORT STORY: FRONTIER
ADULT
Gem
Indian Life
Storyteller
Studio

CHILDREN
Eternal Ink
Kids' Ark
SHINE brightly

TEEN/YOUNG ADULT
Home Times
Storyteller

SHORT STORY: FRONTIER/ROMANCE
Gem
Studio

SHORT STORY: HISTORICAL
ADULT
CBN.com
Gem
Home Times
Indian Life
New Writer's Mag.
Partners
Seek
Storyteller
Studio

CHILDREN
Christian Ranchman
Focus/Clubhouse
Focus/Clubhouse Jr.
Home Times
Kids' Ark
Partners
SHINE brightly

TEEN/YOUNG ADULT
Christian Ranchman
Home Times
Partners

SHINE brightly
Storyteller

SHORT STORY: HISTORICAL/ROMANCE
CBN.com
Gem
Studio

SHORT STORY: HUMOROUS
ADULT
CBN.com
Christian Courier/
    Canada
Christian Journal
Gem
Glory & Strength
Home Times
Mature Living
Mature Years
Men of the Cross
New Writer's Mag.
Seek
Storyteller
Studio
Vista

CHILDREN
Christian Ranchman
Eternal Ink
Focus/Clubhouse
Home Times
SHINE brightly
Skipping Stones

TEEN/YOUNG ADULT
Christian Ranchman
Home Times
Storyteller

SHORT STORY: JUVENILE
CBN.com
Church Herald & Holiness
Focus/Clubhouse
Focus/Clubhouse Jr.
Keys for Kids
Kids' Ark
Partners
Pockets
Seek

SHINE brightly
Skipping Stones

SHORT STORY: LITERARY
ADULT
Christian Courier/
    Canada
Gem
Perspectives
Relief Journal
Seek
Storyteller
Studio

CHILDREN
Skipping Stones

TEEN/YOUNG ADULT
Home Times
Storyteller

SHORT STORY: MYSTERY/ROMANCE
Gem
Studio

SHORT STORY: MYSTERY/SUSPENSE
ADULT
Best New Writing
CBN.com
Gem
Relief Journal
Storyteller
Studio

CHILDREN
Kids' Ark
SHINE brightly

TEEN/YOUNG ADULT
SHINE brightly
Storyteller

SHORT STORY: PARABLES
ADULT
Christian Courier/Canada
Christian Journal
Gem
Glory & Strength
Perspectives
Seek

Studio
Testimony

CHILDREN
Eternal Ink
Focus/Clubhouse Jr.

TEEN/YOUNG ADULT
Home Times
SHINE brightly
Testimony

SHORT STORY: PLAYS
SHINE brightly
Studio

SHORT STORY: ROMANCE
ADULT
Bridal Guides
CBN.com
Gem
Storyteller
Studio

SHORT STORY: SCIENCE FICTION
ADULT
Gem
Storyteller
Studio

CHILDREN
Kids' Ark
SHINE brightly

TEEN/YOUNG ADULT
Home Times
SHINE brightly
Storyteller

SHORT STORY: SENIOR ADULT FICTION
ADULT
Live
Mature Living
Mature Years
Seek
Vista

SHORT STORY: SKITS
CHILDREN
Focus/Clubhouse Jr.
SHINE brightly

TEEN/YOUNG ADULT
SHINE brightly

SHORT STORY:
SPECULATIVE
ADULT
Relief Journal
Studio

TEEN/YOUNG ADULT
Home Times

SHORT STORY:
TEEN/YOUNG ADULT
CBN.com
Seek
Skipping Stones
Storyteller
Testimony

SHORT STORY:
WESTERNS
ADULT
Bridal Guides
Storyteller
Studio

CHILDREN
Christian Ranchman
Kids' Ark

TEEN/YOUNG ADULT
Christian Ranchman
Storyteller

SINGLES' ISSUES
ADULT/GENERAL
Brink Magazine
CBN.com
Christian Examiner
Christian Online
Christian Ranchman
Columbia
Faith Today
Gem
Genuine Motivation
Home Times
Kyria
Light & Life
Live
Lookout
Our Sunday Visitor

Penned from the Heart
Power for Living
Priscilla Papers
Seek
Testimony
War Cry

DAILY DEVOTIONALS
Brink Magazine
Penned from the Heart

PASTORS/LEADERS
Ministry Today

TEEN/YOUNG ADULT
Boundless Webzine
Genuine Motivation
Single! Young Christian Woman
Young Salvationist

WOMEN
Glory & Strength
Single! Young Christian Woman
Women of the Cross

SMALL-GROUP HELPS
ADULT/GENERAL
Kyria
Ministry Today
SmallGroups.com

SOCIAL JUSTICE
ADULT/GENERAL
Brink Magazine
Canada Lutheran
CBN.com
Christian Courier/Canada
Christianity Today
Christian Online
Christian Standard
Columbia
Faith Today
Gem
Genuine Motivation
Guide
Indian Life
Kyria
Light & Life
Lookout
Our Sunday Visitor
Penned from the Heart
Perspectives

Prairie Messenger
Priscilla Papers
Seek
Testimony

CHILDREN
Guide
Pockets
Skipping Stones

PASTORS/LEADERS
Christian Century
Sharing the Practice

TEEN/YOUNG ADULT
Boundless Webzine
Genuine Motivation
Single! Young Christian Woman
Young Salvationist

WOMEN
Single! Young Christian Woman

SOCIOLOGY
ADULT/GENERAL
Christian Courier/Canada
Christian Online
Gem
Light & Life
Our Sunday Visitor
Perspectives
Priscilla Papers
Testimony

TEEN/YOUNG ADULT
Boundless Webzine

WOMEN
Women of the Cross

SPIRITUAL GIFTS
ADULT/GENERAL
Bible Advocate
Brink Magazine
CBN.com
Christian Home & School
Christianity Today
Christian Online
Christian Quarterly
Christian Ranchman
Christian Standard
Columbia
Guide

Home Times
Kyria
Light & Life
Live
Mature Years
Penned from the Heart
Priscilla Papers
Seek
Testimony
Vista

CHILDREN
Guide

DAILY DEVOTIONALS
Penned from the Heart

PASTORS/LEADERS
Ministry Today

WOMEN
P31 Woman
Virtuous Woman

SPIRITUALITY
ADULT/GENERAL
American Tract
Angels on Earth
Bible Advocate
Brink Magazine
CBN.com
Christian Courier/Canada
Christianity Today
Christian Journal
Christian Online
Columbia
Faith Today
Gem
Genuine Motivation
Good News
Guideposts
Indian Life
Leaves
Light & Life
Live
Lookout
Mature Years
Our Sunday Visitor
Penned from the Heart
Prairie Messenger
Presbyterians Today
Priscilla Papers

Seek
Testimony
Vista
War Cry
Weavings

CHILDREN
Skipping Stones

DAILY DEVOTIONALS
Penned from the Heart

PASTORS/LEADERS
Christian Century
Diocesan Dialogue
Leadership
Ministry Today
Sharing the Practice

TEEN/YOUNG ADULT
Boundless Webzine
Genuine Motivation
Single! Young Christian Woman

WOMEN
Single! Young Christian Woman
Women of the Cross

SPIRITUAL LIFE
ADULT/GENERAL
Bible Advocate
Brink Magazine
CBN.com
Christian Examiner
Christian Home & School
Christian Journal
Christian Online
Christian Quarterly
Christian Ranchman
Christian Research
Columbia
Eternal Ink
Faith Today
Guide
Home Times
Light & Life
Live
Lookout
Mature Living
Our Sunday Visitor
Penned from the Heart
Perspectives

Presbyterians Today
Priscilla Papers
Seek
Testimony
Weavings

CHILDREN
Guide

DAILY DEVOTIONALS
Brink Magazine
Penned from the Heart

PASTORS/LEADERS
Leadership
Ministry Today
SmallGroups.com

TEEN/YOUNG ADULT
Boundless Webzine
Genuine Motivation
Single! Young Christian Woman
Young Salvationist

WOMEN
Glory & Strength
P31 Woman
Right to the Heart
Single! Young Christian Woman

SPIRITUAL RENEWAL
ADULT/GENERAL
Bible Advocate
Brink Magazine
Canada Lutheran
CBN.com
Christian Home & School
Christian Online
Christian Quarterly
Christian Ranchman
Columbia
Eternal Ink
Faith Today
Genuine Motivation
Home Times
Light & Life
Live
Lookout
Manna
Pentecostal Evangel
Seek
Testimony

PASTORS/LEADERS
Christian Century
Leadership
Ministry Today

TEEN/YOUNG ADULT
Boundless Webzine
Genuine Motivation
Single! Young Christian Woman
Young Salvationist

WOMEN
Glory & Strength
Right to the Heart
Single! Young Christian Woman
Virtuous Woman

SPIRITUAL WARFARE
ADULT/GENERAL
Angels on Earth
Believers Bay
Bible Advocate
Brink Magazine
CBN.com
Christian Home & School
Christianity Today
Christian Online
Christian Quarterly
Christian Ranchman
Christian Research
Columbia
Gem
Good News
Leaves
Light & Life
Live
Lookout
Manna
Penned from the Heart
Seek
Testimony

DAILY DEVOTIONALS
Penned from the Heart

MISSIONS
Operation Reveille

PASTORS/LEADERS
Growth Points
Ministry Today
Small Groups.com

TEEN/YOUNG ADULT
Young Salvationist

WOMEN
Glory & Strength

SPORTS/RECREATION
ADULT/GENERAL
Angels on Earth
CBN.com
Gem
Guide
Guideposts
Home Times
Lookout
Our Sunday Visitor
Storyteller
Testimony

CHILDREN
Guide
SHINE brightly

TEEN/YOUNG ADULT
Boundless Webzine
Young Salvationist

STEWARDSHIP
ADULT/GENERAL
Angels on Earth
Bible Advocate
Canada Lutheran
CBN.com
Christian Courier/Canada
Christian News NW
Christian Online
Christian Ranchman
Christian Standard
Columbia
Faith Today
Gem
Genuine Motivation
Guide
Home Times
Light & Life
Live
Lookout
Manna
Our Sunday Visitor
Penned from the Heart
Perspectives

Power for Living
Seek
Testimony

CHILDREN
Guide
SHINE brightly

DAILY DEVOTIONALS
Penned from the Heart

PASTORS/LEADERS
InSite
Ministry Today
Sharing the Practice

TEEN/YOUNG ADULT
Boundless Webzine
Genuine Motivation
Single! Young Christian Woman
Young Salvationist

WOMEN
P31 Woman
Single! Young Christian Woman

TAKE-HOME PAPERS
ADULT/GENERAL
Gem
Gems of Truth
Live
Power for Living
Seek
Vision
Vista

CHILDREN
Guide
JuniorWay
Partners

THEOLOGICAL
ADULT/GENERAL
America
Bible Advocate
Brink Magazine
CBN.com
Christian Courier/Canada
Christianity Today
Christian Online
Christian Ranchman
Christian Research
Christian Standard

Faith Today
Light & Life
Lookout
Movieguide
Our Sunday Visitor
Perspectives
Prairie Messenger
Priscilla Papers
Testimony

DAILY DEVOTIONALS
Brink Magazine
Penned from the Heart

PASTORS/LEADERS
Christian Century
Diocesan Dialogue
Growth Points
Sharing the Practice
SmallGroups.com

TEEN/YOUNG ADULT
Boundless Webzine
Young Salvationist

THINK PIECES
ADULT/GENERAL
Brink Magazine
Christian Courier/Canada
Christianity Today
Christian Online
Faith Today
Gem
Genuine Motivation
Light & Life
Lookout
Manna
Men of the Cross
Our Sunday Visitor
Penned from the Heart
Seek
Testimony

CHILDREN
Skipping Stones

PASTORS/LEADERS
Enrichment
Ministry Today

TEEN/YOUNG ADULT
Boundless Webzine
Genuine Motivation

Single! Young Christian Woman
Young Salvationist

WOMEN
MomSense
Single! Young Christian Woman
Women of the Cross

TIME MANAGEMENT
ADULT/GENERAL
Bridal Guides
Brink Magazine
CBA Retailers
CBN.com
Christian Online
Gem
Genuine Motivation
Home Times
Light & Life
Live
Lookout
Men of the Cross
Penned from the Heart
Testimony

DAILY DEVOTIONALS
Brink Magazine
Penned from the Heart

PASTORS/LEADERS
Enrichment

TEEN/YOUNG ADULT
Boundless Webzine
Genuine Motivation
Single! Young Christian Woman

WOMEN
Glory & Strength
P31 Woman
Single! Young Christian Woman
Virtuous Woman

WRITERS
Adv. Christian Writer
Christian Communicator
Fellowscript
Writer

TRAVEL
ADULT/GENERAL
Angels on Earth
Bridal Guides

Brink Magazine
Capper's
CBN.com
Gem
Genuine Motivation
Mature Living
Mature Years
Movieguide
Seek
Testimony

CHILDREN
SHINE brightly
Skipping Stones

TEEN/YOUNG ADULT
Boundless Webzine
Genuine Motivation
Single! Young Christian Woman

WOMEN
Single! Young Christian Woman

TRUE STORIES
ADULT/GENERAL
Angels on Earth
Bridal Guides
Brink Magazine
CBN.com
Christian Online
Christian Quarterly
Christian Ranchman
Columbia
Eternal Ink
Gem
Gems of Truth
Genuine Motivation
Guide
Guideposts
Home Times
Indian Life
Kyria
Light & Life
Live
Lutheran Digest
Mature Living
Men of the Cross
Now What?
On Mission
Partners
Penned from the Heart

Pentecostal Evangel
Power for Living
Priority!
Seek
Storyteller
Testimony
Vision
Vista
War Cry

CHILDREN
Focus/Clubhouse Jr.
Guide
Partners
Pockets
SHINE brightly
Skipping Stones

MISSIONS
Operation Reveille

PASTORS/LEADERS
Leadership
Sharing the Practice

TEEN/YOUNG ADULT
Boundless Webzine
Genuine Motivation
Single! Young Christian Woman
Young Salvationist

WOMEN
Glory & Strength
MomSense
Single! Young Christian Woman

VIDEO REVIEWS
ADULT/GENERAL
CBN.com
Eternal Ink
Genuine Motivation
Home Times
Movieguide
Our Sunday Visitor
Presbyterians Today
Testimony

**CHRISTIAN EDUCATION/
LIBRARY**
Church Libraries

PASTORS/LEADERS
Christian Century
Ministry Today

TEEN/YOUNG ADULT
Genuine Motivation
Single! Young Christian Woman

WOMEN
Dabbling Mum
Glory & Strength
Single! Young Christian Woman
Virtuous Woman

WEBSITE REVIEWS
ADULT/GENERAL
CBN.com
Christianity Today
Eternal Ink
On Mission
Our Sunday Visitor

MISSIONS
Operation Reveille

WOMEN
Glory & Strength

WOMEN'S ISSUES
ADULT/GENERAL
Brink Magazine
CBA Retailers
CBN.com
Chicken Soup Books
Christian Courier/Canada
Christian Examiner
Christian Journal
Christian News NW
Christian Online
Christian Quarterly
Christian Ranchman
Columbia
Faith Today
Gem
Indian Life
Kyria
Light & Life
Live
Lookout
Manna
Our Sunday Visitor
Penned from the Heart
Perspectives
Prairie Messenger
Priscilla Papers
Seek

Share
Single! Young Christian Woman
Storyteller
Testimony
War Cry

CHILDREN
Skipping Stones

DAILY DEVOTIONALS
Penned from the Heart

PASTORS/LEADERS
SmallGroups.com

TEEN/YOUNG ADULT
Boundless Webzine

WOMEN
Dabbling Mum
Glory & Strength
MomSense
P31 Woman
Right to the Heart
Share
Single! Young Christian Woman
Virtuous Woman
Women of the Cross

WORKPLACE ISSUES
ADULT/GENERAL
CBN.com
Christian Examiner
Christian Online
Christian Ranchman
Christian Retailing
Faith Today
Light & Life
Live
Lookout
Manna
Our Sunday Visitor
Penned from the Heart
Perspectives
Seek
Testimony

**CHRISTIAN EDUCATION/
LIBRARY**
Group

MISSIONS
Operation Reveille

TEEN/YOUNG ADULT
Boundless Webzine

WOMEN
Glory & Strength

WRITERS
Adv. Christian Writer

WORLD ISSUES
ADULT/GENERAL
American Tract
Brink Magazine
CBN.com
Christian Examiner
Christian Online
Columbia
Faith Today
Gem
Genuine Motivation
Guide
Home Times
Indian Life
Light & Life
Lookout
Movieguide
Our Sunday Visitor
Penned from the Heart
Perspectives
Seek
Testimony
War Cry

CHILDREN
Guide
Skipping Stones

MISSIONS
Operation Reveille

PASTORS/LEADERS
Christian Century
Ministry Today

TEEN/YOUNG ADULT
Boundless Webzine
Genuine Motivation
Single! Young Christian
    Woman

WOMEN
Single! Young Christian
    Woman

WORSHIP
ADULT/GENERAL
Angels on Earth
Bible Advocate
Brink Magazine
Canada Lutheran
CBN.com
Christian Examiner
Christianity Today
Christian Online
Christian Ranchman
Christian Standard
Columbia
Eternal Ink
Kyria
Light & Life
Live
Lookout
Manna
Penned from the Heart
Perspectives
Power for Living
Presbyterians Today
Priscilla Papers
Seek
Testimony
Time of Singing
Vista
War Cry

CHILDREN
Keys for Kids

CHRISTIAN EDUCATION/
LIBRARY
Group

DAILY DEVOTIONALS
Brink Magazine
Penned from the Heart

PASTORS/LEADERS
Enrichment
Growth Points
Leadership
Ministry Today
Parish Liturgy
Preaching
Sharing the Practice

TEEN/YOUNG ADULT
Boundless Webzine

WOMEN
Glory & Strength
Virtuous Woman

WRITING HOW-TO
ADULT/GENERAL
Canada Lutheran
CBA Retailers
CBN.com
Christian Online
Home Times

CHILDREN
Skipping Stones

CHRISTIAN EDUCATION/
LIBRARY
Group

PASTORS/LEADERS
Newsletter Newsletter

TEEN/YOUNG ADULT
Boundless Webzine

WOMEN
Dabbling Mum
Right to the Heart

WRITERS
Adv. Christian Writer
Best New Writing
Christian Communicator
Fellowscript
Freelance Writer's Report
New Writer's Mag.
Poets & Writers
Writer
Writer's Chronicle
Writer's Digest

YOUNG-WRITER
MARKETS
Note: These publications have
indicated they will accept
submissions from children or
teens (C or T).

ADULT/GENERAL
Bridal Guides (C or T)
CBN.com (T)
Christian Home & School
    (C or T)
Christian Journal (C or T)

Christian Online (C or T)
Church Herald & Holiness
    (C or T)
Eternal Ink (C or T)
Home Times (T)
Indian Life (C or T)
Light & Life (C or T)
Manna (C or T)
Men of the Cross (T)
Penned from the Heart (C or T)
Priority! (C or T)
Storyteller (C or T)
Vista (C or T)

CHILDREN
Focus/Clubhouse (C)
Kids' Ark (C or T)
Pockets (C)

DAILY DEVOTIONALS
Penned from the Heart (C or T)

TEEN/YOUNG ADULT
Boundless Webzine (T)
Take Five Plus (T)

WOMEN
Dabbling Mum (T)
Women of the Cross (T)

WRITERS
Fellowscript (T)

YOUTH ISSUES
ADULT/GENERAL
American Tract
Canada Lutheran
CBN.com
Chicken Soup Books
Christian Examiner
Christian Home & School
Christian News NW
Christian Online
Christian Ranchman
Columbia
Guide
Home Times
Indian Life
Lookout
Manna

Our Sunday Visitor
Penned from the Heart
Seek
Testimony

CHILDREN
Guide
Keys for Kids
SHINE brightly
Skipping Stones

CHRISTIAN EDUCATION/ LIBRARY
Group

PASTORS/LEADERS
InSite
Plugged In

TEEN/YOUNG ADULT
Boundless Webzine
Susie
Young Salvationist

WOMEN
P31 Woman

6

Alphabetical Listings of Periodicals

Request writer's guidelines and a recent sample copy or visit a periodical's website before submitting.
   If you do not find the publication you are looking for, look in the General Index.
   For a detailed explanation of how to get the most out of these listings, as well as marketing tips, see "How to Use This Book." Unfamiliar terms are explained in the Glossary.

(*) before a listing indicates unconfirmed information or no information update.

ADULT/GENERAL MARKETS

AMERICA, 106 W. 56th St., New York NY 10019-3893. (212) 581-4640. Fax (212) 399-3596. E-mail: articles@americamagazine.org. Website: www.americamagazine.org. Catholic. Submit to Editor-in-Chief. For thinking Catholics and those who want to know what Catholics are thinking. Weekly mag. & online version; 32+ pgs.; circ. 46,000. Subscription $56. 100% unsolicited freelance. Complete ms/cover letter; fax/e-query OK. **Pays $150-300** on acceptance. Articles 1,500-2,000 wds. Responds in 6 wks. Seasonal 3 mos. ahead. Does not use sidebars. Guidelines by mail/website; copy for 9 x 12 SAE. Incomplete topical listings. (Ads)
   Poetry: Buys avant-garde, free verse, light verse, traditional; 20-35 lines; $2-3/line.

*AMERICAN TRACT SOCIETY, Box 462008, Garland TX 75046-2008. (972) 276-9408. Fax (972) 272-9642. Website: www.ATStracts.org. Submit to Tract Ed. Majority of tracts written to win unbelievers. New tract releases bimonthly; 40 new titles produced annually. Complete ms/cover letter; e-query OK. **PAYS IN COPIES** on publication for exclusive tract rts. Tracts 600-1,200 wds. Responds in 6-8 wks. Seasonal 1 yr. ahead. Accepts simultaneous submissions & reprints (tell when/where appeared). Accepts requested ms on disk or by e-mail (attached or copied into message). Prefers NIV, KJV. Guidelines by mail/e-mail/website ("Ways to Contribute"/"How to write a tract"); free samples for #10 SAE/1 stamp. (No ads)
   Special needs: Youth issues, African American, cartoonists, critical issues.
   Tips: "Read our current tracts; submit polished writing; relate to people's needs and experiences. Follow guidelines—almost no one does."

*ANGELS ON EARTH, 16 E. 34th St., New York NY 10016. (212) 251-8100. Fax (212) 684-1311. E-mail: submissions@angelsonearth.com. Website: www.angelsonearth.com. Guideposts. Colleen Hughes, ed-in-chief; Meg Belviso, depts. ed. for features and fillers. Presents true stories about God's angels and humans who have played angelic roles on earth. Bimonthly mag.; 75 pgs.; circ. 550,000. Subscription $19.95. 90% unsolicited freelance. Complete ms/cover letter; no phone/fax/e-query. **Pays $25-400** on publication for all rts. Articles 100-2,000 wds. (100/yr.); all stories must be true. Responds in 13 wks. Seasonal 6 mos. ahead. E-mail submissions from website. Guidelines on website (www.angelsonearth.com/writers_Guidelines.asp); copy for 7 x 10 SAE/4 stamps.
   Fillers: Buys many. Anecdotal shorts of similar nature (angelic); 50-250 wds. $50-100.
   Columns/Departments: Buys 50/yr. Messages (brief, mysterious happenings), $25. Earning Their Wings (good deeds), 150 wds. $50. Only Human? (human or angel?/mystery), 350 wds. $100. Complete ms.

Tips: "We are not limited to stories about heavenly angels. We also accept stories about human beings doing heavenly duties."

*ANSWERS MAGAZINE & ANSWERSMAGAZINE.COM, PO Box 510, Hebron KY 41048. (859) 727-2222. Fax (859) 727-4888. E-mail: nationaleditor@answersmagazine.com. Website: www .answersmagazine.com. Answers in Genesis. Mike Matthews, exec. ed-in-chief. Bible-affirming, creation-based. Quarterly mag. Subscription $24. Articles 300-600 wds. Responds in 30 days. Details on website ("Contact"/"Write for Answers Magazine"/"Writers Guidelines").
   **2010 EPA Award of Merit: General.

BELIEVERS BAY, 1202 S. Pennsylvania St., Marion IN 46953. (765) 997-1736. E-mail: editor@ BelieversBay.com. Website: www.BelieversBay.com. Tim Russ, pub. To share the love of God with common sense. Monthly online mag. Mostly freelance. Complete ms by e-mail only (attached); e-query OK. **NO PAYMENT** for 1st & electronic rts. (permanently archives pieces). Articles 500-1,000 wds. Guidelines listed at www.believersbay.com/submissions.
   Columns/Departments: Columns 300-500 wds.
   Special needs: Living in Responsible Grace.
   Tips: "Only accepts on-site submissions."

BIBLE ADVOCATE, Box 33677, Denver CO 80233. (303) 452-7973. Fax (303) 452-0657. E-mail: bibleadvocate@cog7.org. Website: http://baonline.org. Church of God (Seventh-day). Calvin Burrell, ed.; Sherri Langton, assoc. ed. Adult readers; 50% not members of the denomination. Bimonthly (6X) mag.; 32 pgs.; circ. 10,000. Subscription free. 25-35% unsolicited freelance. Complete ms/cover letter; no phone/fax/e-query. **Pays $25-55** on publication for 1st, reprint, electronic, simultaneous rts. Articles 600-1,200 wds. (10-20/yr.). Responds in 4-10 wks. Seasonal 9 mos. ahead (no Christmas or Easter pieces). Accepts simultaneous submissions & reprints (tell when/where appeared). Accepts requested ms by e-mail (attached). Regularly uses sidebars. Prefers NIV, NKJV. Guidelines/theme list by mail/website ("Writer's Guidelines" right side); copy for 9 x 12 SAE/3 stamps. (No ads)
   Poetry: Buys 6-8/yr. Free verse, traditional; 5-20 lines; $20. Submit max. 5 poems.
   Fillers: Buys 5/yr. Prose; 100-400 wds. $20.
   Special needs: Articles centering on upcoming themes (see website).
   Tips: "If you write well, all areas are open to freelance. Articles that run no more than 1,100 words are more likely to get in. Also, fresh writing with keen insight is most readily accepted."

BRIDAL GUIDES, 2660 Peterborough St., Oak Hill VA 20171. E-mail: bridalguides@yahoo.com. Website: http://bridalguidesmagazineguidelines.doodlekit.com. Tellstar Publishing. Shannon Bridget Murphy, ed. Theme-based wedding/reception ideas and planning for Christian wedding planners. Quarterly mag. 85% unsolicited freelance. Complete ms/cover letter; e-query OK. **Pays .02-.05/wd.** on acceptance for 1st, onetime, reprint, simultaneous rts. Articles to 2,000 wds.; fiction to 2,000 wds. Responds in 2-8 wks. Accepts simultaneous submissions & reprints (tell when/where appeared). Accepts disk or e-mail submissions (attached or copied into message). No kill fee. Regularly uses sidebars. Also accepts submissions from children/teens. Prefers KJV. Guidelines by e-mail. (No ads)
   Poetry: Buys variable number. Avant-garde, free verse, haiku, light verse, traditional; any length. Pays variable rates. Submit any number.
   Fillers: Buys most types, to 1,000 wds.; .02-.05/wd.
   Special needs: "Most open to wedding and planning articles that show readers how to successfully complete plans for their events. Illustrations and art either with or without manuscript packages. Romance fiction related to weddings, travel, and home."

THE BRINK MAGAZINE, 114 Bush Rd., Nashville TN 37217. Toll-free (800) 877-7030. (615) 361-1221. Fax (615) 367-0535. E-mail: thebrink@randallhouse.com or through the website: www .thebrinkonline.com. Randall House. David Jones, ed. Devotional magazine for young adults; focusing on Bible studies, life situations, discernment of culture, and relevant feature articles. Quarterly & online mag.; 64 pgs.; circ. 8,000. Subscription $6.99. Estab. 2008. 30% unsolicited freelance; 70% assigned. Query, query/clips; prefers e-query. Accepts full mss by e-mail. **Pays $50-150** on acceptance for all rts. Articles 500-2,000 wds. (10-15/yr.). Responds in 1-2 wks. Seasonal 6 mos. ahead. Accepts simultaneous submissions & reprints (tell when/where appeared). Requires accepted articles by e-mail (attached file). No kill fee. Regularly uses sidebars. Does not accept freelance devotions. Guidelines/theme list on website (under "The Magazine"/"Write for the Brink"). (No ads)

   Fillers: Buys 4/yr. Ideas, newsbreaks, book reviews, app reviews, quizzes; 50-100 wds. Pays $50-100.

   Tips: "Pitch articles that are specific and relevant to young adults."

CANADA LUTHERAN, 302—393 Portage Ave., Winnipeg MB R3B 3H6, Canada. Toll-free (888) 786-6707, ext. 172. (204) 984-9172. Fax (204) 984-9185. E-mail: editor@elcic.ca, or canaluth@elcic.ca. Website: www.elcic.ca/clweb. Evangelical Lutheran Church in Canada. Provides information and inspiration to help our readers relate their faith to everyday life and foster a connection with their congregation, synods, and national office. Trina Gallop, ed. dir. (tgallop@elcic.ca); Susan McIlveen, ed. Denominational. Monthly (8X) mag.; 32 pgs.; circ. 14,000. Subscription $22.60 Cdn.; $49.89 US. E-query or complete ms. **Pays $.20/wd. Cdn.** on publication for 1st rts. Articles 700-1,200 wds. Responds in 1-2 wks. Seasonal 6 mos. ahead. No simultaneous submissions; accepts reprints (tell when/where appeared). Prefers e-mail submission (attached file). Sometimes pays kill fee. Regularly uses sidebars. Prefers NRSV. Guidelines on website ("Contribute"/"Writing Guide"); no copy. (Ads)

   Columns/Departments: Buys 16/yr. Practicing Our Faith (how-to piece to help readers deepen or live out their faith); 600 wds. Pays .20/wd.

   Tips: "Canadians/Lutherans receive priority here; others considered but rarely used. Want material that is clear, concise, and fresh. Primarily looking for how-to articles."

THE CANADIAN LUTHERAN, 3074 Portage Ave., Winnipeg MB R3K 0Y2, Canada. Toll-free (800) 588-4226. (204) 895-3433. Fax (204) 897-4319. E-mail: communications@lutheranchurch.ca or through website: www.lutheranchurch.ca. Lutheran Church—Canada. Matthew Block, ed. Bimonthly (6X) mag. Subscription $20. Open to unsolicited freelance. Not in topical listings. (Ads)

*CAPPER'S, 1503 S.W. 42nd St., Topeka KS 66609. (785) 274-4300. Fax (785) 274-4305. E-mail: cappers@cappers.com or through website: www.cappers.com. Ogden Publications. K. C. Compton, ed-in-chief. Timely news-oriented features with positive messages. Monthly mag.; 40-56 pgs.; circ. 150,000. Subscription $18.95. 40% unsolicited freelance. Complete ms/cover letter by mail only. **Pays about $2.50/printed inch for nonfiction** on publication. Articles to 1,000 wds. (50/yr.). Responds in 2-6 mos. Seasonal 6 mos. ahead. No simultaneous submissions or reprints. Prefers requested ms by e-mail. Uses some sidebars. Guidelines by mail/website; copy $4/9 x 12 SAE/4 stamps. (Ads)

   Columns/Departments: Buys 12/yr. Garden Path (gardens/gardening), 500-1,000 wds. Payment varies. This column most open.

   Tips: "Our publication is all original material either written by our readers/freelancers or occasionally by our staff. Every department, every article is open. Break in by reading at least 6 months of issues to know our special audience. Most open to nonfiction features and garden stories." Submissions are not acknowledged or status reports given.

*CATHOLIC NEW YORK, 1011 First Ave., Ste. 1721, New York NY 10022. (212) 688-2399. Fax (212) 688-2642. E-mail: cny@cny.org. Website: www.cny.org. Catholic. John Woods, ed-in-chief. To inform New York Catholics. Biweekly newspaper; 40 pgs.; circ. 132,680. Subscription $26. 2% unsolicited freelance. Query or complete ms/cover letter. **Pays $15-100** on publication for onetime rts. Articles 500-800 wds. Responds in 5 wks. Copy $3.

   Tips: "Most open to columns about specific seasons of the Catholic Church, such as Advent, Christmas, Lent, and Easter."

*CBA RETAILERS + RESOURCES, 9240 Explorer Dr., Colorado Springs CO 80920. Toll-free (800) 252-1950. (719) 272-3555. Fax (719) 272-3510. E-mail: ksamuelson@cbaonline.org. Website: www.cbaonline.org. Christian Booksellers Assn. Submit queries to Kathleen Samuelson, publications dir. To provide Christian retail store owners and managers with professional retail skills, product information, and industry news. Monthly trade journal (also in digital edition); 48-100 pgs.; circ. 5,000. Subscription $59.95 (for nonmembers). 10% unsolicited freelance; 80% assigned. Query/ clips; fax/e-query OK. **Pays .30/wd.** on publication for all rts. Articles 800-2,000 wds. (30/yr. assigned); book/music/video reviews, 150 wds. ($35). Responds in 8 wks. Seasonal 4-5 mos. ahead. Prefers requested ms e-mailed in MS Word file. Regularly uses sidebars. Accepts any modern Bible version. (Ads/Dunn & Dunn/856-582-0690)

> **Special needs:** Trends in retail, consumer buying habits, market profiles. By assignment only.
> **Tips:** "Looking for writers who have been owners/managers/buyers/sales staff in Christian retail stores. Most of our articles are by assignment and focus on producing and selling Christian products or conducting retail business. We also assign reviews of books, music, videos, giftware, kids products, and software to our regular reviewers."

*CBN.COM (CHRISTIAN BROADCASTING NETWORK), 977 Centerville Turnpike, Virginia Beach VA 23463. (757) 226-3557. Fax (757) 226-3575. E-mail: chris.carpenter@cbn.org or through website: www.CBN.com. Christian Broadcasting Network. Chris Carpenter, dir. of internal programming; Belinda Elliott, books ed. Online mag.; 1.6 million users/mo. Free online. Open to unsolicited freelance. E-mail submissions (attached as a Word document). Query/clips; e-query OK. **NO PAYMENT.** Devotions 500-700 wds. Spiritual Life Teaching, 700-1,500 wds. Living Features (Family, Entertainment, Health, Finance), 700-1,500 wds. Movie/TV/Music Reviews, 500-1,000 wds. Hard News, 300-700 wds. News Features, 700-1,500 wds. News Interviews, 1,000-2,000 words; fiction. Accepts reprints (tell when/where appeared). Also accepts submissions from teens. Prefers NLT/NAS/ NKJV. Guidelines by e-mail; copy online. (No ads)

> **Special needs:** Adoption stories/references, world religions from Judeo-Christian perspective.
> **Tips:** "In lieu of payment, we link to author's website and provide a link for people to purchase the author's materials in our Web store."

*CHARISMA, 600 Rinehart Rd., Lake Mary FL 32746. (407) 333-0600. Fax (407) 333-7100. E-mail: charisma@charismamedia.com. Website: www.charismamag.com. Communications. Marcus Yoars, ed.; Jimmy Stewart, mng. ed.; Felicia Mann, online ed.; submit to J. Lee Grady. Primarily for the Pentecostal and Charismatic Christian community. Monthly & online mag.; 100+ pgs.; circ. 250,000. Subscription $14.97. 80% assigned freelance. Query only; no phone query, e-query OK. **Pays up to $1,000** (for assigned) on publication for all rts. Articles 2,000-3,000 wds. (40/yr.); book/music reviews, 200 wds. ($20-35). Responds in 8-12 wks. Seasonal 5 mos. ahead. Kill fee $50. Prefers accepted ms by e-mail. Regularly uses sidebars. Guidelines on website (click on "Writers Guidelines" at the bottom of Home page); copy $4. (Ads)

> **Tips:** "Most open to news section, reviews, or features. Query (published clips help a lot)."

CHICKEN SOUP FOR THE SOUL BOOK SERIES, PO Box 700, Cos Cob CT 06807. Fax (203) 861-7194. E-mail: webmaster@chickensoupforthesoul.com. Website: www.chickensoup.com. Chicken Soup for the Soul Publishing, LLC. Submit questions/requests to Web master's e-mail. *No submissions to Web master's e-mail.* A world leader in self-improvement, helps real people share real stories of hope, courage, inspiration, and love that is open to all ages, races, etc. Quarterly trade paperback books; 385 pgs.; circ. 60 million. $14.95/book. 98% unsolicited freelance. Make submissions via website only. **Pays $200 (plus 10 free copies of the book, worth more than $110)** on publication for reprint, electronic, and nonexclusive rts. Articles 300-1,200 wds. Seasonal anytime. Accepts simultaneous submissions & sometimes reprints (tell when/where appeared). Submissions only through the website: Go to www.chickensoupforthesoul.com and click on "Submit Your Story" on the left tool bar. No kill fee. Accepts submissions from children & teens. Guidelines/themes on website; free sample. (No ads)

Special needs: See website for a list of upcoming titles.

Contest: See website for list of current contests.

Tips: "Visit our website and be familiar with our book series. Send in stories via our website, complete with contact information. Submit story typed, double-spaced, max. 1,200 words, in a Word document."

CHRISTIAN COURIER (Canada), 5 Joanna Dr., St. Catherines ON L2N 1V1, Canada. (US address: Box 110, Lewiston NY 14092-0110.) Toll-free (800) 969-4838. (905) 682-8311. Toll-free fax (800) 969-4838. (905) 682-8313. E-mail: editor@christiancourier.ca or through website: www.christian courier.ca. Reformed Faith Witness. Angela Reitsma Bick, ed.; Cathy Smith, features ed. Mission: To present Canadian and international news, both religious and general, from a Reformed Christian perspective. Biweekly newspaper; 20-24 pgs.; circ. 2,500. Subscription $58 Cdn.; 20% unsolicited freelance; 80% assigned. Send queries to editor@christiancourier.ca. **Pays $75-120 ms., up to .10/wd.** for assigned; 30 days after publication for onetime, reprint, or simultaneous rts. Not copyrighted. Articles 700-1,200 wds. (40/yr.); fiction to 1,200-2,500 wds. (6/yr.); book reviews 750 wds. Responds in 1-2 wks. Seasonal 3 mos. ahead. Accepts simultaneous submissions & reprints (tell when/where appeared). Prefers accepted ms by e-mail (attached file). No kill fee. Uses some sidebars. Prefers NIV. Guidelines/deadlines on website (under "Writers"); no copy. (Ads)

Poetry: Buys 12/yr. Avant-garde, free verse, light verse, traditional; 10-30 lines; $20-30. Submit max. 5 poems.

Tips: "Suggest an aspect of the theme which you believe you could cover well, have insight into, could treat humorously, etc. Show that you think clearly, write clearly, and have something to say that we should want to read. Have a strong biblical worldview and avoid moralism and sentimentality." Responds only if material is accepted.

CHRISTIAN EXAMINER, PO Box 2606, El Cajon CA 92021. (619) 668-5100. Fax (619) 668-1115. E-mail: info@christianexaminer.com. Website: www.christianexaminer.com. Selah Media Group. Lori Arnold, ed. Reports on current events from an evangelical Christian perspective, particularly traditional family values and church trends. Focus is on ministries in S. California and Minneapolis. Monthly & online newspaper; 24-36 pgs.; circ. 150,000. Subscription $19.95. 5% assigned. Query/clips. **Pays .10/wd.,** on publication for 1st & electronic rts. Articles 600-900 wds. Responds in 4-5 wks. Seasonal 3 mos. ahead. No simultaneous submissions or reprints. Prefers e-mail submissions (copied into message). No kill fee. Uses some sidebars. Guidelines by e-mail; copy $1.50/9 x 12 SAE. (Ads)

Tips: "We prefer news stories."

** 2010 EPA Award of Merit: Online; 2010, 2011 EPA Award of Excellence: Newspaper; 2012 EPA Award of Excellence: Online; 2012 EPA Award of Merit: Newspaper. Member of Association of Christian Newspapers (ACN).

CHRISTIAN HOME & SCHOOL, 3350 East Paris Ave. S.E., Grand Rapids MI 49512. Toll-free (800) 635-8288. (616) 957-1070, ext. 240. Fax (616) 957-5022. E-mail: rheyboer@CSIonline .org. Website: www.CSIonline.org. Christian Schools Intl. Rachael Heyboer, mng. ed. Promotes and explains the concept of Christian education. Encourages Christian parents in their daily walk and helps them improve their parenting skills as a form of discipleship. Biannual mag.; 40 pgs.; circ. 66,000. Subscription $13.95. 25% unsolicited; 75% assigned. Complete ms or e-query. Accepts full mss by e-mail. **Pays $50-250** on publication for 1st rts. Articles 1,000-2,000 wds. (30/yr.); book reviews $25 (assigned). Responds in 4 wks. Seasonal 6 mos. ahead (no Christmas or summer). Accepts simultaneous query. Prefers mss by e-mail (attached). Regularly uses sidebars. Accepts submissions from children/teens. Prefers NIV. Guidelines/theme list by mail/website ("About CSI"/

"What We Have to Offer"/"CSI Publications"/"Christian Home & School"/ "Writers Guidelines"; copy for 7 x 10 SAE/4 stamps. (Ads)

> **Tips:** "Writers can break in by submitting articles based on the CH&S editorial calendar, geared from a Christian perspective and current with the times." Check out website for updated editorial calendar: www.csionline.org/chs.
>
> ** 2007 EPA Award of Merit: Organizational. This periodical was #46 on the 2010 Top 50 Christian Publishers list (#41 in 2009, #36 in 2008, #44 in 2007, #32 in 2006).

*CHRISTIANITY TODAY, 465 Gundersen Dr., Carol Stream IL 60188-2498. (630) 260-6200. Fax (630) 260-8428. E-mail: cteditor@christianitytoday.com. Website: www.christianitytoday.com/ctmag. Christianity Today Int. Mark Galli, ed. For evangelical Christian thought leaders who seek to integrate their faith commitment with responsible action. Monthly & online mag.; 65-120 pgs.; circ. 155,000. Subscription $19.95. Prefers e-query or complete ms. **Pays .25-.35/wd.** on publication for 1st rts. Articles 1,000-4,000 wds. (60/yr.); book reviews 800-1,000 wds. (pays per-page rate). Responds in 13 wks. Seasonal 8 mos. ahead. Accepts reprints (tell when/where appeared—payment 25% of regular rate). Kill fee 50%. Does not use sidebars. Prefers NIV. Guidelines on website ("Contact Us"/"Writers Guidelines"); copy for 9 x 12 SAE/3 stamps. (Ads)

> **Tips:** "Read the magazine." Does not return unsolicited manuscripts.
>
> ** 2010, 2006 EPA Award of Merit: Online (for *Christianity Today Online*); 2008, 2006 EPA Award of Excellence: General; 2010, 2009 EPA Award of Merit: General.

THE CHRISTIAN JOURNAL, 1032 W. Main, Medford OR 97501. (541) 773-4004. Fax (541) 773-9917. E-mail: info@thechristianjournal.org. Website: www.TheChristianJournal.org. Chad McComas, ed. Dedicated to sharing encouragement with the body of Christ in Southern Oregon and Northern California. Monthly & online newspaper; 16-24 pgs.; circ. 17,000. Subscription $20; most copies distributed free. Paper is sent to inmates across the country free. 50% unsolicited freelance; 50% assigned. Complete ms; phone/fax query OK. **NO PAYMENT** for onetime rts. Articles & fiction to 500 words; reviews to 500 wds.; children's stories 500 wds. Prefers articles by e-mail to info@thechristian journal.org (attached file). Also accepts submissions from children/teens. Guidelines/theme list by e-mail/website ("Writer's Info"); copy online. (Ads)

> **Poetry:** Accepts 12-20/yr. Free verse, haiku, light verse, traditional; 4-12 lines. Submit max. 2 poems.
>
> **Fillers:** Accepts 50/yr. Anecdotes, cartoons, jokes, kid quotes, newsbreaks, prayers, quotes, short humor, or word puzzles; 100-300 wds.
>
> **Columns/Departments:** Accepts 6/yr. Youth; Seniors; Children's stories; all to 500 wds.
>
> **Tips:** "Send articles on themes; each issue has a theme. Theme articles get first choice."
>
> ** This periodical was #40 on the 2010 Top 50 Christian Publishers list.

*CHRISTIAN NEWS NORTHWEST, PO Box 974, Newberg OR 97132. Phone/fax (503) 537-9220. E-mail: cnnw@cnnw.com. Website: www.cnnw.com. John Fortmeyer, ed./pub. News of ministry in the evangelical Christian community in western and central Oregon and southwest Washington; distributed primarily through evangelical churches. Monthly newspaper; 24-32 pgs.; circ. 29,000. Subscription $22. 10% unsolicited freelance; 5% assigned. Query; phone/fax/e-query OK. **NO PAYMENT.** Not copyrighted. Articles 300-400 wds. (100/yr.). Responds in 4 wks. Seasonal 3 mos. ahead. Accepts reprints (tell when/where appeared). Accepts e-mail submissions. Regularly uses sidebars. Guidelines by mail/e-mail; copy $1.50. (Ads)

> **Tips:** "Most open to ministry-oriented features. Our space is always tight, but stories on lesser-known, Northwest-based ministries are encouraged. Keep it very concise. Since we focus on the Pacific Northwest, it would probably be difficult for anyone outside the region to break into our publication."
>
> ** 2006 EPA Award of Merit: Newspaper.

CHRISTIAN ONLINE MAGAZINE, PO Box 262, Wolford VA 24658. E-mail: submissions@chris tianmagazine.org. Website: www.ChristianMagazine.org. Darlene Osborne, pub. (darlene@christian magazine.org). Strictly founded on the Word of God, this magazine endeavors to bring you the best Christian information on the net. Monthly e-zine. Subscription free. 10% unsolicited freelance; 90% assigned. E-query. Articles 500-700 wds. Responds in 1 wk. Seasonal 2 mos. ahead. Prefers accepted ms by e-mail (attached file). **NO PAYMENT.** Regularly uses sidebars. Also accepts submissions from children/teens. Prefers KJV. Guidelines on website ("Submit an Article: Writer's Guidelines"). (Ads)
>   **Fillers:** Accepts 50/yr. Prayers, prose, quizzes, short humor; 500 wds.
>   **Columns/Departments:** Variety Column, 700-1,000 wds. Query.
>   **Tips:** "Most open to solid Christian articles founded on the Word of God."

CHRISTIAN QUARTERLY, PO Box 311, Palo Cedro CA 97073. Phone/fax (530) 247-7500. E-mail: ChristQtly@aol.com. Nondenominational. Cathy Jansen, pub. Uplifting and encouraging articles. Quarterly tabloid; 28 pgs; circ. 15,000. Subscription free. 100% unsolicited freelance. Phone or e-query. Accepts full mss by e-mail. **NO PAYMENT.** Not copyrighted. Articles under 800 wds. Responds immediately. Accepts reprints (tell when/where appeared). Accepts e-mail (attached or copied into message). Never uses sidebars. Also accepts submissions from children/teens. Guidelines by e-mail; copy for 10 x 13 SAE/$2 postage. (Ads)
>   **Poetry:** Accepts 6-10/yr. Free verse, traditional.
>   **Fillers:** Accepts anecdotes, cartoons, ideas, quotes, short humor, and word puzzles.
>   **Columns/Departments:** Uses many. Marriage & Family; Health; Financial; Testimonies.
>   **Special needs:** "Articles helping people grow in their Christian walk."

THE CHRISTIAN RANCHMAN/COWBOYS FOR CHRIST, 3011 FM 718, Newark TX 76071, or PO Box 7557, Fort Worth TX 76111. (817) 236-0023. Fax (817) 236-0024. E-mail: cwb4christ@cow boysforchrist.net, or CFCmail@cowboysforchrist.net, or through website: www.CowboysforChrist.net. Interdenominational. Ted Pressley, ed. Monthly tabloid; 16 pgs.; circ. 15,000. No subscription. 85% unsolicited freelance. Complete ms/cover letter. **NO PAYMENT** for all rts. Articles 350-1,000 wds.; book/video reviews (length open). Does not use sidebars. Guidelines on website ("Contact Us"/ "Submit an Article"); sample copy.
>   **Poetry:** Accepts 40/yr. Free verse. Submit max. 3 poems.
>   **Fillers:** Accepts all types.
>   **Tips:** "We're most open to true-life Christian stories, Christian testimonies, and Christian or livestock news. Contact us with your ideas first."

*CHRISTIAN RESEARCH JOURNAL, PO Box 8500, Charlotte NC 28271-8500. (704) 887-8200. Fax (704) 887-8299. E-mail: submissions@equip.org. Website: www.equip.org. Christian Research Institute. Elliot Miller, ed-in-chief; Melanie Cogdill, ed. Probing today's religious movements, promoting doctrinal discernment and critical thinking, and providing reasons for Christian faith and ethics. Quarterly mag.; 64 pgs.; circ. 30,000. Subscription $39.50. 75% freelance. Query or complete ms/ cover letter; fax query OK; e-query & submissions OK. **Pays .16/wd.** on publication for 1st rts. Articles to 4,200 wds. (25/yr.); book reviews 1,100-2,500 wds. Responds in 4 mos. Accepts simultaneous submissions. Kill fee to 50%. Guidelines by mail/e-mail (guidelines@equip.org); copy $6. (Ads)
>   **Columns/Departments:** Effective Evangelism, 1,700 wds. Viewpoint, 875 wds. News Watch, to 2,500 wds.
>   **Special needs:** Viewpoint on Christian faith and ethics, 1,700 wds.; news pieces, 800-1,200 wds.
>   **Tips:** "Be familiar with the *Journal* in order to know what we are looking for. We accept freelance articles in all sections (features and departments). E-mail for writer's guidelines."

*CHRISTIAN RETAILING, 600 Rinehart Rd., Lake Mary FL 32746. (407) 333-0600. Fax (407) 333-7133. E-mail: Christian.Retailing@charismamedia.com. Website: www.christianretailing.com. Charisma Media (formerly Strang Communications). Christine D. Johnston, ed. (chris.johnston@

charismamedia.com). For Christian product industry manufacturers, distributors, retailers. Trade & online journal published monthly; circ. 6,200 (print), 9,000 (digital). Subscription $45 print/$25 digital. 10% assigned. Query/clips; no phone/fax/e-query. **Pays .25/wd.** on publication for articles (various lengths); book reviews (no payment), 160 wds. No simultaneous submissions. Accepts requested mss by e-mail (attached file). Kill fee. Uses some sidebars. Prefers NIV. Guidelines by e-mail; catalogs primarily for assigned book reviews. (Ads)

> **Tips:** "Notify the managing editor, Christine D. Johnson (chris.johnson@charismamedia.com), of your expertise in the Christian products industry." Also publishes 2 supplements: *The Church Bookstore* and *Inspirational Gift Trends*, both quarterly.

CHRISTIAN STANDARD, 8805 Governor's Hill Dr., Ste. 400, Cincinnati OH 45249. (513) 931-4050. Fax (513) 931-0950. E-mail: christianstandard@standardpub.com. Website: www.christianstandard .com. Standard Publishing/Christian Churches/Churches of Christ. Mark A. Taylor, ed. Devoted to the restoration of New Testament Christianity, its doctrines, its ordinances, and its fruits. Weekly & online mag.; 16 pgs.; circ. 30,000. Subscription $45. 40% unsolicited freelance; 60% assigned. Complete ms; no phone/fax/e-query. **Pays $20-200** on publication for onetime, reprint, & electronic rts. Articles 800-1,600 wds. (200/yr.). Responds in 9 wks. Seasonal 8-12 mos. ahead. Accepts reprints (tell when/where appeared). Guidelines/copy on website. (Ads)

> **Tips:** "We would like to hear ministers and elders tell about the efforts made in their churches. Has the church grown? developed spiritually? overcome adversity? succeeded in missions?"

CHURCH HERALD AND HOLINESS BANNER, 7407 Metcalf, Overland Park KS 66212. Fax (913) 722-0351. E-mail: HBeditor@juno.com. Website: www.heraldandbanner.com. Church of God (Holiness)/Herald and Banner Press. Mark D. Avery, ed. Offers the conservative holiness movement a positive outlook on their church, doctrine, future ministry, and movement. Monthly mag.; 24 pgs.; circ. 1,100. Subscription $12.50. 5% unsolicited freelance; 50% assigned. Query; e-query OK. Accepts full mss by e-mail. **NO PAYMENT** for onetime, reprint, or simultaneous rts. Not copyrighted. Articles 600-1,200 wds. (3-5/yr.). Responds in 9 wks. Seasonal 6 mos. ahead. Accepts simultaneous submissions & reprints (tell when/where appeared). Accepts requested ms on disk or by e-mail (attached file). Uses some sidebars. Prefers KJV. Also accepts submissions from children/teens. No guidelines; copy for 9 x 12 SAE/2 stamps. (No ads)

> **Fillers:** Anecdotes, quizzes; 150-400 wds.

> **Tips:** "Most open to short inspirational/devotional articles. Must be concise, well written, and get one main point across; 200-600 wds. Be well acquainted with the Wesleyan/Holiness doctrine and tradition. Articles which are well written and express this conviction are very likely to be used."

COLUMBIA, 1 Columbus Plaza, New Haven CT 06510-3326. (203) 752-4398. Fax (203) 752-4109. E-mail: columbia@kofc.org. Website: www.kofc.org/columbia. Knights of Columbus. Alton Pelowski, mng. ed. Geared to a general Catholic family audience; most stories must have a Knights of Columbus connection. Monthly & online mag.; 32 pgs.; circ. 1.5 million. Subscription $6; foreign $8. 25% unsolicited freelance; 75% assigned. Query; e-query OK. Accepts full mss by e-mail. **Pays $250-1,000** on acceptance for 1st & electronic rts. Articles 500-1,500 wds. (12/yr.). Responds in 4-6 wks. Seasonal 4 mos. ahead. Accepts e-mail submission (attachment preferred). Sometimes pays kill fee. Regularly uses sidebars. Prefers NAS. Guidelines by mail/e-mail; free copy. (No ads)

> **Special needs:** Essays on spirituality, personal conversion. Catholic preferred. Query first.

> **Tips:** "We welcome contributions from freelancers in all subject areas. An interesting or different approach to a topic will get the writer at least a second look from an editor. Most open to feature writers who can handle church issues, social issues from an orthodox Roman Catholic perspective. Must be aggressive, fact-centered writers for these features."

> ** This periodical was #45 on the 2006 & 2007 Top 50 Christian Publishers list.

CONVERGE MAGAZINE, (888) 899-3777. E-mail: info@convergemagazine.com. Website: www .convergemagazine.com.

CREATION, PO Box 4545, Eight Mile Plains QLD 4113, Australia. 61-07 3340 9888. Fax 61-07 3340 9889. E-mail: mail@creation.info. Website: www.creation.com. Creation Ministries Intl. Carl Wieland, managing dir. A family, nature, science magazine focusing on creation/evolution issues. Quarterly mag.; 56 pgs.; circ. 46,000. Subscription $28. 30% unsolicited freelance. Query; phone/fax/e-query OK. **NO PAYMENT** for all rts. Articles to 1,500 wds. (20/yr.). Responds in 2-3 wks. Prefers requested ms on disk or by e-mail (attached file). Regularly uses sidebars. Guidelines by mail/e-mail; copy $7.50. (No ads)

> **Tips:** "Get to know the basic content/style of the magazine and emulate. Send us a copy of your article, or contact us by phone."

CREATION ILLUSTRATED, PO Box 7955, Auburn CA 95604. (530) 269-1424. Fax (888) 415-1989. E-mail: ci@creationillustrated.com. Website: www.creationillustrated.com. Tom Ish, ed./pub. An uplifting, Bible-based Christian nature magazine that glorifies God; for ages 9-99. Quarterly mag.; 68 pgs.; circ. 20,000. Subscription $19.95. 60% unsolicited freelance; 40% assigned. Query or query/clips; fax/e-query OK (put query submission in subject line). **Pays $75-125** within 30 days of publication for 1st rts. (holds North American Serial Rights, Archival Rights, and Internet Duplication of the Magazine in PDF Format). Articles 1,000-2,000 wds. (20/yr.). Response time varies. Seasonal 6 mos. ahead. Accepts simultaneous submissions & reprints (tell when/where appeared). Prefers e-mail submission (attached file or copied into message). Kill fee 25%. Uses some sidebars. Prefers NKJV. Guidelines/theme list on website or by e-mail; copy $3/9 x 12 SAE/$3 postage. (Some ads)

> **Poetry:** Short, usually 4 verses. Needs to have both nature and spiritual thoughts. Pays about $15.
>
> **Columns/Departments:** Creation Up Close feature, 1,500-2,000 wds. $100; Re-Creation and Restoration Through Outdoor Adventure, 1,500-2,000 wds. $100; Creatures Near and Dear to Us, 1,500-2,000 wds. $100; Children's Story, 500-1,000 wds. $50-75; My Walk with God, 1,000-1,500 wds. $75; Gardens from Eden Around the World, 1,000-1,500 wds., $75; Creation Day (a repeating series), 1,500-2,000 wds. $100.
>
> **Tips:** "Most open to an experience with nature/creation that brought you closer to God and will inspire the reader to do the same. Include spiritual lessons and supporting Scriptures— at least 3 or 4 of each."

ETERNAL INK, 4706 Fantasy Ln., Alton IL 62002. E-mail: eternallyours8@yahoo.com. Non-denominational. E-mail publication; open to any serious effort or submission. Mary-Ellen Grisham, ed. (meginrose@gmail.com); Ivie Bozeman, features ed. (ivie@rose.net); Pat Earl, devotions ed. Biweekly e-zine; 1 pg.; circ. 450. Subscription free. 25% unsolicited freelance; 75% assigned. Complete ms/cover letter by e-mail only. **NO PAYMENT** for onetime rts. Not copyrighted. Articles/ devotions 300-500 wds. (26/yr.); reviews 300-500 wds. Responds in 6 wks. Seasonal 2 mos. ahead. Accepts simultaneous submissions & reprints. Accepts e-mail submissions (copied into message). No kill fee or sidebars. Prefers NIV. Occasionally accepts submissions from children/teens. Guidelines/ copy by e-mail. (No ads)

> **Poetry:** Elizabeth Pearson, poetry ed. (roybet@comcast.net). Accepts 24-30/yr. Free verse, traditional, inspirational; to 30 lines. Submit max. 3 poems.
>
> **Fillers:** Ivie Bozeman, features and fillers ed. (ivie@rose.net). Accepts 24-30/yr. Anecdotes, jokes, kid quotes, prayers, prose, short humor; 150-250 wds.
>
> **Columns/Departments:** Accepts many/yr. See information in e-zine. Query.
>
> **Contest:** Annual Prose/Poetry Contest in November-December, with 1st, 2nd, and 3rd-place winners in each category. Book awards for first-place winners.
>
> **Tips:** "Please contact Mary-Ellen Grisham by e-mail with questions."

FAITH TODAY: To Connect, Equip and Inform Evangelical Christians in Canada, PO Box 5885, West Beaver Creek, Richmond Hill, ON L4B 0B8, Canada. (905) 479-5885. Fax (905) 479-4742. E-mail: editor@faithtoday.ca. Website: www.faithtoday.ca. Evangelical Fellowship of Canada. Gail Reid, mng. ed.; Bill Fledderus, sr. ed.; Karen Stiller, assoc. ed. A general-interest publication for Christians in Canada; almost exclusively about Canadians, including Canadians abroad. Bimonthly & online mag.; 56 pgs.; circ. 18,000. US print subscription $35.99, online free. 20% unsolicited freelance; 80% assigned. Query only; fax/e-query preferred. **Pays $80-500 (.20-.25 Cdn./wd.)** on publication for 1st & electronic rts.; reprints .15/wd. Features 800-1,700 words; cover stories 2,000 wds.; essays 650-1,200 wds.; profiles 900 words; reviews 300 wds. (75-100/yr.). Responds in 6 wks. Prefers e-mail submission. Kill fee 30-50%. Regularly uses sidebars. Any Bible version. Guidelines at www.faithtoday.ca/writers; copy at www.faithtoday.ca/digital. (Ads)

Columns/Departments: Guest column (a kind of essay/Canadian focus), 650 wds. Buys 2/yr. Pays $150.

Special needs: Canadian-related content.

Tips: "Most open to short, colorful items, statistics, stories, profiles for Kingdom Matters department. Content (not author) must have a Canadian connection." All issues since Jan. 2008 now available free online at www.faithtoday.ca/digital. Unsolicited manuscripts will not be returned.

** This periodical was #42 on the 2006 Top 50 Christian Publishers list.

THE FIT CHRISTIAN MAGAZINE, PO Box 563, Ward Cove, AK 99928. (206) 274-8474. Fax (614) 388-0664. E-mail: editor@fitchristian.com. Website: www.fitchristian.com. His Work Christian Publishing. Angela J. Willard Perez, ed. A Christian rendering health and fitness. Bimonthly mag. Subscription free. Open to unsolicited freelance. Guidelines online at www.fitchristian.com/jobs.html. Features and Articles in the magazine and online. Topics on health, fitness, diet, nutrition, family, faith.

GEM, 700 E. Melrose Ave., Box 926, Findlay OH 45839-0926. (419) 424-1961. Fax (419) 424-3433. E-mail: communications@cggc.org, or through website: www.cggc.org. Churches of God, General Conference. Rachel L. Foreman, ed. To encourage and motivate people in their Christian walk. Monthly (13X) take-home paper for adults; 8 pgs.; circ. 6,000. Subscription $14. 80% unsolicited freelance; 20% assigned. Complete ms/cover letter; phone/fax/e-query OK. **Pays $15** after publication for onetime rts. Articles 300-1,200 wds. (125/yr.); fiction 1,200 wds. (125/yr.). Responds in 12 wks. Seasonal 3 mos. ahead. Accepts simultaneous submissions & reprints (tell when/where appeared). Accepts requested ms on disk or by e-mail. Uses some sidebars. Prefers NIV. Guidelines on website ("Information"/"Periodicals"/scroll down to "Gem Guidelines"); copy for #10 SAE/2 stamps. (No ads)

Poetry: Buys 100/yr. Any type, 3-40 lines; $5-15. Submit max. 3 poems.

Fillers: Buys 100/yr. All types except party ideas; 25-100 words; $5-10.

Special needs: Missions and true stories. Be sure that fiction has a clearly religious/Christian theme.

Tips: "Most open to real-life experiences where you have clearly been led by God. Make the story interesting and Christian."

** This periodical was #13 on the 2010 Top 50 Christian Publishers list (#9 in 2009, #7 in 2008, #9 in 2007, #37 in 2006).

GEMS OF TRUTH, PO Box 4060, 7407-7415 Metcalf Ave., Overland Park KS 66204. (913) 432-0331. Fax (913) 722-0351. E-mail: sseditor1@juno.com. Website: www.heraldandbanner.com. Church of God (Holiness)/Herald & Banner Press. Arlene McGehee, Sunday school ed. Denominational. Weekly adult take-home paper; 8 pgs.; circ. 14,000. Subscription $2.45. Complete ms/cover letter; phone/fax/e-query OK (prefers mail or e-mail). **Pays .005/wd.** on publication for 1st rts. Fiction 1,000-2,000 wds. Seasonal 6-8 mos. ahead. Accepts simultaneous submissions & reprints (tell when/where appeared). Prefers KJV. Guidelines/theme list/copy by mail. Not in topical listings. (No ads)

GENUINE MOTIVATION: YOUNG CHRISTIAN MAN, PO Box 573, Clarksville AR 72830. (479) 439-4891. E-mail: thebeami@juno.com; Website: www.onmyownnow.com; On My Own Ministries, Inc. Rob Beames, ed. Christian alternative to the men's magazine. For young, single men ages 17-23 who are sincerely seeking to be disciples of Christ. Monthly e-zine; 18 pgs; circ. 1,000. Free subscription. Estb. 2009; 40% unsolicted. 60% assigned. Complete manuscript by e-mail. E-mail query OK. **NO PAYMENT, nonexclusive rights.** Prefer NIV. 800-1200 wds. Accept 24 nonfiction mss/yr. Respond in 2 weeks. Seasonal 2 mo ahead. Accepts simultaneous and previously published submissions. (Tell when/where appeared). Require articles by e-mail. No kill fee. Always inc. bio on feature article. Guidelines on website. Book, Music, Video review 800 wds. Accept submissions from teens. Column: Tool Box (resources for young adult men) 450-550 wds; Faith and Finance (good and godly stewardship) 700-1000 wds; The Recap (review of books, movies, music, etc) 600-1000 wds; Election Year (where faith and politics intersect) 800-1200 wds. Accept 18 mss/yr. Query, send complete manuscript.

   Tips: "Looking for guest columnists for Faith and Finance, Tool Box, and The Recap. Also seek new writers for feature articles." (No ads)

GOOD NEWS, PO Box 132076, The Woodlands TX 77393. Phone/fax (832) 813-5327. E-mail: sbeard@goodnewsmag.org or info@goodnewsmag.org. Website: www.goodnewsmag.org. United Methodist/Forum for Scriptural Christianity, Inc. Steve Beard, ed. Focus is evangelical renewal within the denomination. Bimonthly mag.; 44 pgs.; circ. 25,000. Subscription $25. 20% unsolicited freelance. Query first; no phone/fax/e-query. **Pays $100-150** on publication for onetime rts. Articles 1,500-1,850 wds. (25/yr.). Responds in 24 wks. Seasonal 4-6 mos. ahead. Accepts simultaneous submissions & reprints (tell when/where appeared). Accepts requested ms on disk. Kill fee. Regularly uses sidebars. Prefers NIV. Guidelines by mail/website; copy $2.75/9 x 12 SAE. (Ads)

   Tips: "Most open to features."

*GUIDEPOSTS, 16 E. 34th St., 21st Fl., New York NY 10016-4397. (212) 251-8100. E-mail: submissions@guideposts.com. Website: www.guideposts.com. Interfaith. Submit to Articles Editor. Personal faith stories showing how faith in God helps each person cope with life in some particular way. Monthly mag.; 90-100 pgs.; circ. 8 million. Subscription $16.97. 40% unsolicited freelance; 20% assigned. Complete ms/cover letter by e-mail (attached or copy into message). **Pays $100-500** on publication for all rts. Articles 750-1,500 wds. (40-60/yr.), shorter pieces 250-750 words ($100-250). Responds only to mss accepted for publication in 2 mos. Seasonal 3 mos. ahead. Accepts simultaneous submissions & reprints. Kill fee 20%. Uses some sidebars. Free guidelines on website: www.guideposts.com/tellusyourstory; copy. (Ads)

   Columns/Departments: Mysterious Ways (divine intervention), 250 wds. What Prayer Can Do, 250 wds. Angels Among Us, 400 wds. Divine Touch (tangible evidence of God's help), 400 wds.

   Contest: Writers Workshop Contest held on even years with a late June deadline. Winners attend a weeklong seminar in New York (all expenses paid) on how to write for *Guideposts.*

   Tips: "Be able to tell a good story, with drama, suspense, description, and dialog. The point of the story should be some practical spiritual help that subjects learned through their experience. Use unique spiritual insights, strong and unusual dramatic details. We rarely present stories about deceased or professional religious people." First person only.

HOME TIMES FAMILY NEWSPAPER, PO Box 22547, West Palm Beach FL 33416-2547. (561) 439-3509. Fax (561) 908-6701. E-mail: hometimes2@aol.com. Website: www.hometimes.org. Neighbor News, Inc. Dennis Lombard, ed./pub. Conservative, pro-Christian community newspaper. Monthly tabloid; 12-20 pgs.; circ. 4,000. Subscription $24, 12 issues. 15% unsolicited freelance; 25% assigned. Complete ms only/cover letter; no phone/fax/e-query. **Pays $5-25** on acceptance for onetime rts. Articles 100-1,000 wds. (15/yr.); fiction 300-1,500 wds. (1-2/yr.). Responds in 2-3 wks. Seasonal 2 mos. ahead.

Accepts simultaneous submissions & reprints (tell when/where appeared). No kill fee. Regularly uses sidebars. Also accepts submissions from teens. Any Bible version. Guidelines SASE; 3 issues $3. (Ads)

Poetry: Buys almost none. Free verse, traditional; 2-16 lines; $5. Submit max. 3 poems.

Fillers: Uses a few/yr. Anecdotes, cartoons, facts, ideas, jokes, kid quotes, newsbreaks, prayers, quotes, short humor, tips; to 100 wds. pays 3-6 copies, if requested.

Columns/Departments: Buys 30/yr. See guidelines for departments, to 800 wds. $5-15.

Special needs: Good short stories (creative nonfiction or fiction). Home & Family, parenting, education, etc. More faith, miracles, personal experiences, local people stories.

Tips: "Most open to personal stories or home/family pieces. Very open to new writers, but study guidelines and sample first; we are different. Published by Christians, but not 'religious.' Looking for more positive articles and stories. Occasionally seeks stringers to write local people features with photos. Journalism experience is preferred. E-mail query for more info with your name, background, and address to hometimes2@aol.com. We strongly suggest you read *Home Times*. Also consider our manual for writers: *101 Reasons Why I Reject Your Manuscript* (reduced to $12, reg. $19)."

** This periodical was #47 on the 2010 Top 50 Christian Publishers list.

*INDIAN LIFE, PO Box 3765, Redwood Post Office, Winnipeg MB R2W 3R6, Canada. US address: PO Box 32, Pembina ND 58271. (204) 661-9333. Fax (204) 661-3982. E-mail: ilm.editor@indianlife .org or through website: www.indianlife.org. Indian Life Ministries/nondenominational. Jim Uttley, ed. An evangelistic publication for English-speaking aboriginal people in North America. Bimonthly tabloid newspaper; 20 pgs.; circ. 14,500. Subscription $18. 5% unsolicited freelance; 5% assigned. Query (query or complete ms for fiction); phone/fax/e-query OK. **Pays .15/wd (to $200)** on publication for 1st rts. Articles 150-2,500 wds. (20/yr.); fiction 500-2,000 wds. (8/yr.); reviews, 250 wds. ($40). Responds in 6 wks. Seasonal 4 mos. ahead. Accepts simultaneous submissions & reprints (tell when/where appeared). Accepts requested ms by e-mail (copied into message preferred). Some kill fees 50%. Uses some sidebars. Accepts submissions from children/teens. Prefers New Life Version, NIV. Guidelines by mail/e-mail/website; copy for 9 x 12 SAE/$2 postage (check or money order). (Ads)

Poetry: Buys 4 poems/yr.; free verse, light verse, traditional, 10-100 wds. pays $40. Submit max. 5 poems.

Fillers: Kid quotes, quotes, short humor, 50-200 wds. $10-25.

Special needs: Celebrity pieces must be aboriginal only. Looking for legends.

Tips: "Most open to testimonies from Native Americans/Canadians—either first person or third person—news features, or historical fiction with strong and accurate portrayal of Native American life from the Indian perspective. A writer should have understanding of some Native American history and culture. We suggest reading some Native American authors. Native authors preferred, but some others are published. Aim at a 10th-grade reading level; short paragraphs; avoid multisyllable words and long sentences."

**2010 EPA Award of Merit: Newspaper. This periodical was #6 on the 2010 Top 50 Christian Publishers list (#30 in 2009).

KEYS TO LIVING, 105 Steffens Rd., Danville PA 17821. (570) 437-2891. E-mail: owcam@verizon .net. Website: http://keystoliving.homestead.com. Connie Mertz, ed./pub. Celebrating 20 years of ministry in 2013! Educates, encourages, and challenges readers through devotional and inspirational writings; also nature articles, focusing primarily on wildlife in eastern US. Quarterly newsletter; 12 pgs. Subscription $10. 30% unsolicited freelance (needs freelance). Complete ms/cover letter; prefers e-mail submissions; no phone query. **PAYS 2 COPIES** for onetime or reprint rts. Articles 350-500 wds. Responds in 4 wks. Accepts reprints. No disk; e-mail submission OK (copied into message). Prefers NIV. Guidelines/theme list on website ("Guidelines/Subscription"); copy for 7 x 10 SAE/2 stamps. (No ads)

Poetry: Accepts if geared to family, nature, personal living, or current theme. Traditional with an obvious message.

Special needs: More freelance submissions on themes only.

Tips: "We are a Christ-centered family publication. Seldom is freelance material used unless it pertains to a current theme. No holiday material accepted. Stay within word count."

KINDRED SPIRIT, 3909 Swiss Ave., Dallas TX 75204. (214) 841-3556. Fax (972) 222-1544. E-mail: sglahn@dts.edu. Website: www.dts.edu/ks. Dallas Theological Seminary. Sandra Glahn, ed-in-chief. Publication of Dallas Theological Seminary. Tri-annual & online mag.; 16-20 pgs.; circ. 30,000. Subscription free. 75% unsolicited freelance. Query/clips; fax/e-query OK. **Pays $300 flat fee** on publication for 1st & electronic rts. Articles 1,100 wds.; also accepts biblical fiction. Responds in 6 wks. Seasonal 8 mos. ahead. No simultaneous submissions; accepts reprints. Requires accepted mss by e-mail (attached or copied into message). Regularly uses sidebars. Prefers NIV. Guidelines on website ("Submissions"); copy by mail. (No ads)

Special needs: Profiles/interviews of DTS grads and faculty are open to anyone.

Tips: "Any news or profiles or expositions of Scripture with a link to DTS will receive top consideration; all topics other than interviews need to come from DTS graduates."

** 2010 Award of Merit: Cause of the Year.

LEAVES, PO Box 87, Dearborn MI 48121-0087. (313) 561-2330. Fax (313) 561-9486. E-mail: leaves-mag@juno.com. Website: www.mariannhill.us. Catholic/Mariannhill Fathers of Michigan. Jacquelyn M. Lindsey, ed. For all Catholics; promotes devotion to God and his saints and publishes readers' spiritual experiences, petitions, and thanksgivings. Bimonthly mag.; 24 pgs.; circ. 25,000. Subscription free. 50% unsolicited freelance. Complete ms/cover letter; phone/fax/e-query OK. **NO PAYMENT** for 1st or reprint rts. Not copyrighted. Articles 500 wds. (6-12/yr.). Responds in 4 wks. Seasonal 4 mos. ahead. Accepts reprints. Accepts e-mail submissions (copied into message). Does not use sidebars. Prefers NAB, RSV (Catholic edition). No guidelines or copy. (No ads)

Poetry: Accepts 6-12/yr. Traditional; 8-20 lines. Submit max. 4 poems.

Special needs: Testimonies of conversion or reversion to Catholicism.

Tips: "Besides being interestingly and attractively written, an article should be confidently and reverently grounded in traditional Catholic doctrine and spirituality. The purpose of our magazine is to edify our readers."

*LIGHT & LIFE, Box 535002, Indianapolis IN 46253-5002. (317) 244-3660. Fax (317) 244-1247. E-mail: LLMAuthors@fmcna.org. Website: www.freemethodistchurch.org/Magazine. Free Methodist Church of North America. Cynthia Schnereger, mng. ed.; submit to Margie Newton, ms manager. Interactive magazine for maturing Christians; contemporary-issues oriented, thought-provoking; emphasizes spiritual growth, discipline, holiness as a lifestyle. Bimonthly mag.; 32 pgs. (plus pull-outs); circ. 13,000. Subscription $16. 95% unsolicited freelance. Query first; e-query OK. **Pays .15/wd.** on acceptance for 1st rts. Articles 800-1,500 wds. (24/yr.). Responds in 8-12 wks. Seasonal 12 mos. ahead. No simultaneous submissions. Prefers e-mail submission (attached file) after acceptance. No kill fee. Uses some sidebars. Prefers NIV. Also accepts submissions from children/teens. Guidelines on website ("Writer's Guides"); copy $4. (Ads)

Tips: "Best to write a query letter. We are emphasizing contemporary issues articles, well researched. Ask the question, 'What topics are not receiving adequate coverage in the church and Christian periodicals?' Seeking unique angles on everyday topics."

** This periodical was #48 on the 2010 Top 50 Christian Publishers list.

LIVE, 1445 N. Boonville Ave., Springfield MO 65802-1894. (417) 862-2781. Fax (417) 863-1874. E-mail: rl-live@gph.org. Website: www.gospelpublishing.com. Assemblies of God/Gospel Publishing House. Richard Bennett, adult ed. Inspiration and encouragement for adults. Weekly take-home paper; 8 pgs.; circ. 31,000. Subscription $14.40. 100% unsolicited freelance. Complete ms/cover letter; no phone/fax query; e-query OK. **Pays .10/wd. (.07/wd. for reprints)** on acceptance for onetime or reprint rts. Articles 400-1,100 wds. (80-90/yr.); fiction 400-1,100 wds. (20/yr.). Responds in 4-6 wks. Seasonal 18 mos. ahead. Accepts simultaneous submissions & reprints (tell when/where appeared). Accepts e-mail submissions (attached file). No kill fees. Few sidebars. Prefers NIV. Guidelines by mail/e-mail/website ("Writer's Guides"); copy for #10 SAE/1 stamp. (No ads)

Poetry: Buys 12-18/yr. Free verse, light verse, traditional; 8-25 lines; $60 ($35 for reprints) when scheduled. Submit max. 3 poems.

Tips: "We are often in need of good shorter stories (400-600 wds.), especially true stories or based on true stories. Often need holiday stories that are not 'how-to' stories, particularly for patriotic or nonreligious holidays. All areas open to freelance—human interest, inspirational, and difficulties overcome with God's help. Fiction must be especially good with biblical application. Follow our guidelines. Most open to well-written personal experience with biblical application. Send no more than two articles in the same envelope and send a SASE."

** This periodical was #10 on the 2010 Top 50 Christian Publishers list (#3 in 2009, #5 in 2008, #1 in 2007, #8 in 2006).

*THE LOOKOUT, 8805 Governor's Hill Dr., Ste. 400, Cincinnati OH 45249. (513) 931-4050. Fax (513) 931-0950. E-mail: lookout@standardpub.com. Website: www.lookoutmag.com. Standard Publishing. Shawn McMullen, ed. For adults who are interested in learning more about applying the gospel to their lives. Weekly & online mag.; 16 pgs.; circ. 52,000. Subscription $45. 40% unsolicited freelance; 60% assigned. Query for theme articles; e-query OK. **Pays $145-225** on acceptance (after contract is signed), for 1st rts. Articles 1,000-1,600 wds. Responds in 10 wks. Seasonal 9-12 mos. ahead. Accepts simultaneous submissions; no reprints. No disks or e-mail submissions. Kill fee 50%. Regularly uses sidebars. Prefers NIV. Guidelines/theme list by e-mail/website: www.lookoutmag.com /write/default.asp); copy for #10 SAE/$1. (Ads)

Tips: "Open to feature articles according to our theme list. Get a copy of our theme list and query about a theme-related article at least six months in advance. Request sample copies of our magazine to familiarize yourself with our publishing needs (also available online)."

** This periodical was #22 on the 2010 Top 50 Christian Publishers list (#10 in 2009, #17 in 2008, #10 in 2007, #30 in 2006).

THE LUTHERAN DIGEST, 6160 Carmen Ave. E., Inver Grove MN 55076. (651) 451-9945. E-mail: editor@lutherandigest.com. Website: www.lutherandigest.com. The Lutheran Digest, Nick Skapyak, ed. Blend of general and light theological material used to win nonbelievers to the Lutheran faith. Quarterly literary mag.; 64 pgs.; circ. 60,000. Subscription $16. 100% unsolicited freelance. Query or complete ms/cover letter; phone/fax/e-query OK. **Pays $35-100+ ($25-50 for reprints)** on publication for onetime & reprint rts. Articles to 1,000 wds. or no more than 7,000 characters—3,000 preferred (25-30/yr.). Prefers full mss by e-mail. Responds in 4-9 wks. Seasonal 6-9 mos. ahead. Accepts simultaneous submissions & reprints (tell when/where appeared). Accepts e-mail submissions (attached). No kill fee. Uses some sidebars. Rarely accepts submissions from children/teens. Guidelines by mail/website ("Write for Us"); copy $3.50/6 x 9 SAE. (Ads)

Poetry: Accepts 20+/yr. Light verse, traditional; short/varies; no payment. Submit max. 3 poems/mo.

Fillers: Anecdotes, facts, short humor, tips; length varies; no payment.

Tips: "We want our readers to feel uplifted after reading our magazine. Therefore, short, hopeful pieces are encouraged. We need well-written short articles that would be of interest to middle-aged and senior Christians—and also acceptable to Lutheran Church pastors. We prefer real-life stories over theoretical essays. Personal tributes and testimony articles are discouraged. Please read sample articles and follow our writers' guidelines prior to submission—a little research goes a long way. Too much inappropriate and irrelevant material received."

**This periodical was #31 on the 2010 Top 50 Christian Publishers list (#24 in 2009).

*THE MANNA, PO Box 130, Princess Anne MD 21853. (410) 543-9652. Fax (410) 651-9652. E-mail: wolc@wolc.org. Website: www.wolc.org. Maranatha Inc. Debbie Byrd, ed-in-chief. A free monthly tabloid featuring evangelical articles, and distributed in the marketplace in Delaware, Maryland, and Virginia. Digital online tabloid; 32-40 pgs; circ. 42,000. Subscription free. 10-15% unsolicited freelance; 15% assigned. Query/clips; e-query OK. No full mss by e-mail. **Pays $30-50** on publication for 1st, onetime, or reprint rts. Articles 1,000-1,200 wds. Responds in 1-2 wks. Seasonal 3-4 mos. ahead. No simultaneous submissions. Accepts reprints (tell when/where appeared). Accepted articles on disk or by e-mail (copied into message). Uses some sidebars. Also accepts submissions from children/teens. No guidelines; copy for 9 x 12 SAE/2 stamps. (Ads)

> **Fillers:** Anecdotes, ideas, party ideas, short humor, and tips. No payment.
>
> **Columns/Departments:** Accepts up to 12/yr. Finances (business or personal); Counseling (Q & A); Personal Integrity (scriptural); all 800 wds. No payment.
>
> **Special needs:** Themes: marital fidelity, conquering fear, hypocrites, heaven, showing compassion, and What Is Your Hope? Most open to these theme pieces.
>
> **Tips:** "E-mail your query."
>
> ** 2010 Award of Merit: Newspaper; 2009 Award of Excellence: Newspaper.

*MATURE LIVING, One Lifeway Plaza, MSN 175, Nashville TN 37234-0175. (615) 251-5677. E-mail: matureliving@lifeway.com. Website: www.lifeway.com. LifeWay Christian Resources/Southern Baptist. Rene Holt, content ed. Christian leisure reading for 55+ adults, characterized by human interest and Christian warmth. Monthly mag.; 60 pgs.; circ. 318,000. Subscription $22.50. 90% unsolicited freelance; 10% assigned. Complete ms/cover letter; no phone/fax/e-query. Accepts full mss by e-mail (attached or copied into message). **Pays $85-115** for feature articles ($105-115 for fiction) on acceptance for all rts. Articles 400-1,200 wds. (85/yr.); senior adult fiction 900-1,200 wds. (12/yr.). Responds in 6-8 wks. Seasonal 6-8 mos. ahead. No simultaneous submissions or reprints. No kill fee. Uses some sidebars. Prefers KJV, HCSB. Guidelines by mail/e-mail (rene.holt@lifeway.com); to see sample, www.lifeway.com/matureliving.

> **Fillers:** Accepts 144/yr. Grandchildren stories, 50-100 wds. No payment.
>
> **Columns/Departments:** Buys 300+/yr. Cracker Barrel, 4-line verse, $15; Grandparents' Brag Board, 50-100 wds.; Over the Garden Fence (gardening), 300-350 wds.; Communing with God (devotional), 125-200 wds.; Fun 'n Games (wordsearch/crossword puzzles), 300-350 wds.; Crafts; Recipes; $15-50. Complete ms. See guidelines for full list.
>
> **Tips:** "Almost all areas open to freelancers except medical and financial matters. Study the magazine for its style. Write for our readers' pleasure and inspiration. Fiction for 55+ adults needs to underscore a biblical truth."
>
> ** This periodical was #12 on the 2010 Top 50 Christian Publishers list (#22 in 2009, #44 in 2008, #13 in 2007, #10 in 2006).

*MATURE YEARS, Box 801, Nashville TN 37202. (615) 749-6292. Fax (615) 749-6512. E-mail: matureyears@umpublishing.org. United Methodist. Marvin W. Cropsey, ed. To help persons in and nearing retirement years understand and appropriate the resources of the Christian faith in dealing with specific problems and opportunities related to aging. Quarterly mag.; 112 pgs.; circ. 55,000. Subscription $24. 60% unsolicited freelance; 40% assigned. Complete ms/cover letter; fax/e-query OK. **Pays .07/wd.** on acceptance for onetime rts. Articles 900-2,000 wds. (60/yr.); fiction 1,200-2,000 wds. (4/yr.). Responds in 9 wks. Seasonal 14 mos. ahead. Accepts reprints. Prefers accepted ms by e-mail (copied into message). Regularly uses sidebars. Prefers NRSV, NIV. Guidelines by mail/e-mail; copy $5. (No ads)

> **Poetry:** Buys 24/yr. Free verse, haiku, light verse, traditional; 4-16 lines; .50-1.00/line. Submit max. 6 poems.
>
> **Fillers:** Buys 20/yr. Anecdotes (to 300 wds.), cartoons, jokes, prayers, word puzzles (religious only); to 30 wds. $5-25.

Columns/Departments: Buys 20/yr. Health Hints, 900-1,200 wds. Modern Revelations (inspirational), 900-1,100 wds. Fragments of Life (true-life inspirational), 250-600 wds. Going Places (travel), 1,000-1,500 wds. Money Matters, 1,200-1,800 wds.

Special needs: Articles on crafts and pets. Fiction on older adult situations. All areas open except Bible studies.

** This periodical was #36 on the 2010 Top 50 Christian Publishers list (#30 in 2007, #35 in 2006).

MEN OF THE CROSS, 920 Sweetgum Creek, Plano TX 75023. (972) 517-8553. E-mail: info@ menofthecross.com. Website: www.menofthecross.com. Greg Paskal, content mngr. (greg@greg paskal.com). Encouraging men in their walk with the Lord; strong emphasis on discipleship and relationship. Online community. 50% unsolicited freelance. Query by e-mail. **NO PAYMENT.** Not copyrighted. Articles 500-1,500 wds. (10/yr.). Responds in 2-4 wks. Seasonal 3 mos. ahead. Accepts simultaneous submissions; no reprints. Prefers e-mail submissions (attached or copied into message). Uses some sidebars. Prefers NIV, NKJV, NAS. Also accepts submissions from teens. Guidelines by e-mail; copy online. (No ads)

Poetry: Accepts 1/yr. Avant-garde, free verse; 50-250 lines. Submit max. 1 poem.

Special needs: Christian living in the workplace.

Tips: "Appropriate topic could be a real, firsthand account of how God worked in the author's life. We are looking for humble honesty in hopes it will minister to those in similar circumstances. View online forums for specific topics."

THE MESSENGER, 440 Main St., Steinbach MB R5G 1Z5, Canada. (204) 326-6401. Fax (204) 326-1613. E-mail: messenger@emconf.ca or through website: www.emconf.ca/Messenger. Evangelical Mennonite Conference. Terry M. Smith, ed.; Rebecca Roman, asst. ed. Serves Evangelical Mennonite Conference members and general readers. Monthly mag.; 36 pgs. Subscription $24. Uses little freelance, but open. Query preferred; phone/fax/e-query OK. Accepts full mss by e-mail. **Pays $50-135** on publication for 1st rts. only. Articles. Brief guidelines on website ("Subscriptions, Article Submission Information"). Not included in topical listings.

*MOVIEGUIDE, 1151 Avenida Acaso, Camarillo CA 93012. Toll-free (800) 577-6684. (770) 825-0084. Fax (805) 383-4089. E-mail through website: www.movieguide.org. Good News Communications/Christian Film & Television Commission. Dr. Theodore Baehr, pub. Family guide to media entertainment from a biblical perspective. 10% unsolicited freelance. Query/clips. **PAYS IN COPIES** for all rts. Articles 1,000 wds. (100/yr.); book/music/video/movie reviews, 750-1,000 wds. Responds in 6 wks. Seasonal 6 mos. ahead. Accepts requested ms on disk. Regularly uses sidebars. Guidelines/theme list; copy for SAE/4 stamps. (Ads)

Fillers: Accepts 1,000/yr.; all types; 20-150 wds.

Columns/Departments: Movieguide; Travelguide; Videoguide; CDguide, etc.; 1,000 wds.

Contest: Scriptwriting contest for movies with positive Christian content. Go to www.kairos prize.com.

Tips: "Most open to articles on movies and entertainment, especially trends, media literacy, historical, and hot topics."

NOW WHAT? Box 33677, Denver CO 80233. (303) 452-7973. Fax (303) 452-0657. E-mail: now what@cog7.org. Website: http://nowwhat.cog7.org. Church of God (Seventh-day). Sherri Langton, assoc. ed. Articles on salvation, Jesus, social issues, life problems, that are seeker sensitive. Monthly online mag.; available only online. 100% unsolicited freelance. Complete ms/cover letter; no query. **Pays $25-55** on publication for first electronic, simultaneous, or reprint rts. Articles 1,000-1,500 wds. (10/yr.). Responds in 4-10 wks. Accepts simultaneous submissions & reprints (tell when/where appeared). Accepts requested ms by e-mail. Regularly uses sidebars. Prefers NIV. Guidelines by mail/website ("Send Us Your Story").

Special needs: "Personal experiences must show a person's struggle that either brought him/her to Christ or deepened faith in God. The entire *Now What?* site is built around a personal experience each month."

Tips: "The whole e-zine is open to freelance. Think how you can explain your faith, or how you overcame a problem, to a non-Christian. It's a real plus for writers submitting a personal experience to also submit an objective article related to their story. Or they can contact Sherri Langton for upcoming personal experiences that need related articles."

*ON MISSION, 4200 North Point Pkwy., Alpharetta GA 30022-4176. (770) 410-6382. Fax (770) 410-6105. E-mail: onmission@namb.net. Website: www.onmission.com. North American Mission Board, Southern Baptist. Carol Pipes, ed. Helping readers share Christ in the real world. Quarterly & online mag.; 48 pgs.; circ. 230,000. Subscription free. 1-5% unsolicited freelance; 50-60% assigned. Query (complete ms for fiction); no phone/fax query; e-query OK. Accepts full mss by e-mail. **Pays .25/wd.** on acceptance for 1st rts. Articles 500-1,000 wds. (20/yr.). Responds in 8 wks. Seasonal 8 mos. ahead. No simultaneous submissions or reprints. Accepts e-mail submissions (attached or copied into message). Kill fee. Regularly uses sidebars. Prefers HCSB. Guidelines by mail/e-mail/website (put "Writers Guidelines" in search box); copy for 9 x 12 SAE/$2.38 postage. (Ads)

Columns/Departments: Buys 4-8/yr. The Pulse (outreach/missions ideas); 500 wds. Query.

Special needs: Needs articles on these topics: sharing your faith, interviews/profiles of missionaries, starting churches, volunteering in missions, sending missionaries.

Tips: "We are primarily a Southern Baptist publication reaching out to Southern Baptist pastors and laypeople, equipping them to share Christ, start churches, volunteer in missions, and impact the culture. Write a solid, 750-word, how-to article geared to 20- to 40-year-old men and women who want fresh ideas and insight into sharing Christ in the real world in which they live, work, and play. Send a résumé, along with your best writing samples. We are an on-assignment magazine, but occasionally a well-written manuscript gets published."

** 2010, 2007, 2006 EPA Award of Merit: Missionary.

*OUR SUNDAY VISITOR, 200 Noll Plaza, Huntington IN 46750. Toll-free (800) 348-2440. (260) 356-8400. Fax (260) 356-8472. E-mail: oursunvis@osv.com. Website: www.osv.com. Catholic. John Norton, ed.; Sarah Hayes, article ed. Vital news analysis, perspective, spirituality for today's Catholic. Weekly newspaper; 24 pgs.; circ. 68,000. 10% unsolicited freelance; 90% assigned. Query or complete ms; fax/e-query OK. **Pays $100-800** within 4 wks. of acceptance for 1st & electronic rts. Articles 500-3,500 wds. (25/yr.). Responds in 4-6 wks. Seasonal 2 mos. ahead. No simultaneous submissions; rarely accepts reprints (tell when/where appeared). Kill fee. Regularly uses sidebars. Prefers RSV. Guidelines by mail/e-mail/website (click on "About Us"/"Writers' Guidelines" in left column); copy for $2/10 x 13 SAE/$1 postage. (Ads)

Columns/Departments: Faith; Family; Trends; Profile; Heritage; Media; Q & A. See guidelines for details.

Tips: "Our mission is to examine the news, culture, and trends of the day from a faithful and sound Catholic perspective—to see the world through the eyes of faith. Especially interested in writers able to do news analysis (with a minimum of 3 sources) or news features."

** This periodical was #11 on the 2009 Top 50 Christian Publishers list (#48 in 2006).

*PENTECOSTAL EVANGEL (formerly *Today's Pentecostal Evangel*), 1445 N. Boonville, Springfield MO 65802-1894. (417) 862-2781. Fax (417) 862-0416. E-mail: pe@ag.org. Website: www.pe.ag.org. Assemblies of God. Ken Horn, ed.; submit to Scott Harrup, sr. assoc. ed. Assemblies of God. Weekly & online mag.; 32 pgs.; circ. 170,000. Subscription $28.99. 5% unsolicited freelance; 95% assigned. Complete ms/cover letter; no phone/fax/e-query. Accepts full mss by e-mail. **Pays .06/wd. (.04/wd. for reprints)** on acceptance for 1st & electronic rts. Articles 500-1,200 wds. (10-15/yr.); testimonies 200-300 wds. Responds in 6-8 wks. Seasonal 6-8 mos. ahead. No simultaneous submissions;

accepts reprints (tell when/where appeared). Kill fee 100%. Prefers e-mail submissions (attached file). Uses some sidebars. Prefers NIV, KJV. Guidelines on website (click on "Writer's Guidelines" just under "Customer Service" & "Media"); copy for 9 x 12 SAE/$1.39 postage. (Ads)

Fillers: Anecdotes, facts, personal experience, testimonies; 250-500 wds. Practical, how-to pieces on family life, devotions, evangelism, seasonal, current issues, Christian living; 250 wds. Pays about $25.

Special needs: "The *Pentecostal Evangel* offers a free e-mail/online devotional, *Daily Boost*. Contributors are not paid, but a number of these writers have been published in the magazine."

Tips: "True, first-person inspirational material is the best bet for a first-time contributor. We reserve any controversial subjects for writers we're familiar with. Positive family-life articles work well near Father's Day, Mother's Day, and holidays."

**2010 EPA Award of Excellence: Denominational.

PERSPECTIVES: A Journal of Reformed Thought, 4500—60th Ave. S.E., Grand Rapids MI 49512. (616) 392-8555, ext. 131. Fax (616) 392-7717. E-mail: perspectives@rca.org. Website: www.perspectivesjournal.org. Reformed Church Press. Steve Mathonnet-VanderWell and Arika Theule-Van Dam, eds. To express the Reformed faith theologically; to engage issues that Reformed Christians meet in personal, ecclesiastical, and societal life; and thus to contribute to the mission of the church of Jesus Christ. Monthly (10X) & online mag.; 24 pgs.; circ. 3,000. Subscription $30. 75% unsolicited freelance; 25% assigned. Complete ms/cover letter or query; fax/e-query OK. **PAYS 6 COPIES** for 1st rts. Articles (10/yr.) and fiction (3/yr.), 2,500-3,000 wds.; reviews 1,000 wds. Responds in 20 wks. Seasonal 10 mos. ahead. Accepts reprints (tell when/where appeared). Prefers requested ms by e-mail (attached file). Uses some sidebars. Prefers NRSV. Guidelines on website ("About Us"/"Writer's Guidelines"); no copy. (Ads)

Poetry: Accepts 2-3/yr. Traditional. Submit max. 3 poems.

Columns/Departments: Accepts 12/yr. As We See It (editorial/opinion), 750-1,000 wds. Inside Out (biblical exegesis), 750 wds. Complete ms.

Tips: "Most open to feature-length articles. Must be theologically informed, whatever the topic. Avoid party-line thinking and culture-war approaches. I would say that a reading of past issues and a desire to join in a contemporary conversation on the Christian faith would help you break in here. Also the 'As We See It' column is a good place to start."

*POWER FOR LIVING, #104—Manuscript Submission, 4050 Lee Vance View, Colorado Springs CO 80918. Toll-free (800) 708-5550. (719) 536-0100. Fax (719) 535-2928. Website: www.cook ministries.org. Cook Communications/Scripture Press Publications. Catherine Devries, ed. mgr. To expressly demonstrate the relevance of specific biblical teachings to everyday life via reader-captivating profiles of exceptional Christians. Weekly take-home paper; 8 pgs.; circ. 375,000. Subscription $3.99/ quarter. 50% unsolicited freelance; 50% assigned. Complete ms; no phone/fax/e-query. **Pays up to .15/wd. (reprints up to .10/wd.)** on acceptance for onetime rts. Profiles 700-1,500 wds. (20/yr.). Responds in 10 wks. Seasonal 1 yr. ahead. Accepts simultaneous submissions & reprints (tell when/ where appeared). Accepts requested ms on disk. Kill fee. Requires NIV or KJV. Guidelines on website (click on "About David C. Cook"/"Writers Guidelines"); copy for #10 SAE/1 stamp (use address above, but change to MS #205—Sample Request). (No ads)

Special needs: "Third-person profiles of truly out-of-the-ordinary Christians who express their faith uniquely. We use very little of anything else."

Tips: "Most open to vignettes, 450-1,500 wds. of prominent Christians with solid testimonies or profiles from church history. Focus on the unusual. Signed releases required." Not currently open to freelance submissions; check website for any changes.

PRAIRIE MESSENGER: Catholic Journal, PO Box 190, Muenster SK S0K 2Y0, Canada. (306) 682-1772. Fax (306) 682-5285. E-mail: pm.canadian@stpeterspress.ca. Website: www.prairiemessenger.ca.

Catholic/Benedictine Monks of St. Peter's Abbey. Peter Novecosky, OSB, ed.; Maureen Weber, assoc. ed. For Catholics in Saskatchewan and Manitoba, and Christians in other faith communities. Weekly tabloid (46X); 16-20 pgs.; circ. 5,100. Subscription $35 Cdn. 10% unsolicited freelance; 90% assigned. Complete ms/cover letter; phone/fax/e-query OK. **Pays $55 Cdn. ($2.75/column inch for news items)** on publication for 1st, onetime, simultaneous, reprint rts. Not copyrighted. Articles 800-900 wds. (15/yr.). Responds in 9 wks. Seasonal 3 mos. ahead. Accepts simultaneous submissions & reprints. Regularly uses sidebars. Guidelines by e-mail/website (scroll down left side to "Writers' Guidelines"); copy for 9 x 12 SAE/$1 Cdn./$1.39 US postage. (Ads)

   Poetry: Accepts 15/yr. Avant-garde, free verse, haiku, light verse; 3-30 lines. Pays $25 Cdn.
   Columns/Departments: Accepts 5/yr. Pays $60 Cdn.
   Special needs: Ecumenism; social justice; native concerns.
   Tips: "Comment/feature section is most open; send good reflection column of about 800 words; topic of concern or interest to Prairie readership. It's difficult to break into our publication. Piety not welcome." This publication is limited pretty much to Canadian writers only.

PRESBYTERIANS TODAY, 100 Witherspoon St., Louisville KY 40202-1396. Toll-free (800) 728-7228. (502) 569-5520. (502) 569-8632. E-mail: today@pcusa.org. Website: www.pcusa.org/today. Presbyterian Church (USA). Eva Stimson, ed. Denominational; not as conservative or evangelical as some. Primary focus on mission and ministry of the Presbyterian Church (USA)'s General Assembly Mission Council. Monthly (10X) mag.; 52 pgs.; circ. 40,000. Subscription $24.95. 25% freelance. Query or complete ms/cover letter; phone/fax/e-query OK to eva.stimson@pcusa.org. (502) 569-5635. **Pays $100-300** on acceptance for 1st rts. Articles 800-2,000 wds. (prefers 1,000-1,500); (20/yr.). Also uses short features 250-600 wds. Responds in 2-5 wks. Seasonal 3 mos. ahead. Few reprints. Accepts requested ms by postal mail, on disk, or by e-mail. Kill fee 50%. Prefers NRSV. Guidelines on website: www.presbyterianmission.org/ministries/today/writers-guidelines.

   Tips: "Most open to feature articles about Presbyterians—individuals, churches with special outreach, creative programs, or mission work. Do not often use inspirational or testimony-type articles."
   ** This periodical was #40 on the 2006 Top 50 Christian Publishers list and won a "Best in Class" award (2012) from the Associated Church Press.

PRIORITY! 440 W. Nyack Rd., West Nyack NY 10994. (845) 620-7450. Fax (845) 620-7723. E-mail: linda_johnson@use.salvationarmy.org. Website: www.prioritypeople.org. The Salvation Army. Linda D. Johnson, ed.; Robert Mitchell, assoc. ed. Quarterly & online mag.; 48-56 pgs.; circ. 28,000. Subscription $8.95. 50% assigned. Query/clips; e-query OK. **Pays $200-800** on acceptance for 1st rts. Articles 400-1,700 wds. (8-10/yr.). All articles assigned. Responds in 2 wks. Occasionally buys reprints (tell when/where appeared). Prefers accepted ms by e-mail (in Word or copied into message). Kill fee 50%. Regularly uses sidebars. Prefers NIV. Occasionally buys submissions from children/teens. Guidelines/theme list by e-mail; copy $1/9 x 12 SAE. (Ads)

   Columns/Departments: Buys 5-10/yr. Prayer Power (stories about answered prayer, or harnessing prayer power); Who's News (calling attention to specific accomplishments or missions); My Take (opinion essay); all 400-700 wds. $200-400. Query.
   Special needs: All articles must have a connection to The Salvation Army. Can be from any part of the US. Looking especially for freelancers with Salvation Army connections; Christmas recollections (by August 1); people/program features.
   Tips: "Most open to features on people. Every article, whether about people or programs, tells a story and must feature the Salvation Army. Stories focus on evangelism, holiness, prayer. The more a writer knows about the Salvation Army, the better."
   **This publication was #11 on the 2010 Top 50 Christian Publishers List.

*PRISCILLA PAPERS, 122 W. Franklin Ave., Ste. 218, Minneapolis MN 55404-2451. Send submissions to editor at: 130 Essex St., Gordon-Conwell Theological Seminary, S. Hamilton MA 01982. (612) 872-6898. Fax (612) 872-6891. E-mail: debbeattymel@aol.com. Website: www.cbeinternational.org. Christians for Biblical Equality. William David Spencer, ed.; Deb Beatty Mel, assoc. ed. Addresses biblical interpretation and its relationship to women and men sharing authority and ministering together equally, not according to gender, ethnicity, or class but according to God's gifting. Quarterly jour.; 32 pgs.; circ. 2,000. Subscription $40 (includes subscription to *Mutuality*). 85% unsolicited freelance; 15% assigned. Query preferred; e-query OK. **PAYS 3 COPIES, PLUS A GIFT CERTIFICATE AT CBE'S MINISTRY** for 1st & electronic rts. Articles 600-5,000 wds. (1/yr.); no fiction; book reviews 600 wds. (free book). Slow and careful response. No reprints. Seasonal 12 mos. ahead. Prefers proposed ms on disk or by e-mail (attached file) with hard copy. No kill fee. Uses some sidebars. Guidelines on website; copy for 9 x 12 SAE/$2.07 postage. (Ads)

> **Poetry:** Accepts 1/yr. Avant-garde, free verse, traditional (on biblical gender equality themes); pays a free book.
>
> **Tips:** "P.P. is the academic voice of CBE. Our target is the informed lay reader. All sections are open to freelancers. Any well-written, single-theme article (no potpourri) presenting a solid exegetical and hermeneutical approach to biblical equality from a high view of Scripture will be considered for publication." Seeks original cover art work. Use *Chicago Manual of Style*.

RELIEF JOURNAL: A Christian Literary Expression, 8933 Forestview, Evanston IL 60203. E-mail: editor@reliefjournal.com. Website: www.reliefjournal.com. CC Publishing, NFP. Brad Fruhauff, ed-in-chief; Brady Clark, nonfiction ed.; Michael Dean Clark, fiction ed.; Tania Runyan, poetry ed. Semiannual mag.; 140 pgs.; circ. 300. Subscription $23. 90% unsolicited freelance; 10% assigned. Online submission: e-mail submissions. Complete ms. **PAYS IN COPIES** for 1st rts. Creative nonfiction to 5,000 wds (8/yr); fiction to 8,000 wds. (12/yr.). Poetry to 5 poems (50/yr); images to 5 pieces (8/yr). Responds in 16 wks. Accepts simultaneous submissions & reprints (only when solicited). Any Bible version. Guidelines on website ("Submit Your Work"). Incomplete topical listings. (Ads)

> **Poetry:** Tania Runyan, poetry ed. Accepts 50-60/yr. Poetry that is well-written and makes sense; to 1,000 wds. Submit max. 5 poems.
>
> **CNF:** Brady Clark, cnf ed. Accepts 6-10/yr. Personal essays, nonfiction with a narrative and/or emotional arc; to 5,000 wds.
>
> **Fiction:** Michael Dean Clark, fiction ed. Accepts 9-12/yr. Fiction unafraid of the tough questions and willing to live in the ambiguity that requires faith; to 8,000 wds.
>
> **Images:** Brad Fruhauff, image ed. Accepts 6-10/yr. B/W photos, drawings, or paintings that strike the eye and engage the imagination; to 5 images.

SEEK, 8805 Governor's Hill Dr., Ste. 400, Cincinnati OH 45249. E-mail: seek@standardpub.com. Website: www.Standardpub.com. Standard Publishing. Margaret K. Williams, ed. Light, inspirational, take-home reading for young and middle-aged adults. Weekly take-home paper; 8 pgs.; circ. 29,000. Subscriptions $16.99 (sold only in sets of 5). 75% unsolicited freelance; 25% assigned. Complete ms; no phone/fax/e-query. **Pays .07/wd.** on acceptance for 1st rts., **.05/wd. for reprints.** Articles 750-1,200 wds. (150-200/yr.); fiction 500-1,200 wds. Responds in 18 wks. Seasonal 1 yr. ahead. Accepts reprints (tell when/where appeared). Prefers submissions by e-mail (attached file). Uses some sidebars. Guidelines/theme list by mail/website ("About Standard Publishing"/"View Writer's Guidelines" left side); copy for 6 x 9 SAE/2 stamps. (No ads)

> **Fillers:** Buys 50/yr. Ideas, short humor; $15.
>
> **Tips:** "We now work with a theme list. Only articles tied to these themes will be considered for publication. Check website for theme list and revised guidelines."
>
> ** This periodical was #19 on the 2010 Top 50 Christian Publishers list (#19 in 2009, #11 in 2008, #7 in 2007, #26 in 2006).

SOUTHWEST KANSAS FAITH AND FAMILY, PO Box 1454, Dodge City KS 67801. (620) 225-4677. Fax (620) 225-4625. E-mail: info@swkfaithandfamily.org. Website: www.swkfaithandfamily .org. Independent. Stan Wilson, pub. Dedicated to sharing the Word of God and news and information that honors Christian beliefs, family traditions, and values that are the cornerstone of our nation. Monthly newspaper; circ. 9,000. Subscription $25. Accepts freelance. Prefers e-query; complete ms OK. Articles; no reviews. Guidelines on website ("Submit Articles"). Incomplete topical listings. (Ads)

*ST. ANTHONY MESSENGER, 28 W. Liberty St., Cincinnati OH 45202-6498. (513) 241-5615. Fax (513) 241-0399. E-mail: StAnthony@AmericanCatholic.org. Website: www.AmericanCatholic.org. John Feister, ed. For Catholic adults & families. Monthly & online mag.; 64 pgs.; circ. 180,000. Subscription $28. 55% unsolicited freelance. Query/clips (complete ms for fiction); e-query OK. **Pays .20/wd.** on acceptance for 1st, reprint (right to reprint), and electronic rts. Articles 1,500-3,000 wds., prefers 1,500-2,500 (35-50/yr.); fiction 1,500-2,500 wds. (12/yr.); book reviews 500 wds. $50. Responds in 3-9 wks. Seasonal 6 mos. ahead. Kill fee. Uses some sidebars. Prefers NAB. Guidelines on website ("Contact Us"/"Writer's Guidelines"); copy for 9 x 12 SAE/4 stamps. (Ads)

> **Poetry:** Christopher Heffron, poetry ed. Buys 20/yr. Free verse, haiku, traditional; 3-25 lines; $2/line ($20 min.). Submit max. 2 poems.
>
> **Fillers:** Cartoons.
>
> **Tips:** "Many submissions suggest that the writer has not read our guidelines or sample articles. Most open to articles, fiction, profiles, interviews of Catholic personalities, personal experiences, and prayer. Writing must be professional; use Catholic terminology and vocabulary. Writing must be faithful to Catholic belief and teaching, life, and experience. Our online writers' guidelines indicate the seven categories of articles. Texts of articles reflecting each category are linked to the online writers' guidelines for nonfiction articles."
>
> ** This periodical was #28 on the 2009 Top 50 Christian Publishers list (#25 in 2008, #22 in 2007, #33 in 2006).

THE STORYTELLER, 2441 Washington Rd., Maynard AR 72444. (870) 647-2137. E-mail: story tellermag1@yahoo.com. Website: www.thestorytellermagazine.com. Fossil Creek Publishing. Regina Cook Williams, ed./pub.; Ruthan Riney, review ed. Family audience. Quarterly jour.; 72 pgs.; circ. 850. Subscription $24. 100% unsolicited freelance. Complete ms/cover letter; phone/e-query OK. **NO PAYMENT.** Articles 2,500 wds. (60/yr.); fiction 2,500 wds. (100-125/yr.). Responds in 1 wk. Seasonal 3 mos. ahead. Accepts simultaneous submissions & reprints (tell when/where appeared). Responds in 1-2 wks. No disk or e-mail submissions; does not use sidebars. Also accepts submissions from children/teens (not children's stories). Guidelines by mail/website ("Guidelines"); copy $6/9 x 12 SAE/5 stamps. (Ads)

> **Poetry:** Jamie Johnson, poetry ed. Accepts 100/yr. Free verse, haiku, light verse, traditional; 5-40 lines. Submit max. 3 poems. Pays $1/poem.
>
> **Fillers:** Accepts 10-20/yr. Cartoons, quotes, tips; 25-50 wds. Writing-related only.
>
> **Special needs:** Original artwork. Funny or serious stories about growing up as a pastor's child or being a pastor's wife. Also westerns and mysteries.
>
> **Contest:** Offers 1 or 2 paying contests per year, along with People's Choice Awards, and Pushcart Prize nominations. Go to www.thestorytellermagazine.com for announcements of all forthcoming contests for the year.
>
> **Tips:** "We look for stories that are written well, flow well, have believable dialogue, and good endings. So many writers write a good story but fizzle at the ending. All sections of the magazine are open except how-to articles. Study the craft of writing. Learn all you can before you send anything out. Pay attention to detail, make sure manuscripts are as free of mistakes as possible. Follow the guidelines—they aren't hard." Always looking for B & W photos for front cover.
>
> ** This periodical was #42 on the 2007 Top 50 Christian Publishers list.

STUDIO: A Journal of Christians Writing, 727 Peel St., Albury NSW 2640, Australia. Phone/fax +61 2 6021 1135. E-mail: studio00@bigpond.net.au. Website: http://web.me.com/pdgrover?StudioJournal. Submit to Studio Editor. Quarterly jour.; 36 pgs.; circ. 300. Subscription $60 AUS. 90% unsolicited freelance; 10% assigned. Query. **PAYS IN COPIES** for onetime rts. Articles 3,000 wds. (15/yr.); fiction 3,000 wds. (50/yr.); book reviews 300 wds. Responds in 3 wks. Accepts simultaneous submissions & reprints (tell when/where appeared). No disks; e-mail submissions OK. Does not use sidebars. Guidelines by mail (send IRC); copy for $10 AUS. (Ads)

> **Poetry:** Accepts 200/yr. Any type; 4-100 lines. Submit max. 3 poems.
>
> **Contest:** See copy of journal for details.
>
> **Tips:** "We accept all types of fiction and literary article themes."

SUCCESS/VICTORY NEWS, Franklin Publishing Company, 2723 Steamboat Circle, Arlington TX 76006. (817) 548-1124. E-mail: ludwigotto@sbcglobal.net. Website: www.franklinpublishing.net. Submit to Dr. Ludwig Otto, publisher. Bimonthly journal. 170 pgs; circ. 8,000. Subscription $80. **NO PAYMENT.** 100% unsolicited. Responds in 3 wks. E-mail queries. Send submissions by e-mail attachment. No writer's guidelines. Book reviews 3 pgs. Audience general public with a Christian message.

TESTIMONY, 2450 Milltower Ct., Mississauga ON L5N 5Z6, Canada. (905) 542-7400. Fax (905) 542-7313. E-mail: testimony@paoc.org. Website: www.testimonymag.ca. The Pentecostal Assemblies of Canada. Stephen Kennedy, ed. To encourage a Christian response to a wide range of issues and topics, including those that are peculiar to Pentecostals. Monthly & online mag.; 24 pgs.; circ. 8,000. Subscription $30 US/$24 Cdn. (includes GST). 10% unsolicited freelance; 90% assigned. Query; fax/e-query OK. **Pays $100** on publication for 1st rts. (no pay for reprint rts.). Articles 700-900 wds. Responds in 6-8 wks. Seasonal 4 mos. ahead. Accepts reprints (tell when/where appeared). Prefers e-mail submission (copied into message). Regularly uses sidebars. Prefers NIV. Guidelines/theme list by mail/e-mail/website (click on "Fellowship Services"/ "Publications"/"Testimony"/scroll down to "View our Submission Guidelines Here"); $3 US or $2.50 Cdn./copy 9 x 12 SAE. (Ads)

> **Tips:** "View theme list on our website and query us about a potential article regarding one of our themes. Our readership is 98% Canadian. We prefer Canadian writers or at least writers who understand that Canadians are not Americans in long underwear. We also give preference to members of this denomination, since this is related to issues concerning our fellowship."

*THRIVING FAMILY, 8605 Explorer Dr., Colorado Springs CO 80920. E-mail: thrivingfamily submissions@family.org. Website: www.thrivingfamily.com. Focus on the Family. Submit to The Editor. Focuses on marriage and parenting from a biblical perspective; mostly for families with 4- to 12-year-old children. Monthly & online mag. Open to unsolicited freelance. Complete ms or query; e-query OK (no attachments). **Pays .25/wd.** Feature articles 1,200-2,000 wds.; online articles 800-1,200 wds. Guidelines/theme list; copy online. Incomplete topical listings.

> **Columns/Departments:** Family Stages (practical tips), 50-200 wds. For Fun (marriage or family humor articles), about 500 wds., pays $175. For Him (male perspective), 450 wds. For Her (female perspective), 450 wds. Blended Family (concerns of blended families), 800 wds. Extended Family (relationships with relatives), 450 wds.

TIME OF SINGING: A Magazine of Christian Poetry, PO Box 149, Conneaut Lake PA 16316. E-mail: timesing@zoominternet.net. Website: www.timeofsinging.com. Lora Zill, ed. We try to appeal to all poets and lovers of poetry. Quarterly booklet; 44 pgs.; circ. 250. Subscription $17. 95% unsolicited freelance; 5% assigned. Complete ms; e-query OK. **PAYS IN COPIES** for 1st, onetime, or reprint rts. Poetry only (some book reviews by assignment). Responds in 12 wks. Seasonal 6 mos. ahead. Accepts simultaneous submissions & reprints (tell when/where appeared). Accepts e-mail submission (attached file). Guidelines by mail/e-mail/website ("Guidelines"); copy $4 ea. or 2/$7 (Checks, money orders payable to Wind & Water Press.)

Poetry: Accepts 150-200/yr. Free verse, haiku, light verse, traditional; 3-60 lines. Submit max. 5 poems. Always need form poems (sonnets, villanelles, triolets, etc.) with Christian themes. Fresh rhyme. "Cover letter not needed; your work speaks for itself."

Contest: Sponsors 1-2 annual poetry contests on specific themes or forms ($3 entry fee/poem) with cash prizes (see website or send SASE for rules).

Tips: "Study poetry, read widely—both Christian and non-Christian. Work at the craft. Be open to suggestions and critique. If I have taken time to comment on your work, it is close to publication. If you don't agree, submit elsewhere. I appreciate poets who take chances, who write outside the box. *Time of Singing* is a literary poetry magazine, so I'm not looking for greeting card verse or sermons that rhyme."

THE VISION, 8855 Dunn Rd., Hazelwood MO 63042-2299. (314) 837-7300. Fax (314) 336-1803. E-mail: WAP@upci.org. Website: www.workaflame.org or www.upci.org/wap. United Pentecostal Church. Richard M. Davis, ed.; submit to Karen Myers, administrative aide. Denominational. Weekly take-home paper; 4 pgs.; circ. 6,000. Subscription $3.49/quarter. 95% unsolicited freelance. Complete ms/cover letter; no e-query. **Pays $8-25** on publication. Articles 500-1,600 wds. (to 120/yr.); fiction 1,200-1,600 wds. (to 120/yr.); devotionals 350-400 wds. Seasonal 9 months ahead. Accepts simultaneous submissions & reprints. Guidelines by mail/e-mail/website ("Writer's Guidelines" left side); free copy/#10 SASE. (No ads)

Poetry: Buys 30/yr.; traditional; $3-12.

Columns/Departments: Devotionals 350-400 wds. Requires KJV.

Tips: "Most open to fiction short stories, real-life experiences, and short poems. Whether fiction or nonfiction, we are looking for stories depicting everyday life situations and how Christian principles are used to solve problems, resolve issues, or enhance one's spiritual growth. Be sure manuscript has a pertinent, spiritual application. Best way to break into our publication is to send a well-written article that meets our specifications."

VISTA, PO Box 50434, Indianapolis IN 46250-0434. (317) 774-7900. E-mail: submissions@wesleyan.org. Website: www.wesleyan.org/wg. Wesleyan Publishing House. Jim Watkins, ed. Weekly take-home paper; 8 pgs. 60% unsolicited freelance; 40% assigned. Accepts full mss by e-mail only. **Pays $15-35** on publication for onetime and reprint rts. Articles 500-550 wds.; fiction 500-550 wds.; humor 250 wds. Seasonal 9 mos. ahead. Theme based. E-mail to request theme list. No simultaneous submissions. Requires e-mail submissions (no attachments). No kill fee. Also accepts submissions from children/teens. Prefers NIV. Guidelines on website (www.wesleyan.org/wg).

Tips: "Great market for beginning writers. Any subject related to Christian growth."

WAR CRY, 615 Slaters Ln., Alexandria VA 22314. (703) 684-5500. Fax (703) 684-5539. E-mail: War_cry@USN.salvationarmy.org. Website: www.thewarcry.com. The Salvation Army. Maj. Allen Satterlee, ed-in-chief; Jeff McDonald, mng. ed. Pluralistic readership reaching all socioeconomic strata and including distribution in institutions. 15 issues/yr including special Easter & Christmas issues. 36 pgs. circ. 288,000. Prefers to accept full mss by e-mail (attached or copied into message); e-query OK. **Pays .25/wd.** upon publication. Articles 500-1,000 wds.; fillers 100-400 wds. Limited poetry. Responds in 3-4 wks. Submit material 3 mos in adv for monthly issues, 6 mo for special issues/holidays. Accepts simultaneous submissions or reprints. Guidelines by mail/e-mail; copy for 9 x 12 SASE. Accepts ads.

   ** This periodical was #38 on the 2010 Top 50 Christian Publishers list (#45 in 2009, #40 in 2008, #17 in 2006).

*WEAVINGS, 1908 Grand Ave., PO Box 340004, Nashville TN 37203-0004. (615) 340-7200. E-mail: weavings@upperroom.org. Website: www.upperroom.org. The Upper Room. Submit to The Editor. For clergy, lay leaders, and all thoughtful seekers who want to deepen their understanding of, and response to, how God's life and human lives are being woven together. Quarterly mag. Subscription

$28. Open to freelance. Complete ms. **Pays .12/wd. & up** on acceptance. Articles 1,250-2,000 wds.; sermons & meditations 500-2,000 wds.; stories (short vignettes or longer narratives) to 2,000 wds.; book reviews 750 wds. Responds within 13 wks. Accepts reprints. Accepts requested ms on disk or by e-mail. Guidelines/theme list on website (click on "Weavings" under Publishing column on right side, then "Writing for Weavings"); copy for 7.5 x 10.5 SAE/5 stamps. Incomplete topical listings.

Poetry: Pays $75 & up.

Tips: Note that this publication is transitioning as we go to press and will likely be changing format, as well as other aspects of this listing. Check their website for current information.

WORD & WAY, 3236 Emerald Ln., Ste. 400, Jefferson City MO 65109-3700. (573) 635-5939, ext. 205. Fax (573) 635-1774. E-mail: wordandway@wordandway.org. Website: www.wordandway.org. Baptist. Bill Webb, ed. (bwebb@wordandway.org). Contact: Vicki Brown, Assoc. ed. (vbrown@wordandway.org). Biweekly. Subscription $17.50. To share the stories of God at work through Baptists in Missouri and surrounding areas.

CHILDREN'S MARKETS

*FOCUS ON THE FAMILY CLUBHOUSE, 8605 Explorer Dr., Colorado Springs CO 80920. (719) 531-3400. Website: www.clubhousemagazine.com. Focus on the Family. Jesse Florea, ed.; submit to Ashley Eiman, asst. ed. For children 8-12 years who desire to know more about God and the Bible. Monthly & online mag.; 32 pgs.; circ. 80,000. Subscription $19.99. 15% unsolicited freelance; 25% assigned. Complete ms/cover letter; no phone/fax/e-query. **Pays .15-.25/wd.** for articles, **up to $300 for fiction** on acceptance for nonexclusive license. Articles to 800 wds. (5/yr.); fiction 500-1,800 wds. (30/yr.). Responds in 8 wks. Seasonal 6 mos. ahead. Accepts simultaneous submissions; no reprints. No disk or e-mail submissions. Kill fee. Uses some sidebars. Prefers HCSB. Also accepts submissions from children once a year. Guidelines by mail; copy (call 800-232-6459). (No ads)

Fillers: Buys 6-8/yr. Quizzes, word puzzles, recipes; 200-800 wds., .15-.25/wd.

Tips: "Most open to fiction, personality stories, quizzes, and how-to pieces with a theme. Avoid stories dealing with boy-girl relationships, poetry, and contemporary, middle-class family settings (current authors meet this need). We look for fiction in exciting settings with ethnic characters. Creatively retold Bible stories and historical fiction are easy ways to break in. Send manuscripts with list of credentials. Read past issues."

** 2010, 2009, 2008, 2007, 2006 EPA Award of Merit: Youth.

*FOCUS ON THE FAMILY CLUBHOUSE JR., 8605 Explorer Dr., Colorado Springs CO 80920. (719) 531-3400. Fax (719) 531-3499. E-mail: joanna.lutz@fotf.org. Website: www.clubhousejr.com. Focus on the Family. Jesse Florea, ed.; Joanna Lutz, assoc. ed.; submit to Joanna Lutz, ed. asst. For 3- to 7-year-olds growing up in a Christian family. Monthly & online mag.; 32 pgs.; circ. 65,000. Subscription $19.99. 25% unsolicited freelance; 50% assigned. Complete ms/cover letter; no phone/fax/e-query. **Pays $30-200 ($50-200 for fiction)** on acceptance for nonexclusive rts. Articles 100-500 wds. (1-2/yr.); fiction 250-1,000 wds. (10/yr.); Bible stories 250-800 wds.; one-page rebus stories to 350 wds. Responds in 8 wks. Seasonal 6-9 mos. ahead. Kill fee. Prefers NIrV. Uses some sidebars. Guidelines by mail; copy (call 800-232-6459). (No ads)

Poetry: Buys 4-8/yr. Traditional; 10-25 lines (to 250 wds.); $50-100.

Fillers: Buys 4-8/yr. Recipes/crafts; 100-500 wds. $30-100.

Special needs: Bible stories, rebus, fiction, and crafts.

Tips: "Most open to short, nonpreachy fiction, beginning reader stories, and read-to-me. Be knowledgeable of our style and try it out on kids first. Looking for stories set in exotic places; nonwhite, middle-class characters; historical pieces; humorous quizzes; and craft and recipe features are most readily accepted."

** 2010 EPA Award of Excellence: Youth; 2007 EPA Award of Merit: Youth.

GUIDE, 55 W. Oak Ridge Dr., Hagerstown MD 21740. (301) 393-4037. Fax (301) 393-4055. E-mail: Guide@rhpa.org. Website: www.guidemagazine.org. Seventh-day Adventist/Review and Herald Publishing. Randy Fishell, ed. A Christian journal for 10- to 14-yr.-olds, presenting true stories relevant to their needs. Weekly mag.; 32 pgs.; circ. 26,000. Subscription $54.95/yr. 75% unsolicited freelance; 20% assigned. Complete ms/cover letter; fax/e-query OK. **Pays .07-.10/wd. ($25-140)** on acceptance for 1st, reprint, simultaneous, and electronic rts. True stories only, 500-1,300 wds. (200/yr.). Responds in 4-6 wks. Seasonal 8 mos. ahead. Accepts simultaneous submissions & reprints (tell when/where appeared; pays 50% of standard rate). Prefers requested ms by e-mail (attached or copied into message). Kill fee 20-50%. Regularly uses sidebars. Accepts submissions from children/teens. Prefers NIV. Guidelines on website (link on home page) or by mail; copy for 6 x 9 SAE/ 2 stamps. (Ads)

> **Fillers:** Buys 40-50/yr. Cartoons, games, quizzes, word puzzles on a spiritual theme; 20-50 wds. $20-40. Accepting very few games, only the most unusual concepts.
>
> **Columns/Departments:** All are assigned.
>
> **Special needs:** "Most open to true action/adventure, Christian humor, and true stories showing God at work in a 10- to 14-year-old's life. Stories must have energy and a high level of intrinsic interest to kids. Put it together with dialog and a spiritual slant, and you're on the 'write' track for our readers. School life."
>
> **Tips:** "We are very open to freelancers. Use your best short-story techniques (dialogue, scenes, a sense of 'plot') to tell a true story starring a kid ages 10-14. Bring out a clear spiritual/biblical message. We publish multipart true stories regularly; 3-12 chapters, 1,200 words each. We can no longer accept nature or historical stories without documentation. All topics indicated need to be addressed within the context of a true story."
>
> ** This periodical was #17 on the 2010 Top 50 Christian Publishers list (#23 in 2009, #24 in 2008, #27 in 2007, #44 in 2006).

JUNIORWAY, PO Box 436987, Chicago IL 60643. Fax (708) 868-6759. Website: www.urban ministries.com. Urban Ministries, Inc. K. Steward, ed. (ksteward@urbanministries.com). Sunday school magazine with accompanying teacher's guide and activity booklet for 4th-6th graders. Open to freelance queries; 100% assigned. Query and/or e-query with writing sample and/or clips; no phone queries. **Pays $150** for curriculum, 120 days after acceptance for all rts. Articles 1,200 wds. (4/yr.), pays $80. Responds in 4 wks. No simultaneous submissions. Requires requested material by e-mail (attached file). Guidelines by e-mail. Incomplete topical listings. (No ads)

> **Poetry:** Buys 8/yr.; 200-400 wds. Pays $40.
>
> **Tips:** "*Juniorway* principally serves an African American audience; editorial content addresses broad Christian issues. Looking for those with educational or Sunday school teaching experience who can actually explain Scriptures in an insightful and engaging way and apply those Scriptures to the lives of children 9-11 years old."

KEYS FOR KIDS, PO Box 1001, Grand Rapids MI 49501-1001. (616) 647-4971. Fax (616) 647-4950. E-mail: Hazel@cbhministries.org or geri@cbhministries.org. Website: www.cbh ministries.org. CBH Ministries. Hazel Marett, ed.; Geri Walcott, ed. A daily devotional booklet for children (8-14) or for family devotions. Quarterly booklet & online version; 112 pgs.; circ. 70,000. Subscription free. 100% unsolicited freelance. Complete ms; e-query OK. Accepts full mss by e-mail. **Pays $25** on acceptance for 1st, reprint, or simultaneous rts. Devotionals (includes short fiction story) 375-425 wds. (30-40/yr.). Responds in 4-8 wks. Seasonal 4-5 mos. ahead. Accepts simultaneous submissions & reprints. Prefers NKJV. Guidelines by mail/e-mail; copy for $1.50 postage/ handling. (No ads)

> **Tips:** "We want children's devotions. If you are rejected, go back to the sample and study it some more. We use only devotionals, but they include a short fiction story. Any appropriate topic is fine."

THE KIDS' ARK CHILDREN'S CHRISTIAN MAGAZINE, PO Box 3160, Victoria TX 77903. Toll-free (800) 455-1770. (361) 485-1770. E-mail for queries: editor@thekidsark.com. Website: http://thekidsark.com. Interdenominational. Submit to: Joy Mygrants, sr. ed., @ thekidsarksubmissions@yahoo.com. To give kids, 6-12, a biblical foundation on which to base their choices in life. Quarterly & online mag.; 36 pgs.; circ. 8,000. 100% unsolicited freelance. Complete ms; e-query OK. Accepts full ms by e-mail. **Pays $100 max.** on publication for 1st, reprint ($25), electronic, worldwide rts. Fiction 600 wds. (Buys 4 stories/issue—16/yr., must match issue's theme); no articles. Responds in 3-4 wks. No reprints. Prefers accepted submissions by e-mail (attached file). Kill fee 15%. Uses some sidebars. Also accepts submissions from children/teens. Prefers NIV. Guidelines/theme list on website ("Writer's Guidelines"); paper copy for $1 postage. Sample magazine on website. (Ads—limited)

> **Tips:** "Open to fiction only (any time period). Think outside the box! Must catch children's attention and hold it; be biblically based and related to theme. We want to teach God's principles in an exciting format. Every issue contains the Ten Commandments and the plan of salvation."

PARTNERS, Christian Light Publications Inc., Box 1212, Harrisonburg VA 22803-1212. (540) 434-0768. Fax (540) 433-8896. E-mail: partners@clp.org. Website: www.clp.org. Mennonite. Sue Joy Anderson, ed. Helping 9- to 14-yr.-olds to build strong Christian character. Weekly take-home paper; 4 pgs.; circ. 7,217. Subscription $11.95. 99% unsolicited freelance; 1% assigned. Complete ms; e-query OK. **Pays .04-.06/wd.** on acceptance for 1st, multiuse, or reprint rts. Articles 200-800 wds. (75/yr.); fiction & true stories 400-1,600 wds. (150/yr.); serial stories up to 1,600 wds./installment; short-short stories to 400 wds. Responds in 8 wks. Seasonal 6 mos. ahead. Accepts reprints only 8 yrs. or more after last publication (tell when/where appeared); serials 2-5 parts. Prefers e-mail submissions (attached or copied into message). No kill fee. Requires KJV. Guidelines/theme list by mail/e-mail; copy for 9 x 12 SAE/3 stamps. (No ads)

> **Poetry:** Buys 75/yr. Traditional, story poems; 4-24 lines; .65-.75/line.
> **Fillers:** Buys 150/yr. Prose, quizzes, quotes, word puzzles (Bible-related); 200-800 wds., .04-.06/wd.
> **Columns/Departments:** Character Corner; Cultures & Customs; Historical Highlights; Maker's Masterpiece; Missionary Mail; Torches of Truth; or Nature Nook; all 200-800 wds.
> **Tips:** "Most open to character-building articles and stories that teach a spiritual lesson. New approaches to old themes, or new theme relevant to age level. Please ask for our guidelines before submitting manuscripts. Write in a lively way (showing, not telling) and on a child's level of understanding (ages 9-14). We do not require that you be Mennonite, but we do send a questionnaire for you to fill out if you desire to write for us."
> ** This periodical was #3 on the 2010 Top 50 Christian Publishers list (#2 in 2009, #3 in 2008, #14 in 2007, #15 in 2006).

*POCKETS, PO Box 340004, Nashville TN 37203-0004. (615) 340-7333. Fax (615) 340-7267. E-mail: pockets@upperroom.org or through website: www.pockets.upperroom.org. United Methodist/The Upper Room. Submit to Lynn W. Gilliam, ed. Devotional magazine for children (6-11 yrs.). Monthly (11X) mag.; 48 pgs.; circ. 67,000. Subscription $21.95. 75% unsolicited freelance. Complete ms/brief cover letter; no phone/fax/e-query. **Pays .14/wd.** on acceptance for onetime rts. Articles 400-800 wds. (10/yr.) & fiction 600-1,400 wds. (40/yr.). Responds in 8 wks. Seasonal 1 yr. ahead. Accepts simultaneous submissions & reprints (tell when/where appeared). No mss by e-mail. Uses some sidebars. Prefers NRSV. Also accepts submissions from children through age 12. Guidelines/theme list by mail/e-mail/website (click on "Print Magazine"/"Write for Pockets"); copy for 9 x 12 SAE/4 stamps. (No ads)

> **Poetry:** Buys 25/yr. Free verse, haiku, light verse, traditional; to 25 lines; $25-48. Submit max. 7 poems.
> **Fillers:** Buys 50/yr. Games, word puzzles; $25-50.

Columns/Departments: Buys 20/yr. Complete ms. Kids Cook; Pocketsful of Love (ways to show love in your family), 200-300 wds. Peacemakers at Work (children involved in environmental, community, and peace/justice issues; include action photos and name of photographer), to 600 wds. Pocketsful of Prayer, 400-600 wds. Someone You'd Like to Know (preferably a child whose lifestyle demonstrates a strong faith perspective), 600 wds. Pays .14/wd.

Special needs: Two-page stories for ages 5-7, 600 words max. Need role model stories, retold biblical stories, Someone You'd Like to Know, and Peacemakers at Work.

Contest: Fiction-writing contest; submit between March 1 & August 15 every year. Prize $1,000 and publication in *Pockets*. Length 1,000-1,600 wds. Must be unpublished and not historical fiction. Previous winners not eligible. Send to Pockets Fiction Contest at above address, and include an SASE for return of manuscript and response. Write "Fiction Contest" on envelope and on title/first page of manuscript.

Tips: "Well-written fiction that fits our themes is always needed. Make stories relevant to the lives of today's children and show faith as a natural part of everyday life. All areas open to freelance. Nonfiction probably easiest to sell for columns (we get fewer submissions for those). Read, read, read, and study. Be attentive to guidelines, themes, and study past issues."

** This periodical was #8 on the 2010 Top 50 Christian Publishers list (#6 in 2009, #8 in 2008, #11 in 2007, #12 in 2006).

SHINE BRIGHTLY, Box 7259, Grand Rapids MI 49510. (616) 241-5616, ext. 3034. Fax (616) 241-5558. E-mail: kelli@gemsgc.org. Website: www.gemsgc.org. GEMS Girls Clubs. Kelli Ponstein, mng. ed. (734-478-1596; kelli@gemsgc.org). To show girls ages 9-14 that God is at work in their lives and in the world around them. Monthly (9X) mag.; 24 pgs.; circ. 19,000. Subscription $13.95. 80% unsolicited freelance; 40% assigned. Complete ms; e-mail queries. **Pays .03-.05/wd.** on publication for 1st or reprint rts. Articles 100-400 wds. (35/yr.); fiction 400-900 wds. (30/yr.). Responds in 4-6 wks. Seasonal 10 mos. ahead. Accepts simultaneous submissions & reprints. Accepts requested ms on disk. Regularly uses sidebars. Prefers NIV. Guidelines/theme list on website (click on "Girls" tab/"Shine Brightly"/Magazine cover for SB in the right-hand column/"Writers"); copy $1/9 x 12 SAE/3 stamps. (No ads)

Fillers: Buys 10/yr. Cartoons, games, party ideas, prayers, quizzes, short humor, word puzzles; 50-200 wds. $5-10.

Special needs: Craft ideas that can be used to help others.

Tips: "Be realistic—we get a lot of fluffy stories with Pollyanna endings. We are looking for real-life-type stories that girls relate to. We mostly publish short stories but are open to short reflective articles. Know what girls face today and how they cope in their daily lives. We need angles from home life and friendships, peer pressure, and the normal growing-up challenges girls deal with."

SKIPPING STONES: A Multicultural Literary Magazine, PO Box 3939, Eugene OR 97403. (541) 342-4956. E-mail: editor@skippingstones.org. Website: www.skippingstones.org. Interfaith/multicultural. Arun N. Toké, exec. ed. A multicultural awareness and nature appreciation magazine for young people 7-17, worldwide. In 24th year. Bimonthly (5X) mag.; 36 pgs.; circ. 2,000. Subscription $25. 85% unsolicited freelance; 15% assigned. Query or complete ms/cover letter; no phone query; e-query/submissions OK. **PAYS IN COPIES** (2-4) (40% discount on extra issues) for 1st, electronic, and nonexclusive reprint rts. Articles (15-25/yr.) 750-1,000 wds.; fiction for teens, 750-1,000 wds. Responds in 9-13 wks. Seasonal 2-4 mos. ahead. Accepts simultaneous submissions. Accepts ms on disk or by e-mail. Regularly uses sidebars. Guidelines/theme list by mail/e-mail/website ("Submissions/For Adults" on left side); copy $6. (No ads.) Winner of many awards.

Poetry: Only from kids under 18. Accepts 100/yr. Any type; 3-30 lines. Submit max. 4-5 poems.
Fillers: Accepts 10-20/yr. Anecdotes, cartoons, games, quizzes, short humor, word puzzles; to 250 wds.
Columns/Departments: Accepts 10/yr. Noteworthy News (multicultural/nature/international/ \social, appropriate for youth), 200 wds.
Special needs: Stories and articles on your community and country, peace, nonviolent communication, compassion, kindness, spirituality, tolerance, and giving.
Contest: Annual Book Awards for published books and authors (deadline February 1); Annual Youth Honor Awards for students 7-17 (deadline June 20). Send SASE for guidelines, or check the website.
Tips: "Most of the magazine is open to freelance. We're seeking submissions by minority, multicultural, international, and/or youth writers. Do not be judgmental or preachy; be open or receptive to diverse opinions."

CHRISTIAN EDUCATION/LIBRARY MARKETS

CHURCH LIBRARIES, 9118 W. Elmwood Dr., Ste. 1G, Niles IL 60714-5820. (847) 296-3964. Fax (847) 296-0754. E-mail: linjohnson@ECLAlibraries.org. Website: www.ECLAlibraries.org. Evangelical Church Library Assn. Lin Johnson, mng ed. To assist church librarians in setting up, maintaining, and promoting church libraries and media centers. Quarterly mag.; 28-32 pgs.; circ. 300. Subscription $40. 25% unsolicited freelance. Complete ms or queries by e-mail only. **Pays .05/wd.** on acceptance for 1st or reprint rts. Articles 500-1,000 wds. (24/yr.). Responds in 8-10 wks. Seasonal 6 mos. ahead. Accepts reprints (tell when/where appeared). Requires e-mail submission. Regularly uses sidebars. Prefers NIV. Guidelines by e-mail/website ("Church Libraries Journal"/"Click for Writer's Guidelines"); sample copy on the website. (Ads)
    Tips: "Talk to church librarians or get involved in library or reading programs. Most open to training articles, promotional ideas, and profiles of church libraries."

*GROUP MAGAZINE, Box 481, Loveland CO 80539. (970) 669-3836. Fax (970) 292-4373. E-mail: rlawrence@group.com or sfirestone@group.com or info@group.com. Website: www.group.com or www.youthministry.com. Scott Firestone IV, ed.; submit to Kerri Loesch (kloesche@group.com). For leaders of Christian youth groups; to supply ideas, practical help, inspiration, and training for youth leaders. Bimonthly mag.; 85 pgs.; circ. 25,000. Subscription $29.95. 50% unsolicited freelance; 50% assigned. Query; fax/e-query OK. **Pays $150-350** on acceptance for all rts. Articles 175-2,000 wds. (100/yr.). Responds in 6-9 wks. Seasonal 5 mos. ahead. No simultaneous submissions or reprints. Accepts e-mail submissions (copied into message). No kill fee. Uses some sidebars. Any Bible version. Guidelines on website (click on "Site Map" at bottom of page/scroll down to #27 "Submissions"); copy $2/9 x 12 SAE/3 stamps. (Ads)
    Fillers: Buys 5-10/yr. Cartoons, games, ideas; $40.
    Columns/Departments: Buys 30-40/yr. Try This One (youth group activities), to 300 wds. Hands-on-Help (tips for leaders), to 175 wds. Strange But True (profiles remarkable youth ministry experience), 500 wds. Pays $50. Complete ms.
    Special needs: Articles geared toward working with teens; programming ideas; youth-ministry issues.
    Tips: "We're always looking for effective youth-ministry ideas, especially those tested by youth leaders in the field. Most open to Hands-On-Help column (use real-life examples, personal experiences, practical tips, Scripture, and self-quizzes or checklists). We buy the idea, not the verbatim submission."
    ** This periodical was #28 on the 2010 Top 50 Christian Publishers list (#36 in 2007).

DAILY DEVOTIONAL MARKETS

Due to the nature of the daily devotional market, the following market listings give a limited amount of information. Because most of these markets assign all material, they do not wish to be listed in the usual way.

If you are interested in writing daily devotionals, send to the following markets for guidelines and sample copies, write up sample devotionals to fit each one's particular format, and send to the editor with a request for an assignment. **DO NOT** submit any other type of material to these markets unless indicated.

CHRISTIAN DEVOTIONS, PO Box 6494, Kingsport TN 37663. E-mail: cindy@christiandevotions. us. Website: www.christiandevotions.us. Cindy Sproles & Eddie Jones, eds. Prefers completed devotions; 300-400 wds. Accepts poetry. Accepts reprints & e-mail submissions. Guidelines on website under "Write for Us."

DAILY DEVOTIONS FOR THE DEAF, 21199 Greenview Rd., Council Bluffs IA 51503-4190. (712) 322-5493. Fax (712) 322-7792. E-mail: JoKrueger@deafmissions.com. Website: www.deafmissions.com. Jo Krueger, ed. Published 3 times/yr. Circ. 26,000. Prefers to see completed devotionals; 225-250 wds. **NO PAYMENT.** E-mail submissions OK.

GOD'S WORD FOR TODAY, 1445 N. Boonville Ave., Springfield MO 65802. (417) 831-8000. E-mail: rl-gwft@gph.org. Website: www.GospelPublishing.com. Assemblies of God. Paul W. Smith, dir., ed. services. Assigns all devotions. Contact to see if they are accepting new writers. New writers will need to write a sample. **Pays $25.** Accepts poetry and e-mail submissions. No reprints. Guidelines on website ("God's Word for Today"/down to "Writers Guides").

LIGHT FROM THE WORD, PO Box 50434, Indianapolis IN 46250-0434. (317) 774-7900. E-mail: submissions@wesleyan.org. Website: www.wesleyan.org/wg. Wesleyan. Craig A. Bubeck, ed. dir. Devotions 220-250 wds. **Pays $100 for seven devotions.** Electronic submissions only. Send a couple of sample devotions to fit their format and request an assignment. Accepts e-mail submissions. No reprints.

PENNED FROM THE HEART, 304 Stow Neck Rd., Salem NJ 08079-3431. (856) 339-9422. E-mail: ed4penned@aol.com. Website: www.gloriaclover.com. Son-Rise Publications (toll-free 800-358-0777). Annual daily devotional book; about 240 pgs.; 5,000 copies/yr. 100% unsolicited freelance. Complete ms/cover letter; phone/e-query OK. **PAYS ONE COPY OF THE BOOK.**

***THE QUIET HOUR,** 4050 Lee Vance View, Colorado Springs CO 80918. E-mail: scott.stewart@DavidCCook.com. Website: www.davidccook.com. David C. Cook. Scott Stewart, ed. Subscription $3.99/quarter. Send list of credits only, short bio, and sample suitable for product to be considered for possible assignment. Accepts e-mailed sample devotional. Preferred length 150 wds. **Pay rate varies.** Currently using only writers previously published in this publication.

REFLECTING GOD, 2923 Troost Ave., Kansas City MO 64109. (816) 931-1900. Fax: (816) 412-8306. E-mail: dcbrush@wordaction.com. Website: www.reflectinggod.com. Duane Brush, ed. E-mail for writer's guidelines and application. Daily devotional guide published quarterly.

REJOICE! 35094 Laburnum Ave., Abbotsford BC V2S 8K3, Canada. (778) 549-8544. E-mail: RejoiceEditor@MennoMedia.org. Website: www.faithandliferecoursec.org/periodicals/rejoice. Faith & Life Resources/MennoMedia. Jonathan Janzen, ed. Daily devotional magazine grounded in Anabaptist theology. Quarterly mag.; 112 pgs.; circ. 12,000. Subscription $29.40. 5% unsolicited freelance; 95% assigned. **Pays $100-125 for 7-day assigned meditations,** 250-300 wds. each; on publication for 1st rts. Also accepts testimonies 500-600 wds. (8/yr.). Prefers that you send a couple of sample devotions and inquire about assignment procedures; fax/e-query OK. Accepts assigned mss by e-mail (attached). Responds in 4 wks. Seasonal 8 mos. ahead. No simultaneous submissions or reprints. Some kill fees 50%. No sidebars. Prefers NRSV. Guidelines by e-mail/website (scroll down to "Writing for Rejoice!" center).

Poetry: Buys 8/yr. Free verse, light verse; 60 characters. Pays $25. Submit max. 3 poems.

Tips: "Don't apply for assignment unless you are familiar with the publication and Anabaptist theology."

THE SECRET PLACE, Box 851, Valley Forge PA 19482-0851. (610) 768-2434. Fax (610) 768-2441. E-mail: thesecretplace@abc-usa.org. Website: www.judsonpress.com. Evelyn Heck, ed. Prefers to see completed devotionals, 200 wds. (use unfamiliar Scripture passages). 64 pgs. Circ. 250,000. 100% freelance. **Pays $20** for 1st rts. Accepts poetry. Prefers e-mail submissions. No reprints. Guidelines by mail.

*THE UPPER ROOM, PO Box 340004, Nashville TN 37203-0004. (615) 340-7252. Fax (615) 340-7267. E-mail: TheUpperRoomMagazine@upperroom.org. Website: www.upperroom.org. Mary Lou Redding, ed. dir. 95% unsolicited freelance. **Pays $30/devotional** on publication. 72 pgs. This publication wants freelance submissions and does not make assignments. Phone/fax/e-query OK. Send devotionals up to 250 wds. Buys explicitly religious art, in various media, for use on covers only (transparencies/slides requested); buys onetime, worldwide publishing rts. Accepts e-mail submissions (copied into message). Guidelines by mail/website ("Writers"); copy for 5x7 SAE/2 stamps. (No ads)

Tips: "We do not return submissions. Accepted submissions will be notified in 6-9 wks. Follow guidelines. Need meditations from men." Always include postal address with e-mail submissions.

THE WORD IN SEASON, PO Box 1209, Minneapolis MN 55440-1209. Fax (612) 330-3215. E-mail: rochelle@rightnowcoach.com. Website: www.augsburgfortress.org. Augsburg Fortress. Rev. Rochelle Y. Melander, ed./mngr. 96 pgs. Devotions to 200 wds. **Pays $20/devotion; $75 for prayers.** Accepts e-mail submissions (copied into message) after reading guidelines. Guidelines at www.augsburgfortress.org, type "The Word in Season" in search box.

Tips: "We prefer that you write for guidelines. We will send instructions for preparing sample devotions. We accept new writers based on the sample devotions we request and make assignments after acceptance."

WORSHIPMINISTRYDEVOTIONS.COM, 65 Shepherds Way, Hillsboro MO 63050-2605. (636) 789-4522. E-mail: staff@training-resources.org. Website: www.worshipministrydevotions.com. Tom Kraeuter, ed. Prefer to see completed devotions, 500-750 wds. **Pays $50.** Accepts submissions by e-mail.

Tips: "Please check the website and follow guidelines. We won't consider any submission that does not follow our guidelines."

MISSIONS MARKETS

OPERATION REVEILLE E-JOURNAL, PO Box 3488, Monument CO 80132-3488. (800) 334-0359. Fax (775) 248-8147. E-mail: bside@oprev.org. Website: www.oprev.org. Mission To Unreached Peoples. Bruce T. Sidebotham, dir. Provides information to equip US military Christians for cross-cultural ministry. Bimonthly e-zine. Subscription free. 20% unsolicited freelance; 80% assigned. Query; e-query OK. Accepts full mss by e-mail. **PAYS IN COPIES or up to $99** for electronic, reprint, or nonexclusive rights (negotiable). Articles 500-2,500 wds. (2/yr.); book reviews 700 wds. Responds in 2 wks. Accepts simultaneous submissions & reprints (tell when/where appeared). Accepts requested ms by e-mail (attached file). Uses some sidebars. Prefers NIV. No guidelines; copy online. (Ads)

Fillers: Accepts 4/yr. Facts; newsbreaks; commentary, to 150 wds.

Columns/Departments: Accepts 4/yr. Agency Profile (describes a mission agency's history and work), 200-300 wds. Area Profile (describes spiritual landscape of a military theater of operations), 300-750 wds. Resource Review (describes a cross-cultural ministry tool), 100-200 wds. Query.

Special needs: Commentary on service personnel in cross-cultural ministry situations and relationships.

Tips: "We need insights for military personnel on understanding and relating the gospel to Muslims."

PASTOR/LEADERSHIP MARKETS

THE CHRISTIAN CENTURY, 104 S. Michigan Ave., Ste. 1100, Chicago IL 60603. (312) 263-7510 (no phone calls). Website: http://christiancentury.org. Christian Century Foundation. Submit queries by e-mail to: submissions@christiancentury.org. For ministers, educators, and church leaders interested in events and theological issues of concern to the ecumenical church. Biweekly mag.; 48 pgs.; circ. 30,000. Subscription $59. 10% unsolicited freelance; 90% assigned. **Pays $125** on publication for all or onetime rts. Articles 1,500-3,000 wds. (150/yr.); book reviews, 800-1,500 wds.; music or film reviews 1,000 wds.; pays $0-75. No fiction submissions. Responds in 2-12 wks. Seasonal 4 mos. ahead. No simultaneous submissions. Accepts reprints (tell when/where appeared). No kill fee. Regularly uses sidebars. Prefers NRSV. Guidelines/theme list by e-mail/website (scroll to bottom & click on "Contact Us"); copy $5. (Ads)

> **Poetry:** Poetry Editor (poetry@christiancentury.org). Buys 50/yr. Any type (religious but not sentimental); to 20 lines; $50. Submit max. 10 poems.
>
> **Special needs:** Film, popular-culture commentary; news topics and analysis.
>
> **Tips:** "Keep in mind our audience of sophisticated readers, eager for analysis and critical perspective that goes beyond the obvious. We are open to all topics if written with appropriate style for our readers."

*COOK PARTNERS, 4050 Lee Vance View, Colorado Springs CO 80918. (719) 536-0100. Fax (719) 536-3266. E-mail: Marie.Chavez@davidccook.org. Website: www.cookinternational.org. Cook International. Submit to Marie Chavez. Seeks to encourage self-sufficient, effective indigenous Christian publishing worldwide to spread the life-giving message of the gospel. Bimonthly online publication; circ. 2,000. Subscription free. Open to unsolicited freelance. Query or complete ms. Articles & reviews 400-1,500 wds. Responds in 1-4 wks. **Most writers donate their work, but will negotiate for payment if asked.** Wants all rts. Incomplete topical listings. (No ads)

DIOCESAN DIALOGUE, 16565 S. State St., South Holland IL 60473. (708) 331-5485. Fax (708) 331-5484. E-mail: acp@acpress.org. Website: www.americancatholicpress.org. American Catholic Press. Father Michael Gilligan, editorial dir. Targets Latin-Rite dioceses in the US that sponsor a Mass broadcast on TV or radio. Annual newsletter; 8 pgs.; circ. 750. Free. 20% unsolicited freelance. Complete ms/cover letter; no phone/fax/e-query. Articles 200-1,000 wds. **Pays variable rates** on publication for all rts. Responds in 10 wks. Accepts simultaneous submissions & reprints. Uses some sidebars. Prefers NAB (Confraternity). No guidelines; copy $3/9 x 12 SAE/2 stamps. (No ads)

> **Fillers:** Cartoons, 2/yr.
>
> **Tips:** "Writers should be familiar with TV production of the Mass and/or the needs of senior citizens, especially shut-ins."

ENRICHMENT: A Journal for Pentecostal Ministry, 1445 N. Boonville Ave., Springfield MO 65802. (417) 862-2781, ext. 4095. Fax (417) 862-0416. E-mail: enrichmentjournal@ag.org. Website: www.enrichmentjournal.ag.org. Assemblies of God. George P. Wood, exec. ed.; Rick Knoth, mng. ed. (rknoth@ag.org). Quarterly jour.; 128-144 pgs.; circ. 33,000. Subscription $24;

foreign add $30. 15% unsolicited freelance. Complete ms/cover letter. **Pays up to .15/wd. ($75-350)** on acceptance for 1st rts. Articles 1,000-2,800 wds. (25/yr.); book reviews, 250 wds. ($25). Responds in 8-12 wks. Seasonal 1 yr. ahead. Accepts simultaneous submissions & reprints (tell when/where appeared). Requires requested ms by e-mail (copied into message or attached). Kill fee up to 50%. Regularly uses sidebars. Prefers NIV. Guidelines on website; copy for $7/10 x 13 SAE. (Ads)

Fillers: Buys over 100/yr. Anecdotes, cartoons, facts, short humor, tips; $25-40, or .10-.20/wd.
Columns/Departments: Buys 40/yr. for Women in Ministry (leadership ideas), Associate Ministers (related issues), Managing Your Ministry (how-to), Financial Concepts (church stewardship issues), Family Life (minister's family), When Pews Are Few (ministry in smaller congregation), Worship in the Church, Leader's Edge, Preaching That Connects, Ministry & Medical Ethics; all 1,200-2,500 wds. $75-275. Query or complete ms.
Tips: "Most open to EShorts: short, 150-250 word, think pieces covering a wide range of topics related to ministry and church life, such as culture, worship, generational issues, church/community, trends, evangelism, surveys, time management, and humor."
** 2010, 2009 Award of Merit: Christian Ministries. 2008, 2007 EPA Award of Excellence: Christian Ministry. This periodical was #16 on the 2010 Top 50 Christian Publishers list (#15 in 2009, #43 in 2008, #47 in 2006).

GROWTH POINTS, PO Box 892589, Temecula CA 92589-2589. Phone/fax (951) 506-3086. E-mail: cgnet@earthlink.net. Website: www.churchgrowthnetwork.com. Dr. Gary L. McIntosh, ed. For pastors and church leaders interested in church growth. Monthly newsletter; 2 pgs.; circ. 8,000. Subscription $16. 10% unsolicited freelance; 90% assigned. Query; fax/e-query OK. **Pays $25** for onetime rts. Not copyrighted. Articles 1,000-2,000 wds. (2/yr.). Responds in 4 wks. Accepts simultaneous submissions & reprints. Accepts requested ms on disk. Does not use sidebars. Guidelines by mail; copy for #10 SAE/1 stamp. (No ads)

Tips: "Write articles that are short (1,200 words), crisp, clear, with very practical ideas that church leaders can put to use immediately. All articles must have a pro-church-growth slant, be very practical, have how-to material, and be very tightly written with bullets, etc."

INSITE, PO Box 62189, Colorado Springs CO 80962-2189. (719) 260-9400. Fax (719) 260-6398. E-mail: editor@ccca.org, or info@ccca.org. Website: www.ccca.org. Christian Camp and Conference Assn. Jackie M. Johnson, ed. To inform and inspire professionals serving in the Christian camp and conference center community. Bimonthly mag.; 52 pgs.; circ. 8,200. Subscription $29.95. 15% unsolicited freelance; 85% assigned. Query; e-query OK. **Pays .20/wd.** on publication for 1st and electronic rts. Cover articles 1,500-2,000 wds. (12/yr.); features 1,200-1,500 wds. (30/yr.); sidebars 250-500 wds. (15-20/yr.). Responds in 4 wks. Seasonal 6 mos. ahead. Accepts simultaneous submissions & reprints (tell when/where appeared). Prefers e-mail submission (attached file). Kill fee. Regularly uses sidebars. Prefers NIV. Guidelines on website; copy $4.99/9 x 12 SAE/$1.73 postage. (Ads)

Special needs: Outdoor setting; purpose and objectives; administration and organization; leadership; personnel development; camper/guest needs; programming; health and safety; food service; site/facilities maintenance; business/operations; marketing and PR; relevant spiritual issues; and fund-raising.
Tips: "Most open to how-to pieces; get guidelines, then query first. Don't send general camping-related articles. We print stories specifically related to Christian camp and conference facilities; innovative programs or policies; how a Christian camp or conference experience affected a present-day leader; spiritual renewal and leadership articles. Review several issues so you know what we're looking for." ** 2010, 2008, 2006 EPA Award of Merit: Christian Ministries; 2007 EPA Award of Excellence: Christian Ministries; 2006 EPA Award of Merit: Most Improved Publication.

*LEADERSHIP, 465 Gundersen Dr., Carol Stream IL 60188. (630) 260-6200. Fax (630) 260-0451. E-mail: LJEditor@LeadershipJournal.net. Website: www.leadershipjournal.net. Christianity Today Intl. Marshall Shelley, ed-in-chief. Practical help for pastors/church leaders, covering the spectrum of subjects from personal needs to professional skills. Quarterly & online jour.; 104 pgs.; circ. 48,000. Subscription $24.95. 20% unsolicited freelance; 80% assigned. Query or complete ms/cover letter; fax/e-query OK. Accepts full mss by e-mail. **Pays .15-20/wd.** on acceptance for 1st & electronic rts. Articles 500-3,000 wds. (10/yr.); book reviews 100 wds. (pays $25-50). Responds in 6 wks. Seasonal 6 mos. ahead. Accepts reprints (tell when/where appeared). Accepts requested ms by e-mail (copied into message or attached Word doc). Kill fee 30%. Regularly uses sidebars. Prefers NLT. Guidelines on website; copy for 9 x 12 SAE/$2 postage. (Ads)

>   **Fillers:** Buys 80/yr. Cartoons, short humor; to 150 wds. $25-50.
>
>   **Columns/Departments:** Skye Jethani, mng. ed. Buys 12/yr. Tool Kit (practical stories or resources for preaching, worship, outreach, pastoral care, spiritual formation, and administration); 100-700 wds. Complete ms. Pays $50-250.
>
>   **Tips:** "*Leadership* is a practical journal for pastors. Tell real-life stories of church life— defining moments—dramatic events. What was learned the hard way—by experience. We look for articles that provide practical help for problems church leaders face, not essays expounding on a topic, editorials arguing a position, or homilies explaining biblical principles. We want 'how-to' articles based on first-person accounts of real-life experiences in ministry in the local church."
>
>   ** 2010, 2006 EPA Award of Excellence: Christian Ministries; 2008 EPA Award of Merit: General; 2007 EPA Award of Merit: Christian Ministries. This periodical was #21 on the 2010 Top 50 Christian Publishers list (#21 in 2009, #18 in 2008, #15 in 2007, #14 in 2006).

*MINISTRY TODAY, 600 Rinehart Rd., Lake Mary FL 32746. (407) 333-0600. Fax (407) 333-7133. E-mail: ministrytoday@charismamedia.com. Website: www.ministrytodaymag.com. Charisma Media. Submit to The Editor. Helps for pastors and church leaders, primarily in Pentecostal/Charismatic churches. Quarterly & online mag.; 112 pgs.; circ. 30,000. Subscription $14.97. 60-80% free-lance. Query; fax/e-query preferred. **Pays $50 or $500-800** on publication for all rts. Articles 1,800-2,500 wds. (25/yr.); book/music/video reviews, 300 wds. $25. Responds in 4 wks. Prefers accepted ms by e-mail. Kill fee. Regularly uses sidebars. Prefers NIV. Guidelines on website (scroll to bottom of home page & click on "Writers' Guidelines"); copy $6/9 x 12 SAE. For free subscription to online version go to: www.digital.ministrytoday.com/signup.(Ads)

>   **Tips:** "Most open to columns. Study guidelines and the magazine. Please correspond with editor before sending an article proposal."

THE NEWSLETTER NEWSLETTER, PO Box 36269, Canton OH 44735. Toll-free (800) 992-2144. E-mail: service@newsletternewsletter.com or through website: www.newsletternewsletter.com. Communication Resources. Stephanie Martin, ed. To help church secretaries and church newsletter editors prepare high-quality publications. Monthly & online newsletter; 14 pgs. Subscription $71.80. 100% assigned. Complete ms; e-query OK. **Pays $50-150** on acceptance for all rts. Articles 800-1,000 wds. (12/yr.). Responds in 4 wks. Seasonal 4 mos. ahead. Requires requested ms by e-mail. Guidelines by e-mail.

>   **Tips:** "Most open to how-to articles on various aspects of producing newsletters and e-newsletters—writing, layout and design, distribution, etc."

PARISH LITURGY, 16565 S. State St., South Holland IL 60473. (708) 331-5485. Fax (708) 331-5484. E-mail: acp@acpress.org. Website: www.americancatholicpress.org. American Catholic Press. Father Michael Gilligan, exec. dir. A planning tool for Sunday and holy day liturgy. Quarterly mag.; 40 pgs.; circ. 1,200. Subscription $24. 5% unsolicited freelance. Query; no phone/e-query. **Pays variable rates** for all rts. Articles 400 wds. Responds in 4 wks. Seasonal 4 mos. ahead. Accepts simultaneous submissions & reprints (tell when/where appeared). Uses some sidebars. Prefers NAB. No guidelines; copy available. (No ads)

Tips: "We only use articles on the liturgy—period. Send us well-informed articles on the liturgy."

*PLUGGED IN ONLINE, Colorado Springs CO 80920 (no street address needed). Toll-free (800) 232-6459. (719) 531-3400. Fax (719) 548-5823. E-mail: waliszrs@fotf.org, or pluggedin@ family.org. Website: www.pluggedinonline.com. Focus on the Family. Steven Isaac, online ed.; Bob Smithhouser, sr. ed. To assist parents and youth leaders in better understanding popular youth culture and equip them to impart principles of discernment in young people. Online newsletter. Open to queries only. Articles. Incomplete topical listings. (No ads)

**2010 EPA Award of Excellence: Online.

PREACHING, PREACHING ONLINE & PREACHING NOW, 402 BNA Dr, Ste 400, Nashville TN 37217. (615) 386-3011. Fax (615) 312-4277. E-mail: Alee@SalemPublishing.com. Salem Communications. Dr. Michael Duduit, ed. Bimonthly; circ. 9,000. Subscription $24.95/2 yrs. 50% unsolicited freelance; 50% assigned. Query; fax/e-query OK. **PAYS A SUBSCRIPTION** for one-time & electronic rts. Responds in 1-2 days. Seasonal 10-12 mos. ahead. Reprints from books only. Prefers requested ms by e-mail (attached file). Uses some sidebars. Guidelines on website; copy online. (ads). *Preaching Online* is a professional resource for pastors that supplements *Preaching* magazine. Includes all content from magazine, plus additional articles and sermons. Feature articles, 2,000-2,500, **$50**. Sermons 1,500-2,000 wds. **$35**. *Preaching Now* is a weekly e-mail/e-zine; circ. 43,500. Subscription $39.95. Accepts books for review. Guidelines on website (scroll down to bottom of Home Page and click on "Site Map"/scroll down to "Help"/ "Writing for Us"); Copy $8. (Ads)

THE PRIEST, 200 Noll Plaza, Huntington IN 46750-4304. Toll-free: (800) 348-2440. (260) 356-8400. Fax (260) 359-9117. E-mail: tpriest@osv.com. Website: www.osv.com. Catholic/Our Sunday Visitor Inc. Msgr. Owen F. Campion, ed.; submit to Murray Hubley, assoc. ed. For Catholic priests, deacons, and seminarians; to help in all aspects of ministry. Monthly jour.; 56 pgs.; circ. 6,500. Subscription $43.95. 40% unsolicited freelance. Query (preferred) or complete ms/cover letter; phone/fax/e-query OK. **Pays $50-250** on acceptance for 1st rts. Not copyrighted. Articles to 1,500 wds. (96/yr.); some 2-parts. Responds in 5-13 wks. Seasonal 3 mos. ahead. Uses some sidebars. Prefers disk or e-mail submissions (attached file). Prefers NAB. Guidelines on website (click on "About Us"/"The Priest Writers' Guidelines"; free copy. (Ads)

Fillers: Murray Hubley, fillers ed. Cartoons; $35.

Columns/Departments: Buys 36/yr. Viewpoint, to 1,000 wds. $75.

Tips: "Write to the point, with interest. Most open to nuts-and-bolts issues for priests, or features. Keep the audience in mind; need articles or topics important to priests and parish life. Include Social Security number."

Special needs: Anglican and Episcopal theology, religion, history, doctrine, ethics, homiletics, liturgies, hermeneutics, biography, prayer, practice.

SHARING THE PRACTICE, c/o Central Woodward Christian Church, 3955 W. Big Beaver Rd., Troy MI 48084-2610. (248) 644-0512. Website: www.apclergy.org. Academy of Parish Clergy/Ecumenical/ Interfaith. Rev. Dr. Robert Cornwall, ed-in-chief (drbobcornwall@msn.com); (s.spade@att.net). Growth toward excellence through sharing the practice of parish ministry. Quarterly international jour.; 40 pgs.; circ. 250 (includes 80 seminary libraries & publishers). Subscription $30/yr. (send to APC, 2249 Florinda St., Sarasota FL 34231-1414). 100% unsolicited freelance. Complete ms/cover letter; e-query OK; query/clips for fiction. **NO PAYMENT** for 1st, reprint, simultaneous, or electronic rts. Articles 500-2,500 wds. (25/yr.); reviews 500-1,000 wds. Responds in 2 wks. Seasonal 6 mos. ahead. Accepts simultaneous submissions & reprints (tell when/where appeared). Prefers e-mail submissions (copied into message). Uses some sidebars. Prefers NRSV. Guidelines/theme list by mail/e-mail; free copy. (No ads)

Poetry: Accepts 12/yr. Any type; 25-35 lines. Submit max. 2 poems.

Fillers: Accepts 6/yr. Anecdotes, cartoons, jokes, short humor; 50-100 wds.

Columns/Departments: Academy News; President's.

Contest: Book of the Year Award ($100+), Top Ten Books of the Year list, Parish Pastor of the Year Award ($200+). Inquire by e-mail to DIELPADRE@aol.com.

Tips: "We desire articles and poetry by practicing clergy of all kinds who wish to share their practice of ministry. Join the Academy."

SMALLGROUPS.COM, 465 Gundersen Dr., Carol Steam IL 60188. (630) 260-6200. Fax (630) 260-0451. E-mail: smallgroups@christianitytoday.com. Website: www.smallgroups.com. Christianity Today. Amy Jackson, assoc. ed. Serves small-group leaders and churches and provides training and curriculum that is easy to use. Weekly e-newsletter; circ. 50,000. Subscription $99. 10% unsolicited freelance; 50% assigned. Complete ms/cover letter; e-query OK. Accepts full mss by e-mail. **Pays $75-150 for articles; $350-750 for curriculum;** on acceptance for electronic & nonexclusive rts. Articles 750-1,500 wds. (50/yr.). Responds in 2 wks. Seasonal 2 mos. ahead. Accepts simultaneous submissions & reprints (tell when/where appeared). Prefers requested ms by e-mail (attached file). Some kill fees 50%. No sidebars. Accepts reprints. Prefers NIV. Guidelines/copy by e-mail. (Ads)

Fillers: Icebreakers and other small-group learning activities.

Special needs: Creative, practical ideas for small-group ministry, esp. from experience.

Tips: "It's best to submit articles that you have used to train and support small groups and leaders in your own church."

**2010 EPA Award of Merit: Online; 2012 EPA Award of Excellence: Online Newsletter.

YOUTHWORKER JOURNAL, c/o Salem Publishing, 402 BNA Drive, Suite 400, Nashville TN 37217-2509. (615) 386-3011. Fax (615) 386-3380. E-mail: proposals@youthworker.com. Website: www.Youthworker.com. Salem Communications. Steve & Lois Rabey, eds. For youth workers/church and parachurch. Bimonthly & online jour.; 72 pgs.; circ. 15,000. Subscription $39.95. 100% unsolicited freelance. Query or complete ms (only if already written); e-query preferred. **Pays $50-300** on publication for 1st/perpetual rts. Articles 250-3,000 wds. (30/yr.); length may vary. Responds in 26 wks. Seasonal 6 mos. ahead. No reprints. Kill fee $50. Guidelines/theme list on website: www.youthworker.com/editorial_guidelines.php; copy $5/10 x 13 SAE. (Ads)

Columns/Departments: Buys 10/yr. International Youth Ministry, and Technology in Youth Ministry.

Tips: "Read *YouthWorker*; imbibe its tone (professional, though not academic; conversational, though not chatty). Query me with specific, focused ideas that conform to our editorial style. It helps if the writer is a youth minister, but it's not required. Check website for additional info, upcoming themes, etc. WorldView column on mission activities and trips is about the only one open to outsiders."

TEEN/YOUNG-ADULT MARKETS

BOUNDLESS, Focus on the Family, Colorado Springs CO 80995 (no street address needed). (719) 531-3419. Fax (719) 548-4599. E-mail: editor@boundless.org. Website: www.boundless.org. Focus on the Family. Martha Krienke, ed., producer. For Christian singles up to their mid-30s. Weekly e-zine; 300,000 visitors/mo.; 130 page views/mo. on blog. Free online. 5% unsolicited freelance; 95% assigned. Query/clips; e-query OK. Accepts full ms by e-mail. **Pays** on acceptance for nonexclusive rts. Articles 1,200-1,800 wds. (52/yr.). Responds in 4 wks. Seasonal 4 mos. ahead. Accepts simultaneous submissions & reprints (tell when/where appeared). Requires e-mail submission (attached—preferred—or copied into message). No kill fee. Does not use sidebars. Prefers ESV, NIV. Guidelines by mail/website (click on "About Us"/scroll down to "Write for Us"/"Writers' Guidelines"); copy online. (Ads)

> **Tips:** "See author guidelines on our website. Most open to conversational, winsome, descriptive, and biblical."
>
> ** This periodical was #15 on the 2010 Top 50 Christian Publishers list (#18 in 2009, #12 in 2008, #25 in 2007, #24 in 2006).

DIRECTION MAGAZINE, PO Box 17306, Nashville TN 37217. (615) 361-1221. Fax (615) 367-0535. E-mail: direction@d6family.com. Website: www.randallhouse.com. Randall House. Jonathan Yandell, ed.; submit to Derek Lewis, ed. asst. Bringing junior high students to a closer relationship with Christ through devotionals, relevant articles, and pertinent topics. Quarterly mag.; 56 pgs.; circ. 5,300. Open to freelance. Complete ms/cover letter; query for fiction. Accepts full mss by e-mail. **Pays $35-150 for nonfiction; $35-150 for fiction;** on publication for 1st rts. Articles 600-1,500 wds. (35/yr.); book reviews 500-600 wds. ($35). Responds in 6 wks. Seasonal 6 mos. ahead. Accepts simultaneous submissions; no reprints. Prefers e-mail submissions (attached file). No kill fee. Regularly uses sidebars. Also accepts submissions from teens. Guidelines by e-mail/website; copy for 9 x 12 SAE. (No ads)

> **Columns/Departments:** Buys 10/yr. Changing Lanes (describe how God is changing you; teens only), 500-1000 wds. Between the Lines (review of book approved by Randall House), 500-600 wds. $35-50. Missions (describe a personal opportunity to serve others), 500-1000 wds.
>
> **Tips:** "We are open to freelancers by way of articles and submissions to 'Changing Lanes,' 'Between the Lines,' 'Missions,' and feature articles/interviews. All articles should be about an aspect of the Christian life or contain a spiritual element, as the purpose of this magazine is to bring junior high students closer to Christ. We are happy to accept personal testimonies or knowledgeable articles on current hot topics and how they compare to biblical standards."

*SUSIE: Magazine for Teen Girls, (615) 216-6147. E-mail: susieshell@comcast.net. Susie Shellenberger, owner. A publication appealing and relevant for today's girl. Estab. 2009. Monthly mag. Open to unsolicited freelance. E-mail complete manuscripts labeled "Free Freelance." **NO PAYMENT FOR THE FIRST YEAR.** Nonfiction & fiction. Not included in topical listings.

TAKE FIVE PLUS YOUTH DEVOTIONAL GUIDE, 1445 N. Boonville Ave., Springfield MO 65802-1894. (417) 862-2781, ext. 4357. Fax (417) 862-6059. E-mail: rl-take5plus@gph.org. Assemblies of God. Wade Quick, ed. Devotional for teens. By assignment only. Query. Accepts e-mail submissions. **Pays $25/devotion.** Devotions may range from 210 to 235 wds. (max.). Guidelines on request.

> **Poetry:** Accepts poetry from teens; no more than 25 lines.
>
> **Tips:** "The sample devotions need to be based on a Scripture reference available by query. You will not be paid for the sample devotions." Also accepts digital photos, and artwork from teens.

YOUNG SALVATIONIST, PO Box 269, Alexandria VA 22313-0269. (703) 684-5500. Fax (703) 684-5539. E-mail: ys@usn.salvationarmy.org. Website: http://publications.salvationarmyusa.org. The Salvation Army. Amy Reardon, ed. For teens and young adults in the Salvation Army. Monthly (10X) & online mag.; 24 pgs.; circ. 48,000. Subscription $4.50. 20% unsolicited freelance; 80% assigned. Complete ms preferred; e-query OK. **Pays .25/wd.** on acceptance for 1st, onetime, or reprint rts. Articles (60/yr.); short evangelistic pieces, 350-600 wds. No fiction. Responds in 9 wks. Seasonal 6 mos. ahead. Accepts reprints (tell when/where appeared). Accepts requested ms on disk or by e-mail. Uses some sidebars. Prefers NIV. Guidelines/theme list by mail/website; copy for 9 x 12 SAE/ 3 stamps. (No ads)

> ** This periodical was #2 on the 2010 Top 50 Christian Publishers list (#4 in 2009, # 9 in 2008, #5 in 2007, #3 in 2006).

WOMEN'S MARKETS

THE DABBLING MUM, 508 W. Main St., Beresford SD 57004. (866) 548-9327. E-mail: dm@the dabblingmum.com. Website: www.thedabblingmum.com. Alyice Edrich, ed. Balance your life while you glean from successful entrepreneurs, parents, writers, cooks, and Christians—just like you. Weekly blog; monthly e-zine; circ. 30,000-40,000. Subscription free online. 90% unsolicited freelance; 10% assigned. Complete ms submitted online; e-query OK. Accepts full mss by e-mail. **Pays $20 on acceptance for 1st rts**, and nonexclusive indefinite archival rts. $40 on acceptance for 1st rts with exclusive online indefinite archival rights. $5-15 for reprint rts. Accepts guest posts (donated material). Articles 500-1,500 wds. (48-96/yr.); book & video reviews 500 wds. (no payment). Responds in 4-12 wks. Seasonal 1 mo. ahead. No simultaneous submissions; accepts reprints (tell when/where appeared). Accepts e-mail submissions (copied into message). No kill fee or sidebars. Also accepts submissions from teens. Prefers KJV or NAS. Guidelines/editorial calendar/copy on website ("E-Magazine"/"Women"). (Ads)

> **Special needs:** Simple living articles; small-business ideas; party planning, arts and crafts project tutorials that parents can do with their kids.

> **Tips:** "Please use e-mail and submissions forms when contacting us. We're looking for material that is not readily available on the Internet. When adding a personal twist to your how-to piece, make sure you write in a way that is universal. In other words, it's not enough to say how you did it; we want you to teach others how to do it too. Write in a conversational tone so that readers feel as though you're speaking to them over the kitchen table, but keep it professional."

> ** This periodical was #29 on the 2010 Top 50 Christian Publishers list (#49 in 2008, #39 in 2007).

GLORY AND STRENGTH, 3609 Gere Field Rd, B3, St. Joseph MO 64506. (816) 279-9673. E-mail: admin@gloryandstrength.com. Website: www.gloryandstrength.com. Glory and Strength Ministries. Debra L. Butterfield, pub./ed. Ministers to those who have been impacted by such issues as sexual and physical abuse, pornography, addictions, and crisis; offering godly wisdom and practical advice for overcoming these issues. Monthly e-zine. Subscription free online. Estab. 2009. 98% unsolicited freelance. Query; phone/e-query OK. Accepts full mss by e-mail (after a query). **NO PAYMENT,** but provides a 75-word bio & two links to sites of your choice. Articles 700-1,200 wds. (20-22/mo.); fiction 700-1,000 wds. (12/yr.). Responds in 2 wks. Seasonal 4 mos. ahead. Accepts simultaneous submissions & reprints (tell when/where appeared). Prefers articles by e-mail (attached file). Regularly uses sidebars. Guidelines/theme list by e-mail/website ("Submit" tab); copy on website. (Ads)

> **Poetry:** Accepts few; any type. Submit max. 3-4 poems.

> **Fillers:** Anecdotes, cartoons, facts, prayers, quotes, short humor, and tips.

> **Columns/Departments:** Accepts 20-30/yr. Cheerful Heart (humorous fiction or nonfiction), 700-1,000 wds. Words of Strength (devotional), staff assigned. Growing in Glory (Bible lessons), staff assigned.

> **Tips:** "'Cheerful Heart' is best way to break in. Writers' guidelines list our themes for each issue. Follow those and query and you have a better chance at acceptance."

*KYRIA, 465 Gundersen Dr., Carol Stream IL 60188. (630) 260-6200. Fax (630) 260-0114. E-mail: Kyria@christianitytoday.com. Website: www.kyria.com. Christianity Today Intl. Submit to Acquisitions Editor. To equip and encourage women to use their gifts, take responsibility for their spiritual formation, and fulfill the work God has called them to—through the power of the life-transforming and life-sustaining Spirit. Women's online digizine. Subscription $14.95. Estab. 2009. Open to unsolicited freelance. Query; e-query OK. Does not accepts full mss by e-mail. **Pays $50-150** on acceptance for 1st or reprint rts. Articles 600-1,500 wds. Responds in 8-10 wks. Seasonal 4 mos. ahead. Accepts simultaneous submissions & reprints (tell when/where appeared). No kill fee. Uses some sidebars. Prefers NLT. Guidelines/theme list on website ("Help & Info"/"FAQs"/"Kyria Writer's Guidelines"); no copy. (Ads)

Fillers: Buys 12/yr. Devotions, 150-200 wds. pays $25-50.

Special needs: Spiritual disciplines.

Tips: "See our website for more specifics: kyria.com/help/writersguidelines/kyriawritersguidelines.html."

*MOMSENSE (MomSense), 2370 S. Trenton Way, Denver CO 80231. (303) 733-5353. Fax (303) 733-5770. E-mail: MomSense@mops.org or info@mops.org. Website: www.MomSense.org, or www.MOPS.org. MOPS Intl. Inc. (Mothers of Preschoolers). Mary Darr, ed. Nurtures mothers of preschoolers and school-age kids from a Christian perspective with articles that both inform and inspire on issues relating to womanhood and motherhood. Bimonthly mag.; 32 pgs.; circ. 100,000. Subscription $23.95. 35% unsolicited freelance; 65% assigned. Complete ms/cover letter & bio; e-query OK. Accepts full mss by e-mail. **Pays .15/wd.** on publication for 1st & reprint rts. Articles 450-650 wds. (15-20/yr.). Responds in 12 wks. Seasonal 6 mos. ahead. Accepts simultaneous submissions & reprints (tell when/where appeared). Prefers requested ms by e-mail (attached file or copied into message). Some kill fees 10%. Uses some sidebars. Prefers NIV. Guidelines/theme list by mail/e-mail/or at www.MOPS.org/write; copy for 9 x 12 SAE/$1.39 postage. (Ads)

   Special needs: "We always need practical articles to the woman as a woman, and to the woman as a mom."

   Contest: Sponsors several contests per year for writing and photography. Check website for details on current contests.

   Tips: "Most open to theme-specific features. Writers are more seriously considered if they are a mother with some connection to MOPS (but not required). Looking for original content ideas that appeal to Christian and non-Christian readers."

P31 WOMAN, 616-G Matthews-Mint Hill Rd., Matthews NC 28105. (704) 849-2270. Fax (704) 849-7267. E-mail: editor@proverbs31.org. Website: www.proverbs31.org. Proverbs 31 Ministries. Glynnis Whitwer, ed.; submit to Janet Burke, asst. ed. (janet@proverbs31.org). Seeks to offer a godly woman's perspective on life. Monthly mag.; 16 pgs.; circ. 15,000. Subscription for donation. 50% unsolicited freelance; 50% assigned. Complete ms; e-query OK. **PAYS IN COPIES** for onetime rts. Not copyrighted. Articles 200-1,000 wds. (40/yr.). Responds in 4-6 wks. Seasonal 3 mos. ahead. Accepts simultaneous submissions & reprints (tell when/where appeared). Prefers accepted ms by e-mail (attached file or copied into message). Uses some sidebars. Prefers NIV. Guidelines/theme list by mail/website; copy on website. (No ads)

   Tips: "Looking for articles that encourage women and offer practical advice as well. We tend towards story-driven pieces, but welcome all submissions." Editor's Note: "We are planning to launch a digital magazine with advertising in 2013. Check our website to get the most up-to-date information."

RIGHT TO THE HEART OF WOMEN E-ZINE, PO Box 6421, Longmont CO 80501. (303) 772-2035. Fax (303) 678-0260. E-mail: lswrites@aol.com. Website: www.righttotheheartofwomen.com. Linda Shepherd, ed. Encouragement and helps for women in ministry. Weekly online e-zine; 5 pgs.; circ. 20,000. Subscription free. 10% unsolicited freelance; 90% assigned. Query; e-query OK. **NO PAYMENT** for nonexclusive rts. Articles 100-800 wds. (20/yr.). Responds in 2 wks. Seasonal 2 mos. ahead. Accepts simultaneous submissions & reprints (tell when/where appeared). Requires accepted mss by e-mail (copied into message). Does not use sidebars. No guidelines; copy on website. (Ads)

   Columns/Departments: Accepts 10/yr. Women Bible Teachers; Profiles of Women in Ministry; Women's Ministry Tips; Author's and Speaker's Tips; 100 wds. Query.

   Special needs: Book reviews must be in first person, by the author. Looking for women's ministry event ideas. Topics related to women and women's ministries.

   Tips: "For free subscription, subscribe at website above; also view e-zine. We want to hear from those involved in women's ministry or leadership. Also accepts manuscripts from AWSAs (see www.awsawomen.com). Query with your ideas."

SHARE, 10 W. 71st St., New York NY 10023-4201. (212) 877-3041. Fax (212) 724-5923. E-mail: CDofANatl@aol.com. Website: www.catholicdaughters.org. Catholic Daughters of the Americas. Peggy O'Brien, exec. dir.; submit to Peggy Eastman, ed. For Catholic women. Quarterly mag.; circ. 85,000. Free with membership. Most articles come from membership, but is open. **NO PAYMENT.** Buys color photos & covers. Guidelines/copy by mail. (Ads)
> **Tips:** "We use very little freelance material unless it is written by Catholic Daughters."

SINGLE! YOUNG CHRISTIAN WOMAN, PO Box 573, Clarksville AR 72830. (479) 439-4891. E-mail: donna@onmyownnow.com. Website: www.onmyownnow.com. On My Own Now Ministries, Inc. Donna Lee Schillinger, ed. Christian alternative to the fashion magazine. For young, single women ages 17-23. Monthly e-zine. 18 pgs.; circ. 1,000. Free subscription. Est. 2009. 40% unsolicited, 60% assigned. Query or send complete manuscript by e-mail. **NO PAYMENT.** Nonexclusive rights. Copyrighted. Prefer NIV. 800-1200 wds. Accept 24 nonfiction mss/yr. Respond in 2 wks. Submit holiday 2 mo in advance. Accept simultaneous submissions/prev. published (tell when/where published). Require articles on disk or in e-mail (attached). No kill fee. Some sidebars. Inc. bio on feature articles. Sample copy online. No photos. Book, music, video reviews 800 wds. Accept submissions from teens.
> **Columns:** Just What you Need (resources for young adult women), 450-550 wds; Fashion DIVinA (how to look good and remain godly), 700-1000 wds; The Recap (reviews of books, movies, music, etc.), 600-1000; Accept 18 mss/yr. Query/send complete manuscript.
> **Tips:** Looking for guest columnists for Fashion DIVinA, Just What You Need, and The Recap. Also seek new writers for feature articles. (No ads)

TREASURE, PO Box 5002, Antioch TN 37011. Toll-free (877) 767-7662. (615) 731-6812. Fax (615) 727-1157. E-mail: treasure@wnac.org. Website: www.wnac.org. Women Nationally Active for Christ of National Assn. of Free Will Baptists. Sarah Fletcher, mng. ed. A women's Bible study guide with emphasis on missions and mentoring. Quarterly publication; 48 pgs.; circ. 4,500. Subscription $12. Estab. 2011. 25% unsolicited freelance; 75% assigned. Complete ms/cover letter. Accepts full ms by e-mail. **PAYS IN COPIES** for 1st rts. Articles 750-1,200 wds. (10/yr.). Responds in 8 wks. Seasonal 12 mos. ahead. No simultaneous submissions; accepts reprints (tell when/where appeared). Prefers e-mail submissions (attached file). Regularly uses sidebars. Also accepts submissions from teens. Prefers KJV. Guidelines/theme list by e-mail; copy for 5.35 x 8.5 SAE/$1. (No ads)
> **Columns/Departments:** What Works (practical tips/lists about women's health, homes, fitness, fashion, or finances).
> **Special needs:** Spiritual formation, family issues, life coaching/mentoring, church life, community outreach and global evangelism.
> **Tips:** "Most open to articles. Bulk of material comes from Women Active for Christ or Free Will Baptist writers."

A VIRTUOUS WOMAN, 594 Ivy Hill, Harlan KY 40831. (606) 573-6506. E-mail: submissions@avirtuouswoman.org. Website: www.avirtuouswoman.org. Independent Seventh-day Adventist ministry. Melissa Ringstaff, dir./ed. Strives to provide practical articles for women ages 20-60 years; based on Proverbs 31. Monthly e-zine; circ. 20,000+ online. 80% unsolicited freelance; 20% assigned. Complete ms/cover letter; e-query OK. Accepts full mss by e-mail. **NO PAYMENT** for first, reprint, electronic, anthology rts. Articles 500-2,000 wds. (150+/yr.); reviews 500-1,000 wds. Responds in 6-8 wks. Seasonal 6 mos. ahead. No simultaneous submissions; accepts reprints (tell when/where appeared). Accepts e-mail submissions (attached file in .doc or .txt or copied into message). Uses some sidebars. Prefers KJV, NIV, NLT. Guidelines/theme list on website (click on "Main"/"Writers' Guidelines"); copy for 9 x 12 SAE/$2.02 postage plus $3.50. (Ads)

Poetry: Accepts 5/yr. Free verse, traditional. Submit max. 2 poems.

Fillers: Accepts 12/yr. Anecdotes, facts, ideas, jokes, party ideas, prayers, quizzes, and tips; to 200 wds.

Tips: "Write practical articles that appeal to the average woman—articles that women can identify with. Do not preach. Read our writer's helps for ideas."

WOMEN OF THE CROSS, 920 Sweetgum Creek, Plano TX 75023. (972) 517-8553. Website: www.womenofthecross.com. Greg Paskal, content mngr. (greg@gregpaskal.com). Encouraging women in their walk with the Lord; strong emphasis on discipleship and relationship. Online community. 50% unsolicited freelance. Complete ms by e-mail; e-query OK. **NO PAYMENT.** Articles 500-1,500 wds. (10/yr.). Responds in 2-4 wks. Seasonal 3 mos. ahead. Accepts simultaneous submissions; no reprints. Prefers e-mail submissions (attached or copied into message). Uses some sidebars. Prefers NIV, NKJV, NAS. Also accepts submissions from teens. Guidelines by e-mail. (No ads)

Poetry: Accepts 2/yr. Avant-garde, free verse, haiku, or light verse; 50-250 lines. Submit max. 1 poem.

Columns/Departments: Accepts 10/yr. Features (Christian living, encouragement); article (to other women); all 500-1,500 wds.

Special needs: Personal stories of growing in the Lord; faith-stretching stories about international adoption.

Tips: "Appropriate topics could be firsthand accounts of how God worked in the author's life through a personal or family experience. View online forum for specific topics."

WRITERS' MARKETS

ADVANCED CHRISTIAN WRITER, 9118 W. Elmwood Dr., Ste. 1G, Niles IL 60714-5820. (847) 296-3964. Fax (847) 296-0754. E-mail: ljohnson@wordprocommunications.com. Website: www .ACWriters.com. American Christian Writers/Reg Forder, P.O. Box 110390, Nashville TN 37222. E-mail: ACWriters@aol.com (for samples, advertising, and subscriptions). Lin Johnson, mng. ed. A professional newsletter for published writers. Bimonthly e-mail newsletter; 8 pgs.; circ. 500. Subscription $19.95. 50% unsolicited freelance. Query or complete ms, correspondence, & mss by e-mail only. **Pays $20** on publication for 1st or reprint rts. Articles 700-1,000 wds. (24/yr.). Responds in 6-8 wks. Seasonal 6 mos. ahead. No simultaneous submissions. Accepts reprints (tell when/where appeared). Uses some sidebars. Requires e-mail submission (attached or copied into message). No kill fee. Prefers NIV. Guidelines by e-mail. (Ads)

Special needs: How-to; opinion pieces; time management; workplace issues.

Tips: "We accept articles only from well-published writers and from editors. We need manuscripts about all aspects of building a freelance career and how to increase sales and professionalism; on the advanced level; looking for depth beyond the basics."

BEST NEW WRITING, PO Box 11, Titusville NJ 08560. E-mail: cklim@bestnewwriting.com. Website: www.bestnewwriting.com. Christopher Klim, exec. ed.; Robert Gover, ed. This annual anthology carries the results of the Eric Hoffer Award for Books and Prose and the Gover Prize for short-short writing. Submit books via mail; no queries. Submit prose online. The prose category is for creative fiction and nonfiction less than 10,000 wds. (Hoffer Award) and less than 500 wds (Gover Prize). Annual award for books features 18 categories, including self-help and spiritual. **Pays $250 for winning prose; $2,000 for winning book; $250 for short-short prose; $75 for cover art.** Guidelines at www.HofferAward.com and www.BestNewWriting.com.

CHRISTIAN COMMUNICATOR, 9118 W. Elmwood Dr., Ste. 1G, Niles, IL 60714-5820. (847) 296-3964. Fax (847) 296-0754. E-mail: ljohnson@wordprocommunications.com. Website: www

.ACWriters.com. American Christian Writers/Reg Forder, P.O. Box 110390, Nashville TN 37222. Fax (615) 834-0450. E-mail: ACWriters@aol.com (for samples, advertising or subscriptions). Lin Johnson, mng. ed.; Sally Miller, poetry ed. For Christian writers/speakers who want to improve their writing craft and speaking ability, stay informed about writing markets, and be encouraged in their ministries. Monthly (11X) mag.; 20 pgs.; circ. 3,000. Subscription $29.95. 70% unsolicited freelance. Complete ms/queries by e-mail only. **Pays $5-10** on publication for 1st or reprint rts. Articles 650-1,000 wds. (90-100/yr.). Responds in 6-8 wks. Seasonal 6 mos. ahead. Accepts reprints (tell when/where appeared). Requires e-mail submission. Guidelines by e-mail; copy for 9 x 12 SAE/3 stamps to Nashville address. (Ads)

> **Poetry:** Buys 22/yr. Free verse, haiku, light verse, traditional; to 20 lines. Poems on writing or speaking; $5. Send to Sally Miller: sallymiller@ameritech.net.
> **Columns/Departments:** Buys 35/yr. A Funny Thing Happened on the Way to Becoming a Communicator (humor), 75-300 wds. Interviews (published authors or editors), 650-1,000 wds. Speaking (techniques for speakers), 650-1,000 wds.
> **Tips:** "I need anecdotes for the 'Funny Thing Happened' column and articles on research, creativity, and writing nonfiction."

FELLOWSCRIPT, Canada. E-mail: fellowscript@gmail.com. Website: www.inscribe.org/fellowscript. Bonnie Way, acq. ed. Writer's quarterly newsletter for, by, and about writers/writing. 32 pgs.; circ. 200. Subscription with InScribe membership. Submit complete ms. by e-mail. Pays 2.5 cents per word (Canadian funds) for onetime rights, or 1.5 cents per word for reprint rights, paid by PayPal on publication; an extra half cent paid for publication (with author's permission) on our website for a period of no more than three months. 750-2,000 wds. Responds in 4 weeks. Plans 6 months ahead. Guidelines on website.

> **Tips:** "We always prefer material specifically slanted towards the needs and interests of Canadian Christian writers. We do not publish poetry except as part of an instructional article, nor do we publish testimonials. We give preference to members and to Canadian writers."

FREELANCE WRITER'S REPORT, 45 Main St., PO Box A, North Stratford NH 03590-0167. (603) 922-8338. E-mail: editor@writers-editors.com. Website: www.writers-editors.com. General/CNW Publishing Inc. Dana K. Cassell, ed. Covers marketing and running a freelance writing business. Monthly newsletter; 8 pgs. 25% freelance. Complete ms via e-mail (attached or copied into message). **Pays .10/wd.** on publication for onetime rts. Articles to 900 wds. (50/yr.). Responds within 1 wk. Seasonal 2 mos. ahead. Accepts simultaneous submissions & reprints (tell when/where appeared). Does not use sidebars. Guidelines on website; copy for 6 x 9 SAE/2 stamps (for back copy); $4 for current copy.

> **Fillers:** Prose fillers to 400 wds.
> **Contest:** Open to all writers. Deadline March 15, 2013 (annual). Nonfiction, fiction, children's, poetry. Prizes: $100, $75, $50. Details on website.
> **Tips:** "No articles on the basics of freelancing; our readers are established freelancers. Looking for marketing and business building for freelance writers/editors/book authors."

NEW WRITER'S MAGAZINE, PO Box 5976, Sarasota FL 34277-5976. (941) 953-7903. E-mail: newriters@aol.com. General/Sarasota Bay Publishing. George S. Haborak, ed. Bimonthly mag.; circ. 5,000. 95% freelance. Query or complete ms by mail. **Pays $10-50 ($20-40 for fiction)** on publication for 1st rts. Articles 700-1,000 wds. (50/yr.); fiction 700-800 wds. (2-6/yr.). Responds in 5 wks. Guidelines by mail; copy $3.

> **Poetry:** Buys 10-20/yr. Free verse, light verse; 8-20 lines. Pays $5 min. Submit max. 3 poems.
> **Fillers:** Buys 25-45/yr. Writing-related cartoons; buys 20-30/yr.; pays $10 max. Anecdotes, facts, newsbreaks, short humor; 20-100 wds. buys 5-15/yr. Pays $5 max.
> **Tips:** "We like interview articles with successful writers."

POETS & WRITERS MAGAZINE, 90 Broad St., Ste. 2100, New York NY 10004-2272. (212) 226-3586. Fax (212) 226-3963. E-mail: editor@pw.org. Website: www.pw.org. General. Submit to The Editors. Professional trade journal for poetry, fiction, and nonfiction writers. Subscription $19.95. Bimonthly mag.; circ. 60,000. Query/clips by mail; e-query OK. **Pays $150-500** on acceptance for 1st & nonexclusive rts. Articles 500-3,000 wds. (35/yr.). Responds in 4-6 wks. Seasonal 4 mos. ahead. Some kill fees 25%. Guidelines on website; copy $5.95. (Ads)
   Tips: "Most open to News & Trends, The Literary Life, and The Practical Writer (columns)."

THE WRITER, 21027 Crossroads Cir., Waukesha WI 53187. (262) 796-8776. Fax (262) 798-6468. E-mail: queries@writermag.com. Website: www.writermag.com. General. Jeff Reich, ed.; Ron Kovach, sr. ed. (rkovach@writermag.com); Sarah Lange, assoc. ed. (slange@writermag.com). How-to for writers; lists religious markets on website. Monthly mag.; 60-68 pgs.; circ. 30,000. Subscription $32.95. 80% unsolicited freelance. Query; no phone/fax query (prefers hard copy or e-query). **Pays $250-400** for feature articles; book reviews ($40-80, varies); on acceptance for 1st rts. Features 600-3,500 wds. (60/yr.). Responds in 4-8 wks. Uses some sidebars. Guidelines on website ("The Magazine"/"Submissions"). (Ads)
   Fillers: Prose; writer-related cartoons $50. Send cartoons to slange@writermag.com.
   Columns/Departments: Buys 24+/yr. Freelance Success (shorter pieces on the business of writing); Off the Cuff (personal essays about writing; avoid writer's block stories). All 600-1,600 wds. Pays $100-300 for columns; $25-75 for Take Note. Query 4 months ahead. See guidelines for full list of columns.
   Special needs: How-to on the craft of writing only.
   Contests: Currently running two to three contests a year, generally in personal-essay or short-story categories.
   Tips: "Get familiar first with our general mission, approach, tone, and the types of articles we do and don't do. Then, if you feel you have an article that is fresh and well suited to our mission, send us a query. Personal essays must provide takeaway advice and benefits for writers; we shun the 'navel-gazing' type of essay. Include plenty of how-to, advice, and tips on techniques. Be specific. Query for features six months ahead. All topics indicated must relate to writing."
   ** This periodical was #42 on the 2010 Top 50 Christian Publishers list (#17 in 2009, #45 in 2008).

THE WRITER'S CHRONICLE: The Magazine for Serious Writers, The Association of Writers & Writing Programs, George Mason University, MSN 1E3, 4400 University Dr., Fairfax VA 22030-4444. (703) 993-4301. Fax (703) 993-4302. E-mail: awp@awpwriter.org. Website: www.awpwriter.org. Supriya Bhatnagar, ed. Magazine for serious writers; articles used as teaching tools. Mag. published 6X during academic yr.; 96 pgs.; circ. 35,000. Subscription $20/yr.; $34.2/yr. 90% unsolicited free-lance; 10% assigned. Query; phone/fax/e-query OK. No full mss by e-mail. **Pays .11/wd.** on publication for 1st rts. Articles 3,000-6,000. Responds in 12 wks. Accepts simultaneous submissions. No reprints. No articles on disk or by e-mail. No kill fee. Uses some sidebars. Guidelines/theme list on website ("Magazine"/"Editorial Guidelines"); copy for 10 x 13 SAE/first-class postage. (Ads)
   Special needs: Articles on the craft of writing and interviews with established writers from all over the world. Essays, trends, and literary controversies. No poetry or fiction.
   Contests: Grace Paley Prize for Short Fiction, $6,000 & publication; AWP Prize for Creative Nonfiction, $3,000 & publication; Donald Hall Prize for Poetry, $6,000 & publication; AWP Prize for the Novel, $3,000 & publication. Website: www.awpwriter.org.

*WRITER'S DIGEST, 4700 E. Galbraith Rd., Cincinnati OH 45236. (513) 531-2690, ext. 11483. Fax (513) 891-7153. E-mail: wordsubmissions@fwmedia.com. Website: www.writersdigest.com. General/F & W. Submit to Acquisitions Editor. To inform, instruct, or inspire the freelancer and author. Media (8X) mag.; 84-92 pgs.; circ. 110,000. Subscription $24.96. 20% unsolicited; 60%

assigned. E-mail submissions only. Responds in 8-16 wks. **Pays .30-.50/wd.** on acceptance for 1st & electronic rts. Articles 800-1,500 wds. (75/yr.). Seasonal 8 mos. ahead. Requires requested ms by e-mail (copied into message). Kill fee 25%. Regularly uses sidebars. Guidelines/editorial calendar on website; no copy. (Ads)

Contests: Sponsors annual contest for articles, short stories, poetry, and scripts. Also The International Self-Published Book Awards. Send SASE for rules.

Tips: "We're looking for technique pieces by published authors. The Inkwell section is the best place to break in."

** This periodical was #45 on the 2010 Top 50 Christian Publishers list (#49 in 2009, #38 in 2008).

PART 3
Specialty Markets

7

Greeting Card/Gift/Specialty Markets

This list contains both Christian/religious card publishers and secular publishers that have religious lines or produce some religious or inspirational cards. Secular companies may produce other lines of cards that are not consistent with your beliefs, and for a secular company, inspirational cards usually do not include religious imagery. Support group for greeting card writers can be found at http://groups.yahoo.com/group/GreetingCardWriters.

CARD PUBLISHERS

BLUE MOUNTAIN ARTS INC., PO Box 4549, Boulder CO 80306. (303) 449-0536. Fax (303) 447-0939. E-mail: editorial@sps.com. Website: www.sps.com. Submit to Editorial Department. General card publisher that does a few inspirational cards. Open to freelance; buys 50-100 ideas/yr. Prefers outright submissions. Pays $300 for all rts. for use on a greeting card, or $50 for onetime use in a book, on publication. No royalties. Responds in 12-16 wks. Uses unrhymed or traditional poetry; short or long, but no one-liners. Produces inspirational and sensitivity. Needs anniversary, birthday, Christmas, congratulations, Easter, Father's Day, friendship, get well, graduation, keep in touch, love, miss you, Mother's Day, new baby, please write, reaching for dreams, relatives, sympathy, thank you, valentines, wedding. Holiday/seasonal 6 mos. ahead. Open to ideas for new card lines. Send any number of ideas (1 per pg.). Open to ideas for gift books. Guidelines; no catalog.

Contest: Sponsors a poetry card contest online. Details on website.

Tips: "We are interested in reviewing poetry and writings for greeting cards, and expanding our field of freelance poetry writers."

*DAYSPRING CARDS INC., Editorial Department, Box 1010, 21154 Hwy. 16 East, Siloam Springs AR 72761. Fax (479) 524-9477. E-mail: info@dayspring.com (type "write" in message or subject line). Website: www.dayspring.com. Attn: Freelance Editor. Christian/religious card publisher. Please read guidelines before submitting. Prefers outright submission. Pays $60/idea on acceptance for all rts. No royalty. Responds in 4-8 wks. Uses unrhymed, traditional, light verse, conversational, contemporary; various lengths. Looking for inspirational cards for all occasions, including anniversary, birthday, relative birthday, congratulations, encouragement, friendship, get well, new baby, sympathy, thank you, wedding. Also needs seasonal cards for friends and family members for Christmas, Valentine's Day, Easter, Mother's Day, Father's Day, Thanksgiving, graduation, and Clergy Appreciation Day. Include Scripture verse with each submission. Send 10 ideas or less. Guidelines by phone or e-mail; no catalog.

Tips: Prefers submissions on 8.5 x 11 inch sheets, not 3x5 cards (one idea per sheet).

WARNER PRESS INC., 1201 E. 5th St., PO Box 2499, Anderson IN 46018-9988. (765) 644-7721. Fax (765) 640-8005. E-mail: rfogle@warnerpress.org. Website: www.warnerpress.org. Karen Rhodes, sr. ed.; Robin Fogle, ed. asst. Producer of church resources (greeting cards, bulletins, coloring books, puzzle books). 30% freelance; buys 30-50 ideas/yr. Guidelines on website. Pays $30-35 on acceptance (for bulletins and greeting card copy). No royalties. Responds in 6-8 wks. Uses rhymed, unrhymed, traditional verse, and devotionals for bulletins; 16-24 lines. Accepts 10 ideas/submission. Guidelines for bulletins; no catalog.

Also Does: Also open to ideas for coloring books, bookmarks, charts, postcards, church-resource items.

Photos/Artwork: Accepts freelance photos and queries from freelance artists. E-mail curtis@warnerpress.org, Curtis Corzine, creative director.

GIFT/SPECIALTY-ITEM MARKETS

DESTINY IMAGE, PO Box 310, Shippensburg PA 17257. (717) 532-3040. Fax (717) 532-9291. E-mail: rrr@destinyimage.com, or through website: www.destinyimage.com. Ronda Ranalli, ed. mngr. No unsolicited e-mail submissions; use online submission form (visit website and click on "submit manuscript" button); publishing Christian books that inspire and promote spiritual growth. No poetry.

LORENZ CORP., PO Box 802, Dayton OH 45401. Toll-free (800) 444-1144, ext. 1. (937) 228-6118. Fax (937) 223-2042. E-mail: submit@lorenz.com or through website: www.lorenz.com. Piano, organ, choral, handbell, instrumental, and more. Guidelines online for music submissions; click on "Submissions."

PART 4

Helps for Writers

8

Christian Writers' Conferences and Workshops

(*) before a listing indicates unconfirmed or no information update.

ALABAMA

*SOUTHERN CHRISTIAN WRITERS CONFERENCE. Tuscaloosa/First Baptist Church; early June. Contact: Joanne Sloan, SCWC, PO Box 1106, Northport AL 35473. (205) 333-8603. E-mail: SCWCworkshop@bellsouth.net. Website: http://web.mac.com/wmdsloan/iweb/SCWC. Editors/agents in attendance. Attendance: 200+.

ARIZONA

AMERICAN CHRISTIAN WRITERS PHOENIX CONFERENCE. November 1-2, 2013. Contact: Reg A. Forder, Box 110390, Nashville TN 37222. Toll-free (800) 21-WRITE. E-mail: ACWriters@aol.com. Website: www.ACWriters.com. Attendance: 40-80.

CALIFORNIA

ACT ONE: WRITING PROGRAM. Hollywood. Contact: Terence Berry, 2690 N. Beachwood Dr., Hollywood CA 90068. (323) 464-0815. Fax (323) 468-0315. E-mail: information@actoneprogram .com. Website: www.ActOneProgram.com. Act One offers an intensive training program for screenwriters, taught by professionals working in Hollywood. We also offer a Script Consulting service and run a Screenplay Competition with a $5,000 cash prize. Speakers: Barbara Nicolosi, David McFadzean, Karen Hall, Ron Austin, Bill Marsilli, and more. See website for bios.

CASTRO VALLEY CHRISTIAN WRITERS SEMINAR. Castro Valley; February 22-23, 2013. Contact: Pastor Jon Drury, 19300 Redwood Rd., Castro Valley CA 94546-3465. (510) 886-6300. E-mail: jdrury@redwoodchapel.org. Website: www.christianwriter.org. No editors/agents in attendance. Speaker: Ethel Herr. Offers full or partial scholarships. We offer 36 writing workshops. Written critiques available for fee if website guidelines are followed. CDs of all workshops available after seminar (see list on website).

MOUNT HERMON CHRISTIAN WRITERS CONFERENCE. Mount Hermon (near Santa Cruz); March 22-26, 2013. Website: www.mounthermon.org/writers. (888) MH-CAMPS. Keynote speaker: McNair Wilson. Offering instruction for all levels of writers, professional to beginner (including special track for teen writers). Many well-known editors and agents in attendance. Offers partial scholarships *on tuition only*. Awards for a variety of writing genres. Mentoring Clinic two days before Writers Conference, March 20-22. All details on website November 1 (no brochure). Faculty: 50. Writers: 400. Director: Rachel A. Williams. Registration opens November 1.

MOUNT HERMON HEAD-START MENTORING CLINIC. Mount Hermon; March 20-22, 2013. This mentoring session is held the two days prior to the regular spring conference. See the listing for Mount Hermon Christian Writers Conference for details or www.mounthermon.org.

ORANGE COUNTY CHRISTIAN WRITERS FELLOWSHIP SPRING WRITERS DAY. Orange County. Contact: John DeSimone, dir.; PO Box 1173, Orange CA 92856. (714) 244-0554. E-mail: john@occwf.org. Website: www.occwf.org. Consult with editors, agents, published authors. Offers full and partial scholarships. See website for list of faculty and conference details. Attendance: 150+.

SAN DIEGO CHRISTIAN WRITER'S GUILD FALL CONFERENCE. San Diego; October. Contact: Jennie Gillespie, PO Box 270403, San Diego CA 92198. (760) 294-3269. E-mail: info@sandiegocwg .org. Website: www.sandiegocwg.org. Offers an advanced track. Editors/agents in attendance. Offers some scholarships. Attendance: 200.

SANTA BARBARA CHRISTIAN WRITERS CONFERENCE. Westmont College. Contact: Opal Mae Dailey, PO Box 40860, Santa Barbara CA 93140. Phone/fax (805) 682-0316 (call first for fax). E-mail: opalmaedailey@aol.com. Website: www.CWGSB.com. Offers scholarships to students.

SOCIETY OF CHILDREN'S BOOK WRITERS & ILLUSTRATORS CONFERENCE IN CHILDREN'S LITERATURE. Los Angeles; early August. Society of Children's Book Writers & Illustrators. Contact: Lin Oliver, 8271 Beverly Blvd., Los Angeles CA 90048. (323) 782-1010. Fax (323) 782-1892. E-mail: scbwi@scbwi.org. Website: www.scbwi.org. Includes a track for professionals. Editors/agents in attendance. Attendance: 900.

WRITER'S SYMPOSIUM BY THE SEA. San Diego/Point Loma Nazarene University; February 25-27, 2013. Contact: Dean Nelson, Professor, Journalism Dept., PLNU, 3900 Lomaland Dr., San Diego CA 92106. (619) 849-2592. Fax (619) 849-2566. E-mail: deannelson@pointloma.edu. Website: www .pointloma.edu/writers. Speakers, interviews, and workshops. No scholarships. Attendance: 500.

WRITE TO INSPIRE. Elk Grove; July 19-20, 2013. Contact: Elizabeth M. Thompson, PO Box 276794, Sacramento CA 95827-6794. (916) 607-7796. E-mail: inspiregroup@comcast.net. Website: www.InspireWriters.com. Keynote speakers: Calvin Miller and Davis Bunn. Contests: Fiction and Nonfiction—limited to writers unpublished by traditional publishers, or published only in anthologies, compilations, or periodicals. May have 3rd contest for one sheet (check website). Information about the contests is available at www.InspireWriters.com. Offer full scholarships (pay half the hotel and lunch on Saturday is included. Limited by availability and meeting requirements on website).

COLORADO

COLORADO CHRISTIAN WRITERS CONFERENCE. Estes Park; May 15-18, 2013, at the YMCA of the Rockies. Director: Marlene Bagnull, LittD, 951 Anders Rd., Lansdale PA 19446. Phone/fax (484) 991-8581. E-mail: mbagnull@aol.com. Website: www.writehisanswer.com/Colorado. Conferees choose 6 hour-long workshops from 42 offered or a clinic—fiction, nonnfiction, and speakers— by application) plus one six-hour continuing session from 8 offered. Four 15-minute one-on-one appointments, paid critiques, editors' panels, and general sessions. Early-bird workshops Wednesday afternoon. Teens Write Saturday afternoon, plus teens are welcome to attend the entire conference at 60% off. Contest for published and not-yet-published writers awards—two 50% off 2013 conference registration fee (registered conferees only). Faculty of 50 authors, editors, and agents. Attendance: 225. Offers scholarships.

JERRY B. JENKINS CHRISTIAN WRITERS GUILD WRITING FOR THE SOUL CONFERENCE. The Broadmoor, Colorado Springs; February 14-17, 2013. Sponsored by the Jerry B. Jenkins Christian Writers Guild. Host: Jerry B. Jenkins. Speakers: James MacDonald, Liz Curtis Higgs, Steven James, Christopher Yuan, Dr. Dennis E. Hensley. Appointments with publishers' reps & agents. Editors and agents in attendance. Payment plans available. Special meal rates offered for nonparticipating spouses or parents of teens. General sessions with national keynote speakers and in-depth workshops.

Contact: Christian Writers Guild, 5525 N. Union Blvd., Ste. 200, Colorado Springs CO 80918. Toll-free (866) 495-5177. Fax (719) 495-5181. E-mail: ContactUs@christianwritersguild.com. Website: www.ChristianWritersGuild.com. Attendance: 400.

FLORIDA

AMERICAN CHRISTIAN WRITERS MENTORING RETREAT. November 22-23, 2013. Contact: Reg A. Forder, Box 110390, Nashville TN 37222. Toll-free (800) 21-WRITE. E-mail: ACWriters@aol.com. Website: www.ACWriters.com. Attendance: 40-80.

CHRISTIAN WRITERS GUILD WORD WEAVERS RETREAT. October 2013. Contact: Larry J. Leech II, 911 Alameda Drive, Longwood FL 32750. (407) 925-6411. E-mail: larry@christianwritersguild .com. Website: www.christianwritersguild.com/word-weavers. No editors/agents in attendance. Offers scholarships.

DEEP THINKERS RETREAT. February. Contact: Susan May Warren, PO Box 1290, Grand Marais MN 55604. E-mail: retreats@mybooktherapy.com. Website: http://deepthinkers.mybooktherapy.com. Offers an advanced track. This five-day retreat is for novelists who want to bring their writing to a new level, with deeper characterization, stronger wordsmithing, and a more compelling plot. Speakers: Susan May Warren, Rachel Hauck. No scholarships. Each retreat attendee receives a private consultation about his or her writing. If ready for advanced writing techniques, we teach that. Sponsors the My Book Therapy Frasier Contest. Attendance: 16.

FLORIDA CHRISTIAN WRITERS CONFERENCE. Lake Yale Conference Center/Leesburg; February 28-March 3, 2013. Contact: Billie Wilson, 2344 Armour Ct., Titusville FL 32780. (321) 269-5831. Fax (321) 267-9654. E-mail: billiewilson@cfl.rr.com. Or contact Larry J. Leech II, 911 Alameda Drive, Longwood FL 32750. (407) 925-6411. E-mail: lleech@cfl.rr.com. Website: www .flwriters.org. Offers advanced track (15 hours of class time—by application only) & teen track. Keynote speaker: check website. Editors and agents in attendance. Offers full & partial scholarships. Offers awards in 11 categories. Awards open to registrants; mss. submitted to conference for review are considered for an award. Attendance: 275.

INTERNATIONAL CHRISTIAN RETAIL SHOW. Orlando, FL; July 15-18. (Held in a different location each year.) Contact: Scott Graham. Colorado Springs CO 80962-2000. Toll-free (800) 252-1950. (719) 265-9895. Fax (719) 272-3510. E-mail: info@cbaonline.org. Website: www.christianretailshow .com. Entrance badges available through book publishers or Christian bookstores. Attendance: 5,000.

GEORGIA

AMERICAN CHRISTIAN WRITERS ATLANTA MENTORING RETREAT. July 12-13, 2013. Contact: Reg Forder, Box 110390, Nashville TN 37222. Toll-free (800) 21-WRITE. E-mail: ACWriters@aol .com. Website: www.ACWriters.com. Attendance: 40-80.

CATCH THE WAVE WRITERS CONFERENCE. August 2013. Contact: Cynthia L. Simmons, 322 Homestead Circle, Kennesaw GA 30144. (770) 926-8627. Fax: same number. E-mail: clsimm@ comcast.net. Offer well-rounded curriculum. Keynote speakers: Lin Johnson, Tiffany Colter. Editors and agents attend. Full and partial scholarships offered.

EAST METRO ATLANTA CHRISTIAN WRITERS CONFERENCE. Meets the second Saturday of each month from 10:00 a.m. to noon at Georgia Piedmont Technical College, 8100 Bob Williams Parkway, Covington, GA 30014. Call for information and dates regarding our 2013 two-day annual conference and writing contest. (404) 444-7514. Website: www.emacw.org. EMACW is a chapter of the American Christian Writers. Dues $60.00 annually. Our mission is to educate, encourage, and engage the writer.

ILLINOIS

KARITOS CHRISTIAN ARTS CONFERENCE. The 19th Annual Karitos Christian Arts Conference is scheduled for July 2013 in Chicago. Karitos is unique among conferences for Christian artists in that it brings all of the arts together. In 2012, a 50-person faculty offered workshops in Literary Arts, Music, Dance/Mime, Visual Arts, Film, Theater, and Worship. Three-hour evening celebrations saw the different disciplines coming together on stage for times of extravagant worship, exciting performances, and powerful teaching. More information is available at www.karitos.com.

WRITE-TO-PUBLISH CONFERENCE. Wheaton (Chicago area); June 5-8, 2013. Contact: Lin Johnson, 9118 W. Elmwood Dr., Ste. 1G, Niles IL 60714-5820. (847) 296-3964. Fax (847) 296-0754. E-mail: lin@writetopublish.com. Website: www.writetopublish.com. Offers freelance career track (prerequisite: 1 published book). Majority of faculty are editors and agents. Offers full and partial scholarships. Attendance: 250.

INDIANA

AMERICAN CHRISTIAN WRITERS FORT WAYNE MENTORING RETREAT. April 5-6, 2013. Contact: Reg A. Forder, Box 110390, Nashville TN 37222. Toll-free (800) 21-WRITE. E-mail: ACWriters@aol.com. Website: www.ACWriters.com. Attendance: 40-80.

MIDWEST WRITERS WORKSHOP. Muncie/Ball State University Alumni Center; July 25-27, 2013 (always the last Thursday, Friday, and Saturday of July). Our 40th summer workshop! Contact: Dept. of English, Ball State University, Muncie IN 47306-0484. Director: Jama Kehoe Bigger. (765) 282-1055. E-mail: midwest writers@yahoo.com. Website: www.midwestwriters.org. Sponsors a contest. Editors/agents in attendance. Attendance: 150.

IOWA

CHRISTIAN WRITERS SEMINAR. Arnolds Park. Contact: Denise Triggs, PO Box 709, Arnolds Park IA 51331. (712) 332-7191. E-mail: waterfalls42@hotmail.com. Website: www.waterfallsretreats.com. No editors/agents in attendance. Scholarships. Attendance: 20-30.

KANSAS

CALLED TO WRITE. Pittsburg. Contact: April 4-6, 2013. Contact: Joyce Love, 1676 Express Rd, Fort Scott KS 66701. (620) 547-2596; E-mail: clove@ckt.net.. Website: www.christianwritersfellowship. blogspot.com. Contest for attendees only. Offers full and partial scholarships. Attendance: 75.

MICHIGAN

AMERICAN CHRISTIAN WRITERS GRAND RAPIDS MENTORING RETREAT. June 7-8, 2013. Contact: Reg Forder, Box 110390, Nashville TN 37222. Toll-free (800) 21-WRITE. E-mail: ACWriters@ aol.com. Website: www.ACWriters.com. Attendance: 40-80.

FAITH WRITERS CONFERENCE. Faith Writers' 2013 international writing conference is the second weekend in August. Join us for a time of fellowship and teaching from Faith Writers' own skilled members. These conferences are known for being different—as much about support and encouragement as about writing facts and skills. US location to be announced. Check www.faithwriters.com/conference.php for more information.

FESTIVAL OF FAITH & WRITING. Grand Rapids; April 2014 (exact dates TBD, held every other year). Contact: Shelly LeMahieu Dunn, 1795 Knollcrest Circle S.E., Grand Rapids MI 49546. (616) 526-6770. E-mail: ffw@calvin.edu. Website: festival.calvin.edu. Editors/agents in attendance; no scholarships. Attendance: 1,800.

MARANATHA CHRISTIAN WRITERS' CONFERENCE. Located on the shore of Lake Michigan. September 23-27, 2013. Contact: Verna Kokmeyer, 4759 Lake Harbor Rd., Muskegon MI 49441-5299. (231) 798-2161. E-mail: info@writewithpurpose.org. Website: www.WriteWithPurpose.org. Offers contests, advanced tracks, continuing courses, manuscript makeovers, and many elective workshops. Check website for faculty. Consultations, agents, editors, and publishers included in tuition. Scholarships available. Attendance: 125.

MINNESOTA

AMERICAN CHRISTIAN WRITERS MINNEAPOLIS MENTORING RETREAT. August 2-3, 2013. Contact: Reg Forder, Box 110390, Nashville TN 37222. Toll-free (800) 21-WRITE. Website: www .ACWriters.com. Attendance: 40-80.

STORYCRAFTERS RETREAT. Minneapolis MN. Contact: Susan May Warren, PO Box 1290, Grand Marais MN 55604. (218) 387-2853. E-mail: retreats@mybooktherapy.com. Website: http://story crafters.mybooktherapy.com. This private coaching retreat is for writers at all levels. We focus on storycrafting—starting with an idea, and leaving with a plotted story. Sponsors the My Book Therapy Frasier Contest (winner attends retreat for free). Limit 16.

MISSOURI

*HEART OF AMERICA CHRISTIAN WRITERS NETWORK CONFERENCES. Kansas City. Check website for dates of additional events. Contact: Jeanette Littleton, 3706 N.E. Shady Lane Dr., Gladstone MO 64119. Phone/fax (816) 459-8016. E-mail: HACWN@earthlink.net. Website: www.HACWN.org. Offers classes for new and advanced writers. Editors/agents in attendance. Contest details on brochure. Attendance: 125.

NEW HAMPSHIRE

WRITERS WORKSHOPS FOR ADULTS & YOUNG WRITERS BY MARY EMMA ALLEN. Taught on request by writers' groups, conferences, schools, and libraries. Topics include Workshops for Young Writers (for schools and home-schooling groups); Writing Your Family Stories; Scrapbooking Your Stories. Contact: Mary Emma Allen (instructor), 55 Binks Hill Rd., Plymouth NH 03264. (603) 536-2641. E-mail: me.allen@juno.com. Blogs: http://maryemmallen.blogspot.com.

NEW MEXICO

CLASS CHRISTIAN WRITERS CONFERENCE. Ghost Ranch/Abiquiu NM; November 2013. Editors and agents in attendance. Contact: Linda Gilden, director, PO Box 36551, Albuquerque NM 87176. E-mail: linda@lindagilden.com. Website: www.classeminars.org. Scholarships available. Attendance: 150.

SOUTHWEST WRITERS MINI WORKSHOPS. Albuquerque; various times during the year (check website for dates). Contact: Conference Chair, 3721 Morris St. N.E., Ste. A, Albuquerque NM 87111-3611. (505) 265-9485. E-mail: swwriters@juno.com. Website: www.southwestwriters.com. General conference. Sponsors the Southwest Writers Contests annually and bimonthly (see website). Agents/editors in attendance. Attendance: 50.

NEW YORK

*SOCIETY OF CHILDREN'S BOOK WRITERS & ILLUSTRATORS CONFERENCE IN CHILDREN'S LITERATURE. New York City; early February. Society of Children's Book Writers & Illustrators. Contact: Lin Oliver, 8271 Beverly Blvd., Los Angeles CA 90048. (323) 782-1010. Fax (323) 782-1892. E-mail: scbwi@scbwi.org. Website: www.scbwi.org. Includes a track for professionals. Editors/agents in attendance. Attendance: 900.

NORTH CAROLINA

AMERICAN CHRISTIAN WRITERS CHARLOTTE MENTORING RETREAT. May 17-18, 2013. Contact: Reg A. Forder, Box 110390, Nashville TN 37222. Toll-free (800) 21-WRITE. E-mail: ACWriters@aol.com. Website: www.ACWriters.com. Attendance: 30-45.

BLUE RIDGE MOUNTAINS CHRISTIAN WRITERS CONFERENCE. LifeWay Ridgecrest Conference Center; May 19-23, 2013. Contact: Alton Gansky, 4721 W. Princeton Ave., Fresno CA 93722. (760) 220-1075. E-mail: alton@ganskycommunications.com. Website: www.brmcwc.com, or http://ridgecrestconferencecenter.org/event/blueridgemountainchristianwritersconference. Offers an advanced track. Editors and agents in attendance. Sponsors three contests (details at www.brmcwc.com). Offers limited scholarships. Attendance: 350.

OHIO

PEN TO PAPER LITERARY SYMPOSIUM. Dayton; October 5, 2013. Contact: Valerie L. Coleman, Pen of the Writer, 893 S. Main St., PMB 175, Englewood OH 45322. (937) 307-0760. E-mail: info@penofthewriter.com. Website: www.penofthewriter.com. Editors in attendance. No scholarships. Event is free to public. Attendance: 30.

OKLAHOMA

AMERICAN CHRISTIAN WRITERS OKLAHOMA CITY CONFERENCE. March 22-23, 2013. Contact: Reg Forder, Box 110390, Nashville TN 37222. Toll-free (800) 21-WRITE. E-mail: ACWriters@aol.com. Website: www.ACWriters.com. Attendance: 40-80.

OREGON

OREGON CHRISTIAN WRITERS SUMMER COACHING CONFERENCE. Portland; August 12-15, 2013. Liz Curtis Higgs keynoting. Contact: Lindy Jacobs. E-mail: summerconference@oregonchristianwriters.org. Website: www.OregonChristianWriters.org. Includes about 7 hours of training under a specific coach/topic and more than 30 hour-long afternoon workshops on a variety of writing-related topics. Editors/agents in attendance. Offers partial scholarships to members who apply. Attendance: 250. OCW also offers 3 one-day Saturday conferences—winter in Salem, spring in Eugene, and fall in Portland. Check the website for more information on all conferences.

PENNSYLVANIA

GREATER PHILADELPHIA CHRISTIAN WRITERS CONFERENCE. Philadelphia Biblical University, Langhorne; July 31-August 3 or August 7-10, 2013. Founder and director: Marlene Bagnull, LittD, 951 Anders Rd., Lansdale PA 19446. Phone/fax (484) 991-8581. E-mail: mbagnull@aol.com. Website: www.writehisanswer.com/Philadelphia. Conferees choose 6 hour-long workshops from 42 offered or a clinic by application (beginning novelists, advanced novelists, nonfiction) plus one six-hour continuing session from 8 offered. Four 15-minute one-on-one appointments, paid critiques, editors panels, and general sessions. Contest (registered conferees only) awards 50% off 2013 conference registration to a published and not-yet-published conferee. Especially encourages African American writers. Faculty of 50 authors, editors, and agents. Partial scholarships offered. Attendance: 250.

MONTROSE CHRISTIAN WRITERS CONFERENCE. Montrose; July 21-26, 2013. Patti Souder, dir. Contact: Donna Kosik, Montrose Bible Conference, 218 Locust St., Montrose PA 18801-1473. (570) 278-1001. Fax (570) 278-3061. E-mail: mbc@montrosebible.org. Website: www.montrosebible.org. Tracks for beginners, advanced writers, and teens (some years). Editors/agents in attendance. Attendance: 100. Provides a few partial scholarships.

*ST. DAVIDS CHRISTIAN WRITERS' CONFERENCE. Grove City College, Grove City; June 2012. Lora Zill, director. Contact: Audrey Stallsmith, registrar, 87 Pines Rd. E., Hadley PA 16130-1019. (724) 253-2738. E-mail: registrar@stdavidswriters.com. Website: www.stdavidswriters.com. Offers track for advanced writers. Contest for participants; guidelines on website. Editors in attendance. Offers partial scholarships. See website for information on their Writers' Colony. Attendance: 60-70.

SUSQUEHANNA VALLEY WRITERS WORKSHOP. Lewisburg; Contact: Marsha Hubler, 1833 Dock Hill Rd., Middleburg PA 17842. (570) 837-0002. (570) 374-8700. E-mail: marshahubler@wildblue .net. Website: www.susquehannavalleywritersworkshop.wordpress.com.

SOUTH CAROLINA

*CAROLINA CHRISTIAN WRITERS CONFERENCE. Spartanburg; First Baptist Church, 250 East Main Street, Spartanburg SC 29306. April 19-20, 2013. Editors and agents in attendance. Contact: Linda Gilden, director, PO Box 2928, Spartanburg SC 29304. E-mail: linda@lindagilden.com. Website: www.fbs.org/writersconference. Scholarships available. Attendance: 100.

CHRISTIAN COMMUNICATORS CONFERENCE. The Billy Graham Training Center at The Cove; Fall 2013 and more. Contact: Vonda Skelton, 205 White Meadow Court, Simpsonville SC 29681. (864)906-2256. E-mail: vondaskelton@gmail.com. Website: http://christiancommunicators.com. Christian Communicators Conference's mission is to educate, validate, and launch women in their speaking ministry. Fourteen classes, high tea, professional videotape of attendee presentations. Scholarships. Space is limited.

TENNESSEE

AMERICAN CHRISTIAN WRITERS NASHVILLE MENTORING RETREAT. April 12-13, 2013. Contact: Reg Forder, Box 110390, Nashville TN 37222. Toll-free (800) 21-WRITE. E-mail: ACWriters@ aol.com. Website: www.ACWriters.com. Attendance: 40-80.

TEXAS

AMERICAN CHRISTIAN WRITERS DALLAS MENTORING RETREAT. March 15-16, 2013. Contact: Reg Forder, Box 110390, Nashville TN 37222. Toll-free (800) 21-WRITE. E-mail: ACWriters@aol .com. Website: www.ACWriters.com. Attendance: 40-80.

EAST TEXAS CHRISTIAN WRITERS CONFERENCE. Marshall; October 25-26, 2013 (last weekend of October annually). Contact: Dr. Jerry Hopkins, East Texas Baptist University, One Tiger Drive, Marshall TX 75670. (903) 923-2083. Fax (903) 923-2077. E-mail: jhopkins@etbu.edu. Website: www.etbu.edu/news/CWC. Offers an advanced & teen track. Sponsors a Writers Contest in three categories—Short Story, Poetry, Essay (Grand prize, 1st–3rd Place winners; cash awards). Speakers: Bill Keith, Becca Anderson, Conn Taylor, Terry Burns, Lexie Smith, and others. Editors/agents in attendance. Partial scholarships for students only. Attendance: 200+.

NORTH TEXAS CHRISTIAN WRITERS CONFERENCE. Ft. Worth; June 2013. Contact: NTCW Conference, PO Box 820802, Fort Worth TX 76182. (817) 715-2597. E-mail: info@NTChristianWriters .com. Website: www.NTChristianWriters.com. Offers track for advanced writers. No editors or agents in attendance. Offers partial scholarships. Sponsors a contest for conference registrants only. Attendance: 250.

WASHINGTON

AMERICAN CHRISTIAN WRITERS SPOKANE MENTORING RETREAT. September 27-28, 2013. Contact: Reg Forder, Box 110390, Nashville TN 37222. Toll-free (800) 21-WRITE. E-mail: ACWriters@ aol.com. Website: www.ACWriters.com. Attendance: 40-80.

NORTHWEST CHRISTIAN WRITERS RENEWAL CONFERENCE. Redmond; May 17-18, 2013. Contact: Judy Bodmer, 11108 N.E. 141 Pl., Kirkland WA 98034. Phone/fax (425) 488-2900. E-mail: jbodmer@msn.com. Website: www.nwchristianwriters.org. Speaker: Jane Kirkpatrick. Editors/agents in attendance. Offers 3 scholarships. Attendance: 200.

WISCONSIN

*WRITING WORKSHOPS & RETREATS. La Crosse; check our website for dates. Contact: Franciscan Spirituality Center, 920 Market St., La Crosse WI 54601. E-mail: FSCenter@fspa.org. Website: www .FSCenter.org.

CANADA/FOREIGN

AMERICAN CHRISTIAN WRITERS CARIBBEAN CRUISE. November 30-December 7, 2013. Contact: Reg A. Forder, Box 110390, Nashville TN 37222. Toll-free (800) 21-WRITE. E-mail: ACWriters@aol.com. Website: www.ACWriters.com. Attendance: 15-30.

COMIX35 CHRISTIAN COMICS TRAINING SEMINAR. Various international locations & dates. Contact: Nate Butler, PO Box 27470, Albuquerque NM 87125-7470. E-mail: comix35@comix35.org. Website: www.comix35.org /comix35_home.html. Speakers: Nate Butler and others. Sometimes has editors/agents in attendance. Attendance: 15-20. Sponsors contests (details at www.comix35.org /competitions.html).

INSCRIBE CHRISTIAN WRITERS' FELLOWSHIP FALL CONFERENCE. Wetaskiwin AB, Canada; last weekend of September 2013. Contact: Gwen Mathieu, Box 6201, Wetaskiwin, AB T9A 2E9. (780) 352-4006. E-mail: mathieug@xplornet.com. Website: www.inscribe.org/events/fall-conference/. Some editors in attendance. No agents. Hosted by Inscribe Christian Writer's Fellowship, a Canada-wide organization for Christians who write. Contests for members (see http://www.inscribe.org /contests/inscribe-fall-competition/ for details). Attendance: 100.

*WRITE! CANADA. Guelph, Ontario; Contact: N. J. Linddquist, The Word Guild, PO Box 1243, Trenton ON K8V 5R9, Canada. E-mail: info@thewordguild.com. Website: www.writecanada.org. Hosted by The Word Guild, an association of Canadian writers and editors who are Christian. Offers an advanced track. Editors/agents in attendance. God Uses Ink Contest. No scholarships offered. Attendance: 250.

CONFERENCES THAT CHANGE LOCATIONS

ACT ONE: SCREENWRITING WEEKENDS. Two-day workshops; see website for dates and locations. Contact: Conference Coordinator, 2690 Beachwood Dr., Lower Fl., Hollywood CA 90068. (323) 464-0815. Fax (323) 468-0315. E-mail: info@ActOneProgram.com. Website: www.ActOneProgram .com. Open to anyone who is interested in learning more about the craft of screenwriting. No editors/ agents in attendance. Attendance: 75.

AMERICAN CHRISTIAN FICTION WRITERS CONFERENCE. Rotates cities. Contact: Robin Miller, conf. dir., PO Box 101066, Palm Bay FL 32910-1066. E-mail: cd@acfw.com. Website: www.ACFW.com. Offers varied skill-level tracks for published and unpublished writers. Editors/ agents in attendance. Sponsors 3 contests (details on website). Offers scholarships each year to ACFW members only.

AMERICAN CHRISTIAN WRITERS CONFERENCES. Various dates and locations (see individual states where held). Also sponsors an annual Caribbean cruise November 30-December 7, 2013. Contact: Reg A. Forder, Box 110390, Nashville TN 37222. Toll-free (800) 21-WRITE. E-mail: ACWriters@aol.com. Website: www.ACWriters.com. Attendance 30-40.

AUTHORIZEME. Various locations and dates. Contact: Sharon Norris Elliott, PO Box 1519, Inglewood CA 90308-1519. (310) 508-9860. Fax (323) 567-8557. E-mail: AuthorizeMe@sbcglobal .net. Website: www.AuthorizeMe.net. AuthorizeMe is a 12-hour, hands-on seminar that helps writers get their book ideas out of their heads, down onto paper, and into a professional book proposal format ready to submit to an acquisitions editor. Seminars offered nationwide. For a list of scheduled seminars, or to sponsor a seminar in your area, check website. No editors or agents in attendance. Attendance: 10-50.

*CHRISTIAN LEADERS AND SPEAKERS SEMINARS (The CLASSeminar). PO Box 36551, Albuquerque NM 87176. (702) 882-0638. Website: www.classeminars.org. Sponsors several seminars across the country each year. Check website for CLASSeminar dates and locations. For anyone who wants to improve his or her communication skills for either the spoken or written word, for professional or personal reasons. Speakers: Florence Littauer and others. Attendance: 75-100.

EVANGELICAL PRESS ASSOCIATION CONVENTION. Various locations. Nashville, May 1-3, 2013. Contact: Doug Trouten, dir., PO Box 28129, Minneapolis MN 55428. (763) 535-4793. E-mail: director@epassoc.org. Website: www.epassoc.org. Attendance: 350. Annual convention for editors of evangelical periodicals; freelance communicators welcome. Editors in attendance. Contest open to members only.

INTERNATIONAL CHRISTIAN RETAIL SHOW. (Held in a different location each year.) Orlando FL; July 2012. Contact: Scott Graham. Colorado Springs CO 80962-2000. Toll-free (800) 252-1950. (719) 265-9895. Fax (719) 272-3510. E-mail: info@cbaonline.org. Website: www.christianretailshow.com. Entrance badges available through book publishers or Christian bookstores. Attendance: 5,000.

THE SCRIMMAGE (PROPOSAL, PROMOTION, PITCH) SEMINAR. Before the ACFW conference. Contact: Susan May Warren, PO Box 1290, Grand Marais MN 55604 . (218) 387-2853 . E-mail: scrim mage@mybooktherapy.com. Website: http://scrimmage.mybooktherapy.com. This one-day seminar, hosted right before the annual ACFW conference, helps authors plan their pitch during the conference, hone their proposal, and create a marketing plan for their book. Sponsors the My Book Therapy Frasier Contest (winner attends conference free). Attendance: 25.

"WRITE HIS ANSWER" SEMINARS & RETREATS. Various locations around US; dates throughout the year; a choice of focus on periodicals or books (includes self-publishing or mastering the craft). Contact: Marlene Bagnull, LittD, 951 Anders Rd., Lansdale PA 19446. (484) 991-8581. E-mail: mbag null@aol.com. Website: www.writehisanswer.com/Writing_Seminars.htm. Attendance: 20-60. One- and two-day seminars by the author of *Write His Answer: A Bible Study for Christian Writers.*

9

Area Christian Writers' Clubs, Fellowship Groups, and Critique Groups

(*) before a listing indicates unconfirmed or no information update.

ALABAMA

CHRISTIAN FREELANCERS. Tuscaloosa. Contact: Joanne Sloan, 4195 Waldort Dr., Northport AL 35473. (205) 333-8603. E-mail: cjosloan@bellsouth.net. Membership (30-40) open.

ARIZONA

CHANDLER WRITERS GROUP. Chandler. Contact: Jenne Acevedo. (480) 510-0419. E-mail: jenne acevedo@cox.net. http://chandlerwriters.wordpress.com. ACW Chapter.

WORD WEAVERS NORTHERN ARIZONA. Cottonwood. Contact: Joy Gage, chapter president. E-mail: joypg@swiftnaz.net. Website: www.word-weavers.com. Membership (30+) open. Meeting time: Second Saturday, 9:30-noon. Meeting address: Verde Baptist Church, 102 S. Willard Street, Cottonwood AZ 86226.

ARKANSAS

LITTLE ROCK CHAPTER AMERICAN CHRISTIAN WRITERS/LRACW. Little Rock. Contact: Carole Geckle, 5800 Ranch Dr., Little Rock AR 72223. (501) 228-2477. E-mail: cgeckle@familylife .com. Membership open.

CALIFORNIA

AMADOR FICTION WRITERS CRITIQUE GROUP. Four groups meet every other week in Ione. Contact: Kathy Boyd Fellure, PO Box 1209, Ione CA 95640-1209. (209) 274-0205. E-mail: kathy fellure2@juno.com. Website: www.amadorfictionwriters.com. Membership (16); open to readers. Sponsors an annual Literary Read and an annual Children's Read.

CASTRO VALLEY CHRISTIAN WRITERS GROUP. Contact: Pastor Jon Drury, 19300 Redwood Rd., Castro Valley CA 94546-3465. (510) 886-6300. E-mail: jdrury@redwoodchapel.org. Website: www .christianwriter.org. Membership (8-12) open. Sponsors the Christian Writers Seminar, February 22-23, 2013. Ethel Herr, keynoter, and 36 writing workshops.

CHAIRS: The Christian Authors, Illustrators, & Readers Society. Chino Hills. Contact: Jo Ann Langston-Harlan, 13393 Noble Place, Chino CA 91710-4745. E-mail: jaharlan_1@hotmail.com. Website: www.chairs8.wordpress.com. Membership (15-20) open.

INSPIRE CHRISTIAN WRITERS: Equipping Writers to Inspire the World. Meetings in Auburn, El Dorado Hills, Elk Grove, Fair Oaks, Sacramento, & Roseville, and now in Reno NV. Contact: Elizabeth Thompson, PO Box 276794, Elk Grove CA 95827. (916) 670-7796. E-mail: elizabethmthompson@comcast.net. Group e-mail: inspiregroup@comcast.net. Website: www

.inspirewriters.com. Membership (90) open. Hosts annual Write to Inspire Conference and frequent workshops. Check website for details.

MENTORING MEETINGS. For writers and occasional writing classes. Chino. Contact: Nancy L. Sanders, 6361 Prescott Ct., Chino CA 91710-7105. (909) 590-7105. E-mail: jeffandnancys@gmail .com. Website: www.nancyisanders.com. Open to new participants. Contact to have your name put on a mailing list for upcoming events.

SACRAMENTO CHRISTIAN WRITERS. Citrus Heights. Contact: Beth Miller Self, 2012 Rushing River Ct., Elverta CA 95626-9756. (916) 992-8709. E-mail: cwbself@msn.com. Website: www .scwriters.org. Membership (32) open. Sponsors a contest for members. Next seminar 2015.

SAN DIEGO COUNTY CHRISTIAN WRITERS GUILD. Contact: Jennie & Bob Gillespie, PO Box 270403, San Diego CA 92198. Phone/fax (760) 294-3269. E-mail: info@sandiegocwg.org. Website: www.sandiegocwg.org. Membership (200) open. To join their Internet newsgroup, e-mail your name and address to info@sandiegocwg.com. Sponsors 10 critique groups, fall seminar, and spring fellowship brunch.

TEMECULA CHRISTIAN WRITERS CRITIQUE GROUP. Contact: Rebecca Farnbach, 41403 Bitter Creek Ct., Temecula CA 92591-1545. (951) 699-5148. Fax (951) 699-4208. E-mail: sunbrook@ hotmail.com. Membership (18) open. Part of San Diego Christian Writers Guild.

THE WRITE BUNCH. Stockton. Contact: Shirley Cook, 3123 Sheridan Way, Stockton CA 95219-3724. (209) 477-8375. E-mail: shirleymcp@sbcglobal.net. Membership (8) not currently open.

COLORADO

*ACFW COLORADO GROUP & 3 CHAPTERS. Website: www.acfwcolorado.com. Sponsors ongoing blog, annual retreat, 2 miniconferences/yr., plus the following 3 chapters: HIS Writers, North Denver; www.HisWriters.acfwcolorado.com. Colorado Springs; www.worshipwriterswitness.acfwcolorado .com. Mile High Scribes, South Denver. www.MileHighScribes.acfwcolorado.com.

*SPRING WRITERS. Woodmen Valley Chapel/Colorado Springs. Contact: Scoti Domeij. E-mail: scotidomeij@gmail.com. Offers free monthly workshop; boot camps (2/yr.), critique group training. Membership open.

WORD WEAVERS COLORADO SPRINGS. Contact: Amy Swierczek, chapter president. E-mail: allis grace@msn.com. Website: www.word-weavers.com. Membership (20+) open. Additional information: Meeting time: Second Saturday, 10:00 am–noon (May, July, October excluded). Third Saturday 10 am–noon (May, July, October). Meeting address: New Life Church, 11025 Voyager Parkway, Colorado Springs CO 80921.

WORD WEAVERS NORTH DENVER. Contact: Linda Abels, chapter president. E-mail: suzv2@ comcast.net. Website: www.word-weavers.com. Membership (20+) open. Additional information: Meeting time: Fourth Thursday, 6:00–8:30 pm. Meeting address: Crossroads Church, 10451 Huron St., Northglenn CO 80234.

CONNECTICUT

WORD WEAVERS BERKSHIRES. Contact: Carol Barnier, chapter president. E-mail: carol@carol barnier.com. Website: www.word-weavers.com. Membership (15+) open. Additional information: Meeting time: Third Saturday, 9:00 am–noon. Meeting address: Sherman Congregational, 6 Church Road, Sherman CT 06784.

DELAWARE

DELMARVA CHRISTIAN WRITERS' FELLOWSHIP. Georgetown. Contact: Candy Abbott, PO Box 777, Georgetown DE 19947-0777. (302) 856-6649. Fax (302) 856-7742. E-mail: cfa@candyabbott .com. Website: www.delmarvawriters.com. Membership (20+) open.

FLORIDA

HOBE SOUND WRITERS GROUP/ACW CHAPTER. Hobe Sound. Contact: Faith Tofte, 9342 Bethel Way, Hobe Sound FL 33455. (772) 545-4023. E-mail: faithtofte@bellsouth.net. Membership (5) open.

PALM BEACH CHRISTIAN WRITERS ASSN. West Palm Beach. Contact: Natalie Kim Rodriguez, 964 Imperial Lake Rd., West Palm Beach FL 33413. (561) 293-5725. E-mail: palmbeachacwpres@ live.com. Website: http://palmbeachacw.wordpress.com. Membership open. ACW Chapter.

SUNCOAST CHRISTIAN WRITERS. Seminole. Contact: Elaine Creasman, 13014—106th Ave. N., Largo FL 33774-5602. Phone/fax (727) 595-8963. E-mail: emcreasman@aol.com. Membership (10-15) open.

WORD WEAVERS FIRST COAST. Contact: Tina Givens, chapter president. E-mail: tgivens74@att .net. Website: www.word-weavers.com. Membership (15+) open. Additional information: Meeting time: Second Saturday, 10:00 am–1:00 pm. Meeting address: Alternates between locations in Jacksonville and St. Augustine. Contact chapter president for details.

WORD WEAVERS GAINESVILLE. Contact: Lori Roberts, chapter president. E-mail: llwroberts@ cox.net. Website: www.word-weavers.com. Membership (10+) open. Additional information: Meeting time: Second Sunday, 2:00–4:30 pm. Meeting address: Creekside Church, 2640 NW 39th Ave., Gainesville FL 32605.

WORD WEAVERS ORGANIZATION. Executive chairman Larry J. Leech II, 911 Alameda Dr., Longwood FL 32750. (407) 925-6411. E-mail: larry@christianwritersguild.com. Website: www .word-weavers.com. Membership (400+) open in thirty-one chapters. Sponsors a writing contest for paid members. Regional retreats in October 2013.

WORD WEAVERS ORLANDO. Contact: Edwina Perkins, chapter president. E-mail: perkster6@ earthlink.net. Website: www.word-weavers.com. Membership (80+) open. Additional information: Meeting time: Second Saturday, 10:00 am–12:30 pm. Address: Northland, A Church Distributed, 530 Dog Track Road, Longwood FL 32750.

WORD WEAVERS PALM BEACH. Contact: Natalie Rodriguez, chapter president. E-mail: word-weaverspb@gmail.com. Website: www.word-weavers.com. Membership (20+) open. Additional information: Meeting time: Second Saturday, 9:30 am–noon. Meeting address: 1417 Villa Juno Drive, South Juno Beach FL 33408.

WORD WEAVERS SOUTH FLORIDA. Contact: Anitra Parmele, chapter president. E-mail: Anitra@ REACHFM.ORG. Website: www.word-weavers.com. Membership (25+) open. Additional information: Meeting time: Second Saturday, 8:30–11:30 am. Meeting address: Calvary Chapel, 2401 W. Cypress Creek Rd., Ft. Lauderdale FL 33309.

WORD WEAVERS SPACE COAST. Contact: Gail Golden, chapter president. E-mail: gail.golden@ yahoo.com. Website: www.word-weavers.com. Membership (20+) open. Additional information: Meeting time: Second Sunday, 2:00–4:30 pm. Meeting address: First United Methodist Church, 825 Forrest Ave., Cocoa FL 32922.

WORD WEAVERS TAMPA. Contact: Janet Rockey, chapter president. E-mail: rockeyjanet@yahoo.com. Website: www.word-weavers.com. Membership (20+) open. Additional information: Meeting time: First Saturday, 9:30 am–12:30 pm. Meeting address: 3333 S. Bayshore Blvd., Tampa FL 33629.

WORD WEAVERS TREASURE COAST. Contact: Perry Learned, chapter president. E-mail: perry .learned@wellsfargoadvisors.com. Website: www.word-weavers.com. Membership (20+) open. Additional information: Meeting time: First Saturday, 9:30 am–noon. Meeting address: First Church of God Vero Beach, Room D51, 1105 58th Ave., Vero Beach FL 32966.

WORD WEAVERS VOLUSIA COUNTY. Contact: Mark Hancock, chapter president. E-mail: mthancock@bellsouth.net. Website: www.word-weavers.com. Membership (15+) open. Additional information: Meeting time: First Monday, 7:00–9:00 pm. Meeting address: Java Jungle, 4606 Clyde Morris Ave., Port Orange FL 32129.

GEORGIA

CHRISTIAN AUTHORS GUILD. Meets at Prayer and Praise Christian Fellowship, 6409 Bells Ferry Rd., Woodstock GA 30188. First and third Mondays. Website: www.christianauthorsguild.org. In the spring we also have a Saturday meeting called Coffee and Quill.

CONNEXUS WRITER'S GROUP. Atlanta. Contact: Ricardo Jolly, 2055 Mount Paran Road, Atlanta GA 30327. 678-371-6194. E-mail: ric.jolly@gmail.com. Website: www.connexuswritersgroup.word press.com. Membership open. Meets first and third Saturdays of month at Mount Paran Church of God, Walker Center, Rm. 105, Atlanta, GA.

EAST METRO ATLANTA CHRISTIAN WRITERS/ACW CHAPTER. Covington. Contact: Colleen Jackson, PO Box 2896, Covington GA 30015. (404) 444-7514. E-mail: colleenjackson@charter.net. Website: www.emacw.org. Membership (40) open. Check website for monthly meetings and speakers.

WORD WEAVERS GREATER ATLANTA. Contact: Jorja Davis, chapter president. E-mail: jorja.davis@ gmail.com. Website: www.word-weavers.com. Membership (10+) open. Additional information: Meeting time: First Saturday, 9:30 am–noon. Meeting address: 2315 Rocky Mountain Road NE, Atlanta GA 30066-2113.

ILLINOIS

WORD WEAVERS AURORA. Contact: Cindy Huff, chapter pres. E-mail: cindyshuff@comcast.net. Website: www.word-weavers.com. Membership (10+) open. Additional information: Meeting time: First Monday, 7:00–9:00 pm. Meeting address: Hope Fellowship Church, 221 Locust St.. Aurora IL 60506.

WORD WEAVERS LAND OF LINCOLN. Contact: Celia Milslagle, chapter president. E-mail: wlml-books@msn.com. Website: www.word-weavers.com. Membership (15+) open. Additional information: Meeting time: Second Saturday, 10:00 am–noon. Meeting address: 209 Hudson St., Lincoln IL 62656.

WORD WEAVERS NAPERVILLE. Contact: Kristina Cowan, chapter president. E-mail: kristina. cowan@gmail.com. Website: www.word-weavers.com. Membership (15+) open. Additional information: Meeting time: Third Saturday, 1:00–4:00 pm. Meeting address: Naperville Community Christian Church, 1635 Emerson Lane, Naperville IL 60540.

IOWA

CEDAR RAPIDS CHRISTIAN WRITER'S GROUP. Contact: Susan Fletcher, 513 Knollwood Dr. S.E., Cedar Rapids IA 52403. (319) 365-9844. E-mail: skmcfate@msn.com. Membership (4) open.

IOWA SCRIBES. Contact: Ed Dickerson, 1764 62nd St., Garrison IA 52229-9628. (319) 477-3011. E-mail: edickers@netins.net. Facebook: www.facebook.com/KimnGollnick#!/groups/2154003418 81935/. Website: www.kimn.net/scribes.htm. Membership (6-10) open.

LOUISIANA

*SOUTHERN CHRISTIAN WRITERS GUILD. Mandeville (City Hall, 3101 E Causeway Approach, Mandeville LA 70448). Contact chairman: Marlaine Peachey, 419 Juliette Ln., Mandeville LA 70448. (985) 630-1798. Meets second Saturday of month at 10:00 am. Dues $25/year. Educational classes, critiquing, retreats, conference and speaker training. Has monthly speakers. Membership (25-30) open.

MARYLAND

BALTIMORE AREA CHRISTIAN WRITERS. Owings Mills. Contact: Theresa V. Wilson, MEd, PO Box 47182, Windsor Mill MD 21244-3571. (443) 622-4907. E-mail: writerseminar@aol.com. Website: www.writersinthemarketplace.org. Social networking sites: www.twitter.com/WritersCoach21; www .facebook.com/writersinthemarketplaceupdates. Webinar conferencing. Focused on building author platform. Writers Milestone Cruise, March 21–April 7, 2013. Seeking workshop presenters. Membership (74) open.

MICHIGAN

FIRST FRIDAY'S WRITERS GROUP. Critique group meets the first Friday of each month. Davison Free Methodist Church, 502 Church Street, Davison, MI 48423. Contact Arlene Knickerbocker for details. (810) 793-0316 or writer@thewritespot.org.

WORD WEAVERS WEST MICHIGAN. Contact: Tim Burns, chapter president. E-mail: tim.burns@ usa.com. Website: www.word-weavers.com. Membership (60+) open. Additional information: Meeting time: First and third Tuesday, 7:00–9:00 pm. Meeting address: Russ' Restaurant, 4440 Chicago Dr., Grandville MI 49418.

MISSISSIPPI

BYHALIA CHRISTIAN WRITERS/ACW CHAPTER. Contact: Marylane Wade Koch, Byhalia MS. E-mail: bcwriters@gmail.com. Has a BCW online Yahoo group. Has on-ground, online Yahoo group, and Facebook group. Membership (60) open.

MISSOURI

HEART OF AMERICA CHRISTIAN WRITERS NETWORK. Kansas City metro area. Contact: Mark and Jeanette Littleton, 3706 N.E. Shady Lane Dr., Gladstone MO 64119. Phone/fax (816) 459-8016. E-mail: HACWN@earthlink.net. Website: www.HACWN.org. Membership (150) open. Sponsors monthly meetings, weekly critique groups, professional writers' fellowships, a contest (open to non-members), a newsletter, marketing e-mails, and a conference in November.

OZARKS CHAPTER OF AMERICAN CHRISTIAN WRITERS. Springfield. Meets monthly, Sept. to May. Contact: Jeanetta Chrystie, pres., OCACW, 5042 E. Cherry Hills Blvd., Springfield MO 65809-3301. (417) 832-8409. E-mail: DrChrystie@mchsi.com. Susan Willingham, newsletter ed. Submit articles to OzarksACW@yahoo.com. Guidelines on website: www.OzarksACW.org. Sponsors an annual contest (open to nonmembers); genre, dates, and guidelines on website. See website for other events. Membership (47) open. Newsletter-only subscriptions available.

NEW HAMPSHIRE

WORD WEAVERS MERRIMACK VALLEY. Contact: Clarice James, chapter president. E-mail: wordweaversnashuanh@comcast.net. Website: www.word-weavers.com. Membership (30+) open. Additional information: Meeting time: Second Tuesday, 6:30–9:00 pm. Meeting address: Bonhoeffer's Café & Espresso, 8 Franklin St., Nashua NH 03060.

NEW YORK

THE SCRIBBLERS/ACW CHAPTER. Riverhead. Contact: Bill Batcher, pres., c/o First Congregational Church, 103 First St., Riverhead NY 11901. E-mail: bbatcher@optonline.net. Membership (12) open. Meets monthly and sponsors annual writing retreat.

SOUTHERN TIER CHRISTIAN WRITERS' FELLOWSHIP. Johnson City. Contact: Jean Jenkins, 3 Snow Ave., Binghamton NY 13905-3810. (607) 797-5852. E-mail: jean.d.jenkins@gmail.com. Membership (7) open.

WORD WEAVERS WESTERN NEW YORK. Contact: Rachel E. Dewey, chapter president. E-mail: wnywordweavers@gmail.com. Website: www.word-weavers.com. Membership (10+) open. Additional information: Meeting time: Second Tuesday, 6:30–9:00 pm. Meeting address: Victory Church, 32 Wildbriar Lane, Rochester NY 14623.

NORTH CAROLINA

NEW COVENANT WRITERS. Lincolnton. Contact: Robert Redding, 3392 Hwy. 274, Cherryville NC 28021-9634. (704) 445-4962. E-mail: minwriter@yahoo.com. Membership (10) open.

WORD WEAVERS WILMINGTON. Contact: Andy Lee, chapter president. E-mail: andylee71647@gmail.com. Website: www.word-weavers.com. Membership (30+) open. Additional information: Meeting time: First Monday, 7:00–9:00 pm. Meeting address: Myrtle Grove Presbyterian Church, 800 Piner Rd., Wilmington NC 28412.

WRITE2IGNITE! (ACW). Contact: Jean Hall, pres., PO Box 1101, Indian Trail NC 28079. (704) 238-0491. E-mail: write2ignite@jeanmatthewhall.com.

OKLAHOMA

OKC CHRISTIAN FICTION WRITERS (ACFW CHAPTER). Edmond/Oklahoma City. Contact: Lacy Williams. (405) 229-5851. E-mail: ocfwchapter@gmail.com. Website: www.okcchristianfictionwriters .com. Membership open; includes members-only discussion e-mail loop and discounted special events.

WORDWRIGHTS, OKLAHOMA CITY CHRISTIAN WRITERS. Contact: Milton Smith, 6457 Sterling Dr., Oklahoma City OK 73132-6804. (405) 721-5026. E-mail: HisWordMatters@yahoo .com. Website: www.shadetreecreations.com. Membership (20+) open. Occasional contests for members only. Hosts an annual writers' conference with American Christian Writers, March 22–23, 2013, in Oklahoma City. Send an SASE for information.

OREGON

OREGON CHRISTIAN WRITERS. Contact: president at president@oregonchristianwriters.org or business manager at business@oregonchristianwriters.org or write to 1075 Willow Lake Rd. N., Keizer OR 97303. Website: www.oregonchristianwriters.org. Celebrating our 50th anniversary in 2013. Meets for three all-day Saturday conferences annually: winter in Salem (March 16, 2013—Davis Bunn keynoting); spring in Eugene (May 18, 2013—Melody Carlson and Sally Stuart keynoting); and fall in Portland (October 12, 2013—Brandilyn Collins keynoting). Print newsletter published six weeks before each one-day conference, and monthly e-news sent to members. Annual four-day Summer Coaching Conference with editors and agents held mid to late summer (August 12–15, 2013—Liz Curtis Higgs keynoting), in Portland metro area. Membership (300) open.

SALEM I CHRISTIAN WRITERS GROUP (NOVICE WRITERS) & WRITERS ON DEADLINE (ADVANCED WRITERS). Contact: Sam Hall, 6840 Macleay Rd. S.E., Salem OR 97301. (503) 363-7586. E-mail: samhallarch@msn.com. Membership (9) not currently open.

WORD WEAVERS PORTLAND EAST. Contact: Terry Murphy, chapter president. E-mail: email-4terry@gmail.com. Website: www.word-weavers.com. Membership (10+) open. Additional information: Meeting time: Second Wednesday, 9:30 am–noon. Meeting address: The Abiding Place, 10340 N.E. Weidler St., Portland OR 97220.

WORDWRIGHTS. Gresham (near 182nd & Powell). Contact: Susan Thogerson Maas, 27526 S.E. Carl St., Gresham OR 97080-8215. (503) 663-7834. E-mail: susan.maas@frontier.com. Membership (5) possibly open.

PENNSYLVANIA

FIRST WRITES. Chambersburg. Contact: Dawn Hamsher. 225 S. Second Street, Chambersburg PA 17201. E-mail: 1stwrites@gmail.com. Website: www.1stwrites.blogspot.com. Membership open.

GREATER PHILADELPHIA CHRISTIAN WRITERS FELLOWSHIP. Newton Square. Contact: Marlene Bagnull, 951 Anders Rd., Lansdale PA 19446-5419. (484) 991-8581. E-mail: Mbagnull@aol.com. Website: www.writehisanswer.com. Membership (25) open. Meets one Thursday morning a month, September–June. Sponsors annual writers' conference (August 2013) and contest (open to registered conferees only).

INSPIRATIONAL WRITERS' FELLOWSHIP. Brookville. Contact: Patty Zion (814) 648-2672. E-mail: pattyzion@hotmail.com. Membership (15) open. Sometimes sponsors a contest.

JOHNSTOWN CHRISTIAN WRITERS' GUILD. Contact: Betty Rosian, 102 Rustic Ave., Johnstown PA 15904-2122. (814) 255-4351. E-mail: brosian@ymail.com. Membership (17) open.

LANCASTER CHRISTIAN WRITERS/ACW CHAPTER. Central PA. Contact: Jeanette Windle, 121 E. Woods Dr., Lititz PA 17543. E-mail: jeanette@jeanettewindle.com. Website: www.lancasterchristian writerstoday.blogspot.com. Membership (100+) open. Sponsors a one-day conference in spring.

LANSDALE CHRISTIAN WRITERS FELLOWSHIP/CRITIQUE GROUP. Contact: Marlene Bagnull, 951 Anders Rd., Lansdale, PA 19446-5419. (484) 991-8581. E-mail: mbagnull@aol.com. Membership (8) open. Women only.

WORD WEAVERS PITTSBURGH. Contact: Heather Kreke, chapter president. E-mail: h.kreke@gmail.com. Website: www.word-weavers.com. Membership (10+) open. Additional information: Meeting time: Third Saturday, 9:30 am–noon. Meeting address: Panera Bread, 12071 Perry Highway, Pittsburgh PA 15090.

SOUTH CAROLINA

CAROLINA CHRISTIAN WRITERS, LOCAL CHAPTER OF ACFW. SC AND NC. Founded 2007. E-mail: carolinaacfw@gmail.com. Website: www.carolinachristianwriters.com. Facebook: www.facebook.com/CarolinaChristianWriters. Twitter: @carolinacfw. Membership (14). CCW meets quarterly, requires an annual member fee of $10 (in addition to membership in ACFW). Welcomes all ages. Consists of published and unpublished Christian authors, writers, magazine editors, columnists, freelance writers, and bloggers in various genres—fiction and nonfiction.

PALMETTO CHRISTIAN WRITER'S NETWORK. Lexington/Columbia SC. Contact: Linnette R. Mullin. E-mail: PCWN@live.com; Website: http://pcwn.blogspot.com/. Facebook: www.facebook .com/pages/Palmetto-Christian-Writers-Network/134405679969599. Twitter hashtag: #PCWN. Membership (15) open. PCWN meets monthly. No member fee. Welcomes all ages. Consists of published and unpublished Christian authors, writers, magazine editors, columnists, freelance writers and bloggers in various genres—fiction and nonfiction. We write for the glory of God. Founded March 2011 by Linnette R. Mullin, author and freelance writer.

WORD WEAVERS SIMPSONVILLE. Contact: Sue Carter Stout, chapter president. E-mail: author suecarterstout@yahoo.com. Website: www.word-weavers.com. Membership (20+) open. Additional information: Meeting times: Second Thursday, 10:00 am–noon and 6:30–8:30 pm. Meeting address: First Baptist Church, 101 Church St., Room B201, Simpsonville SC 29681.

WORD WEAVERS SUMMERVILLE. Contact: Tim Owens, chapter president. E-mail: timowens author@gmail.com. Website: www.word-weavers.com. Membership (15+) open. Additional information: Meeting time: First Monday, 8:00–9:00 pm. Meeting address: Summerville Presbyterian Church, 407 South Laurel St., Summerville SC 29483.

WRITE2IGNITE! ACW CHAPTER FOR CHRISTIAN WRITERS OF LITERATURE FOR CHILDREN AND YOUNG ADULTS. Conferences held at North Greenville University near Greenville SC. Contact: Jean Hall, chairperson. Also offers one-day workshops and the Two-4-One Critiques Service. E-mail: write2ignite@jeanmatthewhall.com. Website: www.write2ignite.com.

WRITE2IGNITE! TWO-4-ONE CRITIQUES. We offer two simultaneous written critiques from Write2Ignite! team members for one reasonable price. Specialize in manuscripts for children and young adults. Not an editing service. Details at www.write2ignite.com. Contact Jean Hall at write2 ignite@jeanmatthewhall.com.

WRITING 4 HIM. Spartanburg. Contact: Linda Gilden, PO Box 2928, Spartanburg SC 29304. E-mail: linda@lindagilden.com. Meets twice a month at Christian Supply. Membership open.

TENNESSEE

COLLIERVILLE AMERICAN CHRISTIAN WRITERS (CCWriters2)/ACW CHAPTER. Collierville. Contact: Susan Reichert, 2400 Linkenholt Dr., Collierville TN 38017-8822. (901) 853-4470. E-mail: tnlms44@aol.com. Membership (36) open.

GERMANTOWN CHRISTIAN WRITERS (ACW). Contact: Earl Adams, PO Box 750484, Germantown TN 38175-0484. (901) 751-3311. E-mail: erladms@wmconnect.com.

TEXAS

CROSS REFERENCE WRITERS. A chapter of American Christian Fiction Writers. Brazos Valley. E-mail: CrossRefWriters@yahoo.com. Website: http://sites.google.com/site/crossreference writers. Membership open.

DFW READY WRITERS/ACFW BRANCH. Colleyville. Contact: Janice Olson, president, (214) 415-6967. E-mail: mailto:janice@jkolson.com. Blog: www.dfwreadywriters.blogspot.com. Meeting info on Blog. Membership open.

INSPIRATIONAL WRITERS ALIVE! Group meets in Houston. Contact: Martha Rogers, 6038 Greenmont, Houston TX 77092-2332. (713) 686-7209. E-mail: marthalrogers@sbcglogal.net. Website: inspirationalwritersalivehouston.org. Membership (130 statewide) open. Sponsors summer seminar, August 3, 2013, monthly newsletter, and annual contest (January 1–May 15) open to nonmembers.

INSPIRATIONAL WRITERS ALIVE!/AMARILLO CHAPTER. Contact: Jerry McClenagan, pres., 6808 Cloud Crest, Amarillo TX 79124. (806) 674-3504. E-mail: jerrydalemc@sbcglobal.net. Membership open. Sponsors a contest open to members, and a seminar the Saturday after Easter.

NORTH TEXAS CHRISTIAN WRITERS/ACW CHAPTERS. Meetings held in Argyle, Arlington, Burleson, Cedar Hill, Dallas, Denton, Fort Worth, Granbury, Henderson, Keller, Lake Worth, Lewisville, Lindale, N. Richland Hills, and Plainview. Contact: NTCW, PO Box 820802, Fort Worth TX 76182-0802. (817) 715-2597. E-mail: info@ntchristianwriters.com. Website: www.NTChristianWriters .com. Membership (250+) open. Sponsors an annual conference in June, one-day seminars in March and September, and three-day mentoring clinics throughout the year.

WORD WEAVERS BAY AREA. Contact: Lynn Ammons, chapter president. E-mail: cla6112@ comcast.net. Website: www.word-weavers.com. Membership (10+) open. Additional information: Meeting time: Second Monday, 6:30–9:00 pm. Meeting address: United Texas Realtors, 17000 El Camino Real, Suite 107, Houston TX 77058.

WORD WEAVERS NORTH TEXAS. Contact: Henry McLaughlin, chapter president. E-mail: henry mclaughlin@att.net. Website: www.word-weavers.com. Membership (25+) open. Additional information: Meeting time: Third Tuesday, 6:30–8:30 pm. Meeting address: Northwood Church, 1870 Rufe Snow Drive, Keller TX 76248.

WORD WEAVERS PINEY WOODS. Contact: Robin Bryce, chapter president. E-mail: robin@ robinbryce.com. Website: www.word-weavers.com. Membership (10+) open. Additional information: Meeting time: Fourth Friday, 6:30–9:00 pm. Meeting address: The Lexington, 679 Interstate 45 S, Huntsville, TX 77340.

WRITERS ON THE STORM. The Woodlands TX. Chapter of SCFW. Contact: Linda P. Kozar, 7 South Chandler Creek Cir., The Woodlands TX 77381. (281) 362-1791. Prefers cell (832) 797-7522. E-mail: zarcom1@aol.com. Blog: http://acfwwritersonthestorm.blogspot.com. Visitors welcome (e-mail contact).

VIRGINIA

CAPITAL CHRISTIAN WRITERS. Fairfax. Director: Betsy Dill, PO Box 2332, Centreville VA 20122-0873. Phone/fax (703) 803-9447. E-mail: ccwriters@gmail.com. Website: www.ccwriters.org. Meets second Monday of odd-numbered months. Sponsors a Saturday workshop and a prose & poetry party most years. Membership (40) open.

NEW COVENANT WRITER'S GROUP. Newport News. Contact: Mary Tatem, 451 Summer Dr., Newport News VA 23606-2515. (757) 930-1700. E-mail: rwtatem@juno.com. Membership (8) open.

WASHINGTON

SPOKANE CHRISTIAN WRITERS. Contact: Ruth McHaney Danner, PO Box 18425, Spokane WA 99228-0425. (509) 328-3359. E-mail: ruth@ruthdanner.com. Membership (20) open.

WALLA WALLA VALLEY CHRISTIAN SCRIBES. College Place. Contact: Helen Heavirland, PO Box 146, College Place WA 99324-0146. Phone/fax (541) 938-3838. E-mail: hlh@bmi.net. Membership (8) open.

WISCONSIN

LIGHTHOUSE CHRISTIAN WRITERS. Klondike. Contact: Lois Wiederhoeft, 901 Aubin St., Lot 115, Peshtigo WI 54157. (715) 582-1024. E-mail: lois-ann67@hotmail.com. Or, Mary Jansen, PO Box 187, Mountain WI 54149. (715) 276-1706. Membership (8) open.

PENS OF PRAISE CHRISTIAN WRITERS. Manitowoc. Contact: Cofounders Becky McLafferty, 9225 Carstens Lake Rd., Manitowoc WI 54220. (920) 758-9196; or Sue Kinney, 4516 Laurie Ln., Two Rivers WI 54241. (920) 793-2922. E-mail: mclafferty@lakefield.net, or cal-suek@charter.net. Membership (8–10) open. Meets monthly.

WORD WEAVERS FOX VALLEY. Contact: Caleb Rocke, chapter president. E-mail: caleb.rocke@ utmosthighest.com. Website: www.word-weavers.com. Membership (10+) open. Additional information: Meeting time: Third Saturday, 8:00–10:00 am. Meeting address: Copper Rock, 210 W. College Ave., Appleton WI 54911.

CANADIAN/FOREIGN

MANITOBA CHRISTIAN WRITERS ASSN. Winnipeg MB. Contact: Irene LoScerbo, 78 River Elm Dr., West St. Paul MB R2V 4G1, Canada. (204) 334-7780. E-mail: solonoi@shaw.ca. Membership (25) open.

SWAN VALLEY CHRISTIAN WRITERS GUILD. Swan River. Contact: Addy Oberlin, Box 132, Swan River MB R0L 1Z0, Canada. Phone/fax (204) 734-4269. E-mail: waltadio@mymts.net. Membership (8) open. May sponsor a contest open to nonmembers.

*THE WORD GUILD. An organization of Canadian writers and editors who are Christian. We meet in various cities and online. We sponsor an annual conference in Guelph Ontario, Canada, in June. Write! Canada www.writecanada.org. We sponsor contests open to nonmembers who are Canadian citizens: http://canadianchristianwritingawards.com. Website: www.thewordguild.com. PO Box 1243, Trenton ON K8V 5R9, Canada. E-mail: mailto:info@thewordguild.com.

WORD WEAVERS MISSISSAUGA. Contact: Ann Peachman Stewart, chapter president. E-mail: Peachie01@sympatico.ca. Website: www.word-weavers.com. Membership (15+) open. Additional information: Meeting time: Second Monday, 7:00–9:00 pm. Meeting address: Portico Community Church Room 212, 1814 Barbertown Rd., Mississauga ON L5M 2M5, Canada.

WORD WEAVERS WATERLOO. Contact: Helena Smrcek, chapter president. E-mail: helena_ smrcek@yahoo.ca. Website: www.word-weavers.com. Membership (15+) open. Additional information: Meeting time: First Tuesday, 7:00–9:00 pm. Meeting address: The Art Studio, 22 Regina St. N., Waterloo ON N2J 3A1, Canada.

NATIONAL/INTERNATIONAL GROUPS (NO STATE LOCATION)

*AMERICAN CHRISTIAN FICTION WRITERS. PO Box 101066, Palm Bay FL 32910. Phone/fax (321) 984-4018. E-mail: Publicity Officer, Angela Breidenbach, 200 Horseshoe Ln., Missoula MT 59803, pr@acfw.com. Website: www.ACFW.com. E-mail loop, online courses, critique groups, and e-newsletter for members. Send membership inquiries to membership@acfw.com. Membership (2,000+) open. Sponsors contests for published and unpublished members. Sponsors annual seminar in September.

*AMERICAN CHRISTIAN WRITERS SEMINARS. Sponsors conferences in various locations around the country (see individual states for dates and places). Call or write to be placed on mailing list for any conference. Events are Friday and Saturday unless otherwise noted. Brochures usually mailed three months prior to event. Contact: Reg Forder, Box 110390, Nashville TN 37222. Toll-free (800) 21-WRITE. Website: www.ACWriters.com.

JERRY B. JENKINS CHRISTIAN WRITERS GUILD. Contact: Janice Mitchell, 5525 N. Union Blvd., Ste. 101, Colorado Springs CO 80918. Toll-free (866) 495-5177. Fax (719) 495-5181. E-mail: ContactUs@ChristianWritersGuild.com. Website: www.ChristianWritersGuild.com. This international organization of 1,800 members offers annual memberships, mentor-guided correspondence courses for adults (two-year Apprentice; advanced one-year Journeyman; and Craftsman) and youth (Pages: ages 9-12, and Squires: 13 and up), writing contests, conferences, critique service, writers resource books, monthly newsletter, and more. Critique service accepts prose samples of 1-15 pages. Professional writing assessment covers proper language usage, pacing, presentation, purpose, and persuasiveness.

PEN-SOULS (prayer and support group, not a critique group). Conducted entirely by e-mail. Contact: Janet Ann Collins, Grass Valley CA. E-mail: jan@janetanncollins.com. Membership (12) open by application.

10

Editorial Services

It is often wise to have a professional editor critique your manuscript before you submit it to an agent or publisher—some agents even require a written evaluation. The following people offer this kind of service. We recommend asking for references or samples of their work.

Abbreviations of work they offer:

B brochures
BCE book contract evaluation
CA coauthoring

GE general editing/manuscript
   evaluation
GH ghostwriting
LC line editing or copyediting

NL newsletters
PP PowerPoint
SP special projects
WS website development

Abbreviations of the types of material they evaluate:

A articles
BP book proposals
BS Bible studies
D devotionals
E essays
F fillers

GB gift books
JN juvenile novels
N novels
NB nonfiction books
P poetry
PB picture books

QL query letter
S scripts
SS short stories
TM technical material
YA young adults

AMI EDITING/ANNETTE M. IRBY, PO Box 7162, Covington WA 98042-7162. (425) 433-8676. E-mail: editor@AMIediting.com. Website: www.AMIediting.com. E-mail contact. GE/LC/B/NL/critiques. Edits: A/SS/F/N/NB/BS/GB/TM/E/D/website copyedits. Published author; freelance and acquisitions editor. Has been writing for nearly 20 years, has edited manuscripts for well-published and new authors, as well as publishing houses (Summerside Press). See website for testimonials from Susan May Warren, Rachel Meisel, and others. Rates: $25/hr. for general jobs; $35/hr. for rush jobs. Send a $25 deposit with first 15 pages for a job estimate for general job; $35 deposit/15 pages for rush job. Deposit covers first hour in both cases.

ANDY SCHEER EDITORIAL SERVICES, 5074 Plumstead Dr., Colorado Springs CO 80920. (719) 282-3729. E-mail: Andy@AndyScheer.com. Prefers e-mail. GE/LC/GH/CA. Edits: A/SS/N/NB/BP/BS/GB. 25+ years' experience in Christian writing, editing, and publishing. Has served as a judge for national fiction and nonfiction contests. Rates negotiable, depending on size and condition of project.

ANGAH CREATIVE SERVICES/DANIELLE CAMPBELL-ANGAH, 961 Taylor Dr., Folcroft PA 19032. (610) 457-8300. E-mail: dcangah@angahcreative.com, or blessingsofgod77@verizon.net. Website: www.angahcreative.com. Ten years' writing experience; 5 years' editing experience.

B. K. NELSON EDITORIAL SERVICES/JOHN W. BENSON (editorial director), 1565 Paseo Vida, Palm Springs CA 92264-9508. (760) 778-8800. Fax (760) 778-6242. E-mail: bknelson4@cs.com. Website: www.bknelson.com. E-mail or mail contact. GE/LC/SP/BCE. Edits: A/SS/P/F/N/NB/BP/QL/JN/PB/BS/GB/TM/E/D/S. Has been a literary agent for 22 years and has sold more than 2,000 books to royalty publishers. We do not deal with self-publishing. Contact for rates.

BLUE MOUNTAIN EDITORIAL SERVICE/BARBARA WARREN, 4721 Farm Road 2165, Exeter MO 65647. (417) 835-3235. E-mail: barbarawarren@hughes.net. Website: www.barbarawarrenblue mountainedit.com. E-mail/call. GE/LC/B/NL writing coach. Edits: A/SS/N/NB/BP/QL/JN/BS/GB/E/D. Charges $20/hr. Twenty-three years' experience.

CARLA'S MANUSCRIPT SERVICE/CARLA BRUCE, 10229 W. Andover Ave., Sun City AZ 85351-4509. Phone/fax (623) 876-4648. E-mail: Carlaabruce@cox.net. Call/e-mail. GE/LC/GH/typesetting/ PDF files for publishers. Edits: A/SS/P/F/N/NB/BP/QL/BS/GB/TM/E/D. Charges $2/page copyedit, $25/hr., or gives a project estimate after evaluation. Does ghostwriting for pastors and teachers; professional typesetting. Twenty-five years' ghostwriting/editing; 14 years typesetting.

CHRISTIAN COMMUNICATOR MANUSCRIPT CRITIQUE SERVICE/SUSAN TITUS OSBORN, 3133 Puente St., Fullerton CA 92835-1952. (714) 990-1532. E-mail: Susanosb@aol.com. Website: www.christiancommunicator.com. Call/e-mail/write. For book, send material with $160 deposit. Staff of 18 editors. GE/LC/GH/CA/SP/BCE. Edits: A/SS/P/F/N/NB/BP/JN/PB/QL/BS/GB/TM/E/D/S/ YA screenplays. $100 for short pieces/picture books. Three-chapter book proposal $160 (up to 40 pgs.). Additional editing $40/hr. Over thirty years' experience.

CHRISTIAN EDITOR NETWORK/KATHY IDE, Brea CA. E-mail: Kathy@kathyide.com. An editorial matchmaking service to connect authors, publishers, and agents with qualified professional editorial freelancers. Free to authors, publisher, and agents. Website: www.christianeditor.com.

CHRISTIAN MANUSCRIPT EDITING SERVICES/LEE WARREN, 4311 S. 38th St., Omaha NE 68107-1236. (401) 884-4074. E-mail: lee.warren@rocketmail.com. Website: www.christian manuscriptediting.com. Prefer e-mail. GE/LC/GH/writing coach. Edits: A/N/NB/BP/QL/BS/GB/D. Has written 6 royalty books and hundreds of articles in newspapers, magazines, and websites. Also edited more than 30 fiction and nonfiction manuscripts for self-publishing company and edited/ critiqued another 50 manuscripts or proposals for a manuscript-critique service. For rates, see www.christianmanuscriptediting.com/p/services.

CHRISTIAN MANUSCRIPT SUBMISSIONS.COM, An online manuscript submission service operated by the Evangelical Christian Publishers Association (ECPA). ChristianManuscriptSubmissions .com is the only manuscript service created by the top Christian publishers looking for unsolicited manuscripts in a traditional royalty-based relationship. It allows authors to submit their manuscript proposals in a secure, online format for review by editors from publishing houses that are members of the ECPA. Website: www.ChristianManuscriptSubmissions.com.

CHRISTIAN WRITERS INSTITUTE MANUSCRIPT CRITIQUE SERVICE, PO Box 110390, Nashville TN 37222. Toll-free (800) 21-WRITE. E-mail: ACWriters@aol.com. Website: www.AC Writers.com. Call/write. GE/LC/GH/CA/SP/BCE. Edits: A/SS/P/F/N/NB/BP/JN/PB/BS/TM/E/D/S. Send SASE for rate sheet and submission slip.

DEDICATED PUBLICATION SERVICES/TAMMY L. HENSEL, PO Box 382, College Station TX 77841-0382. (979) 204-0674. Fax (979) 823-6252. E-mail: thensel@DedicatedPublicationServices .com. Website: DedicatedPublicationServices.com. E-mail. GE/LC/B/NL/SP/WS/articles, press releases, ads, and other documents, writing coach. Edit:A/SS/F/N/NB/BP/QL/JN/PB/BS/GB/TM/E/D/S/academic books/papers, depending on subject. Bachelor's degree in journalism and history from Baylor University, plus more than 25 years' writing, editing, and public-relations experience in print media. Very strong writing, editing, and communication skills. Experienced in both content and line-by-line editing, page design, manuscript preparation, newsletters, proposals, advertising, and more. Proficient in use of *The Chicago Manual of Style, The AP Stylebook, APA Publication Manual*, and *The Christian Writer's Manual of Style*. Published works include newspaper and magazine features, devotions, and inspirational articles. Rates are determined by the individual needs of the project and based on those recommended by the Editorial Freelancers Association (www.the-efa.org/res/rates.php). A deposit is required for first project but may be waived on return business. Customary rates from magazine and book publishers are accepted if within industry standards.

EDITOR FOR YOU/MELANIE RIGNEY, 4201 Wilson Blvd., #110328, Arlington VA 22203-1859. (703) 863-3940. E-mail: editor@editorforyou.com. Website: www.editorforyou.com. E-mail contact. GE/LC/writing coach. Edits: SS/N/NB/BP/QL/E/D. Charges $65/hr. for content editing & coaching (provides a binding ceiling on number of hours); fees vary for ms. evaluation; generally $200-500 depending on ms. length. Eight years of freelance edition and consulting for hundreds of writers, publishers, and agents. Editor of *Writer's Digest* magazine for 5 years; book editor/manager of Writer's Digest Books for 1 year; 3.5 years with Macmillan Computer Publishing and Thomsen Financial Publishing in books; 35 years' editing experience; frequent conference speaker/contest judge.

EDITORIAL SERVICES/BETTY L. WHITWORTH, 11740 S. Hwy. 259, Leitchfield KY 42754. (270) 257-2461. E-mail: Blwhit@bbtel.com. Call/e-mail. Editing for fiction and nonfiction books/articles and short stories. Retired English teacher, currently working as a newspaper columnist/journalist and independent editor. Worked with 45+ writers. Send 50 pages, SASE for return of ms. with $25.00. Will give estimate for entire project after viewing those pages.

EDITORIAL SERVICES/DIANE E. ROBERTSON, Bradenton FL. Contact via (941) 928-5302 or by e-mail: pswriter1@netzero.net. Website: www.freelancewritingbydiane.com. E-mail contact is best. GE/GH/SP/writing coach. Edits: A/SS/F/N/NB/BP/QL/JN/PB/BS/E/S. Has written 2 novels, 1 book on all types of creative writing, 2 children's books, 200+ articles, short stories, and children's stories; previously served as associate editor of 2 magazines; presently teaches Short Story, Novel Writing, Magazine Writing, and Nonfiction creative writing classes at several colleges and independent living centers. Charges $30/hr.

EDITORIAL SERVICES/JEANETTE HANSCOME, 3201 Heights Dr., Reno NV 89503. (775) 787-1263. E-mail: jeanettehanscome@sbcglobal.net. Website: www.jeanettehanscome.com. E-mail contact. GE/writing coach. Edits: A/SS/F/N/NB/QL/JN/E/D/S/YA novels & nonfiction. Author of 3 YA books with Focus on the Family; editor for almost 10 years; 350+ published articles, devotions, and stories; teaches and critiques online, locally, and at writers' conferences. Charges $30-35/hr; flat fees negotiable.

EDITORIAL SERVICES/KATHY IDE, Brea CA. E-mail: Kathy@kathyide.com. Website: www.Kathy Ide.com. GE/LC/GH/CA/B/NL/SP/WS, writing coach. Edits: A/SS/F/N/NB/BP/QL/JN/BS/GB/D/S. Charges by the hour (mention this listing and get a $5/hr. discount). Freelance author, editor (full time since 1998), and speaker. Has done proofreading and editing for Moody, Thomas Nelson, Barbour/Heartsong, and other publishers.

EDITORIAL SERVICES/KELLY KAGAMAS TOMKIES, 36 N. Cassady Rd., Columbus OH 43209. Phone/fax (614) 732-4860. E-mail: kellytomkies@gmail.com. Call, e-mail, or write. GE/LC/GH/CA/ NL writing coach. Edits: A/SS/N/NB/BP/QL/JN/PB/BS/GB/TM/E/D. An author/editor with 20 years' experience. Written and/or edited for individuals, websites, magazines, and publishing houses, such as Barbour Publishing and McGraw-Hill. Prefers to negotiate a flat fee per project.

*EDITORIAL SERVICES/KIM PETERSON, 1114 Buxton Dr., Knoxville TN 37922. E-mail: petersk@ BethelCollege.edu or peterskus@yahoo.com. Write/e-mail. GE/LC/GH/CA/B/NL/SP/PP/mentoring/ writing coach. Edits: A/P/F/N/NB/BP/QL/JN/PB/GB/TM/E/D. Freelance writer; college writing instructor; freelance editor; conference speaker. MA in print communication. Charges $25-35/hr.

EDITORIAL SERVICES/LESLIE SANTAMARIA, 1024 Walnut Creek Cove, Winter Springs FL 32708. (407) 497-5365. Fax: same number, call first. E-mail: leslie@lesliesantamaria.com. Website: www .lesliesantamaria.com. Prefer e-mail. GE/LC/WS. Writing coach. Edits: A/QL/JN/PB/GB/TM/E/D/S. Published author and book reviewer with 20+ years' book and magazine editing experience and a BA in English. Also experienced editor of technical proposals. Specializes in children's materials, as well as fiction and nonfiction for adults. Critiques: $50 for short pieces/picture books; $100 for 3-chapter book proposals. Editing services fee: by the project after free initial consultation.

EDITORIAL SERVICES/MARILYN A. ANDERSON, 127 Sycamore Dr., Louisville KY 40223-2956. (502) 244-0751. Fax (502) 452-9260. E-mail: shelle12@aol.com. Call/e-mail. GE/LC. Edits: A/F/NB/BS/TM/E/D. Charges $15-20/hr. for proofreading, $25/hr. for extensive editing, or negotiable by the job or project. Holds an MA and a BA in English; former high school English teacher; freelance consultant since 1993. References available. Contributing member of The Christian PEN.

*EDITORIAL SERVICES/MARION DUCKWORTH, 15917 N.E. 41st St., Vancouver WA 98682-7473. (360) 609-1583. E-mail: mjduck@comcast.net. Website: www.MarionDuckworthMinistries .com. E-mail/write. GE/writing coach. Edits: A/NB/BP/QL/BS; also does consultations. Charges $25/hr. for critique or consultation. Negotiates on longer projects. Author (for over 25 years) of 17 books and 300 articles; writing teacher for over 25 years; extensive experience in general editing and manuscript evaluation.

EDITORIAL SERVICES/MELISSA JUVINALL, 1518 Augusta, Normal IL 61761. (309) 452-8917. E-mail: kangaj1@hotmail.com. Website: www.bearla.com. E-mail contact. GE/LC. Edits: N/NB/JN/PB/BS/GB/TM. Has a BA & MA in English; specializes in children's lit.; more than 10 years' editing experience; judge for Christy Awards. Charges by the page for proofreading and copyediting; by the hour for critiquing.

EDITORIAL SERVICES/SKYLAR HAMILTON BURRIS, PO Box 7505, Fairfax Station VA 22039. (703) 944-1530. E-mail: SSburris@cox.net. Website: www.editorskylar.com. E-mail contact. LC/B/NL/WS. Edits: A/SS/P/F/N/NB/JN/BS/GB/TM/E/D/S. Charges authors $3/double-spaced page for editing. Charges $40/hr. for newsletter editing, writing, and design. Primarily works with authors who are planning either to self-publish or to submit their work to traditional publishing houses and who have completed books that require line-by-line copyediting prior to final proofreading and publication. BA and MA in English. Fourteen years as a magazine editor; 15 years' newsletter editing and design. Free sample edit of 2 pages.

EDITORIAL SERVICES/STERLING DIMMICK, 311 Chemung St., Apt. 5, Waverly NY 14892-1463. (607) 565-4247. E-mail: sterlingdimmick@hotmail.com. Call. GE/LC/GH/CA/SP. Edits: A/SS/P/F/N/NB/BP/QL/JN/PB/BS/GB/TM/E/D/S. Has an AAS in Journalism; BA in Communication Studies. Charges $20/hr. or by the project. Website under construction.

EPISTLEWORKS CREATIONS/JOANN RENO WRAY, Helping Writers Reach Their High Call. Originally in OK, now in the Pittsburgh, PA, area. Cell (918) 695-4528 (may change—check website for contact). E-mail: epedit@epistleworks.com. Website: http://epistleworks.com. E-mail preferred. GE/LC/GH/CA/B/NL/SP/Research. Edits: A/SS/P/F/N/NB/BP/D. Creates graphic art: covers, logos, cartoons. Does website design, site content management. PR materials: (static or animated) brochures, booklets, and Web ads including animated. Uses signed contracts with clients. Experienced writer, editor, and artist since 1974, including work as editor for two Tulsa monthly Christian newspapers, publishing an online magazine, business columnist, editing clients' work. Edited pastors' and ministers' material, including books. Have spoken and taught at national Christian Writers' conferences. Had over 3,000 articles published, and articles included in 14 compilation books. Charges start at $30/hr. Required $45 nonrefundable consulting fee (deducted from total). Gives binding estimates. Provides a detailed time-clock report. Discounts available. Accepts checks, money orders, or PayPal. See website for detailed information on services.

FAITHFULLY WRITE EDITING/DAWN KINZER, 25914—188th Ave. S.E., Covington WA 98042-6021. (253) 630-7617. E-mail: dawnkinzer@comcast.net. Website: www.faithfullywriteediting.com.

E-mail contact. GE/LC. Edits: A/SS/N/NB/D. Published writer with short stories, articles, and devotions. Experience in editing both fiction and nonfiction. Created and edited department newsletter for national telecommunications corporation. Serves as a judge for contests that award excellence in Christian fiction. Member of The Christian PEN, The Christian Editor Network, and American Christian Fiction Writers. Rates are by page and depend on type of work required. Payment is made in advance of each block of work being completed. Complimentary 2-page sample edit offered with initial contact.

FAITHWORKS EDITORIAL & WRITING, INC./NANETTE THORSEN-SNIPES, PO Box 1596, Buford GA 30515. Phone/fax (770) 945-3093. E-mail: nsnipes@bellsouth.net. Website: www.faith workseditorial.com. E-mail contact. Freelance editor, copyeditor/line editor, proofreader, work-for-hire projects. Edits juvenile fiction/short stories, picture books/devotions, juvenile or adult nonfiction/articles/business/humor. Author of more than 500 articles/stories; has stories in more than 55 compilation books. Member: The Christian PEN (Proofreaders & Editors Network) and CEN (Christian Editors Network). Proofreader for *Cross & Quill* newsletter (CWFI) for two years. Proofreading corporate newsletters for past 7 years. 25+ years' editing experience. Edit for ghostwriters, children's fiction writers, and writers of adult nonfiction.

FICTION FIX-IT SHOP/MEREDITH EFKEN, 2885 Sanford Ave. S.W., #17598, Grandville MI 49418. E-mail: editor@fictionfixitshop.com. Website: www.fictionfixitshop.com. E-mail contact. Edit any work of fiction—any genre—that is novella length or longer, either adult fiction or young adult fiction. Provide all levels of editing as well as coaching. Editing based on flat fee estimated on per-project basis, not hourly, and rates or estimates are listed on website. Coaching rates on per-session basis.

BONNIE C. HARVEY, PhD, 309 Carriage Place Ct., Decatur GA 30033. (404) 299-6149. Cell (404) 580-9431. E-mail: Boncah@aol.com. Website: www.Bookimprove.com. Call/e-mail/write to discuss terms and payment. Has doctorate in English; Bible school credits from Montreat, NC. Edits academic, theology, and general-interest books and articles. Fifteen years' experience teaching writing and English/college level, especially at Kennesaw University, Georgia; 30 years' editorial experience (including Xulon A +Editor); writing coach, fiction and nonfiction; ghostwrites books and authored 22 books—many available nationwide in schools and libraries. Ghostwrote *The Judge…to the Beat of a Different Drummer* (by George W. Trammell, California superior court judge). Also has The Harvey Literary Agency, LLC.

DR. DENNIS E. HENSLEY, 6824 Kanata Ct., Fort Wayne IN 46815-6388. Phone/fax (260) 485-9891. E-mail: dnhensley@hotmail.com. E-mail/write. GE/LC/GH/CA/SP. Edits: A/SS/P/F/N/NB/BP/QL/JN/E/D/comedy/academic articles/editorials/Op-Ed pieces/columns/speeches/interviews. Rate sheet for SASE or by e-mail. Author of 53 books and 3,000 articles and short stories; PhD in English; Taylor University professor of professional writing; columnist for *Metro Business North* and *Advanced Christian Writer*.

HESTERMAN CREATIVE, V. L. Hesterman, PhD, PO Box 6788, San Diego CA 92166. E-mail: vhes@mac.com (cc to vhes@earthlink.net). E-mail first contact; include phone number if you want follow-up call. Editing, writing, photography. Twenty-five years' experience as book editor, author, writing teacher and coach, journalist, curriculum developer, photographer. Edits/develops nonfiction material, including books, essays, memoirs, and photo books; works with publishers, agents, and writers as coauthor, line editor, or in editorial development. Will do line edits of fiction. Standard industry rates; depends on scope and condition of project. Will give binding quote with sample of writing and query/proposal.

HONEST EDITING, Bill Carmichael and editing team. E-mail: bill.honestediting@gmail.com. Website: www.honestediting.com. Cost-effective manuscript and proposal evaluations by professional editors. Check website for full list of services and instructions.

*IZZY'S OFFICE/DIANE STORTZ, PO Box 31239, Cincinnati OH 45231. (513) 602-6720. E-mail: diane.stortz@gmail.com. Website: www.dianestortz.com. E-mail contact. GE/LC/GH/CA. Edits: A/NB/BP/JN/N/PB/QL/BS/GB/E/D. Former editorial director for a Christian publisher (10 yrs.); published author, experience as children's editor and magazine copy editor. See website for client list and partial list of projects. Copyediting or substantive editing by the hour or per-project basis; book proposal package $750; evaluation and 2-chapter critique $350. One-half payment amount due before work begins.

JAMES WATKINS/XARISCOM, 318 N. Lenfesty Ave., Marion IN 46952. E-mail: jim@jameswatkins .com. Website: www.jameswatkins.com. E-mail contact. GE/LC/GH/WS. Edits: A/NB/BP/QL/BS/D/S. Award-winning author of 16 books, 2,000+ articles, and an editor; winner of four editing and 2 book awards. 20+ years' experience. Charge $40 for 2,000 words of critique, editing, market suggestions; $5/pg. for content editing; $15/pg. for rewriting/ghosting; $50/hr. for website evaluation/consulting.

JOY MEDIA/JULIE-ALLYSON IERON, PO Box 1099, Park Ridge IL 60068. E-mail: j-a@joy mediaservices.com. Website: joymediaservices.com. Contact by e-mail. GE/GH/CA/B/NS/SP/PP/ writing coach. Edits: A/NB/BP/BS/GB/D. Master's degree in journalism and 25+ yrs. experience in Christian publishing. Charges $40 per hour; negotiates for larger projects. Half of fee up front.

JRH EDITING/JENNIFER HAMILTON, No. California. E-mail: jennifer@jrhediting.com or through website: www.jrhediting.com. $3 per double-spaced page. Coaching, mentoring, in-depth critiques with explanations and plenty of examples. For Substantive Editing, JRH EDITING. "Your Work, My Heart."

KAREN O'CONNOR COMMUNICATIONS/KAREN O'CONNOR, 10 Pajaro Vista Ct., Watsonville CA 95076. E-mail: karen@karenoconnor.com. Website: www.karenoconnor.com. E-mail. GE/LC. Book proposal commentary/editing. Edits: A/F/NB/BP/QL/D. One-hour free evaluation; $90/hr. or flat fee depending on project. Has 35 years of writing/editing; 25+ years teaching writing; 70 published books and hundreds of magazine articles.

KMB COMMUNICATIONS INC./LAURAINE SNELLING, PO Box 1530, Tehachapi CA 93581. (661) 823-0669. Fax (661) 823-9427. E-mail: TLsnelling@yahoo.com. Website: www.LauraineSnelling .com. E-mail contact. GE. Edits: SS/N/JN. Charges $100/hr. with $100 deposit, or by the project after discussion with client. Award-winning author of 70 books (YA and adult fiction, 2 nonfiction); teacher at writing conferences.

LIGHTHOUSE EDITING/DR. LON ACKELSON, 13326 Community Rd., #11, Poway CA 92064-4754. (858) 748-9258. Fax (858) 748-7431. E-mail: Isaiah68LA@sbcglobal.net. Website: www .lighthouseedit.com. E-mail/write. GE/LC/GH/CA/B/NL/BCE. Edits: A/SS/N/NB/BP/QL/BS/E/D. Charges $35 for article/short-story critique; $60 for 3-chapter book proposal. Send SASE for full list of fees. Editor since 1981; senior editor 1984–2012.

LOGOS WORD DESIGNS INC./LINDA L. NATHAN, PO Box 735, Maple Falls WA 98266-0735. (360) 599-3429. Fax (360) 392-0216. E-mail: linda@logosword.com. Website: www.logosword .com. Call/e-mail. GE/LC/GH/CA/B/NL/SP/publishing consultation/writing assistance/writes proposals/manuscript submission services. Edits: A/BP/BS/TM/E/D/F/JN/N/NB/PB/QL/SS/TM/YA/academic/legal/apologetics/conservative political. Over 30 years' experience in wide variety of areas, including publicity, postdoctoral; BA Psychology/some MA. Member: Editorial Freelance Assn.; NW Independent Editors Guild; American Christian Fiction Writers. Quote per project. See website, or e-mail for rates.

NOBLE CREATIVE, LLC/SCOTT NOBLE, PO Box 131402, St. Paul MN 55113. (651) 494-4169. E-mail: snoble@noblecreative.com. Website: www.noblecreative.com. E-mail contact. GE/LC/GH/B/NL/SP/WS. Edits: A/SS/F/N/NB/BP/QL/BS/GB/TM/E/D. More than a decade of experience, including several years as asst. ed. at *Decision* magazine. Masters degree in Theological Studies. Charges by the hour or the project.

PERFECT WORK EDITING SERVICES/LINDA HARRIS, 2617 Montebello Dr. W, Colorado Springs CO 80919-1917. (719) 264-9385. E-mail: lharris@perfectwordediting.com. Website: www.PerfectWordEditing.com. Prefers e-mail contact. GE/LC/GH/CA/B/NL/SP. Edits: A/SS/F/N/NB/BP/QL/BS/E/D. Over 30 yrs. experience. Charge by the page. $2–$20 a page. Free evaluation. First 10 pages free for book clients, no obligation.

PICKY, PICKY INK/SUE MIHOLER, 1075 Willow Lake Road N., Keizer OR 97303-5790. (503) 393-3356. E-mail: suemiholer@comcast.net. E-mail contact. LC/B. Edits: A/NB/BS/D. Charges $30 an hour or $50 for first 10 pages of a longer work; writer will receive a firm completed-job quote based on the first 10 pages. Freelance editor for several book publishers since 1998. Will help you get your manuscript ready to submit.

PWC EDITING/PAUL W. CONANT, 527 Bayshore Pl., Dallas TX 75217-7755. (972) 286-2882. Cell (214) 289-3397. E-mail: elance.com. Website: www.EditorWorld.com. E-mail contact preferred. LC/NL/SP/PP. Edits: SS/N/NB/BS/TM/E/D/S/Sci-Fi. Writer, editor; proofreader for magazines and book publishers. Member of Christian Editor's Network, The Christian PEN. Terms negotiable for long works. Charges publishers up to $25/hr. Prefers to work up a page rate based on a minimum 5-page sample, giving new clients up to one hour of free editing. Has edited 3 high school science textbooks; technical books on geology, manufacturing, and hypobaric inventions; and numerous books by new or ESL writers.

SALLY STUART, 15935 S.W. Greens Way, Tigard OR 97224. Phone/fax: (503) 642-9844. E-mail: stuartcwmg@aol.com. Website: www.stuartmarket.com. Blog: www.stuartmarket.blogspot.com. Call/e-mail. GE/BCE/agent contracts. Edits: A/SS/N/NB/BP/GB/JN. No poetry or picture books. Charges $40/hr. for critique; $45/hr. for phone/personal consultations. For books, send a copy of your book proposal: cover letter, chapter-by-chapter synopsis for nonfiction (5-page overall synopsis for fiction), and the first three chapters, double-spaced. Comprehensive publishing contract evaluation $75-175. Author of 37 books (including 26 editions of the *Christian Writers' Market Guide*) and 40+ years' experience as a writer, teacher, marketing expert.

SCRIBBLE COMMUNICATIONS/BRAD LEWIS, Colorado Springs CO. (719) 649-4478. Fax (866) 542-5165. E-mail: brad.lewis@scribblecommunications.com. Website: www.scribblecommunications.com. E-mail contact. GE/LC/GH/substantive editing/developmental editing. Edits: A/NB/BP/QL/BS/D/website content. Edited more than 100 nonfiction books; senior editor of the *New Men's Devotional Bible* (Zondervan); content editor for *New Living Translation Study Bible* (Tyndale). Charges by project, mutually agreed upon with publisher or author, and stated in editor/author agreement.

SHIRL'S EDITING SERVICES/SHIRL THOMAS, 9379 Tanager Ave., Fountain Valley CA 92708-6557. (714) 968-5726. E-mail: Shirlth@verizon.net. Website: shirlthomas.com. E-mail (preferred)/write, and send material with $100 deposit. GE/LC/GH/SP/review/rewriting. Edits: A/SS/P/F/N/NB/BP/QL/GB/D/greeting cards/synopses. Consultation, $75/hr.; evaluation/critique, $75/hr.; mechanical editing $65/hr.; content editing/rewriting $75/hr.

SPREAD THE WORD COMMERCIAL WRITING/KATHERINE SWARTS, Houston TX. (832) 573-9501. E-mail: ks@houstonfreelancewriter.com. Website: www.houstonfreelancewriter.com. Blog: http://strengthfortheweary.wordpress.com; http://newsongsfromtheheart.blogspot.com. E-mail contact preferred. Blogs/articles projects related to Christian encouragement and mental health. Per-project rates. MA in written communications from Wheaton College; over 100 published articles.

THE CHRISTIAN PEN: PROOFREADERS AND EDITORS NETWORK, Kathy Ide, Brea, CA. Website: www.TheChristianPEN.com. Contact: Kathy@KathyIde.com. Provides proofreaders and editors with a venue for "cooperative competition" through mutual support and exchange of information. E-mail discussion loop, online courses, resources and suggestions, tips and tools. Contributing members can post their bios/ads on The Christian PEN website, receive a quarterly e-newsletter, get discounts on online courses, receive active job leads, and more. Open to anyone who is a full-time or part-time proofreader or editor (at any level), is seriously planning to become an editorial freelancer, or is investigating the possibility. If you're a writer looking for an editor or proofreader, contact Kathy Ide at Kathy@KathyIde.com for a referral.

THE WRITE SPOT/ARLENE KNICKERBOCKER, Where Quality and Economy Unite, PO Box 424, Davison MI 48423-9318. (810) 793-0316. E-mail: writer@thewritespot.org. Website: www.the writespot.org. E-mail/write. GE/LC/GH/CA/B/NL/classes and speaking/writing coach. Edits: A/SS/P/ NB/BP/QL/BS/D. Published credits since 1996; references available. Prices on website.

THE WRITE WAY EDITORIAL SERVICES/JANET K. CREWS/B. KAY COULTER, 806 Hopi Trl., Temple TX 76504-5008. (254) 778-6490 or (254) 939-1770. E-mails: janetcrews@sbcglobal.net or bkcoulter@sbcglobal.net. Website: www.writewayeditorial.com. Call/e-mail. GE/LC/GH/CA/B/NL/ SP/scan to Word document/voice to Word document/graphics. Edits: A/SS/N/NB/BP/QL/JN/BS/GB/D. Published author of 3 books; contributor to 2 books; 14 years' combined experience; certified copy-editor. Free estimate; 50% of estimate as a deposit; $30/hr. Contact for additional details.

*THE WRITING SPA/MARY DEMUTH, PO Box 1503, Rockwall TX 75087. (214) 475-9083. E-mail: mary@marydemuth.com. Website: www.thewritingspa.com. E-mail contact. GE/LC/GH/CA/NL/writing coach. Edits: A/SS/P/N/NB/BP/QL/BS/GB/E/D. Published author of 6 nonfiction books, 6 novels; teaches, keynotes, and mentors at national writers' conferences. Has 3 people on staff. Initial consultation: 5 pgs., double-spaced $75. Writing coach: $75/hr. E-mail for additional package prices.

TOPNOTCH WRITING SOLUTIONS/MARYANN DIORIO, PhD, PO Box 1185, Millville NJ 08109. (856) 488-0366. Fax: (856) 488-0291. E-mail: DrMaryAnn@TopNotchWritingSolutions.com. Website: www.TopNotchWritingSolutions.com or www.maryanndiorio.com. E-mail contact. GE/SP/ NL/WS/writing coach (www.TopNotchLifeandCareerCoaching.com). Edits: A/SS/P/F/BP/QL. 25+ years' experience; award winner; 5 published books, contributed to 5 others; hundreds of published articles, short stories, and poems. Rate sheet available on request.

*TWEEN WATERS EDITORIAL SERVICES/TERRI KALFAS, PO Box 1233, Broken Arrow OK 74013-1233. (918) 346-7960. E-mail: tlkalfas@cox.net. E-mail contact. GE/LC/GH/CA/B/SP/BCE. Edits: A/N/ NB/BP/QL/BS/TM/D/project management/book doctoring. Multiple editorial and freelance writing services. Over 25 years' writing and publishing experience. Writing instructor. Available as conference speaker and workshop teacher. Charges $3 per pg./$25 per hr./negotiable on special projects.

WALLIS EDITORIAL SERVICES/DIANA WALLIS, 547 Cherry St. S.E., #6C, Grand Rapids MI 49503-4755. (616) 459-8836. E-mail: WallisEdit@gmail.com. Call/e-mail. GE/LC/SP/WS/proof-reading. Edits: A/N/NB/JN/BS/TM/D/advertising and promotional copy, website content, educational materials for students and parents/teachers, catalog copy. Calvin College graduate, 17 years freelancing for publishers, corporations, and ad agencies; details on request.

WINGS UNLIMITED/CRISTINE BOLLEY, Broken Arrow OK. (918) 250-9239. Fax: (918) 250-9597. E-mail: WingsUnlimited@aol.com. Website: www.wingsunlimited.com. E-mail contact. GE/LC/GH/CA/ SP. Edits: BP/NB/D. All fees negotiated in advance: developmental edits (format/house-style/clarity) range from $1,500-$3,000; 100-250 pgs.; substantive rewrite averages $5,000/250 pgs. Specializes in turning sermon series into books for classic libraries. Author/coauthor/ghostwriter of 30+ titles. Over 25 years' experience in development of bestselling titles for major Christian publishing houses.

WRITE HIS ANSWER MINISTRIES/MARLENE BAGNULL, LittD, 951 Anders Rd., Lansdale PA 19446. Phone/fax: (484) 991-8581. E-mail: mbagnull@aol.com. Website: www.writehisanswer .com. Call/write. GE/LC/typesetting. Edits: A/SS/N/NB/BP/JN/BS/D. Charges $35/hr.; estimates given. Call or write for information on At-Home Writing Workshops, a correspondence study program. Author of 5 books; compiler/editor of 3 books; over 1,000 sales to Christian periodicals.

WRITE NOW SERVICES/KAREN APPOLD, 2012 Foxmeadow Cir., Royersford PA 19468. (610) 948-1961. Fax: (917) 793-8609. E-mail: KAppold@msn.com. Website: www.writenowservices.com. Call/e-mail. GE/LC/GH/CA/B/NL/SP/WS. Edits: A/SS/F/QL/BS/E/D. Professional editor, writer, consultant since 1993 for magazines, journals, and online content. Hundreds of published articles and extensive editing of magazine and newspaper, journal, and website content. Rates determined after free evaluation of project.

WRITER'S RELIEF, INC./RONNIE L. SMITH, 409 S. River St., Hackensack NJ 07601. (866) 405-3003. Fax: (201) 641-1253. E-mail: info@wrelief.com. Website: www.WritersRelief.com. Call or e-mail. LC/NL/targeting submissions. Proofs: A/SS/P/F/N/NB/JN/E. Eighteen years' experience as an author's submission service. Subscribe to their e-publication, *Submit Write Now! Leads & Tips for Creative Writers*. Contact for rates.

WRITING COACH/LINDA WINN, 138 Bluff Dr., Winchester TN 37398. E-mail: lhwinn@comcast .net. Writing coach.

CANADIAN/FOREIGN

AOTEAROA EDITORIAL SERVICES/VENNESSA NG, PO Box 228, Oamaru 9444, New Zealand. +64224346995. (A US-based number is available to clients.) E-mail: editor@aotearoaeditorial.com. Website: www.aotearoaeditorial.com. E-mail contact. GE/LC. Edits: SS/N. Page rates vary depending on project: start from $2/critique, $2/basic proofread, and $4/copyedit. (Rates are in US dollars and can be paid by PayPal or Western Union.) Ten years' critiquing experience.

AY'S EDIT/ALAN YOSHIOKA, PhD, 801-21 Maynard Ave., Toronto ON M6K 2Z8, Canada. (416) 531-1857. Fax number upon request. E-mail: ay1@aysedit.com. Website: www.aysedit.com. E-mail contact. GE/LC/PP. Edits: A/NB/TM/E. Certified proofreader and copy editor. Member of Editors' Association of Canada since 1999. In ninth year as freelance editor, writer, and indexer, following four years in-house as medical writer at a major pharmaceutical company. Clients include a large international Christian humanitarian organization. Math degree and PhD in history of science, technology, and medicine. Expertise in orthodox Christian responses to homosexuality. Payment negotiable, starting from basic rate of US $50/hour for clients in US with nonmedical material.

CHESTNUT LANE CREATIVE/ADELE SIMMONS, PO Box 116, Whitby ON L1N 5R7, Canada. (905) 263-4211. E-mail: AdeleCLCreative@bell.net. Website: www.AdeleSimmons.WordPress.com. E-mail/ write. GE/LC/GH/CA/B/NL/SP/substantive editing/rewriting/writing/writing coach. Edits: A/SS/P/F/NB/ PB/BS/GB/TM/E/D/S/songs/speeches. Decades of experience, award-winning, published writer/author. Editor for business, mental health, tourism, marketing, ministry, creative ministry arts, newspaper, television, radio, books, education, nonfiction, how-tos, songs. Freelance and contract work. Member of Editors Association of Canada. Topics mostly nonfiction. Rates negotiated based on project and services required.

DORSCH EDITORIAL/AUDREY DORSCH, 90 Ling Road, PH 302, Toronto ON M1E 4Y3, Canada. (416) 439-4320. E-mail: audrey@dorschedit.ca. Website: www.dorschedit.ca. Audrey Dorsch, ed. Editorial services: substantive editing, copyediting, indexing, proofreading.

EDITORIAL SERVICES/DARLENE OAKLEY, Kemptville ON K0G 1J0, Canada. (613) 816-3277. E-mail: darlene@darscorrections.com. Website: www.darscorrections.com. E-mail contact. GE/LC/

GH/B/NL/SP/WS/PP/reviews/critiques/Web copy. Edits: A/SS/N/NB/QL/BP/BS/GB/E/D/synopses/Web copy. Substantive editor and proofreader with Lachesis Publishing & Glasshouse Publishing. The Word Guild; judge for Silicon Valley Romance Writers of America Gotcha! Contest 2008–2011 (inspirational category). Detailed (substantive) edit $5/pg. or .02/wd. Proofread: .012/wd. Manuscript critique: $1/page. Payment plans negotiable. See website for details.

EDITORIAL SERVICES/AIMEE REID, 1063 King St. W, Suite 301, Hamilton ON L8S 4S3, Canada. (905) 526-8794. E-mail: areid@aimeereid.com. Website: www.aimeereid.com. E-mail or call for contact. GE/CA/SP/(developmental, substantive, stylistic editing). Edits: A/NB/PB/BS/GB/D. Has published nonfiction for youth and adults, both in print and on wiki format. Has done editing for ages 5 to adult; tasks include incorporating reviewer's comments, rewriting as needed, suggesting images and layout, and creating illustration lists. Charges according to individual project depending on length and complexity. Manuscript evaluations are a set fee.

WENDY SARGEANT, 4 Lyall Clse, RIVERHILLS, QLD 4074, Australia. E-mail: wordfisher52@gmail .com. Website: www.editorsqld.com/freelance/Wendy_Sargeant.htm. E-mail contact. GE/LC/GH/CA/B/NL/SP/WS(writing & evaluation)/PP/instructional design/writing coach. Edits: A/SS/F/N/NB/BP/QL/JN/PB/BS/GB/TM/E/D/S. Copywriting. Special interests: technical material, business humor, children's books, educational books (primary, secondary, tertiary, and above), fiction, history, legal. Manuscript assessor and instructional designer with The Writing School. Award-winning author published in major newspapers and magazines. Editing educational manuals. Project officer and instructional designer for Global Education Project, United Nationals Assoc. Information specialist for Australian National University. Charges $55/hr. for articles/short stories; .02/wd. for copywriting; $300-400+ for book assessment.

11

Christian Literary Agents

Asking editors and other writers is a great way to find a good, reliable agent. You might also want to visit www.agentresearch.com and www.sfwa.org/beware/agents for tips. For a database of more than 500 agencies, go to www.literaryagent.com.

The site for the Association of Authors' Representatives, www.aaronline.org, carries a list of agents who don't charge fees, except for office expenses. Their website will also provide information on how to receive a list of approved agents. Some of the listings below indicate which agents belong to the Association of Authors' Representatives, Inc. Those members have subscribed to a set code of ethics. Lack of such a designation, however, does not indicate the agent is unethical; most Christian agents are not members. For a full list of member agents, go to www.publishersweekly.com/aar.

(*) before a listing indicates unconfirmed or no information update.

---

*AGENT RESEARCH & EVALUATION INC., 425 N. 20th St., Philadelphia PA 19130. (215) 563-1867. Fax (215) 563-6797. E-mail: info@agentresearch.com. Website: www.agentresearch.info. This is not an agency but a service that tracks the public record of literary agents and helps authors use the data to obtain effective literary representation. Charges fees for this service. Offers a free "agent verification" service at the site. (Answers the question of whether or not the agent has created a public record of sales.) Also offers a newsletter, *Talking Agents E-zine*, free if you send your e-mail address.

ALIVE COMMUNICATIONS, 7680 Goddard St., Ste. 200, Colorado Springs CO 80920. (719) 260-7080. Fax (719) 260-8223. E-mail: submissions@alivecom.com. Website: www.alivecom.com. Agents: Rick Christian, president; Lee Hough, Joel Kneedler, Andrea Heinecke. Well known in the industry. Estab. 1989. Represents 175 clients. Not open to unpublished authors. New clients by referral only. Handles adult & teen novels and nonfiction, gift books, and crossover books. Deals in both Christian (70%) and general market (30%). Member Author's Guild & AAR.
> **Contact:** E-mail to: submissions@alivecom.com. Accepts simultaneous submissions.
> Responds in 6 wks. to referrals only. May not respond to unsolicited submissions.
> **Commission:** 15%
> **Fees:** Only extraordinary costs with client's pre-approval; no review/reading fee.
> **Tips:** "If you have a referral, send material by mail, and be sure to mark envelope 'Requested Material.' Unable to return unsolicited materials without postpaid envelope."

*AMBASSADOR AGENCY, PO Box 50358, Nashville TN 37205. (615) 370-4700, ext. 230. E-mail: Wes@AmbassadorAgency.com. Website: www.AmbassadorAgency.com. Agent: Wes Yoder. Estab. 1973. Recognized in the industry. Represents 25 clients. Open to unpublished authors and new clients. Handles adult nonfiction, crossover books. Also has a Speakers Bureau.
> **Contact:** E-mail.

*BOOKS & SUCH/JANET KOBOBEL GRANT, 52 Mission Circle #22, PMB 170., Santa Rosa CA 95409. (707) 538-4184. E-mail: representation@booksandsuch.biz. Website: www.booksandsuch .biz. Agents: Janet Kobobel Grant, Wendy Lawton, Rachel Kent, Mary Keeley. Well recognized in industry. Estab. 1997. Member of AAR. Represents 150 clients. Open to new or unpublished authors (with recommendation only). Handles fiction and nonfiction for all ages except children's, picture books, gift books, crossover, and general books.

Contact: E-mail query (no attachments); no phone query. Accepts simultaneous submissions. Responds in 6-8 wks.

Commission: 15%.

Fees: No fees.

Tips: "Especially looking for fiction."

*CURTIS BROWN LTD., 10 Astor Pl., New York NY 10003-6935. (212) 473-5400. Website: www .curtisbrown.com. Agents: Maureen Walters, Laura Blake Peterson, and Ginger Knowlton. Member AAR. General agent; handles religious/inspirational novels for all ages, adult nonfiction, and crossover books.

Contact: Query with SASE; no fax/e-query. Submit outline or sample chapters. Responds in 4 wks. to query; 8 wks. to ms.

Fees: Charges for photocopying & some postage.

*BROWNE & MILLER LITERARY ASSOCIATES, 410 S. Michigan Ave., Ste. 460, Chicago IL 60605. (312) 922-3063. Fax (312) 922-1905. E-mail: mail@browneandmiller.com. Website: www.browne andmiller.com. Agent: Danielle Egan-Miller. Estab. 1971. Recognized in the industry. Represents 150 clients, mostly general, but also select Christian fiction writers. Open to new clients and talented unpublished authors, but most interested in experienced novelists looking for highly professional, full-service representation including rights management. Handles teen and adult fiction, adult nonfiction, and gift books for the general market; adult Christian fiction only. Member AAR, RWA, MWA, and The Author's Guild.

Contact: E-query to mail@browneandmiller.com, or mailed query letter/SASE. No unsolicited mss. Prefer no simultaneous submissions. Responds in 6 wks.

Commission: 15%, foreign 20%.

PEMA BROWNE LTD., 71 Pine Road, Woodbourne, NY 12788. E-mail: ppbltd@optonline.net. Website: www.pemabrowneltd.com. Agent: Pema Browne. Recognized in industry. Estab. 1966. Represents 20 clients (2 religious). Open to unpublished authors; very few new clients at this time. Handles novels and nonfiction for all ages; picture books/novelty books, gift books, crossover books. Only accepts mss not previously sent to publishers; no simultaneous submissions. Responds in 6-8 wks.

Contact: Letter query with credentials; no phone, fax, or e-query. Must include SASE. No simultaneous submissions. No attachments.

Commission: 20% US & foreign; illustrators 30%.

Fees: None.

Tips: "Check at the library in reference section, in *Books in Print*, for books similar to yours. Have good literary skills, neat presentation. Know what has been published and research the genre that interests you."

KEITH CARROLL, AGENT, PO Box 428, Newburg PA 17257. (717) 423-6621. Fax: (717) 423-6944. E-mail: keith@christianliteraryagent.com. Website: www.christianliteraryagent.com. Estab. 2009, as an author coach since 2000. Represents 86 clients. New clients welcome. Specializes in helping new authors prepare for publication, as a coach. Handles adult and teen nonfiction, adult fiction, picture books, e-books, crossover books. Accepts simultaneous submissions. Responds in 4 weeks.

Contact: Phone & e-mail.

Commission: 10%

Fees: Small fee for introductory consultation w/ unpublished authors, which includes a review/analysis of author's material, a two-hour personal phone call to advise and recommend regarding publishability.

CREDO COMMUNICATIONS LLC, 3148 Plainfield Ave NE, Ste 111, Grand Rapids MI 49525. (616) 363-2686. Fax (616) 363-7821. E-mail: connect@credocommunications.net. Website: www.credo communications.net. Agents: Tim Beals, founder and pres.; Ann Byle; Karen Neumair; David Sanford. Recognized and recommended in the industry. Estab. 2005. Represents 60+ clients. Have current contracts with 40+ publishers. New clients by referral only. Handles adult and young-adult religious/inspirational nonfiction and fiction. Other services offered: coaching for self-published authors on production, marketing, sales, and distribution.

> **Contact:** E-mail connect@credocommunications.net. No simultaneous submissions. Responds in one month.
> **Commission:** 15%; foreign 20%.
> **Fees:** No fees or expenses.
> **Tips:** Work with Christian ministry leaders to develop life-changing books, Bible-related products, and other Christian resources. Seeking new voices with thoughtful nonfiction and creative fiction.

*THE BLYTHE DANIEL AGENCY INC., PO Box 64197, Colorado Springs CO 80962-4197. (719) 213-3427. E-mail: blythe@theblythedanielagency.com. Website: www.theblythedanielagency .com. Agent: Blythe Daniel. Recognized in the industry. Estab. 2005. Represents 30 clients. Open to unpublished authors with an established platform/network and previously published authors. Handles adult religious/inspirational novels, adult nonfiction, limited children's books, and cross-over books.

> **Contact:** By e-mail or mail. Accepts simultaneous submissions. Responds in 3 weeks.
> **Commission:** 15%; foreign 20%.
> **Fees:** Agreed-upon expenses outside normal expenses.
> **Also:** Provides publicity and marketing campaigns to clients as a separate service from literary representation.
> **Tips:** "Authors must have a solid proposal on the topic of their book, including research on their audience, comparison to competitor's books, and what the author uniquely brings to the topic. Authors need to have a ready-made marketing plan to promote their book and the ability to promote their own book. Currently only handling a minimal number of new clients."

DANIEL LITERARY GROUP, 1701 Kingsbury Dr., Ste. 100, Nashville TN 37215. No phone calls. E-mail: greg@danielliterarygroup.com. Website: www.danielliterarygroup.com. Agent: Greg Daniel. Estab. 2007. Recognized in the industry. Represents 30 clients. Open to unpublished authors and new clients. Handles nonfiction, crossover & secular books.

> **Contact:** E-mail only. Accepts simultaneous submissions. Responds in 3 wks.
> **Commission:** 15%; foreign 20%.
> **Fees:** None.

*JAN DENNIS LITERARY SERVICES, 19350 Glen Hollow Cir., Monument CO 80132. (719) 559-1711. E-mail: jpdennislit@msn.com. Agent: Jan Dennis. Estab. 1995. Represents 20 clients. Open to unpublished authors and new clients. Handles teen/YA & adult religious/inspirational novels, adult nonfiction, crossover, and general books.

DYSTEL & GODERICH LITERARY MANAGEMENT INC., 1 Union Square W., Ste. 904, New York NY 10003. (212) 627-9100. Fax (212) 627-9313. E-mail: Miriam@dystel.com. Website: www.dystel .com. Agents: Jane Dystel, Miriam Goderich, Stacey Glick, Michael Bourret, Jim McCarthy, Lauren Abramo, Jessica Papin, and John Rudolph. Estab. 1994. Recognized in the industry. Represents 5-10 religious book clients. Open to unpublished authors and new clients. Handles fiction and nonfiction for adults, gift books, general books, crossover books. Member AAR.

> **Contact:** Query letter with bio. Brief e-query; no simultaneous queries. Responds to queries in 3-5 wks.; submissions in 2 mos.

Commission: 15%; foreign 19%.

Fees: Photocopying is author's responsibility.

Tips: "Send a professional, well-written query to a specific agent."

*FINE PRINT LITERARY MANAGEMENT, 240 W. 35th St., Ste. 500, New York NY 10001. (212) 279-1282. Fax (212) 279-0927. E-mail: peter@fineprintlit.com. Website: www.fineprintlit.com. Agent: Peter Rubie and 7 other agents. Open to unpublished authors and new clients. General agent. Handles adult religion/spirituality nonfiction for teens and adults.

> **Contact:** Query/SASE; accepts e-query. Responds in 2-3 mos.
> **Commission:** 15%; foreign 20%.

GARY D. FOSTER CONSULTING, 733 Virginia Ave., Van Wert OH 45891. (419) 238-4082. E-mail: gary@garydfoster.com. Website: www.garydfoster.com. Agent: Gary Foster. Estab. 1989. Represents 25 clients. Recognized in the industry. Open to unpublished authors and new clients. Handles adult religious/inspirational novels & nonfiction for all ages, picture books, and gift books.

> **Contact:** E-mail. Responds in 6 wks.
> **Commission:** 15%
> **Fees:** Charges a nominal fee upon signing of representation agreement, plus expense reimbursement.

*SAMUEL FRENCH INC., 45 W. 25th St., New York NY 10010-2751. (212) 206-8990. Fax (212) 206-1429. E-mail: publications@samuelfrench.com. Website: www.samuelfrench.com, www.bakers plays.com. Agent: Roxane Heinze-Bradshaw. Estab. 1830. Open to new clients. Handles rights to some religious/inspirational stage plays. Owns a subsidiary company that also publishes religious plays.

> **Contact:** Query online or by mail. See website for full submission information. Accepts simultaneous submissions; responds in 10 wks.
> **Commission:** Varies.
> **Fees:** None.

*GLOBAL TALENT REPS, INC./NATIONAL WRITERS LITERARY AGENCY, 3140 S. Peoria St., #295, Aurora CO 80014. (720) 851-1959. E-mail: Info@globaltalentreps.com. Website: www.global talentreps.com. Agent: Andrew J. Whelchel III (a.whelchel@globaltalentreps.com). Estab. 1982. Recognized in the industry. Open to unpublished authors and new clients. Handles religious/inspirational novels for all ages, nonfiction for teens & adults, screenplays, movie scripts, gift books, and crossover/secular books.

> **Contact:** Query by e-mail (use online form). Accepts simultaneous submissions; responds in 8 wks.
> **Commission:** 10% film; 15% books; 5% scouting.
> **Fees:** Postage charged to new, unknown authors.

*SANFORD J. GREENBURGER ASSOCIATES INC., 55 Fifth Ave., New York NY 10003. (212) 206-5600. Fax (212) 463-8718. Website: www.greenburger.com. Agents: Heide Lange, Dan Mandel, Matthew Bialer, Brenda Bowen, Faith Hamlin, Michael Harriot, Lisa Gallagher, Courtney Miller-Callihan. Estab. 1945. Represents 500 clients. Open to unpublished authors and new clients. General agent; handles adult religious/inspirational nonfiction. Member of AAR.

> **Contact:** Query/proposal/3 sample chapters to Heide Lange by mail with SASE, or by fax; no e-query. Accepts simultaneous queries. Responds in 6-8 wks. to query; 2 mos. to ms.
> **Commission:** 15%; foreign 20%.
> **Fees:** Charges for photocopying and foreign submissions.

HARTLINE LITERARY AGENCY, 123 Queenston Dr., Pittsburgh PA 15235. (412) 829-2483. Fax (888) 279-6007. E-mail: joyce@hartlineliterary.com. Website: www.hartlineliterary.com. Blog: www.hartlineliteraryagency.blogspot.com. Agents: Joyce A. Hart, adult novels (romance, mystery/

suspense, women's fiction) and nonfiction; Tamela Hancock Murray, adult fiction (romance, mystery/suspense, women's) and nonfiction, tamela@hartlineliterary.com; Terry Burns, adult fiction & nonfiction, YA, terry@hartliterary.com; Diana Flegal, adult novels & nonfiction, diana@hartline literary.com. Andy Scheer, adult fiction & nonfiction, andy@hartlineliterary.com; Linda Glaz, adult fiction & nonfiction, linda@hartlineliterary.com. Recognized in industry. Estab. 1992. Represents 150+ clients. Open to new clients. Handles adult nonfiction, gift books. No poetry, children's books, fantasy, or science fiction.

    Contact: E-mail/phone/letter; e-mail preferred. Accepts simultaneous submissions; responds in 6-8 wks.

    Commission: 15%; foreign 20%; films 20% and 25%.

    Fees: No reading fees or expenses.

    Tips: "Please look at our website before submitting. Guidelines are listed, along with detailed information about each agent. Be sure to include your biography and publishing history with your proposal. The author/agent relationship is a team effort. Working together we can make sure your manuscript gets the exposure and attention it deserves."

THE HARVEY LITERARY AGENCY, LLC., 309 Carriage Place Ct, Decatur GA 30033. (404) 299-6149. Cell: (404) 589-9431. E-mail: BoncaH@aol.com; Website: www.bookimprove.com. Agent: Dr. Bonnie C. Harvey, PhD. Recognized in the industry. Open to unpublished authors and new clients. Handles adult novels—fiction & nonfiction, juvenile & young adult—some children's books.

HAZELRIGG, ROBERTS & EASLEY, P.C., 2202 W. Chesterfield Blvd., Ste. 100, Springfield MO 65807. (417) 881-0800 Fax: (417) 881-6776. E-mail: jroberts@hrelawyers.com. Website: www.hrelawyers.com. Agent: Joshua K. Roberts. Established 2010. Open to unpublished authors. Open to new clients.

    Contact: E-mail or phone. Accepts simultaneous submissions. Responds in 4 weeks.

    Commission: 10%; 15% foreign.

    Fees: No reading fee.

    Tips: "Prefer query letter, book proposal with 3-5 sample chapters."

*JEFF HERMAN AGENCY, PO Box 1522, Stockbridge MA 01262. (413) 298-0077. Fax (413) 298-8188. E-mail: Jeff@jeffherman.com. Website: www.jeffherman.com. Agents: Jeff Herman and Deborah Herman. Estab. 1987. Recognized in the industry. Represents 20+ clients with religious books. Open to unpublished authors and new clients. Handles adult nonfiction (recovery/healing, spirituality), gift books, general books, crossover.

    Contact: Query by mail/SASE, or by e-mail or fax. Accepts simultaneous submissions & e-queries.

    Commission: 15%; foreign 10%.

    Fees: No reading or management fees; just copying and shipping.

    Tips: "I love a good book from the heart. Have faith that you will accomplish what has been appointed to you."

HIDDEN VALUE GROUP, 1240 E. Ontario Ave., Ste. 102-148, Corona CA 92881. Phone/fax (951) 549-8891. E-mail: bookquery@hiddenvaluegroup.com. Website: www.HiddenValueGroup.com. Agents: Jeff Jernigan & Nancy Jernigan. Estab. 2001. Recognized in the industry. Represents 20+ clients with religious books. Open to previously published authors only. Handles adult fiction and nonfiction, gift books, and crossover books. No poetry, articles, or short stories.

    Contact: Letter or e-mail. Accepts simultaneous submissions. Responds in 4-6 wks.

    Commission: 15%; foreign 15%.

    Fees: None.

    Tips: "Looking for romance and suspense fiction projects as well as women's nonfiction. Make sure the proposal includes author bio, 2 sample chapters, and manuscript summary. Marketing plan to promote your project is a must."

*HIGHER LIFE PUBLISHING AND MARKETING, 400 Fontana Cir., Bldg. 1, Ste. 105, Oviedo FL 32765. (407) 563-4806. Fax (407) 574-2699. Website: www.ahigherlife.com. Agent: Hope Flinchbaugh; hope@ahigherlife.com. Estab. 2006. Represents 6 clients. Recognized in the industry. Open to unpublished authors and new clients. Handles religious/inspirational novels & nonfiction for all ages, picture books, crossover books.

> **Contact:** By e-mail. Open to simultaneous submissions; responds in 4 wks.
> **Commission:** 15%.
> **Fees:** Fees to cover copying or postage occasionally apply.
> **Tips:** "Due to recent downsizing in traditional publishing houses, it is becoming increasingly difficult to place new authors. However, if your writing is strong, it will stand out above the rest. We are very picky!"

*HORNFISCHER LITERARY MANAGEMENT, PO Box 50544, Austin TX 78763. E-mail: queries@ hornfischerlit.com or jim@hornfischerlit.com. Website: www.hornfischerlit.com. Agent: James D. Hornfischer. Estab. 2001. Represents 45 clients. Open to unpublished authors and new clients (with referrals from clients). Considers simultaneous submissions. Responds in 1 mo. General agent; handles adult religious/inspirational nonfiction.

> **Contact:** E-query only for fiction; query or proposal for nonfiction (proposal package, outline, and 2 sample chapters). Considers simultaneous queries. Responds to queries in 5-6 wks.
> **Commission:** 15%; foreign 25%.

D. C. JACOBSON & ASSOCIATES, 3689 Carman Drive, Suite 200 C, Lake Oswego OR 97035. (503) 850-4800. Fax (503) 850-4805. E-mail: submissions@dcjacobson.com. Website: www.djacobson .com. Agents: Don Jacobson, Jenni Burke, David Van Diest, Blair Jacobson. Estab. 2006. Represents 70+ clients. Recognized in the industry (former owner of Multnomah Publishers). Open to unpublished authors and new clients. Handles adult & teen religious/inspirational novels & nonfiction, crossover books.

> **Contact:** Submissions & queries through website form only. Accepts simultaneous submissions; responds in 8 wks.
> **Commission:** 15%.
> **Fees:** No reading fees.
> **Services:** Offers literary consulting services on a fee basis to nonrepresented clients.
> **Tips:** "Looking for fresh writing that will redeem culture and renew the church. Please review our website thoroughly before submitting your proposal."

*JELLINEK & MURRAY LITERARY AGENCY, 47-722 Hui Kelu St., Apt. 4, Kaneohe HI 96744. Phone/fax (808) 239-8451. E-mail: rgr.jellinek@gmail.com. Blog: www.hawaiireaders.com. Agent: Roger Jellinek. Estab. 1995. Represents a few Christian clients. Not recognized in the industry. Open to unpublished authors; new clients by personal reference (otherwise only June through December). Handles adult religious/inspirational nonfiction, crossover books, secular books.

> **Contact:** E-mail only. Accepts simultaneous submissions; responds in 6 wks.
> **Commission:** 15%; foreign 20%.
> **Fees:** No, except for unusual travel or Express Mail.

*WILLIAM K. JENSEN LITERARY AGENCY, 119 Bampton Ct., Eugene OR 97404. Phone/fax (541) 688-1612. E-mail: queries@wkjagency.com. Website: www.wkjagency.com. Agent: William K. Jensen. Estab. 2005. Recognized in the industry. Represents 38 clients. Open to unpublished authors and new clients. Handles adult fiction (no science fiction or fantasy), nonfiction for all ages, picture books, gift books, crossover books.

> **Contact:** E-mail only using online form; no phone queries. Accepts simultaneous submissions. Responds in 12 wks.
> **Commission:** 15%.
> **Fees:** No fees.

*NATASHA KERN LITERARY AGENCY INC., PO Box 1069, White Salmon WA 98672. Website: www.natashakern.com. Agent: Natasha Kern. Well-recognized member of Author's Guild, ACFW, RWA. Estab. 1987. Represents 36 religious clients. Open to unpublished authors and new clients. Handles adult religious/inspirational fiction (romance, romantic suspense, women's fiction, historical fiction, mystery, suspense, thrillers, and general market novels).

> **Contact:** Accepts e-queries at queries@natashakern.com only; 3-pg. synopsis & 1 chapter. Responds in 2-4 wks. to queries, if interested. Also meets at conferences or through current clients.
> **Commission:** 15%; 20% foreign (includes foreign-agent commission).
> **Fees:** No reading fee.
> **Tips:** "I have personally sold over 1,000 books, many of them bestsellers and award winners. See submission guidelines on our website before sending a query."

K J LITERARY SERVICES, LLC, 1540 Margaret Ave., Grand Rapids MI 49507. (616) 551-9797. E-mail: kim@kjliteraryservices.com. Agent: Kim Zeilstra.

> **Contact:** E-query preferred; phone query OK.
> **Commission:** 15%.
> **Tips:** "Taking new authors by referral only."

KRIS LITERARY AGENCY, 34 Oguntona Crescent, Phase 1, Gbagada Estate, Lagos, Nigeria. +2348067628017. E-mail: krisliterary@yahoo.com. Agent: Chris Agada. Estab. 2009. Represents 50 clients. Building recognition in the industry. Open to unpublished authors and new clients. Handles all types of material.

> **Contact:** Query by e-mail or phone. Accepts simultaneous submissions; responds in 2 wks.
> **Commission:** 15%; foreign 15%.
> **Fees:** No fees.

THE STEVE LAUBE AGENCY, 5025 N. Central Ave., #635, Phoenix AZ 85012-1502. (602) 336-8910. E-mail: info@stevelaube.com. Website: www.stevelaube.com. Agents: Steve Laube (pres.), Tamela Hancock Murray, Karen Ball. Estab. 2004. Well recognized in the industry. Represents 170+ clients. Open to new and unpublished authors. Handles adult Christian fiction and nonfiction, theology, how-to, health, Christian living, and selected YA. No children's books, end-times literature, or poetry. Accepts simultaneous submissions. Responds in 6-8 wks.

> **Contact:** Please use guidelines on website: www.stevelaube.com/guidelines. If guidelines are not followed, the proposal will not receive a response.
> **Commission:** 15%; foreign 20%.
> **Fees:** No fees.
> **Tips:** "Looking for fresh and innovative ideas. Make sure your proposal contains an excellent presentation."

*LEVINE GREENBERG LITERARY AGENCY INC., 307—7th Ave., Ste. 2407, New York NY 10001. (212) 337-0934. Fax (212) 337-0948. Website: www.levinegreenberg.com. Agent: James Levine. Agent: Arielle Eckstut. Estab. 1989. Represents 250 clients. Open to unpublished authors and new clients. General agent; handles adult religious/inspirational nonfiction. Member AAR.

> **Contact:** See guidelines/submission form on website; requires e-query; does not respond to mailed queries.
> **Commission:** 15%; foreign 20%.
> **Fees:** Office expenses.
> **Tips:** "Our specialties include spirituality and religion."

*THE LITERARY GROUP INTL., 14 Penn Plaza, Ste. 925, New York NY 10122. (646) 442-5896. E-mail: js@theliterarygroup.com. Website: www.theliterarygroup.com. Agent: Frank Weimann. Recognized in the industry. Estab. 1986. Represents 300 clients (120 for religious books). Member of AAR. Open to new clients and unpublished authors. Handles adult novels, teen/young adult novels, picture books, adult nonfiction, teen/young adult nonfiction. Children's nonfiction, gift books, e-books, crossover.

Contact: E-mail.

Commission: 15%; foreign 20%.

Fees: Expenses for overseas postage/FedEx/DHL/UPS.

Tips: "Looking for fresh, original spiritual fiction and nonfiction. We offer a written contract which may be canceled after 30 days."

*LITERARY MANAGEMENT GROUP INC., PO Box 40965, Nashville TN 37204. (615) 812-4445. E-mail: brucebarbour@literarymanagementgroup.com (for nonfiction); lavonne@literary managementgroup.com (for fiction). Website: www.literarymanagementgroup.com. Agents: Bruce R. Barbour (nonfiction), Lavonne Stevens (fiction). Estab. 1995. Well recognized in the industry. Represents 100+ clients. No unpublished authors; open to new clients. Handles adult novels, teen and adult nonfiction, crossover books. Other services offered: book packaging and consulting.

Contact: E-mail preferred. Will review proposals, no unsolicited mss. Accepts simultaneous submissions; responds in 4-6 wks.

Commission: 15%; foreign 20%.

Fees: No fees or expenses on agented books.

Tips: "Follow guidelines, proposal outline, and submissions format on website. Use Microsoft Word. Study the market and know where your book will fit in."

LIVING WORD LITERARY AGENCY/KIMBERLY SHUMATE, PO Box 40974, Eugene OR 97404. E-mail: livingwordliterary@gmail.com. Website: www.livingwordliterary.wordpress.com. Agent: Kimberly Shumate. Estab. 2009. Recognized in the industry. Represents 30 clients. Open to unpublished authors and some additional clients (depends on author). Handles adult fiction and nonfiction (no YA fiction) and some secular books, but primarily CBA.

Contact: E-mail. No simultaneous submissions; responds in 1 week.

Commission: 15%; foreign 20%.

Fees: Please refer to the agency website for submission guidelines. No fees.

Tips: "Looking for creative, relevant material. I'm all about the underdog, so don't be shy. Secular fiction must have underlying redemptive quality and no profanity. Have your material professionally edited before submitting to agents."

*STERLING LORD LITERISTIC INC., 65 Bleecker St., New York NY 10012. (213) 780-6050. Fax (212) 780-6095. E-mail: claudia@sll.com or info@sll.com. Website: www.sll.com. Agent: Claudia Cross. Recognized in the industry. In addition to clients in the general market, she represents 10 clients with Christian/religious books. Open to unpublished clients with referrals and to new clients. Handles adult and teen Christian fiction, including women's fiction, romance novels, adult nonfiction exploring themes of spirituality, gift books, crossover books, general books.

Contact: Letter, fax, or e-query (with referral only). Accepts simultaneous submissions, if informed. Responds in 4-6 wks.

Commission: 15%; foreign 20%.

Fees: "We charge for photocopy costs for manuscripts or any costs above and beyond the usual cost of doing business."

MACGREGOR LITERARY, 2373 N.W. 185th Ave., Ste. 165, Hillsboro OR 97124. E-mail: submis sions@macgregorliterary.com. Website: www.MacGregorLiterary.com. Agents: Chip MacGregor, Sandra Bishop, Amanda Luedeke. Estab. 2006. Member of AAR. Recognized in the industry. Rarely open to unpublished authors and taking on few new clients. Handles teen and adult religious/inspirational novels and nonfiction; crossover and secular books.

Contact: E-mail query. Accepts simultaneous submissions. Responds in 4 wks.

Commission: 15%; foreign 20%.

Fees: No fees or expenses.

Tips: "We represent books that make a difference. Working with a list of established authors, we are always looking for strong nonfiction projects in a variety of genres. Please check the website before submitting."

*MANUS & ASSOCIATES LITERARY AGENCY, 425 Sherman Ave., Ste. 200, Palo Alto CA 94306. (650) 470-5151. Fax (650) 470-5159. E-mail: manuslit@manuslit.com. Website: www.manuslit .com. Agents: Jillian Manus, Penny Nelson, Dena Fischer, and Jandy Nelson. Members AAR. Estab. 1994. Open to unpublished authors and new clients. Handles adult religious/inspirational novels & nonfiction, gift books, crossover & general books.

> **Contact:** Query by mail/fax/e-query (no attachments or phone calls). For fiction, send first 30 pages, bio, and SASE. For nonfiction, send proposal/sample chapters. Responds in 12 weeks, only if interested.
>
> **Commission:** 15%; foreign 20-25%.

*WILLIAM MORRIS LITERARY AGENCY, 1325 Avenue of the Americas, New York NY 10019. (212) 586-5100. Fax (212) 246-3583. E-mail: vs@wma.com. Website: www.wma.com. Agent: Valerie Summers. Recognized in the industry. Estab. 1898. Hundreds of clients with religious books. Not open to unpublished authors or new clients. Handles all types of material. Member AAR.

> **Contact:** Send query/synopsis, publication history by mail/SASE. No fax/e-query. No unsolicited mss.
>
> **Commission:** 15%; foreign 20%.
>
> **Fees:** None.

*MORTIMER LITERARY AGENCY, 43500 Ridge Park Dr., Suite 105-A, Temecula CA 92590. (951) 208-5674. E-mail: kmortimer@mortimerliterary.com. Agent: Kelly Gottuso Mortimer. Estab. 2006. Open to unpublished authors or those not published for 3 yrs. Adult novels, adult nonfiction, crossover books, secular books. Will not represent writers who are members of Romance Writers of America.

> **Contact:** E-mail only. Accepts simultaneous submissions. Responds in 1 week to queries.
>
> **Commission:** 20%
>
> **Fees:** None
>
> **Tips:** "Check website for current submission guidelines before submitting."

NAPPALAND LITERARY AGENCY, PO Box 1674, Loveland CO 80539. (970) 635-0641. Fax (970) 635-9869. E-mail: literary@nappaland.com. Website: www.nappalandliterary.com. Division of Nappaland Communications Inc. Agent: Mike Nappa. Estab. 1995. Recognized in the industry. Represents 10 clients. Prefers published authors; prefers authors who are referred by a current Nappaland author or traditional publishing company professional. Handles literary nonfiction, historical nonfiction, cultural concerns, Christian living, women's issues, suspense fiction, YA fiction, and women's fiction. DOES NOT handle memoirs, children's books, or anything about cats. Submission guidelines and "open submission" periods for unsolictied queries are posted at www .NappalandLiterary.com. Also associated with Author Echo Public Relations (www.AuthorEcho .com), which is available to author clients seeking PR representation in conjunction with literary representation.

> **Contact:** By e-mail. Accepts simultaneous submissions; responds in 2-4 wks. Unsolicited queries are automatically rejected unless sent during "open submission" periods.
>
> **Commission:** 15% for literary represenation; 15% for public-relations representation.
>
> **Fees:** None.
>
> **Tips:** "Authors who apply the advice of Mike Nappa's book *77 Reasons Why Your Book Was Rejected* before sending queries will have a much better chance of rising above the slush pile."

B. K. NELSON LITERARY AGENCY AND LECTURE BUREAU, 1565 Paseo Vida, Palm Springs CA 92264. (760) 778-8800. Fax (760) 778-6242. NY: 914-741-1322. Fax: 914-741-1324. Web sites: www.bknelson.com, bknelsonlecturebureau.com, bknelsoneditorialservices.com. Agent: B. K. Nelson, pres.; ed. asst. dir., John W. Benson. Incorporated in New York, Certificate of Qualification California. Notary Lic., Degree of Bachelors of Laws, Diploma in American Law & Procedure. Sold over 2,000 books. Represents adult & childrens' religious & inspirational fiction & nonfiction, self-help, how-to, movies. Member BBB. 80 clients.

*NUNN COMMUNICATIONS INC., 1612 Ginger Dr., Carrollton TX 75007. (972) 394-6866. E-mail: info@nunncommunications.com. Website: www.nunncommunications.com. Agent: Leslie Nunn Reed. Estab. 1995. Represents 20 clients. Recognized in the industry. Not open to unpublished authors. Handles adult nonfiction, gift books, crossover books, and general books.
> **Contact:** By e-mail. Responds in 4-6 wks.
> **Commission:** 15%.
> **Fees:** Charges office expenses if over $100.

*ALLEN O'SHEA LITERARY AGENCY, LLC, 615 Westover Rd., Stamford CT 06902. (203) 359-9965. E-mail: Marilyn@allenoshea.com. Website: www.allenoshea.com. Agents: Marilyn Allen and Coleen O'Shea. Estab. 2003. Represents 4 clients with religious books. Recognized in the industry. Open to unpublished authors (with credentials & platform) and new clients. Handles adult nonfiction.
> **Contact:** Query by mail or e-mail. No simultaneous submissions. Responds in 4 wks.
> **Commission:** 15%; foreign 15-25%.
> **Fees:** For overseas mailing.
> **Tips:** "We specifically like practical nonfiction."

PATRICK-MEDBERRY ASSOCIATES, 567 W. Channel Islands Blvd. #179, Port Hueneme CA 93041. (661) 251-4428. E-mail: patrickmedberry@sbcglobal.net. Agents: Peggy Patrick & C. J. Medberry. Estab. 2005. Management & production company specializing in Christian writers, directors, and producers, as well as religious and inspirational novels, screenplays, TV/movie scripts, crossover books, general books, and screenplays. Open to unpublished authors and new clients.
> **Contact:** Query by letter, fax, or e-mail; no calls.
> **Commission:** 10%.
> **Fees:** None.

*PELHAM LITERARY AGENCY, PMB 315, 2650 Jamacha Rd., Ste. 147, El Cajon CA 92019. (619) 447-4468. E-mail: jmeals@pelhamliterary.com. Website: www.pelhamliterary.com. Agents: Howard Pelham & Jim Meals. Estab. 1993. Recognized in the industry. Open to unpublished authors and new clients. Handles adult and teen religious/inspirational novels & nonfiction, crossover books.
> **Contact:** Brief query letter; e-query OK. Provides a list of published clients and titles. Accepts simultaneous submissions; responds in 6 wks.
> **Commission:** 15%; foreign 20%.
> **Fees:** Charges for postage and copying only. Offers an optional extensive critique for $200. Information on website.
> **Tips:** "We are actively seeking writers for the Christian fiction market, but also open to nonfiction. We specialize in genre fiction and enjoy working with new authors."

*THE QUADRIVIUM GROUP, 7512 Dr. Phillips Blvd., Ste. 50-229, Orlando FL 32819. Website: www.TheQuadriviumGroup.com. Agents: Steve Blount (SteveBlount@TheQuadriviumGroup.com); Susan Blount (SusanBlount@TheQuadriviumGroup.com). Estab. 2006. Represents 20-30 clients. Recognized in the industry. Open to a limited number of unpublished authors (with credentials, platform, compelling story/idea) and to new clients (mostly by referral). General agent. Handles Christian and general fiction and nonfiction for all ages, gift books, crossover books. Other services offered: consulting on book sales and distribution.

Contact: E-mail preferred; responds in 2-4 wks.
Commission: 15%; foreign 20%.
Fees: Only extraordinary costs with client's permission.

*RED WRITING HOOD INK, 2075 Attala Rd. 1990, Kosciusko MS 39090. (662) 674-5223. Fax (662) 796-3161. E-mail: redwritinghoodink@gmail.com. Website: redwritinghoodink.net. Agent: Sheri Williams. Estab. 1997. Represents 4 clients with religious books. Recognized in the industry. Open to unpublished authors with strong platform; open to new clients. Handles novels & nonfiction for all ages; picture books, gift books, crossover books.
    Contact: E-mail/letter. Accepts simultaneous submissions; responds in 4-6 weeks to e-mail; 1 month for postal.
    Commission: 15%; foreign 20%.
    Tips: See website.

*RLR ASSOCIATES, LTD., Literary Dept., 7 W. 51st St., New York NY 10019. (212) 541-8641. Fax (212) 262-7084. E-mail: sgould@rlrassociates.net. Website: www.rlrliterary.net. Scott Gould, literary assoc. Estab. 1972. Member AAR. Represents 50 clients. Open to unpublished authors and new clients. General agency; handles adult religious/inspirational nonfiction.
    Contact: Query by e-mail, or by mail with SASE. Considers simultaneous submissions. Responds in 4-8 wks.
    Commission: 15%; foreign 20%.

ROSS YOON LITERARY AGENCY, 1666 Connecticut Ave. N.W., #500, Washington DC 20009. (202) 328-3282. Fax (202) 328-9162. Website: www.rossyoon.com. Agent: Gail Ross (gail@rossyoon .com). Contact: Anna Sproul (anna@rossyoon.com). Estab. 1988. Represents 200 clients. Open to unpublished authors and new clients (mostly through referrals). General agent; handles adult religious/inspirational nonfiction, history, health, and business books.
    Contact: No mailed queries; e-queries only. Accepts simultaneous queries.
    Commission: 15%; foreign 25%.
    Fees: Office expenses.

SCHIAVONE LITERARY AGENCY INC., 236 Trails End, West Palm Beach FL 33413-2135. Phone/ fax (561) 966-9294. E-mail: profschia@aol.com. Website: www.publishersmarketplace.com/members/profschia. Agent: James Schiavone, EdD. Recognized in the industry. Estab. 1997. Represents 6 clients. Open to unpublished and new clients. Handles adult, teen, and children's fiction and nonfiction; celebrity biography; general books; crossover books.
    Contact: E-mail only; one-page e-mail query (no attachments).
    Commission: 15%; foreign 20%.
    Fees: No reading fees; authors pay postage only.
    Tips: Works primarily with published authors; will consider first-time authors with excellent material. Actively seeking books on spirituality, major religions, and alternative health. Very selective on first novels.

*SUSAN SCHULMAN LITERARY AGENCY, 454 W. 44th St., New York NY 10036. (212) 713-1633. Fax (212) 581-8830. E-mail: schulman@aol.com. Agent: Susan Schulman. Estab. 1989. Represents 6 clients. Recognized in the industry. Member of AAR. Open to unpublished authors and new clients. Handles adult & teen/YA religious/inspirational novels, adult nonfiction, picture books.
    Contact: Query.
    Commission: 15%; foreign 20%.

*SERENDIPITY LITERARY AGENCY, LLC, 305 Gates Ave., Brooklyn NY 11216. (718) 230-7689. Fax (718) 230-7829. E-mail: rbrooks@serendipitylit.com. Website: www.serendipitylit.com. Agent: Regina Brooks. Member AAR. Estab. 2000. Represents 50 clients; 3 with religious books. Recognized in the industry. Open to unpublished authors and new clients. General agent; handles fiction & nonfiction for all ages, gift books, crossover books, general books. No science fiction. No picture books for now.

> **Contact:** By e-mail or letter; no faxes. Accepts simultaneous submissions. Responds in 8-12 wks.
> **Commission:** 15%; foreign 20%.
> **Fees:** None.

THE SEYMOUR AGENCY, 475 Miner Street Rd., Canton NY 13617. (315) 386-1831. E-mail: mary sue@theseymouragency.com. Website: www.theseymouragency.com. Agent: Mary Sue Seymour. Estab. 1992. Member of AAR, ACFW, The Author's Guild, RWS, WGA. Represents 35 religious clients. Open to unpublished authors and new clients (prefers published authors). Handles Christian romance novels, Christian historical romance, and nonfiction for all ages, general books, crossover books. Co-agent Nicole Resciniti can be reached at nicole@theseymouragency.com. She handles all types of Christian books, including YA.

> **Contact:** Query letter or e-mail with first 50 pages of ms. For nonfiction, send proposal with chapter 1. Simultaneous query OK. Responds in 1 mo. for queries and 2-3 mos. for mss.
> **Commission:** 15% for unpublished authors.
> **Fees:** None.
> **Tips:** "We have multibook sales to Zondervan, Thomas Nelson, Harvest House, Cook Communications, Abingdon Press, Bethany House, Guideposts, and HarperOne."

*KEN SHERMAN & ASSOCIATES, 9507 Santa Monica Blvd., Beverly Hills CA 90210. (310) 273-3840. Fax (310) 271-2875. E-mail: ken@kenshermanassociates.com. Agent: Ken Sherman. Estab. 1989. Represents 50 clients. Open to unpublished authors and new clients. Handles adult religious/ inspirational novels, nonfiction, screenplays, and TV/movie scripts.

> **Contact:** By referral only. Responds in 1 mo.
> **Commission:** 15%; foreign 20%; dramatic rights 15%.
> **Fees:** Charges office expenses and other negotiable expenses.

*WENDY SHERMAN ASSOCIATES, 27 W. 24th St., Ste. 700B, New York NY 10110. (212) 279-9027. Fax (212) 279-8863. Website: www.wsherman.com. Agents: Wendy Sherman, Kimberly Perel. Open to unpublished authors and new clients. General agents. Handle adult religious nonfiction.

> **Contact:** Query by mail/SASE or send proposal/1 chapter. No phone/fax/e-query. Guidelines on website.
> **Commission:** 15%; foreign 20%.

MICHAEL SNELL LITERARY AGENCY, PO Box 1206, Truro MA 02666-1206. (508) 349-3718. E-mail: snell.patricia@gmail.com. Website: http://michaelsnellagency.com. Agent: Patricia Snell. Estab. 1978. Represents 200 clients. Open to unpublished authors and new clients. General agent: handles adult religious.

> **Contact:** Query with SASE. No simultaneous submissions. Responds in 1-2 wks.
> **Commission:** 15%; foreign 15%.

*SPENCERHILL ASSOCIATES, LTD./KAREN SOLEM, Chatham NY. (518) 392-9293. Fax (518) 392-9554. E-mail: submissions@spencerhillassociates.com. Website: www.spencerhillassociates .com. Agent: Karen Solem. Member of AAR. Recognized in the industry. Estab. 2001. Represents 15-20 clients with religious books. Not currently open to unpublished authors; very selective of new clients. Primarily handles adult Christian fiction; no YA, children's, or nonfiction.

> **Contact:** By e-mail.
> **Commission:** 15%; foreign 20%.
> **Fees:** Photocopying and Express Mail charges only.
> **Tips:** "Check website for latest information and needs and how to submit. No nonfiction."

LESLIE H. STOBBE, 300 Doubleday Rd., Tryon NC 28782. (828) 808-7127. E-mail: lhstobbe123@ gmail.com. Website: www.stobbeliterary.com. Agent: Les Stobbe. Well recognized in the industry. Estab. 1993. Represents 71 clients. Open to unpublished authors and new clients. Handles adult fiction, nonfiction, and crossover books.

> **Contact:** By e-mail. Considers simultaneous submissions; responds within 12 weeks.
> **Commission:** 15%
> **Fees:** None.
> **Tips:** "I will not accept clients whose theological positions in their book differ significantly from mine."

SUITE A MANAGEMENT TALENT & LITERARY AGENCY, 120 El Camino Dr., Ste. 202, Beverly Hills CA 90212. (310) 278-0801. Fax (310) 278-0807. E-mail: suite-A@juno.com. Agent: Lloyd D. Robinson. Recognized in the industry. Estab. 2001. Several clients. Open to new and unpublished clients (if published in other media). Specializes in screenplays and novels for adaptation to TV movies.

> **Contact:** By mail or fax only. For consideration of representation, send current bio, and for each screenplay, your WGA registration number, log line, and two-paragraph synopsis only. Complete scripts or e-mail submissions are not read; attachments are deleted. Responds only if interested.
> **Commission:** 10%
> **Comments:** Representation limited to adaptation of novels and true-life stories for film and television development. Work must have been published for consideration.

MARK SWEENEY & ASSOCIATES, 28540 Altessa Way, Ste. 201, Bonita Springs FL 34135. (239) 594-1957. Fax (239) 594-1935. E-mail: sweeney2@comcast.net. Agents: Mark Sweeney; Janet Sweeney. Recognized in the industry. Estab. 2003. Open to unpublished authors and new clients on a restricted basis. Handles adult religious/inspirational nonfiction, crossover books, general books. No new fiction at this time.

> **Contact:** E-mail.
> **Commission:** 15%; foreign 15%.
> **Fees:** None.

*TALCOTT NOTCH LITERARY SERVICES, 276 Forest Rd., Milford CT 06461. (203) 877-1146. Fax (203) 876-9517. Website: www.talcottnotch.net. Agent: Gina Panettieri (gpanettieri@talcottnotch .net). Not yet recognized in the industry; building a Christian presence. Estab. 2003. Represents 25 clients (3 with religious books). Open to unpublished authors and new clients. Handles nonfiction & fiction, crossover & general market books for all ages.

> **Contact:** By e-mail (editorial@talcottnotch.net). Accepts simultaneous submissions; responds in 8 wks.
> **Commission:** 15%; foreign or with co-agent 20%.
> **Fees:** None.
> **Tips:** "While Christian and religious books are not our main focus, we are open to unique and thought-provoking works from all writers. We specifically seek nonfiction in areas of parenting, health, women's issues, arts & crafts, self-help, and current events. We are open to academic/scholarly work as well as commercial projects."

*3 SEAS LITERARY AGENCY, PO Box 8571, Madison WI 53708. (608) 221-4306. E-mail: threeseas lit@aol.com. Website: www.threeseaslit.com. Agent: Michelle Grajkowski. Estab. 2000. Represents 40 clients. Open to unpublished authors and new clients. General agent; handles adult religious/ inspirational novels & nonfiction.

> **Contact:** E-query only with synopsis & 1 chapter (queries@threeseaslit.com). Considers simultaneous submissions. Responds in 2-3 mos.
> **Commission:** 15%; foreign 20%.

*TRIDENT MEDIA GROUP, LLC, 41 Madison Ave., 36th Fl., New York NY 10010. (212) 262-4810. Fax (212) 262-4849. E-mail: dfehr@tridentmediagroup.com. Website: www.tridentmediagroup .com. Agent: Don Fehr. Open to unpublished authors and new clients. General agent. Handles adult religious nonfiction.

    Contact: No unsolicited mss. Query/SASE first; send outline and sample chapters on request. Responds to queries in 3 wks.; mss in 6 wks.

    Commission: 15%.

*VAN DIEST LITERARY AGENCY, PO Box 1482, Sisters OR 97759. (541) 549-0477. Fax (541) 549-1213. E-mail through website: www.ChristianLiteraryAgency.com. Agents: David & Sarah Van Diest. Estab. 2004. Represents 20 clients. Open to unpublished authors and new clients. Recognized in the industry. Handles teen & adult novels, nonfiction for all ages, crossover books.

    Contact: By e-mail. Use online form. Responds in 4 wks.

    Commission: 15%; 25% for first-time authors.

*VERITAS LITERARY AGENCY, 601 Van Ness Ave., Opera Plaza Ste. E, San Francisco CA 94102. (415) 647-6964. Fax (415) 647-6965. E-mail: submissions@veritasliterary.com. Website: www .veritasliterary.com. Agent: Katherine Boyle (kboyle@veritasliterary.com). Member AAR. Handles serious religious nonfiction (no New Age).

    Contact: Query with SASE; e-query OK (no attachments); no fax queries.

*WATERSIDE PRODUCTIONS INC., 2055 Oxford Ave., Cardiff-by-the-Sea CA 92007. (760) 632-9190. Fax (760) 632-9295. E-mail: admin@waterside.com. Website: www.waterside.com. Agent: William E. Brown (webrown@waterside.com). Christian agent in a highly regarded general agency. Interested in handling Christian books, or books which otherwise challenge and engage readers from a Judeo-Christian perspective. Prefers nonfiction, but will look at fiction (the bar is very high). In addition to spiritually oriented books, devotions, theology, chick lit, and mom lit; list includes business books: leadership, marketing, sales, business development.

    Contact: Query via online form (see website). Considers simultaneous submissions.

    Commission: 15%; foreign 25%.

*WINTERS & KING, INC., 2448 E. 81st St., Ste. 5900, Tulsa OK 74137-4259. (918) 494-6868. Fax (918) 491-6297. E-mail: dboyd@wintersking.com. Website: www.wintersking.com. Agent: Thomas J. Winters. Estab. 1983. Represents 100+ clients. Recognized in the industry. Rarely open to unpublished authors; open to qualified new clients with a significant sales history/platform. Handles adult religious/inspirational novels & nonfiction for all ages, screenplays, TV/movie scripts, gift books, e-books, crossover books, secular w/ underlying Christian theme.

    Contact: By fax: (918) 491-6297. No more than 10 pages.

    Commission: 15%; foreign 15%.

    Fees: None

    Tips: "Unsolicited proposals/manuscripts will not be acknowledged, considered, or returned. Solicited proposals/outlines/samples/manuscripts that are not in proper format will not be reviewed or considered for representation. No handwritten submissions."

WOLGEMUTH & ASSOCIATES INC., 8600 Crestgate Cir., Orlando FL 32819. (407) 909-9445. Fax (407) 909-9446. E-mail: rwolgemuth@wolgemuthandassociates.com. Agent: Robert D. Wolgemuth; Andrew D. Wolgemuth (awolgemuth@wolgemuthandassociates.com); Erik S. Wolgemuth (ewolge muth@wolgemuthandassociates.com); Austin Wilson (awilson@wolgemuthandassociates.com). Member AAR. Well recognized in the industry. Estab. 1992. Represents 85 clients. No new clients or unpublished authors. Handles mostly adult nonfiction; most other types of books handled only for current clients.

    Contact: By letter.

    Commission: 15%.

Fees: None.

Tips: "We work with authors who are either bestselling authors or potentially bestselling authors. Consequently, we want to represent clients with broad market appeal."

*WORDSERVE LITERARY GROUP, 10152 S. Knoll Cir., Highlands Ranch CO 80130. (303) 471-6675. E-mail: admin@wordserveliterary.com ("Query" in subject line). Website: www.wordserve literary.com. Agents: Greg Johnson (greg@wordserveliterary.com) and Rachelle Gardner (rachelle @wordserveliterary.com/PO Box 1089, Monument CO 80132). Estab. 2003. Represents 80 clients. Recognized in the industry. Open to new clients. Handles novels & nonfiction for all ages, gift books, crossover books, general books (memoir, military, self-help, adult fiction).

   Contact: By e-mail (no attachments). Visit website for submission guidelines. Responds in 4-8 wks.

   Commission: 15%; foreign 15-20%.

   Fees: None.

   Tips: "Nonfiction: First impressions count. Make sure your proposal answers all the questions on competition, outline, audience, felt need, etc. Fiction: Make sure your novel is completed before you submit a proposal (synopsis, plus 5 chapters)."

*WRITERS HOUSE, 21 W. 26th St., New York NY 10010. (212) 685-2400. Fax (212) 685-1781. E-mail: azuckerman@writershouse.com. Website: www.writershouse.com. Agent: Albert Zuckerman. Estab. 1974. Represents 440 clients. General agency; handles adult religious/inspirational fiction. Member of AAR.

   Contact: One-page query by mail/SASE. No e-mail/fax queries. Responds in 1 mo. to query.

   Commission: 15%; foreign 20%.

   Fees: No fees.

   Tips: "See website for details. Write a compelling query so we'll ask to see your manuscript."

YATES & YATES, 1100 W. Town and Country Rd., Ste. 1300, Orange CA 92868-4654. (714) 480-4000. Fax (714) 480-4001. E-mail: email@yates2.com. Website: www.yates2.com. Agents: Sealy Yates, Matt Yates. Estab. 1989. Recognized in the industry. Represents 50+ clients. No unpublished authors. Handles adult nonfiction.

   Contact: E-mail.

   Commission: Negotiable.

*ZACHARY SHUSTER HARMSWORTH LITERARY AND ENTERTAINMENT AGENCY, 1776 Broadway, Ste. 1405, New York NY 10019. (212) 765-6900. Fax (212) 765-6490. Or 535 Boylston St., Ste. 1103, Boston MA 02116. (617) 262-2400. Fax (617) 262-2468. E-mail: mchappell@zsh literary.com. Website: www.zshliterary.com. Agent: Mary Beth Chappell (Boston office). Recognized in the industry. Represents 15-30 religious clients. Open to unpublished authors and new clients. Handles adult religious/inspirational novels & adult nonfiction, crossover books, general books.

   Contact: E-mail with online form only; no unsolicited submissions.

   Commission: 15%; foreign & film 20%.

   Fees: Office expenses only.

   Tips: "We are looking for inspirational fiction, Christian nonfiction, especially that which focuses on the emerging/emergent church or that which would appeal to readers in their 20s and 30s, and teen/YA series."

12

Contests

A listing here does not guarantee the legitimacy of a contest. For guidelines on evaluating contests and to help determine if a contest is legitimate, go to www.sfwa.org/beware/contests.

CHILDREN/YOUNG-ADULTS CONTESTS, WRITING FOR

THE CHILDREN'S WRITER CONTESTS. Offers a number of contests for children's writers. Website: www.childrenswriter.com.

HIGHLIGHTS FOR CHILDREN FICTION CONTEST. (570) 253-1080. Website: www.highlights .com. Offers 3 prizes of $1,000 each for stories up to 800 words for children; for beginning readers up to 500 words. See website for guidelines and current topic. (To find contest info put "Contest" in search field.) No crime, violence, or derogatory humor. No entry fee or form required. Entries must be postmarked between January 1 and January 31.

CORETTA SCOTT KING BOOK AWARD. Coretta Scott King Task Force, American Library Assn. Toll-free (800) 545-2433. E-mail: olos@ala.org. Website: www.ala.org. Annual award for children's books by African American authors and/or illustrators published the previous year. Books must fit one of these categories: preschool to grade 4; grades 5-8; grades 9-12. Deadline: December 1 each year. Guidelines on website (click on "Awards & Grants"/click on contest name on list). Prizes: a plaque, a set of encyclopedias, and $1,000 cash. Recipients are authors and illustrators of African descent whose distinguished books promote an understanding and appreciation of the "American Dream."

LEE & LOW BOOKS NEW VOICES AWARD. E-mail: info@leeandlow.com. Website: www.lee-and low.com. Annual award for a children's fiction or nonfiction picture book story by a writer of color; up to 1,500 words. Deadline: between May 1 and October 31. Prizes: $1,000 plus publication contract; $500 for Honor Award Winner. Guidelines on website (click on "Creators"/"New Voices Award"). Sign up on website for their newsletter, which will include details for the next contest.

MILKWEED PRIZE FOR CHILDREN'S LITERATURE. Milkweed Editions. (612) 332-3192. E-mail: editor@milkweed.org. Website: www.milkweed.org. Annual prize for unpublished novel intended for readers 8-13; 90-200 pgs. Prize: $10,000 advance against royalties and publication. Guidelines on website (Click on "Submissions Guidelines & Prizes").

POCKETS WRITING CONTEST. (615) 340-7333. Fax (615) 340-7267. E-mail: pockets@upper room.org. Website: www.pockets.org. United Methodist. Lynn W. Gilliam, ed. Devotional magazine for children (6-11 yrs.). Fiction-writing contest; submit between March 1 and August 15 every yr. Prize: $500 and publication in *Pockets*. Length: 750-1,000 words. Must be unpublished and not historical fiction. Previous winners not eligible. Send to Pockets Fiction Contest at above address, designating "Fiction Contest" on outside of envelope. Send SASE for return and response. Details on website (click on "Breaking News"/"Annual Fiction Contest").

SKIPPING STONES 25TH ANNIVERSARY AWARDS. P.O. Box 3939, Eugene OR 97403 USA. (541) 342-4956. E-mail: editor@skippingstones.org. Website: www.skippingstones.org. Interfaith/ multicultural/nature. Arun N. Toké, exec. ed.; literary, multicultural, and nature awareness magazine for young people, worldwide. Now in 25th year. The 25th Anniversary awards are for students 8-18.

Deadline October 2, 2013, Winners announced in January 2014. Guidelines and prizes on website (click to "AWARDS/ 25TH ANNIVERSARY AWARDS" in the sidebar) or e-mail the editor.

SKIPPING STONES YOUTH HONOR AWARDS. PO Box 3939, Eugene OR 97403-0939. Phone/fax: (541)342-4956. E-mail: editor@skippingstones.org. Website: www.skippingstones.org. Annual awards to "promote creativity as well as multicultural and nature awareness in youth." Prize: publication in the autumn issue, honor certificate, subscription to magazine, plus 5 multicultural and/or nature books. Categories: short stories, nonfiction, and poetry. Entry fee: $3; make checks payable to *Skipping Stones*. Cover letter should include name, address, phone, and e-mail. Deadline: June 20. Entries must be unpublished. Length: 1,000 words maximum. Open to any writer between 7 and 17. Guidelines available by SASE, e-mail, or on website. Accepts inquiries by e-mail or phone. "Be creative. Do not use stereotypes or excessive violent language or plots. Be sensitive to cultural diversity." Results announced in the September-October issue. Winners notified by mail. For contest results, visit website. Everyone who enters receives the issue that features the award winners. Acquisitions: Arun N. Toké. Editorial Comments: *Skipping Stones* is a winner of the 2007 NAME award and now in its 25th year.

SOCIETY OF CHILDREN'S BOOK WRITERS & ILLUSTRATORS GOLDEN KITE AWARDS. Website: www.scbwi.org. Offers $2,500 in cash awards. Details on website (click on "Awards & Grants"/"Golden Kite Awards").

FICTION CONTESTS

AMAZON BREAKTHROUGH NOVEL AWARD. In cooperation with Penguin and Hewlett-Packard. Penguin will publish winning novel with a $25,000 advance. November deadline.

AMERICAN CHRISTIAN FICTION WRITERS CONTESTS. Phone/fax (321) 984-4018. E-mail: genesis@ACFW.com, boty@acfw.com, or vp@acfw.com. Website: www.ACFW.com. Sponsors a fiction contest and others. See website for current contests and rules (scroll down to "Contests"/click on name of contest).

ATHANATOS CHRISTIAN MINISTRIES BOOK LENGTH NOVEL CONTEST. (202) 697-4623. E-mail: director@athanatosministries.org. Website: www.christianwritingcontest.com. Novel 40,000-90,000 words. Prizes: 1st prize $1,500 and a possible book contract; 2nd prize $1,000 and a possible book contract. Entry fee: $69.95. Deadline: September 1.

BARD FICTION PRIZE. Awarded annually to a promising, emerging young writer of fiction, aged 39 years or younger. Entries must be previously published. Deadline: July 15. No entry fee. Prizes: $30,000 and appointment as writer in residence for one semester at Bard College, Annandale-on-Hudson NY. E-mail: bfp@bard.edu. Website: www.bard.edu/bfp.

BOSTON REVIEW SHORT STORY CONTEST. *Boston Review*. Website: www.bostonreview.net. Prize: $1,500 (plus publication) for an unpublished short story up to 4,000 words. Entry fee: $20. Deadline: October 1. Details on website (click on "About"/scroll down to "Contest"/"Aura Estrada Short Story Contest").

BULWER-LYTTON FICTION CONTEST. For the worst opening line to a novel. Deadline: April 15. Website: www.bulwer-lytton.com. Rules on website.

CANADIAN WRITER'S JOURNAL SHORT FICTION CONTEST. White Mountain Publications, Box 1178, New Liskeard ON P0J 1P0, Canada. (705) 647-5424. Canada-wide toll-free (800) 258-5451. E-mail: cwc-calendar@cwj.ca. Website: www.cwj.ca. Sponsors semiannual short fiction contests. Deadline: April 30. Length: to 1,500 words. Entry fee: $5. Prizes: $150, $100, $50. All fiction needs for CWJ are filled by this contest. Click on "CWJ Short Fiction Contest."

ALEXANDER PATTERSON CAPPON PRIZE FOR FICTION. New Letters, UMKC, University House, 5101 Rockhill Rd., Kansas City MO 64110. (816) 235-1168. E-mail: newletters@umkc.edu. Website: www.newletters.org. Deadline: May 18. Entry fee: $15. Prize: $1,500. Click on "Awards for Writers."

THE CHRISTY AWARDS. Phone/fax (734) 663-7931. E-mail: CA2000DK@aol.com. Website: www .christyawards.com. Awards in 9 fiction genres for excellence in Christian fiction. Nominations made by publishers, not authors. For submission guidelines and other information, see website (click on "Forms"/"Official Guidelines"). Awards are presented at an annual Christy Awards Banquet held Friday prior to the annual ICRS convention in July.

JACK DYER FICTION PRIZE. Crab Orchard Review, Fiction Contest, Dept. of English, Mail Code 4503, Southern Illinois University–Carbondale, 1000 Faner Dr., Carbondale IL 62901. (618) 453-5321. Website: www.siuc.edu/~crborchd. Entry fee: $10. Prize: $1,500. Deadline: submit between March 1 and May 10 (may vary). Submit fiction up to 6,000 words. See website for guidelines.

GLIMMER TRAIN PRESS FICTION CONTESTS. Glimmer Train Press. Website: www.glimmer train.com. Sponsors a number of contests. Check website for current contests (click on "Writers' Guidelines").

JAMES JONES FIRST NOVEL FELLOWSHIP. (570) 408-4547. E-mail: cwriting@wilkes.edu. Website: www.wilkes.edu/pages/1159.asp. Deadline: March 1. Entry fee: $25. Prizes: $10,000 first prize; $750 for two runners-up. Submit a 2-page outline and the first 50 pages of an unpublished novel. Guidelines on website.

THE MARY MCCARTHY PRIZE IN SHORT FICTION. Sarabande Books. E-mail: sarabandeb@ aol.com. Website: www.sarabandebooks.org. Prize: $2,000 and publication of a collection of short stories, novellas, or a short novel (150-250 pgs.), plus a standard royalty contract. Deadline: submit between January 1 and February 15. Entry fee: $25. Guidelines on website (click on "Submission Guidelines"/scroll to bottom and click on name of contest).

SERENA MCDONALD KENNEDY AWARD. Snake Nation Press. Website: www.snakenationpress .org. Novellas up to 50,000 words, or short-story collection up to 200 pgs. (published or unpub-lished). Deadline: July 30 (check website to verify). Entry fee: $25. Prize: $1,000 and publication. Guidelines on website (click on "Contests").

NATIONAL WRITERS ASSOCIATION NOVEL-WRITING CONTEST. The National Writers Assn., 10940 S. Parker Rd, #508, Parker CO 80134. (303) 841-0246. Website: www.nationalwriters.com. Check website for current contests and guidelines (click on "Contests"/then name of contest).

NATIONAL WRITERS ASSOCIATION SHORT-STORY CONTEST. The National Writers Assn., (303) 841-0246. Website: www.nationalwriters.com. Check website for current contest and guide-lines (click on "Contests"/then name of contest).

THE FLANNERY O'CONNOR AWARD FOR SHORT FICTION. University of Georgia Press. Website: www.ugapress.uga.edu. For collections of short fiction, 50,000-75,000 wds. Prize: $1,000, plus pub-lication under royalty book contract. Entry fee: $25. Deadline: between April 1 and May 31 (post-mark). Guidelines on website (click on "About Us"/"For Prospective Authors"/"Flannery O'Connor Award for Short Fiction").

OPERATION FIRST NOVEL. Sponsored by the Jerry B. Jenkins Christian Writers Guild. For unpublished novelists who are students or annual members of the Christian Writers Guild. Winner receives $20,000 and publication. Length: 75,000-100,000 words. Deadline: September 15. No entry fee. For contest rules, go to www.ChristianWritersGuild.com/contest.asp.

GRACE PALEY PRIZE FOR SHORT FICTION. (703) 993-4301. E-mail: awp@awpwriter.org. Website: www.awpwriter.org. Prize: $4,000 & publication. Entry fee: $25. Deadline: Postmarked between January 1 and February 28, 2012.

KATHERINE ANNE PORTER PRIZE FOR FICTION. Literary Contest/Fiction, *Nimrod Journal*, University of Tulsa. (918) 631-3080. E-mail: nimrod@utulsa.edu. Website: www.utulsa.edu/nimrod /awards.html. Quality prose and fiction by emerging writers of contemporary literature, unpublished. Deadline: submit between January 1 and April 30. Entry fee: $20. Prizes: $2,000 and publication; $1,000 and publication. Guidelines on website (click on "Nimrod Literary Awards").

THE SILVER QUILL SOCIETY SHORT FICTION 2013 CONTEST. Website: www.thestoryteller magazine.com/. Entry fee: $5. Deadine: September 25, 2013. Prizes: 1st place: $50, 2nd place: $25, 3rd place: $15, 4th place: $10. Open genre contest. Writers may enter as often as they wish, but entry fee must accompany each entry. Name, address, phone, e-mail, title of story, and word count should be on cover page. Name should not appear anywhere else on ms. No pornography, graphic anything, New Age, or children's stories will be accepted.

TOBIAS WOLFF AWARD IN FICTION. Western Washington University, Bellingham WA. E-mail: bhreview@cc.wwu.edu. Website: www.bhreview.org. Short story or novel excerpt up to 8,000 words. Deadline: postmarked between December 1 and March 15. Entry fee: $18 for first story/chapter; $10 each additional. Prize: $1,000, plus publication. Details on website.

WRITER'S JOURNAL ANNUAL FICTION CONTEST. E-mail: writersjournal@writersjournal.com. Website: www.writersjournal.com. Sponsors several contests; see website (click on "Contests"/scroll down to "Contest Entry Manuscript Format").

WRITE TO INSPIRE. July 19-20, 2013. Elk Grove CA. Contact Elizabeth Thompson. Inspire Christian Writers, PO Box 276794, Sacramento, CA 95827. (916) 607-7796. Limited to writers unpublished by traditional publishers, or published only in anthologies, compilations, or periodicals.

NONFICTION CONTESTS

AMY WRITING AWARDS. A call to present spiritual truth reinforced with biblical references in general, nonreligious publications. First prize is $10,000 with a total of $34,000 given annually (additional prizes of $1,000-5,000). To be eligible, submitted articles must be published either in print or online in a general, nonreligious publication (either printed or online) and must be rein-forced with at least one passage of Scripture. Deadline is January 31 of following year. Winners are notified by May 1. For details and a copy of last year's winning entries, contact: The Amy Foundation, PO Box 16091, Lansing MI 48901-6091. (517) 323-6233. E-mail: amyfoundtn@aol.com. Website: www.amyfound.org.

AWP CREATIVE NONFICTION PRIZE. Assoc. of Writers and Writing programs, George Mason University, Fairfax VA. E-mail: awp@awpwriter.org. Website: www.awpwriter.org. For authors of book-length manuscripts; submit only 150-300 pgs. Deadline: February 28. Entry fee: $15 for members; $30 for nonmembers. Prize: $2,000. Guidelines on website (click on "Contests"/"AWP Award Series").

THE BECHTEL PRIZE. *Teachers and Writers Magazine* Contest. E-mail: info@twc.org. Website: www.twc.org/publications/bechtel-prize. Contemporary writing articles (unpublished) to 3,500 words. Deadline: June 30 (varies). Entry fee: $20. Prize: $1,000, plus publication.

DOROTHY CHURCHILL CAPON PRIZE FOR ESSAY. New Letters, UMKC, University House. (816) 235-1168. E-mail: newletters@umkc.edu. Website: www.newletters.org. Deadline: May 18. Entry fee: $15. Prize: $1,500. Guidelines on website (scroll down and click on "New Letters Writing Contests").

ANNIE DILLARD AWARD IN CREATIVE NONFICTION. Essays on any subject to 8,000 words. Deadline: between December 1 and March 15. Entry fee: $18 for first; $10 each additional. First prize: $1,000. Unpublished works only, up to 8,000 words. E-mail: bhreview@cc.wwu.edu. Website: www .wwu.edu/~bhreview. Details on website (click on "Contests"/"Contest Submission Guidelines").

EVENT CREATIVE NONFICTION CONTEST. Deadline: mid-April, annually. $1,500 in prizes. Judges reserve the right to award either two prizes valued at $750 or three at $500. Plus winners get published in *EVENT*. Must be creative nonfiction and must not exceed the 5,000-word limit. Entry fee is $34.95, including a one-year subscription to *EVENT*. See www.eventmags.com for details.

GRAYWOLF PRESS NONFICTION PRIZE. (651) 641-0036. Website: www.graywolfpress .org/Company_Info/Submission_Guidelines/Graywolf_Press_Nonfiction_Prize_Submission_ Guidelines. For the best literary nonfiction book by a writer not yet established in the genre. Deadline: between June 1 & June 30 (varies). Entry fee: none. Prize: $12,000 advance and publication. Guidelines on website (click on "Submission Guidelines").

GUIDEPOSTS CONTEST. Website: www.guideposts.org. Interfaith. Writers Workshop Contest held on even years, with a late June deadline. True, first-person stories (yours or someone else's), 1,500 words. Needs one spiritual message, with scenes, drama, and characters. Winners attend a week-long seminar in New York (all expenses paid) on how to write for *Guideposts*.

RICHARD J. MARGOLIS AWARD. Blue Mountain Center, Margolis & Assocs. E-mail: hsm@margolis .com. Website: www.award.margolis.com. Given annually to a promising young journalist or essayist whose work combines warmth, humor, wisdom, and concern with social justice. Deadline: July 1. Prize: $5,000. Guidelines on website.

MASTER BOOKS SCHOLARSHIP ESSAY CONTEST. PO Box 726, Green Forest AR 72638. (870) 438-5288. Fax (870) 438-5120. E-mail: submissions@newleafpress.net. Essay contest; $3,000 college scholarship; www.newleafpublishinggroup.com/store/scholarship.htm. Details on website.

WRITE TO INSPIRE. July 19-20, 2013. Elk Grove CA. Contact Elizabeth Thompson. Inspire Christian Writers, PO Box 276794, Sacramento, CA 95827. (916) 607-7796. Limited to writers unpublished by traditional publishers, or published only in anthologies, compilations, or periodicals.

PLAY/SCRIPTWRITING/SCREENWRITING CONTESTS

AMERICAN ZOETROPE SCREENPLAY CONTEST. E-mail: contests@zoetrope.com. Website: www .zoetrope.com/contests. Deadline: August 1 (early), September 6 (final). Entry fees: $35 (early), $50 (final). Prizes: First prize $5,000. That winner and 10 finalists will be considered for film option and development.

AUSTIN FILM FESTIVAL SCREENWRITERS COMPETITION. (512) 478-4795. E-mail: info@ austinfilmfestival.com. Website: www.austinfilmfestival.com. Offers a number of contest categories for screenplays. See current details on website.

BAKER'S PLAYS HIGH SCHOOL PLAYWRITING COMPETITION. Plays may be about any subject and any length as long as the play can be reasonably produced by high school students on a high school stage. Deadline: January 30. Prizes: $500, $250, and $100. Guidelines on website: www .bakersplays.com (go down to "Information" box & click on "Contests & Festivals").

KAIROS PRIZE FOR SPIRITUALLY UPLIFTING SCREENPLAYS. John Templeton Foundation. E-mail: contact@kairosprize.com. Website: www.kairosprize.com. Annual. For first-time screenwriters with a religious message. Prizes: $25,000, $15,000, $10,000. Guidelines on website (click on "Guidelines").

MOONDANCE INTERNATIONAL FILM FESTIVAL COMPETITION. E-mail: director@moon dancefilmfestival.com. Website: www.moondancefilmfestival.com. Open to films, screenplays, and features. Deadline: May 30. Entry fees:$50-100. Prize: winning entries screened at festival. Details on website.

NICHOLL FELLOWSHIPS IN SCREENWRITING. (310) 247-3010. E-mail: nicholl@oscars.org. Website: www.oscars.org/nicholl/index.html. International contest held annually, open to any writer who has not optioned or sold a treatment, teleplay, or screenplay for more than $5,000. Up to five $30,000 fellowships offered each year to promising authors. Deadline: May 1. Entry fee: $30. Guidelines/required application form on website (scroll down to "About the Competition" and click on "More").

MILDRED & ALBERT PANOWSKI PLAYWRITING AWARD. Award Coordinator, Forest Roberts Theatre, Northern Michigan University, Marquette MI. Website: www.nmu.edu/theatre. Unpublished, unproduced, full-length plays. Deadline: September 1. Prizes: $2,000, a summer workshop, a fully mounted production, and transportation to Marquette. Guidelines on website (click on "Playwriting Award").

SCRIPTAPALOOZA ANNUAL INTERNATIONAL SCREENPLAY COMPETITION. (323) 654-5809. E-mail: info@scriptapalooza.com. Website: www.scriptapalooza.com. Over $25,000 in prizes and over 90 producers reading all the entries. Entry fees are from $40-55, plus you can get feedback on your entry now. Deadlines: January 7th, March 5th, and April 15th.

POETRY CONTESTS

ANHINGA PRIZE FOR POETRY. E-mail: info@anhinga.org. Website: www.anhinga.org. A $2,000 prize for original poetry book in English. Winning manuscript published by Anhinga Press. For poets trying to publish a first or second book of poetry. Submissions: 48-80 pgs. Number pages and include $25 reading fee. Deadline: between February 15 and May 1 each year. Details on website (click on contest name).

MURIEL CRAFT BAILEY MEMORIAL POETRY AWARD. E-mail: poetry@comstockreview.org. Awarded annually. Deadline: July 1. Prizes: $100 to $1,000. Finalists published in the *Comstock Review*. Unpublished poems up to 40 lines. Entry fee: $5 for each poem (no limit on number of submissions). Details on website: www.comstockreview.org.

BALTIMORE REVIEW POETRY CONTEST. All styles and forms of poetry. April 1-July 1. Entry fee: $10. Prizes: $300 & publication; $150; $50; plus publication in the *Baltimore Review*. Details on website: www.baltimorereview.org. Click on "Contests" on main menu.

BLUE MOUNTAIN ARTS/SPS STUDIOS POETRY CARD CONTEST. (303) 449-0536. E-mail: poetrycontest@sps.com. Website: www.sps.com. Biannual contest. Next deadlineS: June 30, December 31. Use online form for submissions. Rhymed or unrhymed original poetry (unrhymed preferred). Poems also considered for greeting cards or anthologies. Prizes: $300, $150, $50. Details on website ("Poetry Contest").

BOSTON REVIEW ANNUAL POETRY CONTEST. Deadline: June 1. First prize: $1,500, plus publication. Submit up to 5 unpublished poems. Entry fee: $20 (includes a subscription to *Boston Review*). Submit manuscripts in duplicate with cover note. Website: www.bostonreview.net. Details on website (click on "About"/"Contests"/name of contest).

CAVE CANEM POETRY PRIZE. Supports the work of African American poets with excellent manuscripts who have not found a publisher for their first book. Deadline: April 30 (varies). Prize: $1,000, publication by a national press, and 15 copies of the book. Entry fee: $15. Details on website: www.cavecanempoets.org (click on "Book Awards"/click on name of contest/scroll down and click on "Competition Guidelines"). E-mail: ccpoets@verizon.net.

49TH PARALLEL POETRY AWARD. Mail Stop 9053, Western Washington University, Bellingham WA. (360) 650-4863. E-mail: bhreview@cc.wwu.edu. Website: www.wwu.edu/~bhreview. Poems in any style or on any subject. Deadline: submit between December 1 and March 15. Entry fee: $18 for first entry; $10 for each additional entry. First prize: $1,000 and publication. Details on website.

FLO GAULT STUDENT POETRY COMPETITION. Sarabande Books. E-mail: info@sarabande books.org. Website: www.sarabandebooks.org. Prize: $500. Submit up to 3 poems. Deadline: October 30. Details on website (click on "Student Poetry Prize").

GRIFFIN POETRY PRIZE. (905) 618-0420. E-mail: info@griffinpoetryprize.com. Website: www .griffinpoetryprize.com. Prizes: two $65,000 awards (one to a Canadian and one to a poet from anywhere in the world) for a collection of poetry published in English during the preceding year; plus additional prizes ($200,000 in prizes total). All submissions must come from publishers. Deadline: December 31. Details on website.

DONALD HALL PRIZE FOR POETRY. (703) 993-4301. E-mail: awp@awpwriter.org. Website: www.awpwriter.org. Prize: $4,000 & publication. Entry fee: $25. Deadline: postmarked between January 1 and February 28, 2012.

TOM HOWARD/JOHN H. REID POETRY CONTEST. Website: www.winningwriters.com/tompoetry .htm. Deadline: between December 15 and September 30. Poetry in any style or genre. Published poetry accepted. Entry fee: $7 for every 25 lines. Prizes: $3,000 first prize; total of $5,550 in cash prizes. Details on website.

THE LEDGE ANNUAL POETRY CHAPBOOK CONTEST. E-mail: info@theledgemagazine.com. Website: www.theledgemagazine.com. Submit 16-28 pages of poetry with title page, bio, and acknowledgments. Entry fee: $12 for first three poems; $3.00 each additional. Prizes: $1,000, $250, and $100, plus publication. Deadline: April 30.

BARBARA MANDIGO KELLY PEACE POETRY AWARDS. Nuclear Age Peace Foundation. (805) 965-3443. E-mail: wagingpeace@napf.org. Website: www.wagingpeace.org. Annual series of awards to encourage poets to explore and illuminate positive visions of peace and the human spirit. Deadline: July 1. Prizes: $1,000 for Adult; $200 for Youth 13-18 years; and $200 for Youth ages 12 and under. Adult entry fee: $15 for up to 3 poems; $5 for youth; no fee for 12 and under. Details on website (see right-hand column).

NARRATIVE MAGAZINE POETRY CONTEST. Closes July 17, 2013. Website: http://narrative magazine.com/node/181953. Prizes: $1,500/750/300, plus 10 finalists receive $75 each. Submission fee: $22. See website for details.

NEW LETTERS PRIZE FOR POETRY. New Letters, UMKC. (816) 235-1168. E-mail: newletters@ umkc.edu. Website: www.newletters.org. Deadline: May 18. Entry fee: $15 for first entry; $10 ea. for additional. Prize: $1,500 for best group of 3 to 6 poems.

*JESSE BRYCE NILES CHAPBOOK CONTEST. Submit 25-34 pages of poetry. August 1-September 30. Entry fee: $25. Prizes: $1,000, plus 50 copies of chapbook. Details on website: www.comstock review.org.

PEARL POETRY PRIZE. Pearl Editions. Website: www.pearlmag.com. Deadline: submit between May 1 and June 30. Entry fee: $20. Prizes: $1,000 and publication in *Pearl Editions*.

RICHARD PETERSON POETRY PRIZE. *Crab Orchard Review*, Poetry Contest, Dept. of English, Mail Code 4503, Southern Illinois University–Carbondale, 1000 Faner Dr., Carbondale IL 62901.

(618) 453-5321.Website: www.siuc.edu/~crborchd. Entry fee: $15. Prize: $1,500. Deadline: submit between March 1 and May 10 (may vary). Submit up to 3 poems; 100-line limit.

POETRY SOCIETY OF VIRGINIA POETRY CONTESTS. Website: www.poetrysocietyofvirginia .org. Categories for adults and students. Prizes: $20-250. Entry fee per poem for nonmembers: $4. Deadline: March 15. List of contests on website.

SLIPSTREAM ANNUAL POETRY CHAPBOOK COMPETITION. Website: www.slipstreampress .org/contest.html. Prize: $1,000, plus 50 copies of chapbook. Deadline: December 1. Send up to 40 pages of poetry. Reading fee: $20. Guidelines on website.

SOUL-MAKING LITERARY COMPETITION. National League of American Pen Women. E-mail: pennobhill@aol.com. Website: www.soulmakingcontest.us. One-page poems only (single- or double-spaced). Up to 3 poems/entry. Deadline: November 30. Entry fee: $5. Prizes $25, $50, $100.

HOLLIS SUMMERS POETRY PRIZE. Ohio University Press. (740) 593-1155. E-mail: oupress@ ohio.edu. For unpublished collection of original poems, 60-95 pgs. Entry fee: $25. Deadline: October 31. Prize: $1,000, plus publication in book form. Details on website: www.ohiou.edu/oupress/poetry prize.htm (scroll down to "About OU Press" and click on "Poetry Prize").

SUMMERTIME BLUES POETRY CONTEST. Website: www.thestorytellermagazine.com/. Entry fee $5 per 3 poems. Deadline: July 15, 2013. Prizes: 1st place: $25; 2nd place: $15; 3rd place: $10. Poems may be rhyming or nonrhyming, any style. Writers may enter as often as they wish, but entry fee must accompany each entry. Name, address, phone, e-mail, title of story, and word count should be on cover page. Name should not appear anywhere else on ms. No pornography, graphic anything, New Age, or children's poetry will be accepted.

THE MAY SWENSON POETRY AWARD. Utah State University Press. (435) 797-1362. Website: www.usu.edu/usupress. Collections of original poetry, 50-100 pgs. Deadline: September 30. Prize: $1,000, publication, and royalties. Reading fee: $25. Details on website ("Swenson Poetry Award").

KATE TUFTS DISCOVERY AWARD. Claremont Graduate University. (909) 621-8974. E-mail: tufts@cgu.edu. Presented annually for a first or very early work by a poet of genuine promise. Prize: $10,000. Deadline: September 15. Details and entry form on website: www.cgu.edu/tufts.

KINGSLEY TUFTS POETRY AWARD. Claremont Graduate University. (909) 621-8974. E-mail: tufts@cgu.edu. Presented annually for a published book of poetry by a midcareer poet. Prize: $100,000. Deadline: September 15. Details and entry form on website: www.cgu.edu/tufts.

UTMOST NOVICE CHRISTIAN POETRY CONTEST. Utmost Christian Writers Foundation, Canada. E-mail: nnharms@telusplanet.net. Website: www.utmostchristianwriters.com/poetry-contest/poetry -contest-rules.php. Nathan Harms. Entry fee: $10/poem. Prizes: $500, $300, $200; Best Rhyming Poem $150. Deadline: August 31. Details and entry form on website.

WINNING WRITERS. Variety of poetry contests. Website: www.winningwriters.com.

MULTIPLE-GENRE CONTESTS

AMERICAN LITERARY REVIEW CONTESTS. University of North Texas. E-mail: americanliter aryreview@yahoo.com. Website: www.engl.unt.edu/alr. Now sponsors three contests: short fiction, creative nonfiction, and poetry. Prize: $1,000 and publication in spring issue of the magazine. Entry fee: $15. Deadline: October 1. Details on website ("Contest").

BAKELESS LITERARY PUBLICATION PRIZES. Bread Loaf Writers' Conference, Middlebury College. E-mail: bakelessprize@middlebury.edu. Website: www.bakelessprize.org. Book series competition for new authors of literary works of poetry, fiction, and nonfiction. Entry fee: $10. Deadline: between September 15 and November 1. Details on website.

BEST NEW CANADIAN CHRISTIAN WRITING AWARDS. The Word Guild, Canada. E-mail: admin@thewordguild.com. Website: www.thewordguild.com. Sponsors a number of contests annually. Check website for any current contests and guidelines (click on "Awards"/"Contests").

BLUE RIDGE CONFERENCE WRITING CONTEST. (760) 220-1075. E-mail: alton@ganskycom munications.com. Website: http://brmcwc.com. Sponsors a book contest. First prize: a trophy plus $200; scholarship toward conference. Fiction or nonfiction. Details on website.

CHRISTIAN SMALL PUBLISHER BOOK OF THE YEAR. Website: www.christianbookaward.com. Christian Small Publisher Book of the Year Award is designed to promote small publishers in the Christian marketplace as well as to bring recognition to outstanding Christian books from small publishers. Awards are given in 12 categories.

COLUMBIA FICTION/POETRY/NONFICTION CONTEST. Website: www.columbiajournal.org /contests.htm. Length: 20 double-spaced pgs. or up to 5 poems. Prize: $500 in each category, plus publication. Deadline: January 15 (varies). Details on website.

ECPA CHRISTIAN BOOK AWARD. (480) 966-3998. E-mail: info@ecpa.org. Website: www .ChristianBookExpo.com. Presented annually to the best books in Christian publishing. Awards recognize books in 6 different categories: Bibles, Fiction, Children, Inspiration, Bible Reference, Nonfiction, and New Author. Only ECPA members in good standing can nominate products. Submit between September 1 and October 2 (verify on website). Books submitted must have been published between October 2011 and October 2012. Awards are presented annually at the ECPA Executive Leadership Summit. Verify all details on Evangelical Christian Publishers Association website: www.ecpa.org.

EVANGELICAL PRESS ASSOCIATION ANNUAL CONTEST. PO Box 28129, Crystal MN 55428. (763) 535-4793. E-mail: director@epassoc.org. Website: www.epassoc.org. Sponsors annual contest for member publications. Submit in September.

WILLIAM FAULKNER–WILLIAM WISDOM CREATIVE WRITING COMPETITION. Offers significant cash prizes in seven categories: Novel, Novella, Novel-in-Progress, Short Story, Essay, Poem, and Short Story by a High School Student. For details, visit www.wordsandmusic.org and download guidelines and entry form. Or e-mail the Society at Faulkhouse@aol.com.

GOD USES INK NOVICE CONTEST (for nonpublished writers). Opens in September of 2010. Prizes are available in three age categories: ages 14 to 19; 20 to 39; and age 40 and over. First prize: Registration to Write! Canada Christian Writers' Conference (approximate value nearly $400.00), held in June. (Please check website for details: www.writecanada.org.) Second prize: A $100 gift certificate for The Word Guild (can be used for conference registration, membership, etc.). Third prize: A $50 gift certificate for The Word Guild (can be used for conference registration, membership, etc.).

ERIC HOFFER AWARD. *Best New Writing.* E-mail: info@hofferaward.com. Website: www .HofferAward.com. Submit books via mail; no queries. Submit prose online only. The prose category is for creative fiction and nonfiction less than 10,000 words. Annual award for books features 14 categories. Pays $250-2,000. Guidelines at www.HofferAward.com.

INSCRIBE CHRISTIAN WRITERS' CONTEST. Edmonton AB, Canada. (780) 542-7950. Fax (780) 514-3702. E-mail: query@inscribe.org. Website: www.inscribe.org. Sponsors contests open to nonmembers; details on website.

INSIGHT WRITING CONTEST. (301) 393-4038. Fax (301) 393-4055. E-mail: insight@rhpa.org. Website: www.insightmagazine.org. Review and Herald/Seventh-day Adventist. A magazine of positive Christian living for Seventh-day Adventist high schoolers. Sponsors short story and poetry contests; includes a category for students 22 or under. Prizes: $50-$250. Deadline: June 1. Submit by e-mail. Details on website (click on "Writing Contest").

GRACE IRWIN AWARD. Website: canadianchristianwritingawards.com. All shortlisted finalists in fiction and nonfiction book categories in The Word Guild Canadian Christian Writing Awards will contend for the Grace Irwin Award. Prize $5,000. A separate round of independent judging will determine the prizewinner.

MINISTRY & LITURGY VISUAL ARTS AWARDS. (408) 286-8505. Fax (408) 287-8748. E-mail: vaa@rpinet.com. Website: www.rpinet.com/vaaentry.pdf. Visual Arts Awards held in 4 categories throughout the year. Best in each category wins $100. Entry fee: $30. Different deadline for each category (see website).

NARRATIVE MAGAZINE FALL STORY CONTEST. Website: www.narrativemagazine.com. Fiction and nonfiction. Submission fee: $22. Prizes $2,500/$1,000/$500, plus 10 finalists will receive $100 each. Deadline: Nov. 30, 2013. Complete guidelines on website.

NARRATIVE MAGAZINE 30 BELOW. www.narrativemagazine.com. Fiction, Nonfiction, Poetry, Graphic Art, Audio, Video, Photography. Submission fee: $22. Prizes $1,500/$750/$300, plus 10 finalists will receive $100 each. Deatline Oct. 30, 2013. Complete guidelines on website.

NARRATIVE MAGAZINE SPRING STORY CONTEST. Website: www.NarrativeMagazine.com. Fiction & nonfiction. Submission fee: $22. Prizes $2,500/$1,000/$500, plus 10 finalists at $100 ea. Deadline: July 31, 2013. Also sponsors a fall contest. Complete guidelines on website.

NEW MILLENNIUM AWARDS. Website: www.newmillenniumwritings.com/awards.html. Prizes: $1,000 award for each category. Best Poem, Best Fiction, Best Nonfiction, Best Short-Short Fiction (fiction and nonfiction 6,000 words; short-short fiction up to 1,000 words; 3 poems to 5 pgs. total). Entry fee: $17 each. Deadline: June 17. Guidelines on website. Enter online or off.

NEW MILLENNIUM WRITINGS SEMIANNUAL WRITING CONTESTS. Contact: Steve Petty (steve petty@live.com). Website: www.newmillenniumwritings.com. Includes fiction, short-short fiction, poetry, and creative nonfiction. Entry fee: $17. Prizes: $1,000 in each category. Deadlines: June 17 & November 30.

ONCE WRITTEN CONTESTS. Fiction and poetry contests. Website: www.oncewritten.com.

THE EUPLE RINEY MEMORIAL AWARD. Website: www.thestorytellermagazine.com. Entry fee $5. Deadline: June 20, 2013. Prizes: 1st place: $50; 2nd place: $25; 3rd place: $15; 4th place: $10. Plus an Editor's Choice Award. Open genre contest, but must be about family—good or bad. Can be fiction or nonfiction. Writers may enter as often as they wish, but entry fee must accompany each entry. Name, address, phone, e-mail, title of story, and word count should be on cover page. Name should not appear anywhere else on ms. No pornography, graphic anything, New Age, or children's stories will be accepted.

MONA SCHREIBER PRIZE FOR HUMOROUS FICTION AND NONFICTION. E-mail: brash cyber@pcmagic.net or brad.schreiber@att.net.. Website: www.brashcyber.com or or www.brad schreiber.com.. Humorous fiction and nonfiction to 750 words. Prizes: $500, $250, and $100. Entry fee: $5. Deadline: December 1. Details on website (click on contest name at bottom of illustration).

SOUL-MAKING KEATS LITERARY COMPETITION. Entering its twentieth year, Soul-Making Keats Literary Competition consists of thirteen categories with cash prizes awarded to first, second, and third place in each. Annual deadline is November 30th (postmarked), and winners and honorable mentions are invited to read at the Awards Event at the Koret Auditorium, San Francisco Mail Library, Civic Center. Complete details are available at the website: www.soulmakingcontest.us or via an SASE to The Webhallow House, 1544 Sweetwood Dr., Broadmoor Vlg., CA 94015.

THE STORYTELLER CONTESTS. (870) 647-2137. E-mail: storyteller1@hightowercom.com. Contest website: www.thestorytellermagazine.com. Fossil Creek Publishing. Offers 1 or 2 paying contest/yr., along with People's Choice Awards, and Pushcart Prize nominations.

TICKLED BY THUNDER CONTESTS. Canada. (604) 591-6095. E-mail: info@tickledbythunder .com. Website: www.tickledbythunder.com. Sponsors several writing contests each year in various genres. Entry fee $10 for nonsubscribers. Prizes: Based on point system. See website for details.

THE WORD GUILD CANADIAN CHRISTIAN WRITING AWARDS. (For published writers.) Thirty-five awards, encompassing 19 book categories and 16 article/short piece categories, including song lyrics, scripts or screenplays, and blog posts. Round One deadline is September 30 and Round Two deadline is December 31. The fee structure is available on the website for members and non-members. Categories of books and articles, etc., can be found on the website: http://canadianchristian writingawards.com.

WRITER'S DIGEST COMPETITIONS. (715) 445-4612, ext. 13430. E-mail: WritersDigestWriting Competition@fwmedia.com. Website: www.writersdigest.com. Sponsors annual contests for articles, short stories (multiple genres), poetry, children's and young adult fiction, inspirational writing, memoirs/personal essays, self-published books, and scripts (categories vary). Deadlines: vary according to contest. Prizes: up to $3,000 for each contest. Some contests also offer a trip to the annual Writer's Digest Conference in New York City. See website for list of current contests and rules.

WRITERS-EDITORS NETWORK ANNUAL WRITING COMPETITION. E-mail: editor@writers-editors.com. Website: www.writers-editors.com. Open to all writers. Deadline: March 15. Nonfiction, fiction, children's, poetry. Prizes: $100, $75, $50. Details on website (see right-hand column).

WRITERS' UNION OF CANADA AWARDS & COMPETITIONS. Canada. (416) 703-8982. Fax (416) 504-9090. E-mail: info@writersunion.ca. Website: www.writersunion.ca. Various competitions. Prizes: $500-10,000. Details on website.

RESOURCES FOR CONTESTS

ADDITIONAL CONTESTS. You will find some additional contests sponsored by local groups and conferences that are open to nonmembers. See individual listings in those sections.

FREELANCE WRITING: WEBSITE FOR TODAY'S WORKING WRITER. Website: www.freelance writing.com/writingcontests.php.

KIMN SWENSON GOLLNICK'S WEBSITE. Contest listings. Website: www.KIMN.net/contests.htm.

OZARK CREATIVE WRITERS CONTESTS. E-mail submissions only: ozarkcreativewriters@earth link.net. Website: www.ozarkcreativewriters.org. Lists a number of contests on website.

THE WRITER CONTEST. *The Writer* magazine. (262) 796-8776. E-mail: editor@writermag.com. Website: www.writermag.com. General. How-to for writers. Occasionally sponsors a contest and lists multiple contests. Check website.

MAJOR LITERARY AWARDS

AUDIES: www.audiopub.org

CALDECOTT MEDAL: www.ala.org

CAROL AWARDS: www.acfw.com

EDGAR: www.mysterywriters.org

HEMINGWAY FOUNDATION/PEN AWARD: www.pen-ne.org

HUGO: http://worldcon.org/hugos.html

NATIONAL BOOK AWARD: www.nationalbook.org

NATIONAL BOOK CRITICS CIRCLE AWARD: www.bookcritics.org

NEBULA: http://dpsinfo.com/awardweb/nebulas

NEWBERY: www.ala.org

NOBEL PRIZE FOR LITERATURE: www.nobelprize.org

PEN/FAULKNER AWARD: www.penfaulkner.org

PULITZER PRIZE: www.pulitzer.org

RITA: www.rwanational.org/cs/contests_and_awards

13

Denominational Book Publishers and Periodicals

ASSEMBLIES OF GOD
Book Publisher
Gospel Publishing House

Periodicals
Enrichment Journal
Live
Pentecostal Evangel
Testimony

BAPTIST, FREE WILL
Book Publishers
Randall House
Randall House Digital

BAPTIST, SOUTHERN
Book Publishers
B&H Publishing
New Hope Publishers

Periodicals
Mature Living
On Mission

BAPTIST (OTHER)
Book Publishers
Earthen Vessel Publishing
Judson Press (American)

Periodical
Secret Place (American)

CATHOLIC
Book Publishers
American Catholic Press
Canticle Books
HarperOne (Cath. bks.)
Loyola Press
Our Sunday Visitor
Pauline Books

Periodicals
America
Catholic New York
Columbia
Diocesan Dialogue
Leaves
Our Sunday Visitor
Parish Liturgy
Prairie Messenger
Priest
Share
St. Anthony Messenger

CHRISTIAN CHURCH/ CHURCH OF CHRIST
Book Publisher
CrossLink Publishing

CHURCH OF GOD (HOLINESS)
Periodicals
Church Herald and Holiness Banner
Gems of Truth

CHURCH OF GOD (OTHER)
Periodicals
Bible Advocate (Seventh-day)
The Gem
Now What? (Seventh-day)

LUTHERAN
Book Publishers
Concordia
Langmarc Publishing
Lutheran University Press

Periodicals
Canada Lutheran (ELCC)
Canadian Lutheran
Lutheran Digest

MENNONITE
Periodicals
The Messenger
Partners
Rejoice!

METHODIST, FREE
Periodical
Light and Life

METHODIST, UNITED
Book Publisher
Abingdon Press

Periodicals
Good News (TX)
Mature Years
Pockets
Upper Room

PRESBYTERIAN
Periodical
Presbyterians Today

REFORMED
Periodical
Perspectives

SEVENTH-DAY ADVENTIST
Book Publisher
Pacific Press

Periodical
Guide Magazine

WESLEYAN CHURCH

Book Publisher

Wesleyan Publishing House

Periodicals

Light from the Word

Vista

MISCELLANEOUS DENOMINATIONS

Antiochian Orthodox

Conciliar Press

Church of God (Anderson IN)

Warner Press

Grace Brethren Churches

BMH Books

Glossary

Advance: Amount of money a publisher pays to an author up front, against future royalties. The amount varies greatly from publisher to publisher and is often paid in two or three installments (on signing contract, on delivery of manuscript, and on publication).

All rights: An outright sale of your material. Author has no further control over it.

Anecdote: A short, poignant, real-life story, usually used to illustrate a single thought.

Assignment: When an editor asks a writer to write a specific piece for an agreed-upon price.

As-told-to story: A true story you write as a first-person account but about someone else.

Audiobooks: Books available on CDs or in other digital formats.

Avant-garde: Experimental; ahead of the times.

Backlist: A publisher's previously published books that are still in print a year after publication.

B & W: Abbreviation for a black-and-white photograph.

Bar code: Identification code and price on the back of a book read by a scanner at checkout counters.

Bible versions: AMP—Amplified Bible; ASV—American Standard Version; CEV—Contemporary English Version; ESV—English Standard Version; GNB—Good News Bible; HCSB—Holman Christian Standard Bible; ICB—International Children's Bible; KJV—King James Version; MSG—The Message; NAB—New American Bible; NAS—New American Standard; NEB—New English Bible; NIrV—New International Reader's Version; NIV—New International Version; NJB—New Jerusalem Bible; NKJV—New King James Version; NLT—New Living Translation; NRSV—New Revised Standard Version; RSV—Revised Standard Version; TLB—*The Living Bible*; TNIV—Today's New International Version.

Bimonthly: Every two months.

Bio sketch: Information on the author.

Biweekly: Every two weeks.

Bluelines: Printer's proofs used to catch errors before a book is printed.

Book proposal: Submission of a book idea to an editor; usually includes a cover letter, thesis statement, chapter-by-chapter synopsis, market survey, and 1-3 sample chapters.

Byline: Author's name printed just below the title of a story, article, etc.

Camera-ready copy: The text and artwork for a book that are ready for the press.

Chapbook: A small book or pamphlet containing poetry, religious readings, etc.

Circulation: The number of copies sold or distributed of each issue of a publication.

Clips: See "Published clips."

Column: A regularly appearing feature, section, or department in a periodical using the same heading; written by the same person or a different freelancer each time.

Concept statement: A 50-150 word summary of your proposed book.

Contributor's copy: Copy of an issue of a periodical sent to the author whose work appears in it.

Copyright: Legal protection of an author's work.

Cover letter: A letter that accompanies some manuscript submissions. Usually needed only if you have to tell the editor something specific or to give your credentials for writing a piece of a technical nature. Also used to remind the editor that a manuscript was requested or expected.

Credits, list of: A listing of your previously published works.

Critique: An evaluation of a piece of writing.

Defamation: A written or spoken injury to the reputation of a living person or organization. If what is said is true, it cannot be defamatory.

Derivative work: A work derived from another work, such as a condensation or abridgement. Contact copyright owner for permission before doing the abridgement and be prepared to pay that owner a fee or royalty.

Devotional: A short piece that shares a personal spiritual discovery, inspires to worship, challenges to commitment or action, or encourages.

Editorial guidelines: See "Writers' guidelines."

Electronic submission: The submission of a proposal or article to an editor by electronic means, such as by e-mail or on disk.

Endorsements: Flattering comments about a book; usually carried on the back cover or in promotional material.

EPA/Evangelical Press Assn.: A professional trade organization for periodical publishers and associate members.

E-proposals: Proposals sent via e-mail.

E-queries: Queries sent via e-mail.

Eschatology: The branch of theology that is concerned with the last things, such as death, judgment, heaven, and hell.

Essay: A short composition usually expressing the author's opinion on a specific subject.

Evangelical: A person who believes that one receives God's forgiveness for sins through Jesus Christ, and believes the Bible is an authoritative guide for daily living.

Exegesis: Interpretation of the Scripture.

Feature article: In-depth coverage of a subject, usually focusing on a person, an event, a process, an organization, a movement, a trend or issue; written to explain, encourage, help, analyze, challenge, motivate, warn, or entertain as well as to inform.

Filler: A short item used to "fill" out the page of a periodical. It could be a timeless news item, joke, anecdote, light verse or short humor, puzzle, game, etc.

First rights: Editor buys the right to publish your piece for the first time.

Foreign rights: Selling or giving permission to translate or reprint published material in a foreign country.

Foreword: Opening remarks in a book introducing the book and its author.

Freelance: As in 50% freelance: means that 50% of the material printed in the publication is supplied by freelance writers.

Freelancer or freelance writer: A writer who is not on salary but sells his or her material to a number of different publishers.

Free verse: Poetry that flows without any set pattern.

Galley proof: A typeset copy of a book manuscript used to detect and correct errors before the final print run.

Genre: Refers to type or classification, as in fiction or poetry. Such types as westerns, romances, mysteries, etc., are referred to as genre fiction.

Glossy: A black-and-white photo with a shiny, rather than matte, finish.

Go-ahead: When a publisher tells you to go ahead and write up or send your article idea.

Haiku: A Japanese lyric poem of a fixed 17-syllable form.

Hard copy: A typed manuscript, as opposed to one on disk or in an e-mail.

Holiday/seasonal: A story, article, filler, etc., that has to do with a specific holiday or season. This material must reach the publisher the stated number of months prior to the holiday/season.

Homiletics: The art of preaching.

Honorarium: If a publisher indicates they pay an honorarium, it means they pay a small flat fee, as opposed to a set amount per word.

Humor: The amusing or comical aspects of life that add warmth and color to an article or story.

Interdenominational: Distributed to a number of different denominations.

International Postal Reply Coupon: See "IRC."

Interview article: An article based on an interview with a person of interest to a specific readership.

IRC or IPRC: International Postal Reply Coupon: can be purchased at your local post office and should be enclosed with a manuscript sent to a foreign publisher.

ISBN: International Standard Book Number; an identification code needed for every book.

Journal: A periodical presenting news in a particular area.

Kill fee: A fee paid for a completed article done on assignment that is subsequently not published. Amount is usually 25-50% of original payment.

Libel: To defame someone by an opinion or a misquote and put his or her reputation in jeopardy.

Light verse: Simple, lighthearted poetry.

Little/Literary: Small circulation publications whose focus is providing a forum for the literary writer, rather than on making money. Often do not pay, or pay in copies.

Mainstream fiction: Other than genre fiction, such as romance, mystery, or science fiction. Stories of people and their conflicts handled on a deeper level.

Mass market: Books intended for a wide, general market, rather than a specialized market. These books are produced in a smaller format, usually with smaller type, and are sold at a lower price. The expectation is that their sales will be higher.

Ms: Abbreviation for manuscript.

Mss: Abbreviation for more than one manuscript.

Multiple submissions: Submitting more than one piece at a time to the same publisher, usually reserved for poetry, greeting cards, or fillers, not articles. Also see "Simultaneous submissions."

NASR: Abbreviation for North American Serial Rights.

Newsbreak: A newsworthy event or item sent to a publisher who might be interested in publishing it because it would be of interest to his particular readership.

Nondenominational: Not associated with a particular denomination.

Not copyrighted: Publication of your piece in such a publication will put it into the public domain and it is not then protected. Ask that the publisher carry your copyright notice on your piece when it is printed.

Novella: A short novel starting at 20,000 words—35,000 words maximum. Length varies from publisher to publisher.

On acceptance: Periodical or publisher pays a writer at the time the manuscript is accepted for publication.

On assignment: Writing something at the specific request of an editor.

Onetime rights: Selling the right to publish a story one time to any number of publications (usually refers to publishing for a nonoverlapping readership).

On publication: Publisher pays a writer when his or her manuscript is published.

On speculation/On spec: Writing something for an editor with the agreement that the editor will buy it only if he or she likes it.

Overrun: The extra copies of a book printed during the initial print run.

Over the transom: Unsolicited articles that arrive at a publisher's office.

Payment on acceptance: See "On acceptance."

Payment on publication: See "On publication."

Pen name/pseudonym: Using a name other than your legal name on an article or book in order to protect your identity or the identity of people included, or when the author wishes to remain anonymous. Put the pen name in the byline under the title, and your real name in the upper, left-hand corner.

Permissions: Asking permission to use the text or art from a copyrighted source.

Personal experience story: A story based on a real-life experience.

Personality profile: A feature article that highlights a specific person's life or accomplishments.

Photocopied submission: Sending an editor a photocopy of your manuscript, rather than an original. Some editors prefer an original.

Piracy: To take the writings of others just as they were written and put your name on them as the author.

Plagiarism: To steal and use the ideas or writings of another as your own, rewriting them to make them sound like your own.

Press kit: A compilation of promotional materials on a particular book or author, usually organized in a folder, used to publicize a book.

Print-on-Demand (POD): A printing process where books are printed one at a time instead of in quantity. The production cost per book is higher, but no warehousing is necessary. Bookstores typically will not carry POD books.

Public domain: Work that has never been copyrighted, or on which the copyright has expired. Subtract 75 from the current year, and anything copyrighted prior to that is in the public domain.

Published clips: Copies of actual articles you have had published, from newspapers or magazines.

Quarterly: Every three months.

Query letter: A letter sent to an editor telling about an article you propose to write and asking if he or she is interested in seeing it.

Reporting time: The number of weeks or months it takes an editor to get back to you about a query or manuscript you have sent in.

Reprint rights: Selling the right to reprint an article that has already been published elsewhere. You must have sold only first or onetime rights originally, and wait until it has been published the first time.

Review copies: Books given to book reviewers or buyers for chains.

Royalty: The percentage an author is paid by a publisher on the sale of each copy of a book.

SAE: Self-addressed envelope (without stamps).

SAN: Standard Account Number, used to identify libraries, book dealers, or schools.

SASE: Self-addressed, stamped envelope. Should always be sent with a manuscript or query letter.

SASP: Self-addressed, stamped postcard. May be sent with a manuscript submission to be returned by publisher indicating it arrived safely.

Satire: Ridicule that aims at reform.

Second serial rights: See "Reprint rights."

Semiannual: Issued twice a year.

Serial: Refers to publication in a periodical (such as first serial rights).

Sidebar: A short feature that accompanies an article and either elaborates on the human interest side of the story or gives additional information on the topic. It is often set apart by appearing within a box or border.

Simultaneous rights: Selling the rights to the same piece to several publishers simultaneously. Be sure everyone is aware that you are doing so.

Simultaneous submissions: Sending the same manuscript to more than one publisher at the same time. Usually done with nonoverlapping markets (such as denominational or newspapers) or when you are writing on a timely subject. Be sure to state in a cover letter that it is a simultaneous submission and why.

Slander: The verbal act of defamation.

Slanting: Writing an article so that it meets the needs of a particular market.

Slush pile: The stack of unsolicited manuscripts that have arrived at a publisher's office.

Speculation: See "On speculation."

Staff-written material: Material written by the members of a magazine staff.

Subsidiary rights: All those rights, other than book rights, included in a book contract such as paperback, book club, movie, etc.

Subsidy publisher: A book publisher who charges the author to publish his or her book, as opposed to a royalty publisher who pays the author.

Synopsis: A brief summary of work from one paragraph to several pages long.

Tabloid: A newspaper-format publication about half the size of a regular newspaper.

Take-home paper: A periodical sent home from Sunday school each week (usually) with Sunday school students, children through adults.

Think piece: A magazine article that has an intellectual, philosophical, or provocative approach to a subject.

Third world: Reference to underdeveloped countries of Asia and Africa.

Trade magazine: A magazine whose audience is in a particular trade or business.

Traditional verse: One or more verses with an established pattern that is repeated throughout the poem.

Transparencies: Positive color slides, not color prints.

Unsolicited manuscript: A manuscript an editor didn't specifically ask to see.

Vanity publisher: See "Subsidy publisher."

Vignette: A short, descriptive literary sketch of a brief scene or incident.

Vitae/Vita: An outline of one's personal history and experience.

Work-for-hire: Signing a contract with a publisher stating that a particular piece of writing you are doing for the publisher is work-for-hire. In the agreement you give the publisher full ownership and control of the material.

Writers' guidelines: An information sheet provided by a publisher that gives specific guidelines for writing for the publication. Always send an SASE with your request for guidelines.

Index

This index includes periodicals, books, distributors, greeting cards/specialty markets, and agents, as well as some of the organizations/resources you may need to find quickly. Conferences and groups are listed alphabetically by state in those sections.

BEST ADVICE ON WRITING *INSPIRATIONAL* FICTION.

With contributions from bestselling authors }

Jerry B. Jenkins
Francine Rivers
Karen Kingsbury
Randy Alcorn
Terri Blackstock
Robin Jones Gunn
Angela Hunt
. . . and more

Expert advice from successful fiction writers who have published thousands of novels, with more than 70 million copies sold.

Whether you're a novice or have been writing for years, learn the best ways to plan, perfect, and promote your writing. Discover what makes a novel Christian, and master the art of writing about tough topics.

This valuable guide contains tips on

> plotting,
> dialogue,
> point of view,
> characterization,

> marketing,
> social networking,
> and more. . . .

For the first time, bestselling Christian novelists have joined together to bring you this comprehensive guide on the craft of writing. If you've always wanted to write the next great novel or felt compelled to tell the story that's burning inside you, *A Novel Idea* will give you the tools you need.

CP0373